Political Economy of Tourism

Political economy, in its various guises and transfigurations, is a research philosophy that presents both social commentary and theoretical progress and is concerned with a number of different topics: politics, regulation and governance, production systems, social relations, inequality and development amongst many others. As a critical theory, political economy seeks to provide an understanding of societies – and of the structures and social relations that form them – in order to evoke social change towards more equitable conditions.

Despite the early influence of critical development studies and political economy on tourism research, political economy has received relatively little attention in tourism research. *Political Economy of Tourism* is the first volume to bring together different theoretical perspectives and discourse in political economy related to tourism. Written by leading scholars, the text is organized into three sequential parts, linked by the principle that 'the political' and 'the economic' are intimately connected. Part I presents different approaches to political economy, including Marxist political economy, regulation, comparative political economy, commodity chain research and alternative political economies; Part II links key themes of political economy, such as class, gender, labour, development and consumption, to tourism; and Part III examines the political economy at various geographical scales and focuses on the outcomes and processes of the political act of planning and managing tourism production.

This engaging volume provides insights and alternative critical perspectives on political economy theory to expand discussions of tourism development and policy in the future. *Political Economy of Tourism* is a valuable text for students, researchers and academics interested in tourism and related disciplines.

Jan Mosedale is Senior Lecturer in Tourism, Hospitality and Events at the University of Sunderland, UK. His research interests lie in the analysis of multiple forms of economic practices across space, focussing on tourism commodity chains as well as non-capitalist exchanges. Jan is co-editor for the 'Current Developments in the Geographies of Leisure and Tourism' book series.

Contemporary Geographies of Leisure, Tourism and Mobility

Series Editor: C. Michael Hall, Professor at the Department of Management, College of Business and Economics, University of Canterbury, Private Bag 4800, Christchurch, New Zealand

The aim of this series is to explore and communicate the intersections and relationships between leisure, tourism and human mobility within the social sciences.

It will incorporate both traditional and new perspectives on leisure and tourism from contemporary geography, e.g. notions of identity, representation and culture, while also providing for perspectives from cognate areas such as anthropology, cultural studies, gastronomy and food studies, marketing, policy studies and political economy, regional and urban planning, and sociology, within the development of an integrated field of leisure and tourism studies.

Also, increasingly, tourism and leisure are regarded as steps in a continuum of human mobility. Inclusion of mobility in the series offers the prospect to examine the relationship between tourism and migration, the sojourner, educational travel, and second home and retirement travel phenomena.

The series comprises two strands:

Contemporary Geographies of Leisure, Tourism and Mobility aims to address the needs of students and academics, and the titles will be published in hardback and paperback. Titles include:

The Moralisation of Tourism
Sun, sand . . . and saving the world?
Jim Butcher

The Ethics of Tourism Development
Mick Smith and Rosaleen Duffy

Tourism in the Caribbean
Trends, development, prospects
Edited by David Timothy Duval

Qualitative Research in Tourism
Ontologies, epistemologies and methodologies
Edited by Jenny Phillimore and Lisa Goodson

The Media and the Tourist Imagination
Converging cultures
Edited by David Crouch, Rhona Jackson and Felix Thompson

Tourism and the Consumption of Wildlife
Hunting, shooting and sport fishing
Edited by Brent Lovelock

Tourism, Creativity and Development
Edited by Greg Richards and Julie Wilson

Tourism at the Grassroots
Edited by John Connell and Barbara Rugendyke

Tourism and Innovation
Michael Hall and Allan Williams

World Tourism Cities
Developing tourism off the beaten track
Edited by Robert Maitland and Peter Newman

Tourism and National Parks
International perspectives on development, histories and change
Edited by Warwick Frost and C. Michael Hall

Tourism, Performance and the Everyday
Consuming the Orient
Michael Haldrup and Jonas Larsen

Tourism and Change in Polar Regions
C. Michael Hall and Jarkko Saarinen

Fieldwork in Tourism
Methods, issues and reflections
Edited by C. Michael Hall

Tourism and India
A critical introduction
Kevin Hannam and Anya Diekmann

Political Economy of Tourism
A critical perspective
Edited by Jan Mosedale

Forthcoming:

Volunteer Tourism
Angela Benson

The Study of Tourism
Richard Sharpley

Children's and Families' Holiday Experience
Neil Carr

Tourism and Agriculture
Rebecca Torres and Janet Momsen

Gender and Tourism
Cara Atchinson

Tourism in China
David Airey and King Chong

Real Tourism
Claudio Minca and Tim Oaks

Tourism and Animal Ethics
David A. Fennell

Tourism and National Identity
Elspeth Frew and Leanne White

Political Economy of Tourism

A critical perspective

Edited by Jan Mosedale

LONDON AND NEW YORK

First published 2011
by Routledge
2 Park Square, Milton Park, Abingdon, Oxfordshire OX14 4RN

Simultaneously published in the USA and Canada
by Routledge
711 Third Avenue, New York, NY 10017

First issued in paperback 2014

Routledge is an imprint of the Taylor & Francis Group, an informa business

© 2011 Jan Mosedale

The right of Jan Mosedale to be identified as author of this work has been
asserted by him in accordance with the Copyright, Designs and Patent Act
1988.

Typeset in Times New Roman by Prepress Projects Ltd, Perth, UK

British Library Cataloguing in Publication Data
A catalogue record for this book is available from the British Library

Library of Congress Cataloguing in Publication Data
Political economy of tourism / edited by Jan Mosedale.
p. cm.
Includes bibliographical references and index.
1. Tourism. 2. Tourism—Government policy. I. Mosedale, Jan.
G155.A1P65 2010
338.4'791—dc22
2010025336

ISBN13: 978-1-138-88068-9 (pbk)
ISBN13: 978-0-415-54802-1 (hbk)

To Christel and Tim

Contents

Illustrations

Figure

Tables

Contributors

Julia N. Albrecht is a Lecturer in Tourism Management at the Victoria Management School, Victoria University of Wellington. Her research interests include tourism policy and planning and the relationships of stakeholders in tourism.

Raoul Bianchi is a Principal Lecturer in Tourism and Leisure at the University of East London, UK. He specialises in the sociology of tourism development and the international political economy of tourism. He has also published on the politics of tourism and cultural heritage, including world heritage, with particular emphasis on Spain and the Canary Islands.

Michael Clancy is Associate Professor of Politics and Government at the University of Hartford, Connecticut, USA. His work focuses on tourism and development, commodity chains and nation branding. His most recent book is *Brand New Ireland: Tourism, Development and National Identity in the Irish Republic.*

Scarlett Cornelissen is an Associate Professor in the Department of Political Science at Stellenbosch University in South Africa. She holds a PhD from the University of Glasgow and conducts research on African international relations and the political economy of tourism and sport mega-events. She is the author of a book on South Africa's place in the global tourism system and has co-edited three books on globalization and politics in Africa.

David Timothy Duval is Associate Professor in the Faculty of Business and Economics at the University of Winnipeg.

C. Michael Hall is Professor in the Department of Management, University of Canterbury, New Zealand; Docent in the Department of Geography, University of Oulu, Finland; and Visiting Professor at the Linnaeus University School of Business and Economics, Kalmar, Sweden. He is co-editor of Current Issues in Tourism and he has published widely in tourism, gastronomy and environmental history.

Steven F. Illum is currently Tourism Specialist and Professor at Missouri State University, Springfield, Missouri, USA. He holds a PhD in Recreation, Park and Tourism Sciences from Texas A&M University – College Station, Texas and serves on the editorial review board for *Anatolia* and *International Journal of Tourism Policy*. His research interests include marketing and rural heritage tourism.

Stanislav Ivanov is currently Academic Director of International University College in Dobrich, Bulgaria. He holds a PhD in Tourism Economics from the University of Economics – Varna and is the editor-in-chief of the *European Journal of Tourism Research*. His research interests include destination marketing, tourism and economic growth, political issues in tourism, and special interest tourism.

Teresa Leopold is a Senior Lecturer in Tourism and Events Studies at the University of Sunderland. Her research interests span from socio-cultural aspects of events and festivals to the political economy of tourist migration and power relations within the social construction of communities.

Kirsten Lovelock is a Research Fellow at the University of Otago. Her research has focused on the immigration industry, immigrant participation in voluntary associations, migrant participation in nature-based outdoor recreation, the migration of children for adoption and temporary migrant worker schemes in agriculture.

John Macilree is Principal Adviser, Air Services in the Aviation and Security Team at the New Zealand Ministry of Transport.

Kevin Meethan is Senior Lecturer in Sociology at the University of Plymouth. He is the author of *Tourism in Global Society* and *Tourism, Consumption and Representation*, and founding editor of the *Journal of Tourism Consumption and Practice*.

Dorothea Meyer is Senior Lecturer in Tourism at Sheffield Hallam University. Her current research interests include tourism as a tool for poverty reduction; development impacts of foreign direct investment in tourism; and power structures and the political economy of tourism.

Janet Momsen is Emerita Professor of Geography at the University of California, Davis and Senior Research Associate in the International Gender Studies Centre and the Centre for the Environment, Oxford University. She is author or editor of fifteen books and edits a series for Routledge on International Studies of Women and Place.

Jan Mosedale is Senior Lecturer in Tourism and Hospitality at the University of Sunderland. He is primarily concerned with analysing the constitution of 'the economy' as multiple forms of economic practices across space. This involves research on the capitalist structures of the economy as well as non-capitalist forms of economic exchanges.

Michihiko Nakata studied at Kyoto University (LLB 1963) and subsequently worked with Mitsubishi Corporation for thirty-six years. After retirement he studied Human Geography at the University of California, Davis (MA 2004, PhD candidate 2007). He is interested in Japanese activities in sub-Saharan Africa.

Nicolai Scherle is Senior Lecturer in the Department of Cultural Geography at the Catholic University of Eichstätt-Ingolstadt, Germany. His monograph on the presentation of cultural aspects in German-language travel guides was awarded a research prize by the International Tourism Fair (ITB) in Berlin in 2000.

Craig Webster earned his doctorate from Binghamton University, USA. He has taught at Ithaca College, and the College of Tourism and Hotel Management. He is currently an Associate Professor at the University of Nicosia. His research interests include human rights, comparative foreign policy, tourism politics and public opinion analysis.

Acknowledgements

Numerous people have contributed in various ways to the production of this book. Foremost, I am grateful to the contributors for their enthusiasm in participating in this volume. Their works address critical issues in tourism research and demonstrate the diversity of political economy approaches. I would like to thank Emma Travis, Faye Leerink and Lisa Salonen of Routledge and Michael Hall as book series editor for "Contemporary Geographies of Leisure, Tourism and Mobility". They were excited about the book from its conception and provided valuable assistance during the process. I have also benefitted from stimulating and enjoyable academic environments at the Department of Tourism of the University of Otago and the University of Sunderland and would like to thank colleagues for their support and encouragement.

Finally, I am grateful to W. W. Norton & Company, Inc. for kindly granting permission to use the table Political Economic Systems from *Essentials of Comparative Politics*, Second Edition, by Patrick O'Neil. Copyright © 2007, 2004.

1 Re-introducing tourism to political economy

Jan Mosedale

Political economy in its earlier stages – as undertaken by Smith (1981 [1776]) and Ricardo (1973 [1817]) – was concerned with the production and accumulation of wealth (what is generally considered to be the economy) and its distribution (the political dimension). Marx later focused in particular on the distribution (or rather lack thereof) of wealth across social classes. Although political economy was deemed to be a 'unified social science' at its inception, a number of methodological ruptures have since fragmented the erstwhile discipline. As the aim of this book is not to give a precise historical account of political economy, I will touch only briefly on developments from the 1960s onwards (see Milonakis and Fine 2009 for an in-depth overview of the evolution of political economy and its links to economic theory), before introducing some of the key approaches to political economy that are currently being drawn on in tourism scholarship.

In the late 1960s and early 1970s, at a time when positivism was *de rigeur*, critics such as Harvey (1973) argued that spatial positivist science was not only unable to answer the questions and solve the pressing problems of the time, but also there was no room in the positivist approach to consider the necessary questions (Kitchin 2006). The civil rights movement in the United States influenced Harvey (1973) to think about capital and space in urban settings and uneven development at different spatial scales. Further, a general decline of the main manufacturing regions in Europe and the United States (notably the Midlands in the United Kingdom, the Ruhrgebiet in Germany and the Midwest in the United States) led to an increasing critical research on regional decline, labour issues and industrial restructuring. The underlying motivation for turning towards a critical political economy was a perceived failure of capitalism to address and solve these *social* problems.

Similarly, the stimulus for a more critical analysis of tourism was given in the 1970s, epitomized by the influential texts of Young (1973), *Tourism: Blessing or Blight?*, and de Kadt (1979), *Tourism: Passport to Development?* Both critically analyse the advantages and disadvantages of tourism by focusing on tourism from the perspective of development and dependency theory. A key theme for dependency theorists is the interdependence of development and underdevelopment. As such there is a clear distinction between dependency theory and modernization theory in that the former situates the periphery in a different historical context from the latter. There is no internal lack of capital or skills that determines lack of development (as stipulated by modernization theory); rather, underdevelopment is the result of external forces – the integration of the periphery into the global capitalist economy and the inherent unequal exchange relationships between the core and periphery within that system.

Dependency theorists argue that incorporating peripheral economies into the global capitalist economy results not only in influencing production to align with the demands of the centre, but also in siphoning the economic surplus to the dominant countries. As the dominant countries in the centre continue to develop based on that surplus, the countries in the periphery struggle with underdevelopment: 'the international, national and local capitalist system generates economic development for the few and underdevelopment for the many' (Frank 1969: 7–8). This system is reproduced as the small local ruling class benefits from exporting raw materials, while the economy is controlled by the dominant nations in the centre. Contemporary dependency theory uses the case of transnational corporations as an example for exerting under- or dependent development (Britton 1980, 1982a,b; Bianchi 2002; Telfer 2002; also see Meyer in Chapter 10 for a re-conceptualization of the semi-periphery).

Dependency theory therefore analyses the macro-relations of production, that is, the position of tourism destinations in 'developing countries' (the periphery) *vis-à-vis* the position of dominant tourist-generating countries in the core. This view allows for a differentiation of development (or lack thereof) between developing countries based on their relation with dominant countries and has contributed greatly to add a critical edge to tourism research: 'Dependency theory opened our eyes and made us see the world from the perspective of the oppressed masses living in its "distant" corners. This is quite a contribution' (Peet 1991: 54).

Political economy as a critical theory still remains important in providing an understanding of societies, but has received relatively little attention in tourism research. A notable exception is Britton (1982a,b, 1991) who realized the importance of political economy in order to uncover the capitalist structures that are driving not only tourism development but also inequalities engrained in the system of uneven development and to position tourism in context to the capitalist system of accumulation. In his seminal paper, Britton (1991) calls for a move from mainly descriptive studies in the tradition of regional geography and spatial analysis towards a re-theorization of tourism geography through the integration of critical theory and political economy. Influenced by the writings of David Harvey, Britton (1991) seeks an analysis of the structural conditions that tourism operates in, a basic characteristic of political economy. Britton's appeal for a more critical geography of tourism and to position tourism firmly within the context of capitalist society has been followed and echoed by a number of tourism geographers, most notably Shaw and Williams (1994, 2002, 2004), Ioannides (1995, 2006), Ioannides and Debbage (1998), Dieke (2000) and Williams (2004). However, despite the early influence of critical development studies and political economy on tourism research, there is still a lack of publications bringing together different approaches to the political economy approach used in tourism, leading Williams (2004: 62) to claim that 'fruitful theoretical developments in political economy have largely bypassed tourism'. The aim of this edited book is therefore to assemble theoretical debates and current issues in the political economy of tourism.

Political economy approaches

'Political economy' in current usage is a term that encompasses a wide variety of approaches to studying the relationship between what is called 'the economy' and its 'non-economic' (i.e. political, socio-cultural, psychological and geographical) context. Peet and Thrift (1989: 3) view economy as 'social economy, or way of life, founded in production. In turn, social production is viewed not as a neutral act by neutral agents but as a political act'. Given the political nature, power is an underlying theme of political economy (albeit discussions of power are not often brought to the fore). Bianchi (2002: 265), for instance, emphasizes 'the systemic sources of power which serve to reproduce and condition different modes of tourism development'. Concepts of power as applied to tourism reseach have been discussed in much more detail elsewhere (see Coles and Church 2007, as well as Macleod and Carrier 2010), so, rather than replicate previous efforts, I will focus instead on some select approaches to political economy that have been used in tourism research.

Although there are a number of approaches to political economy, four seem to be particularly popular in the social sciences: first, Marxian political economists (typified by the early work of David Harvey; see, for instance, Harvey 1973, 1975) who rely on a close interpretation of Marx's writings and historical materialism; second, regulationists who are concerned with the regulatory framework (structure) of capitalism (Boyer 1990); third, comparative and international political economists who analyse the regulatory structures and the trade relationships between nation-states respectively; and, fourth – more recently – poststructural political economists or post-Marxists who are influenced by poststructural concepts and focus on alternatives to capitalism (Gibson-Graham 1996 and 2006). The differences between these strains seem so significant that Barnes (2000: 594) argues that 'only a single common thread seems to connect the many uses of political economy within geography: the belief that the political and the economic are irrevocably linked'.

Marxian political economy and historical materialism

According to Marx, matter and its production (i.e. the formation or transformation of matter) are the basis of social existence and history. 'Production' includes all processes of transformation and associated relationships and an object therefore is the sum or the end result of a process (Swyngedouw 2003). In historical materialism, it is more important to understand objects as the sum of all involved relations and processes rather than as the innate characteristics of the object itself. By analysing the relational processes involved in the production of an object, it is possible to expose the structures of the economic system (in Marx' case, economic exploitation of the working class and the domination of labour by capital). The tensions (e.g. between labour and capital) and intrinsic dynamic and competitive nature of capitalism (because of the need for constant growth) cause the capitalist system to suffer from instability and occasional crises of over-accumulation or over-production (such as the banking crisis of 2009/2010). Yet despite this instability, capitalism manages to regulate and reproduce itself. This resilience to systematic change and the mechanisms of capitalist reproduction are the key questions of concern to regulationist political economists.

Bianchi (2002: 265), in turn, applies a historic-geographical approach of political economy to analyse the structures governing tourism development. He posits that capital restructuring and economic globalization have resulted in a changing configuration within the tourism production system, thus requiring a detailed examination of relationships between all actors in the system in order to unveil the impacts of the 'transnationalization' of the tourism system.

Regulationism

Theories of regulation focus on the transformations in the social relations of capitalist production and the regulatory responses to these transformations. This particular school of thought on understanding economic problems and crises was developed in France in the 1970s by economists such as Aglietta (1979), Lipietz (1979) and Boyer (1978). Dunford (1990) argues that regulation theory comprises four key concepts: regimes of accumulation, industrial trajectories, modes of regulation and hegemonic structures.

As industries are interdependent (in terms of production, distribution, exchange and consumption) a regime of accumulation is the systematic organization of these interdependent processes in order to guarantee the reproduction of the economic system. The last concept of regulation theories is the industrial trajectories, changes in the production process that influence the organization of labour and production and hence the regime of accumulation. A prime example of this influence is the introduction of the semi-automatic assembly line by Ford, which resulted in the mechanization of transfer, rationalized the flow of work and increased divisions of labour (Dunford 1990).

Modes of regulation are therefore established in order to direct and stabilize the process of accumulation: 'it is through these structural forms that multiple, decentralized individual and collective rationalities with their limited horizons result in regular overall processes of economic reproduction' (Dunford 1990: 306). The modes of regulation are institutions or rules (such as structural and legal constraints, collective agreements and general rules of conduct within the economy and society) that ensure the unfolding and coordination of individual and collective behaviour, thus providing a stable and reproducible economic system. The mode of regulation that is applied in any one country depends on the chosen political, economic and institutional strategy. These hegemonic structures arguably extend the economic sphere to encompass civil society as a whole.

Comparative and international political economy

The hegemonic structures analysed by regulationists as one part of the regulatory structures to stabilize capitalism form the point of analysis for comparative political economy. Influenced by political science, comparative political economy is interested in the consequences that differences in ideologies and structural organization (e.g. different legal, political and social institutions) have on economies and civil society as a whole. Originally, most of the attention of the comparative approach was focused on the dual extremes of capitalism and socialism; yet with the capitalist/democratic shift of former centrally planned/socialist countries, some authors declared the triumph of capitalism (Ohmae 1990; Fukuyama 1992). They predicted that the demise of communism coupled with globalization would lead to a 'borderless world', the end of history (Ohmae 1990) and therefore the inevitable emergence of a single capitalist economy.

In contrast to these predictions of a global, homogeneous capitalism devoid of historical connections, comparative political economy has re-focused on understanding the diversity of political-economic systems of governance and regulation by analysing different systems of capitalism. The emphasis is not only on different interpretations of how to practice capitalism by the former centrally planned economies of the transition countries (see Feldmann 2006) but also on the varieties of capitalism within the 'traditional' market economies (Hall and Soskice 2001; Peck and Theodore 2008). These varieties of capitalism are explained by differences in historical context (e.g. in the creation of institutions or the formation of a nation-state). Political-economic systems are thus path-dependent: actions by institutions are not just reactions to contemporary conditions, they are also dependent on the entire series of previous decisions and their resulting outcomes. This institutional history is place-specific as relationships between economic/political/social actors, institutions and structures unfold in particular places (see, for example, Bathelt and Gertler 2005 for a discussion of evolutionary changes to the German Rhineland model).

Whereas comparative political economists are engaged in analysing varieties of capitalism (usually contained within a nation-state or region), international political economy is concerned with the relationship between nation-states or regions. One Marxist approach to international political economy is world systems theory (Wallerstein 1976), which posits that international relations are framed – and largely determined – by a superimposing structure: the global capitalist economy. In this global capitalist structure, nation-states or regions compete for the flow of commodities, labour and capital that are the basis for various forms of power (e.g. economic and military). It is this competition that shapes the relationships between nation-states and results in a hierarchical layering of the capitalist global economy (Wallerstein 2000). Of particular interest to international political economy is the reordering of the global order (e.g. the transition from centrally planned to market economies, China's 'economic opening', and the continued expansion of the European Union) and the resulting changes in international relations between nation-states.

However, one of the key predicaments for international political economy is the disparity between a relational capitalist economy, which crosses geographical scales and involves a variety of different actors, and the static focus of international political economy scholars on the national scale and institutions. This contradiction or 'methodological nationalism' (Hess and Yeung 2006: 1197) has led to a different analysis of the global economy that cuts across the scalar divisions by returning to Marx' materialism and focusing on (re)production processes and the relationships between diverse actors (firms, institutions and individuals). In contrast to analysing the macro-structures of global capitalism, process-based frameworks such as global commodity chains (Gereffi and Korzeniewicz 1994), global value chains (Gereffi *et al.* 2005) and global production networks (Henderson *et al.* 2002) examine the relational connections between actors involved in production processes.

A cultural challenge for political economy

Production and materialism as the focal point for political economy are being challenged by cultural forces and a move (by some) to a political economy that is more sensitive to cultural meanings of material forces (Jessop and Sum 2001). This cultural political economy is based on the 'cultural turn' – encompassing a multitude of different approaches – which is based on the realization that the cultural dimension has been neglected in the analysis of social, economic and political processes. Yet there exist numerous articulations of culture and economy. Crang (1997) lists four alternative views that differ in the type/depth of the relationship: first, the determination of culture by the economy; second, the embeddedness of economic processes in cultural meanings; third, the representation of the economy through cultural media such as symbols, signs and discourses; and, finally, the production, circulation and consumption of cultural materials. These different interpretations of the complex relationship between culture and economy are visible in distinct approaches of cultural political economy (Crang 1997; Sayer 2001; Hudson 2004; Thrift 2004; Jessop and Oosterlynck 2008; Jones 2008; see also Chapter 6, this volume, by Mosedale).

Concurrently with the debate over the articulations of culture and economy, poststructuralists have questioned the discursive practices and resulting manifestations of capitalist power, especially in consolidating the capitalist system (Gibson-Graham 1996). The point that poststructuralists are making is that discourses, which bestow meaning to terms, are subject to the dominant social value and power. Once a structure is seen as being 'normal' – for example patriarchy in the case of Western society – this dominant structure creates the social norms that influence discourses and give meaning to terms, hence reproducing its dominance as it has 'the ability to construct and maintain difference through language and practice' (Dixon and Jones 2006: 49).

Structure of the book

With the advent of cultural studies and the cultural turn, political economy is no longer the most fashionable approach for critical analyses of tourism. Yet political economy (in its various guises and transfigurations) still has much to offer tourism analyses and should not be ignored or indeed written off in favour of a more fashionable approach to studying and analysing tourism. In this introductory chapter I have outlined that the study of political economy is far from being a unified approach to analysing societies and have undertaken to introduce the main approaches to political economy. Inevitably, it is impossible to capture all the nuances of political economy in one edited collection, yet the chapters offer more succinct discussions of various approaches and provide empirical studies in the political economy tradition.

The collection is made up of three parts. Part I broadly presents different approaches to political economy, including discussions on Marxist political economy, regulation, comparative political economy, commodity chain research and alternative political economies. This introduces the reader to the diverse interpretations of and approaches to political economy and helps to explain the differing focal points of the following contributions.

Bianchi (Chapter 2) sets out to apply a Marxian political economy to international tourism and labour relations within it. His chapter introduces historical materialism and Marxian political economy and applies this theoretical lens to analyse tourism in light of capitalism, globalization and labour relations. For Bianchi, Marxian political economy is still very much relevant for the analysis of the global tourism political economy, as apparent in ongoing labour disputes. Marxian political economy is useful for tourism research by focusing on labour relations in tourism, access to travel and equitable distribution in the destination.

Cornelissen (Chapter 3) provides a comprehensive overview of the regulation approach and demonstrates that researchers in tourism have mainly focused their attention on the regime of accumulation (how tourism products are consumed and produced, for example a shift from Fordism to post-Fordism) and largely neglected the institutional structures that direct and stabilize the process of accumulation. She argues that tourism analyses would benefit from a rigorous application of the regulation approach to tourism 'in and of itself': tourism as a capitalist activity is subject to crises with subsequent regulatory fixes. Applying the regulation approach to tourism would highlight how actors and structures interact to stabilize economic processes and thus ensure the reproduction of tourism itself.

In Chapter 4, Webster and colleagues follow a comparative political economy approach by exploring and comparing the institutional organization of tourism across different models of political economies of governance. In their analysis of the organizational structure of tourism across liberal (United States and Canada), social democratic (Finland and Sweden) and mercantilist (South Korea and Japan) political systems, they establish that the paradigms of political systems influence the intensity of response towards tourism and its institutional organization. However, it seems that the social democracies analysed have experienced a shift towards neoliberalism.

In contrast to comparative political economy, which analyses national differences in the institutional organization of regulation, Clancy (Chapter 5) draws on commodity chain research as a particular approach to international political economy, to analyse globalization and development in tourism. He puts forward commodity chain analysis, a systems-based rather than a destination-based approach to analysing tourism, in order to embed tourism in the larger political economy as opposed to being purely tourism-centric. Clancy suggests that commodity chain research has a key role to play in linking upgrading opportunities within the chain to pro-poor tourism initiatives, as upgrading is beneficial for local tourism providers in order to attain a position with more power over production and consumption processes and which generates more income.

To conclude the overview of political economy approaches in Part I, Mosedale (Chapter 6) puts Marxian political economy in the context of the cultural turn. Given the shift of emphasis from structural meta-narrative to cultural micro-narrative, new approaches to political economy have undertaken to incorporate cultural aspects either within (in the case of cultural political economy) or in opposition to (in the case of many poststructural political economists) a Marxian political economy. Mosedale argues that Marxian political economy can be complemented by poststructural theory in order to create an alternative political economy, thus balancing structure and agency by providing space for agency outside and within the dominant capitalist structures.

Part II links key themes of political economy (i.e. class, gender, labour, development and consumption) to tourism in the context of the approaches discussed in Part I. Class was at the forefront of Marx's critique of political economy, yet has received scant interest in tourism studies. Hall (Chapter 7) presents an overview of class as a representation of the stratifying nature of capitalist, socio-economic organization. He argues that the unequal access to time and money are the stratifying causes of unequal mobility (e.g. people, capital, knowledge) and puts forward a strong case for the continued involvement of tourism studies with the concept of class. Class remains an important structural determinant and an explanatory factor, especially in the context of neoliberal strategies.

Class has traditionally been *the* inequality inherent in capitalist social relations with which political economy has struggled. In contrast to class, gender has been integrated into political economy only relatively recently. Gender has received a certain amount of interest in tourism research (see, for instance, Kinnaird and Hall 1994; Aitchison 2001, 2005; Pritchard *et al.* 2007), yet the feminist perspective is still under-represented in the political economy of tourism. In their contribution to this volume, Momsen and Nakata (Chapter 8) offer an overview of the changing approaches towards gender and tourism and reveal the importance of age, class and gender for Japanese mountain tourism.

As expanded by Bianchi in Chapter 2, labour relations are of prime interest for historical materialism. In Chapter 9, Lovelock and Leopold draw on political economic concepts of labour to relate temporary labour migration in New Zealand and the migration–tourism nexus. Their case study of New Zealand demonstrates that the regulation of labour migration is embedded in historical national and international contexts. Competition for labour between nation-states has led to a changing focus of the New Zealand government from permanent settlement towards temporary labour migration. Within the larger context of labour migration, Lovelock and Leopold demonstrate that working holidaymakers occupy a 'privileged niche' (see also Hall's discussion of class in Chapter 7) as they benefit from preferential entry requirements compared, for instance, with labourers from the Pacific.

In Chapter 10, Meyer draws on concepts from world systems theory and development theory by focusing on the relationships between the centre, periphery and semi-periphery. Her research on foreign direct investment in tourism development in Zanzibar highlights the role of foreign direct investment from the global South as an increasingly important source of capital. Because of extensive experience in operating and investing in tourism in the global South, Kenyans and South Africans especially have taken a powerful position and provide an important connection between peripheral destinations and tour operators from the global North. Meyer's analysis highlights a re-configuration of power relationships between the global North and the global South, proving that the 'semi-periphery' should not be ignored in tourism research and merits more detailed analysis.

With the advent of the cultural turn (see Chapter 6), political economy is discovering consumption. Meethan (Chapter 11) sets consumption in the context of political economy by considering Dubai's shift from oil production to leisure and tourism consumption. Dubai has now become a synonym for consumption, Meethan demonstrates that globalization and Dubai's strategic position in air transport have increased the state's power to attract and connect to flows of people and capital, bolstered by increased public–private funding for tourism projects. This rapid transformation from oil to tourism hinges on the government's actions being unconstrained by an opposition and strict labour regulations resulting in a flexible yet strained labour force.

Part III, then, examines the political economy at various geographical scales and focuses on the outcomes and processes of the political act of planning and managing tourism production. Albrecht (Chapter 12) situates decision-making at the heart of political economy. Her analysis of community tourism planning in rural New Zealand encapsulates the decision-making processes and power relations in terms of representation involved in tourism planning. How different actors take part in planning, how they articulate their views on tourism and are represented in the planning process and whether there is such as thing as 'common good' are some of the questions that are highly relevant to local tourism development and planning.

In Chapter 13, Scherle examines current Moroccan tourism policies in light of a changing national and international context (political economy). Morocco offers an interesting case because of its economic system trying to integrate traditional rent capitalism and neoliberalism. Scherle outlines this by examining the Master Plan of Marrakech and focusing particularly on the internationalization agenda, such as the liberalization of air traffic and, linked to this neoliberal strategy, the gentrification of Moroccan medinas by Europeans and North Americans.

Duval and Macilree (Chapter 14) provide an analysis of the international political economy within which international air transport operates. They demonstrate that international air transport relies largely on a complex system of bilateral arrangements governing and negotiating a variety of access rights. Most successful airlines benefit from having strategic geographical positions as stopover points because of the reluctance by some states to grant foreign airlines the right to carry traffic from their airports to a third country. Advancements in technology (i.e. an increase in aircraft range), which lead to a reduction of this competitive advantage, might result in a reshuffle of international relations in the future.

Finally, Mosedale and Albrecht (Chapter 15) discuss the spatialities of political economy and support a relational and discursive perspective of tourism space over hierarchical sets of spatial scales. Given the restructuring of spaces and sites of regulation, they contend that it is necessary to re-theorize the implications for tourism regulation and governance. At the same time, they are conscious that the discourse of spatial organization can be politically motivated. It is therefore imperative for a cultural political economy of tourism regulation to analyse the various discourses on space and to examine how they are represented and employed strategically within a politics of scale. Given discourses on spatiality, Mosedale and Albrecht ask whether territorially bound tourism regulation can still be successful or whether an increasing significance of social relations demands a changing orientation and organization of tourism regulation beyond spatial scales.

References

Aglietta, M. (1979) *A Theory of Capitalist Regulation: The US experience*, London: New Left Books.

Aitchison, C. (2001) 'Theorizing other discourses of tourism, gender and culture: Can the subaltern speak (in tourism)?', *Tourist Studies*, 1: 133–147.

Aitchison, C. (2005) 'Feminist and gender perspectives in tourism studies: The socio-cultural nexus of critical and cultural theories', *Tourist Studies*, 5: 207–224.

Barnes, T. (2000) 'Political economy', in R. J. Johnston, D. Gregory, G. Pratt and M. Watts (eds) *The Dictionary of Human Geography*, 4th edn, Oxford: Blackwell.

Bathelt, H. and Gertler, M. S. (2005) 'The German variety of capitalism: Forces and dynamics of evolutionary change', *Economic Geography*, 81: 1–9.

Bianchi, R. V. (2002) 'Towards a new political economy of global tourism', in R. Sharpley and D. J. Telfer (eds) *Tourism and Development: Concepts and issues*, Clevedon: Channel View.

Boyer, R. (1978) 'Les salaries en longe période', *Economie et Statistique*, 103: 27–57.

Boyer, R. (1990) *The Regulation School: A critical introduction*, New York: Columbia University Press.

Britton, S. G. (1980) 'The spatial organisation of tourism in a neo-colonial economy: A Fiji case study', *Pacific Viewpoint*, 21: 144–165.

Britton, S. G. (1982a) 'International tourism and multinational corporations in the Pacific: The case of Fiji', in M. Taylor and N. Thrift (eds) *The Geography of Multinationals*, Andover: Croom Helm.

Britton, S. G. (1982b) 'The political economy of tourism in the Third World', *Annals of Tourism Research*, 9: 331–359.

Britton, S. G. (1991) 'Tourism, capital and place: Towards a critical geography of tourism', *Environment and Planning D*, 9: 451–478.

Coles, T. and Church A. (eds) (2007) *Tourism, Power and Space*, Abingdon: Routledge.

Crang, P. (1997) 'Cultural turns and the (re)constitution of economic geography: Introduction to section one', in R. Lee and J. Wills (eds) *Geographies of Economies*, London: Edward Arnold.

de Kadt, E. (ed.) (1979) *Tourism: Passport to development? Perspectives on the social and cultural effects of tourism in developing countries*, New York: Oxford University Press.

Dieke, P. U. C. (ed.) (2000) *The Political Economy of Tourism Development in Africa*, New York: Cognizant Communication Corporation.

Dixon, D. P. and Jones, J. P., III (2006) 'Feminist geographies of difference, relation, and construction', in S. Aitken and G. Valentine (eds) *Approaches to Human Geography*, London: SAGE.

Dunford, M. (1990) 'Theories of regulation', *Society and Space*, 8: 297–321.

Emmanuel, A. (1972) *Unequal Exchange: A study of the imperialism of trade*, New York: Monthly Review Press.

Feldmann, M. (2006) 'Emerging varieties of capitalism in transition countries: industrial relations and wage bargaining in Estonia and Slovenia', *Comparative Political Studies* 39, 829–54.

Frank, A. G. (1969) *Capitalism and Underdevelopment in Latin America*, New York: Monthly Review Press.

Fukuyama, F. (1992) *The End of History and the Last Man*, New York: Free Press.

Gereffi, G. and Korzeniewicz, M. (eds) (1994) *Commodity Chains and Global Capitalism*, Westport: Praeger.

Gereffi, G., Humphrey, J. and Sturgeon, T. J. (2005) 'The governance of global value chains', *Review of International Political Economy*, 12: 78–104.

Gibson-Graham, J. K. (1996) *The End of Capitalism (as We Knew It): A feminist critique of political economy*, Oxford: Blackwell.

Gibson-Graham, J. K. (2006) *A Postcapitalist Politics*, London: University of Minnesota Press.

Hall, P. A. and Soskice, D. (2001) *Varieties of Capitalism: The institutional foundations of comparative advantage*, Oxford: Oxford University Press.

Harvey, D. (1973) *Social Justice and the City*, London: Edward Arnold.

Harvey, D. (1975) 'The geography of capitalist accumulation: A reconstruction of the Marxian theory', *Antipode*, 7: 9–21.

Henderson, J., Dicken, P., Hess, M., Coe, N. and Yeung, H. W.-C. (2002) 'Global production networks and the analysis of economic development', *Review of International Political Economy*, 9: 436–464.

Hess, M. and Yeung, H. W.-C. (2006) 'Whither global production networks in economic geography? Past, present and future', *Environment and Planning A*, 38: 1193–1204.

Hudson, R. (2004) 'Conceptualizing economies and their geographies: Spaces, flows and circuits', *Progress in Human Geography*, 28: 447–471.

Ioannides, D. (1995) 'Strengthening the ties between tourism and economic geography: A theoretical agenda', *Professional Geographer*, 47: 49–60.

Ioannides, D. (2006) 'Commentary: The economic geography of the tourist industry: Ten years of progress in research and an agenda for the future', *Tourism Geographies*, 8: 76–86.

Ioannides, D. and Debbage, K. G. (eds) (1998) *The Economic Geography of the Tourist Industry: A supply-side analysis*, London: Routledge.

Jessop, B. and Sum, N. L. (2001) 'Pre-disciplinary and post-disciplinary perspectives in political economy', *New Political Economy*, 6: 89–101.

Jessop, B. and Oosterlynck, S. (2008) 'Cultural political economy: On making the cultural turn without falling into soft economic sociology', *Geoforum*, 39: 1155–1169.

Jones, M. (2008) 'Recovering a sense of political economy', *Political Geography*, 27: 377–399.

Kinnaird, V. and Hall, D. (eds) (1994) *Tourism: A gender analysis*, Chichester: Wiley.

Kitchin, R. (2006) 'Positivistic geographies and spatial science', in S. Aitken and G. Valentine (eds) *Approaches to Human Geography*, London: Sage Publications.

Lipietz, A. (1979) *Crise et Inflation, Pourquoi?* Paris: Maspéro.

Macleod, D. V. L. and Carrier, J. G. (2010) *Tourism, Power and Culture: Anthropological insights*, Bristol: Channel View.

Milonakis, D. and Fine, B. (2009) *From Political Economy to Economics: Method, the social and the historical in the evolution of economic theory*, Abingdon: Routledge.

Ohmae, K. (1990) *The Borderless World: Power and strategy in the interlinked economy*, HarperCollins: London.

Peck J and Theodore N (2008) 'Variegated capitalism', *Progress in Human Geography*, 31: 731–772.

Peet, R. (1991) *Global Capitalism: Theories of societal development*, London: Routledge.

Peet, R. and Thrift, N. (1989) 'Political economy and human geography', in R. Peet and N. Thrift (eds) *New Models in Geography: The political-economy perspective*, London: Unwin Hyman.

Pritchard, A., Morgan, N., Ateljevic, I. and Harris, C. (2007) *Tourism and Gender: Embodiment, sensuality and experience,* Wallingford: CABI.

Ricardo, D. (1973) [1817] *The Principles of Political Economy and Taxation*, Oxford: Oxford University Press.

Sayer, A. (2001) 'For a critical cultural political economy', *Antipode*, 33: 687–708.

Shaw, G. and Williams, A. M. (1994) *Critical Issues in Tourism: A geographical perspective*, Oxford: Blackwell.

Shaw, G. and Williams, A.M. (2002) *Critical Issues in Tourism: A geographical perspective*, 2nd edn, Oxford: Blackwell.

Shaw, G. and Williams, A. M. (2004) *Tourism and Tourism Spaces*, London: Sage Publications.

Smith, A. (1981) [1776] *An Inquiry into the Nature and the Causes of the Wealth of Nations*, Volume 1, Indianapolis: Liberty Fund.

Swyngedouw, E. (2003) 'The Marxian alternative: Historical-geographical materialism and the political economy of capitalism', in E. Sheppard and T. Barnes (eds) *A Companion to Economic Geography*, Oxford: Blackwell.

Telfer, D. J. (2002) 'The evolution of tourism and development theory', in R. Sharpley and
    D. J. Telfer (eds) *Tourism and Development: Concepts and issues*, Clevedon: Channel
    View.
Thrift, N. (2004) *Knowing Capitalism*, London: SAGE.
Wallerstein, I. (1976) *The Modern World-System: Capitalist agriculture and the origins
    of the european world-economy in the sixteenth century*, New York: Academic Press.
Wallerstein, I. M. (2000) 'Introduction to special issue on commodity chains in the world
    economy, 1590–1790', *Review*, 23: 1–13.
Williams, A. M. (2004) 'Toward a political economy of tourism', in A. A. Lew, C. M. Hall
    and A. M. Williams (eds) *A Companion to Tourism*, Oxford: Blackwell.
Young, G. (1973) *Tourism: Blessing or blight?* Harmondsworth: Penguin.

Part I

Approaches to political economy in tourism

2   Tourism, capitalism and Marxist political economy

Raoul V. Bianchi

> I want to argue that in the triumphant resurgence of capitalism – and indeed, its global reach – the one thinker who is vindicated is Karl Marx.
>
> (Meghnad Desai 2004: 3)

There is little doubt that Marxist political economy has made a profound contribution to our understanding and critique of the capitalist political economy. Cox (2002: 27) goes as far as to argue that 'we are all Marxists now, given the demonstrated usefulness of many Marxist, or rather, Marxian models for understanding social processes'. Notwithstanding the constant soundings of its death knell (see Booth 1985; Fukuyama 1989), Marx continues to be relevant for understanding the workings of twenty-first-century capitalism. This chapter thus considers the political economy of international tourism and its labour relations through the conceptual–theoretical lens of Marx's political economy and historical materialism. Where relevant it also draws on broader strands of Marxian enquiry, which have in one way or another contributed to a reappraisal of Marxist political economy in the context of globalization and neoliberalism, and which offer ways of moving beyond the theoretical barricades and ideological enclaves that have often undermined the contribution of radical political economy to recent debates.

The principles of Marxist political economy

It is often argued by his critics that Marx's political economy is underpinned by an intrinsic determinism based on the causal primacy of economic forces, otherwise known as the 'base-superstructure' model (Jack and Phipps 2005: 18). Nowhere is this more evident than in the oft-cited assertion that, 'The country that is more developed industrially only shows to the less developed, the image of its own future' (Marx 1974: 19). Although there are strong grounds for challenging Marxist orthodoxy when it lapses into stagist and linear interpretations of historical social change, in his defence, such interpretations rest largely upon selective quotations from key works as well as the ideological imperatives of Bolshevism, which did a great deal to expunge any nuanced readings of Marx's writings (Desai 2004: 42). Such 'orthodox' readings of Marx ignore the more nuanced and circumspect analyses of capitalism that are evident throughout his work, which emphasize the context-specific tendencies of historical capitalist development (e.g. Marx 1974: 603, 1977a: 576–580), and thus also repudiate any notion of the inevitability of capitalism's demise, which he famously expressed in Chapter 32 of *Capital*, Volume 1 (see Desai 2004: 79–81).

Historical materialism

Marx's theory of capitalist development was never intended as an 'iron law', much less a rigid template upon which the diverse experiences of development could be mapped (see Sweezy 1970: 18–19). Rather, Marxist political economy revolves around the *historical materialist* method, the essence of which can be stated quite simply as an attempt 'to understand what is produced, how, and by and for whom' (Dunn 2009: 73). Historical materialism thus involves the analysis of the manner in which human beings have progressively developed their capacity to exploit the physical world in order to survive, and in doing so forge social relationships and ever more complex divisions of labour that together constitute the 'mode of production'. Moreover, the manner in which these productive forces and social relations combine and shape societies is not immediately apparent to the actors involved (Callinicos 1989: 126). As humans' capacity to control and exploit the physical world (or, rather, the 'forces of production') develops, the minority (capitalist class) appropriates the surpluses produced by the majority (direct producers or workers), over and above that which is necessary to keep everyone at a level just above subsistence (see Harman 1998: 13). It is within these distinctive logics of surplus extraction and class conflict that the essence of Marx's explanation of the workings of capitalist development lies.

Marx on development

For Marx, capitalist societies are underpinned by the antagonistic relationship between capital and labour. This in turn is reflected in the division of classes into the 'bourgeoisie' (capitalist class) and 'proletariat' (working class), and the concentration of the 'means of production' in the hands of the former. Accordingly, private property is the foundation of capitalist development and society, and is the means through which producers are 'alienated' from the products of their labour as well as constituting the motor force behind the continual pursuit of profit. The monopolization of ownership in the form of capitalist enterprise thus enables the capitalist class to exercise control over the division of labour in the context of production and thereby monopolise decisions over what to produce, how much to produce and how to produce. Notwithstanding increasing differentiation within the capitalist classes and the diversity of capitalisms, according to Sklair (2001: 10–16) today's 'transnational capitalist class' shares a common interest in enabling the pursuit of profit and expanding the realms of capital accumulation.

Although in his earlier writings and speeches Marx was a virulent critic of the inhumanity of capitalism and the marked inequalities it had brought about, he was initially favourable towards colonialism (particularly in India) as well as free trade (as was Lenin) (Marx 1977b: 269–270). Specifically, he emphasized the positive effects of capitalist development in terms of dissolving pre-capitalist forms of production that were (in his view) holding back the expansion of capitalism and the development of productive forces in 'backward' societies, the advancement of which would hasten the demise of capitalism itself and bring about the onset of a workers' revolution (Marx 1977c: 332–336). Nevertheless, Marx did emphasize how the growing industrial capacity of European societies was a key factor in the ruination of endogenous systems of production in the colonies, in particular India, converting them into fields for the supply of raw materials for the industrial heartlands of Western Europe (Marx 1974: 424–425). It was, in fact, Lenin who overturned Marx's belief in the progressive nature of capitalism. Rather, he emphasized that imperialism, which he described as the 'highest stage of capitalism', would lead to stagnation and decay, thus stimulating the search for profits abroad through the export of capital to the colonized territories (Lenin 1987: 245–246). In doing so he laid the ground work for later neo-Marxist theories of underdevelopment and dependency, which would exercise a significant degree of influence on the political economy of tourism development during the 1960s and 1970s.

Marx and the workers

Central to Marx's interrogation of capitalism is the *commodity*, which encompasses both intrinsic *use values* regardless of their monetary worth, as well as an economic value that is realized by way of exchange in the commodity economy (*exchange values*), through the medium of money (Sweezy 1970: 26–28). However, it is only in capitalist societies based on the production of commodities for profit that labour itself, or rather the capacity to produce, or *labour power* as Marx calls it, constitutes a commodity in itself. For Marx, the exploitation[1] of labour associated with the production of *surplus value* lies at the heart of capitalist economic development and distinguishes capitalism from other forms of 'extra-economic' coercion (Worsley 2002: 33). Surplus value refers to the difference between the value of commodities produced by the workers and the value of the wages they receive in return for their labour (Sweezy 1970: 59–62). Workers are not paid the full value of the goods (and services) they produce, which enables the owners to appropriate the remaining surplus and to generate a profit. This then sets in train the constant cycle of accumulation and the concentration of capital into fewer and fewer hands.

Competition between workers maintains a constant downwards pressure on wages, thus enabling the process of capital accumulation to be sustained. This results in the existence of what Marx famously termed the 'reserve army of labour', a surplus population of unemployed workers that, during periods of economic stagnation, grows relative to the demand for labour (Marx 1974: 589–600). The exploitative relationship between capital and labour is, however, concealed by the impersonalized sphere of market exchange, which promotes the myth, reinforced discursively within the public realm, that workers are 'free' to move from one employer to another in search of work or the best wage (Marx 1974: 166). Marx refers to this facade as the 'fetish character of commodities' (Marx 1974: 76–87). Putting aside politico-cultural obstacles to labour mobility (see Chapter 9 by Lovelock and Leopold), without the wherewithal to sustain themselves, workers in capitalist societies are compelled to seek work in the labour market, often under conditions that are less than favourable.

The ability of capitalists to extract surpluses from workers is no accident, nor is it the reflection of inherent differences between the classes. Rather it is the outcome of an historical process of 'primitive accumulation', through which the direct or independent producers (peasants, artisans and the self-employed) are deprived of their control over the means of production and the ability to provide for their own subsistence without recourse to wage work (Marx 1974: Chapter 27; Meiksins Wood 2002: 108–109). Although Marx saw primitive accumulation as part of the 'original' moment integral to the beginnings of capitalist development during the transition from feudalism, Marxist geographer David Harvey (2005, 2006) argues that the separation of people from their independent means of livelihood is a continuous process embedded within contemporary (global) capitalism. Referring to this process as 'accumulation by dispossession', Harvey demonstrates that capital continuously seeks to open up new and profitable avenues of investment and, in so doing, avert crises of over-accumulation and declining profitability (see Harvey 2005: Chapter 4).

Perhaps Marx's greatest failing in seeing the root of the dynamic forces and antagonisms in society as derived from the economic realm is the fact that he under-emphasized (but did not ignore altogether) the role of ideas and non-economic forces in sustaining the inequalities of capitalist economics (Worsley 2002: 46). Nonetheless, although distinctive attitudes towards inequality and injustice, and, one might add, the differential propensity to trade leisure for income in different societies (see Woolsey Biggart 1994: 682–684), are cultural and political questions that cannot be explained through the lens of production and the class structure of societies, this does not negate the utility of an historical materialist analysis. Moreover, although factors such as gender and ethnicity shape the organization of production, not to mention consumption, as Perrons (1999: 94–95) explains, the internal dynamic of capitalist societies is still fundamentally tied to the profit motive and the need for the majority of people to engage in wage-work in order to survive.

Finally, one does not have to accept the Marxist–Leninist dictum that the 'proletariat' is the historical agent of the overthrow of capitalism to acknowledge the historical role played by workers in the struggle against the exploitative conditions and injustices perpetrated by capitalist development in different societies (Mason 2008). Subsequent Marxian thought has in fact advanced diverse understandings of class that encompass the core Marxist notion that one's class is linked to both the structure of production as well as the subjective experiences of workers in the formation of class identities (see Munck 2000: 62–63; Wright 2009). Fundamentally, however, Marxist political economy rests upon the core notion that, in capitalist societies in which access to work is mediated by the institution of private property and the organization of work controlled by the capitalists, antagonisms between those who monopolise the benefits of private property and those who are only 'free' to sell their labour are likely to arise.

Marxist political economy and tourism

The dearth of Marxist theorizing in tourism remains something of a mystery, not least because it has often been proclaimed that tourism constitutes one of the world's largest industries. It is all the more surprising when one considers that the possibility of international travel for the relatively wealthy is a by-product of global capitalism and the pervasive social inequalities associated with it (Smith 2009: 274). Although the recent *Handbook of Tourism Studies* (Jamal and Robinson 2009) makes no mention of Marxist thinking in tourism, the influence of Marxist political economy is nevertheless apparent in the economic geography of tourism (see Britton 1991; Hall 1994; Ioannides and Debbage 1998; Mosedale 2006), in recent critiques of tourism and corporate globalization (Bianchi 2002; Duffy 2002; Reid 2003) and sustainable tourism (Sharpley 2009), and in inform-ing analyses of 'commodification' in tourism (Arremberi 2001; Harrison 2001: 29; MacCannell 1992, 1999; Meethan 2001).

This can perhaps be explained by the pervasive influence of an applied busi-ness 'paradigm' in tourism studies (Tribe 2008), and, more recently, the 'critical turn in tourism studies', which has shifted the emphasis of tourism enquiry away from the material configurations of power and inequality towards an emphasis on discourse, consumption and representations (Bianchi 2009). Moreover, studies of tourism development are often disconnected from questions of political economy (Steiner 2006: 165). Marx's belief in the progressive nature of capitalism does resonate with earlier thinking regarding the *commodification* or *commoditization* of host societies; however, the emphasis here has typically been on the allegedly damaging consequences of tourism for the 'authenticity' of destination cultures rather than a critique of the capitalist imperatives of profit-making and the exploi-tation of wage-labour in the realm of tourism enterprise (see Cohen 1988; Smith 1989). Marx himself would no doubt have welcomed the integration of these societies into the mainstream of global capitalism, although he most likely would have expressed concern at the conversion of hospitality from a ritual obligation and social duty into a commercialized profit-driven industry.

Tourism and underdevelopment

The most significant influence of Marxist political economy in tourism has argua-bly been exercised by neo-Marxist theories of underdevelopment and dependency, which drew on classical Marxist theories of imperialism in order to explain the inequalities between core capitalist states and peripheral 'Third World' economies (see Amin 1976; Baran 1957; Emmanuel 1972; Frank 1969; Wallerstein 1974). Dependency theorists argued that the penetration of foreign capital had led to the destruction of indigenous economies, subsequently re-organizing Third World economies to serve the needs of foreign capital. Accordingly, capital accumula-tion in the rich metropolitan states sustained itself through the expropriation of the economic surpluses produced in the Third World, locking them into a relationship of dependency and condemning them to a situation of *under*development.

Britton (1980, 1982) was one amongst several tourism development analysts (see Bryden 1973; Husbands 1981; Pérez 1980; Turner 1976; Weaver 1988) to draw on different strands of underdevelopment and dependency theories to argue that patterns of (neo)colonial domination underpinned the structural relations of inequality in the international tourist industry (Britton 1982: 336). Echoing the line of thought pursued by Marxist economists such as Baran and Sweezy (1966), Britton (1982) argued that the foundations of this unequal system were centred upon vertically integrated metropolitan-based tourism enterprises that exercise monopolistic control over the flow of benefits from the destination tourist industry. Underdevelopment and dependency theories, in fact, departed from classical Marxist political economy by emphasizing *unequal exchange* between nations, rather than *how* surpluses are produced (i.e. *class relations*), and thus did not account for the diverse experiences of capitalist development in the Third World (Kiely 1995: 46–49). Although Britton's historical-geographical analysis of how European colonialism and postcolonial development shaped the economic and spatial organization of tourism in the Pacific avoids many of the generalizations inherent in dependency theories, its proponents have been rightly challenged for postulating a deterministic model of tourism development in which destinations are systematically exploited and underdeveloped as a consequence of the dominance of metropolitan tourism enterprise (Oppermann 1993). In so doing they ignored the geographically uneven nature of tourism and capitalist development and the systematic variations in the local conditions of tourism development.

Tourism, capitalism and globalization

Notwithstanding the shortcomings of dependency and underdevelopment theories, they served a valuable role in demonstrating the tendencies towards uneven development and core–periphery inequalities within the world economy and, by extension, international tourism. However, since the early 1970s the forces of economic globalization and neoliberalism and the restructuring of economies in the capitalist heartlands of Western Europe and North America have intensified capitalist social relations within the so-called 'core' capitalist states as well as stimulated the search for profitable outlets for surplus capital on a truly globalized scale, with a concomitant increase in competitive pressures and inequalities within and between nations (Glyn 2007: 167–170). Despite disagreement over the degree to which capitalism has become truly globalized (see Hirst and Thompson 1996) and the existence of diverse capitalisms, the dynamics of capitalist development continue to be driven by the *imperatives* of accumulation (profit-making) and the exploitation of wage labour (Perrons 1999: 94).

Tourism, as Britton (1991: 451) remarked, 'is an important vehicle of capitalist accumulation', and is overwhelmingly made up of a variety of private enterprise, small and large, driven by the pursuit of profit. The organizational and structural transformations brought about by neoliberal globalization have further encouraged the growth of large, integrated, *transnational* forms of corporate tourism enterprise, exercising considerable monopolistic advantage through their domination of key sectors, markets and distribution channels (Mosedale 2006). Although there is little evidence to suggest that global tourism is directed by a coordinated 'transnational capital class' with common interests (*pace* Sklair 2001), neoliberalism and globalization have stimulated a resurgence of the power of capital (or 'shareholder value') and thereby accentuated the tendencies towards the concentration and centralization of capital emphasized by Marx (1974: Chapter 25, section 2).

Although the organization of global tourism production and consumption is complex and varied (Ioannides and Debbage 1998), since the early 1990s, significant subsectors within the global travel industries have increasingly become dominated by larger corporate entities through a growth in mergers, acquisitions and strategic alliances (see Bywater 1998). Nowhere is this more apparent than in the global cruise industry in which nearly 80 per cent of passenger capacity in the Caribbean is handled by just two corporations (Wood 2004: 159). Additionally, the transformation of German shipping and logistics firm Preussag AG into the tourism giant TUI AG[2] in little over a decade illustrates both the degree to which capital has sought to maximise profit through entrance into key tourism-related sectors, as well as the centralizing tendencies highlighted by Marx.

During the 1990s, neoliberal policies paved the way for the dismantling of barriers to the cross-border mobility of capital and the liberalization of services in the 'South', including tourism (World Development Movement 2003), stimulating further foreign capital involvement in a range of sectors hitherto 'off-limits', including equity participation in hospitality and tourism providers, urban heritage and ecotourism (see Bianchi 2005; Daher 2007; Duffy 2002; Negussie 2006). More specifically, the growth of international financial flows has led to the movement of a range of new corporate investors into the development of luxury resorts in both existing and emergent destinations, with capital raised on financial markets (see Levy and Scott-Clark 2008). The search for profitable outlets for surplus capital was also of course fundamental to an earlier phase of urban regeneration in the 1980s, as former docks, waterfronts and industrial areas in advanced capitalist states were transformed into profitable mixed-use developments combining tourism, leisure, retail, offices and private residences (see Beauregard 1998; Harvey 1990). Capital's relentless drive for profit also continues to make its mark on the reconfiguration of urban spaces in the United Kingdom, as publically controlled urban spaces are converted into profitable commodities and proprietorship is transferred into the hands of multinational corporate investors (see Minton 2009: Chapter 3).

Marx made explicit reference to the globalizing imperative of capitalism throughout his work, not least in the *Grundrisse*, in which he remarks that 'The tendency to create a world market is directly given in the concept of capital itself. Every limit appears as a barrier to be overcome. [. . .], capital drives beyond national barriers and prejudices' (Marx 1973: 408–410). That is not to say that capitalism is a monolithic, homogenizing force, or that markets everywhere will respond in the same way to global flows of capital and trade liberalization. The existence of diverse capitalisms, and, more significantly, distinctive orientations of the state to capital in different countries, renders the globalization of capitalism an uneven and often contested process. Rather, as capital becomes increasingly mobile and flows across borders in search of outlets for profitable investment, new markets are opened up and strong competitive pressures are brought to bear on economic agents at different levels of enterprise.

Marx stresses how the logic of competition compels capitalists (from the smallest entrepreneur to the large transnational corporation) to continuously innovate and drive down costs (wages) in order to produce more cheaply than competitors (and satisfy shareholders), thus setting off constant cycles of destructive competition.

> he [the capitalist] shares with the miser the passion for wealth. But that which in the miser is a mere idiosyncrasy, is, in the capitalist, the effect of the social mechanism, of which he is but one of the wheels. Moreover, the development of capitalist production makes it constantly necessary to keep increasing the amount of capital laid out in a given undertaking, and competition makes the immanent laws of capitalist production to be felt by each individual capitalist, as external coercive laws. It compels him to keep constantly extending his capital, in order to preserve it, but extend it he cannot, except by means of progressive accumulation.
>
> (Marx 1974: 555)

Although today's networked, transnational capitalist economy is a far cry from the limited reach of the world market in Marx's day, capital's search for profits continues to drive the economics of globalization and the constant search for new markets and outlets for profitable investment (e.g. developing new 'tourist' services and opening up new territories for tourism development). The imperative of competition not only imposes a particular 'discipline' on the development of the forces of production, compelling capitalist enterprise to innovate, it also enhances the power of the capitalist vis-à-vis that of the worker (manifest in the intensification of the working day, wage cuts, contractual insecurity and, ultimately, unemployment). This may result in the restructuring of local enterprise along increasingly market-driven lines or force business owners to seek to externalise (social and environmental) costs (e.g. reduction of employee benefits, pollution) as far as is legally possible (see Sharpley 2009: 153). Such pressures also underpin the tension between foreign principals (tour operators) and local providers, the latter of which are often forced to accept less than favourable terms in order to survive (see Buhalis 1999; Mosedale 2006).

Although Marx *did* recognize the historically uneven and contradictory nature of capitalist development (see Marx 1974: 603, 669–670), one must caution against the assumption, which does pervade much of his work, that capitalism will inevitably result in the progressive concentration of corporate power, thus subsuming or forcing small and/or non-capitalist enterprise to sell up or close down (Brennan 2003: 15). Rather than disappear or be subsumed by capital, small independently owned enterprises are often characterized by a diversity of capital/

labour relations cutting across different households, particularly when members combine work in tourism with other forms of wage-work or subsistence farming and fishing (e.g. Bianchi and Santana Talavera 2004). Furthermore, when faced with the entrance of larger, capitalist forms of tourism enterprise, small-scale household forms of tourism enterprise may often thrive by continuing to provide services for a particular niche market. Although, for the most part, household- or family-run tourism enterprise tends to predominate in parts of the world where capitalist enterprise has not fully developed (e.g. Cohen 1982; Michaud 1991), even in the capitalist heartlands of Europe, in particular the southern regions, much of the tourist accommodation sector comprises small to medium-sized tourism enterprises, many of which may be family owned (Smeral 1998).

Small-scale, family-owned tourism enterprises may often be antagonistic towards foreign capital and big business, particularly when their monopoly on the provision of local services is threatened. This does not however contradict the logic of competition acting upon different capitalists and entrepreneurs, as outlined by Marx. All tourism businesses, regardless of size (as opposed to ownership structure), are driven by the profit motive (see Sharpley 2009: 154). Indeed, local entrepreneurs are often just as aggressive in their pursuit of profit, whether running tourism businesses or channelling surpluses into speculative property investments (Bianchi and Santana Talavera 2004). Such competitive pressures are apparent in the Canary Islands where, until recent restrictions came into effect, small-scale local investors were dependent upon a speculative model of tourism and real estate development based on the untrammelled construction of low-quality cheap apartment complexes in order to ensure their economic survival (Bianchi 2004: 515). There is little in the way of Adam Smith's 'invisible hand' here, regulating the balance between supply and demand; as Dunn (2009: 75) states, 'what is good and rational for the individual capitalist may be irrational for collective capital'. Recent events in Spain, where a disproportionate emphasis on labour-intensive industries such as tourism and property (construction) has left Spain's economy particularly exposed to the current economic crisis (Moya 2009), only serve to reinforce Marx's view of capitalism as an uneven and unstable force that contains within it a tendency towards crises of over-accumulation (over-production) and profitability.

Where Marxist political economy has perhaps been found particularly wanting is in its theorization of the state in capitalist development, although Marx did in fact recognize the crucial role of the state in the early development of capitalism in England (Marx 1974: part viii). Capital has nevertheless always worked in tandem with the state in order to create the appropriate conditions for capital accumulation (Harvey 2005: 143). Indeed, neoliberal globalization has not so much been accompanied by the withdrawal of the state from the market, but rather the power of the state has been reconfigured along the lines of a 'market-based free enterprise system' in order to optimize the conditions of capital accumulation (Gill 1995: 400). There are numerous illustrations of where the state has been integral to the restructuring of property relations and the balance of power between private enterprise and public ownership in tourism. For example, interventions by both the state and supra-state authorities have served to restructure both Mediterranean and Middle Eastern economies towards services (and tourism), whilst underwriting the intervention of private (foreign) capital into myriad urban tourism heritage developments (see Bianchi 2005; Daher 2007). However, this does not imply a weakening of state power or indeed the inevitability of foreign capitalist domination. As Steiner (2006) demonstrates, not only is the equity participation of foreign transnationals in Egyptian tourism quite low, the opening up of the tourism sector to foreign investment stabilized Egypt's economy, but also consolidated rather than threatened the power of the regime.

Tourism, work and labour relations in the global economy

The study of class and labour relations in tourism is relatively scarce, notwithstanding the existence of a substantial, largely empirically driven literature on working conditions in tourism and hospitality industries. Many but by no means all of these studies tend to highlight the low-paid, unskilled and, in some cases, exploitative nature of working conditions in these industries (Beddoe 2004; Burns 1993; International Labour Organization 2001; Lee and Seyoung 1998; Radiven and Lucas 1997; Wood 1992). Others take a more circumspect view, arguing that labour conditions in the tourism industries are more complex and differentiated (Baum 1996; Santana Turégano 2003). There are also a small number of notable work-based ethnographies, such as Hochschild's (2003 [1983]) classic study of airline workers, and Adler and Adler's (2004) exploration of the working experiences and occupational subcultures of resort workers in Hawaii. However, these studies inevitably focus on micro-level experiences of work in tourism rather than explore the relationship of work to the wider political economy of tourism and related sectors.

There is perhaps some inevitability in this apparent 'neglect' given that the study of tourism was beginning to find its niche in academia during the 1970s and 1980s, precisely at the time when the sociology of work was moving to the margins (see Halford and Strangleman 2009: 812–813). Where the experience of work has been of interest to tourism analysts, the influence of the 'critical turn' has shifted the analytical gaze onto the 'performative' nature of tourism work, rather than the systemic (structural) inequalities that are produced and reproduced within (and beyond) the workplace (see Edensor 2001). Elsewhere, analyses of organizational restructuring in the airline industry, notably British Airways, have emphasized the successes of 'cultural change' for turning around ailing companies whilst ignoring the wider political economy and its influence on industrial relations (Grugulis and Wilkinson 2002: 180).

There can be little argument that the structure and organization of tourism labour markets are increasingly globalized, cosmopolitan and segmented according to various occupational subcultures defined by ethnicity, nationality and gender (see Church and Frost 2004; Wood 2000). Nonetheless, in both the core capitalist states as well as the capital-intensive resort enclaves in poorer, 'less developed' states, capitalist tourism development and the increasing corporate and/or transnational penetration of hospitality and other related subsectors continue to drive the commodification of labour power and the proletarianization of the workforce. In her ethnographic study of proletarianization and labour relations in the hotel industry in Huatulco, Mexico, Madsen Camacho (1996) describes how the construction of large resorts resulted in the eviction of peasants who were subsequently forced to abandon their independent, family-owned businesses to seek work in the largely foreign-dominated industry. This is not to posit a simplistic divide between locally owned and transnational tourism enterprise. In fact, according to Harrison (2001: 33), because of better levels of unionization, hotels operated by transnational firms in Fiji are characterized by higher wages and better working conditions than local ones. Rather, it is not the nationality of ownership that matters, but to what extent capitalist wage-labour has been extended (and on what terms) throughout different parts of the tourism industry as a country's economy becomes increasingly integrated into wider capitalist markets.

The world of work and labour unrest is indeed far more diverse and contradictory than Marx ever suggested (Munck 2000: 69–72). This much is apparent in the simultaneous decline of manufacturing employment within the capitalist heartlands and the emergence of peripheral centres of industrial production characterized by pluralized forms of working class politics and labour relations (see Mason 2008). *Pace* Marx, much has also been made of the decline of the (industrial) working class as a force for progressive social change (Gorz 1982). Globalization, de-industrialization and the neoliberal drive to dismantle socialized production have indeed signalled the end of the industrial working class as an economic and political force in the West and in turn spurred the rise of an increasingly heterogeneous global workforce (Therborn 2001). According to International Labour Organization figures, industrial employment as a proportion of world employment declined from 19 per cent to 17 per cent between 1960 and 1990, whilst during the same period industrial employment in core capitalist states alone fell from 37 per cent to 26 per cent (Therborn 2001: 99).

Yet despite the pronounced decline of manufacturing and the rise of private sector service industries, of which tourism comprises up to one-third, particularly in the capitalist heartlands, the substitution of service employment has often taken place at the expense of agriculture rather than manufacturing (Callinicos 1989: 122). This pattern has been particularly evident in southern European and Mediterranean states, where peasant agriculturalists and fishermen have either abandoned traditional economic activities (Kousis 1989: 322–323; Jurdao Arrones 1990) or invested in small tourism businesses (van der Werff 1980). Although the degree to which tourism is directly responsible for the decline of agriculture is disputed, there is little doubt that in the 'less developed' countries, with little or no significant industrial activities to speak of, tourism often gradually supplants agriculture as the main revenue generator and employer (Latimer 1985).

Perhaps one of the most consistent weaknesses in Marxist thinking is the treatment of non-economic forms of stratification and exploitation, particularly gender and women's inequality. When it is considered at all the emphasis is on male wage-labour, whereas the exploitation of women is viewed through the lens of capitalist production (Marx 1974: Chapter 15). For the most part, Marx's thinking is dominated by the assumption that (unpaid) women's work in the home is unproductive and hence produces no surplus value, or wealth. Clearly, such a view is untenable in today's globalized and feminized economy, indeed if it ever was. However, as Barrett and McIntosh (1980) argue, women enter the labour market on very differing terms because of the under-valuing of their skills. They are thus often consigned to low-wage ghettos with few opportunities for socio-economic advancement, ample evidence of which can be found throughout the tourism and hospitality industries (see Chin 2008). Although small-scale tourism enterprises may offer valuable opportunities for social advancement and economic independence where traditional economic sectors are dominated by men (Scott 1997), culturally sanctioned forms of exclusion from the labour market (Tucker 2003), and gendered perceptions of (appropriate) types of labour, constrain the scope of available positions for women in the tourism labour market (Sinclair 1991, 1997; Timmo 1993). Additionally, the lack of (well-remunerated) tourism jobs, particularly in poorer destinations, may lead women into the darker side of the (informal) labour market in the form of prostitution (Hickman 2007: Chapter 5).

Although Marx *did* acknowledge the role of ethnic divisions amongst the working classes this was not accorded the same degree of primacy as economic, class-based divisions (Worsley 2002: 48). Not only are different societies characterized by distinct trajectories and experiences of capitalist development – a fact that did not go unremarked by Marx (see 1974: 669–70) – the composition of the workforce, both in the (post)industrial capitalist heartlands as well as in the new centres of industrial production worldwide, has increasingly been intersected by a variety of forms of ethnic stratification and social differentiation (Therborn 2001: 107–108). Capital has always nevertheless sought the fragmentation of labour through a variety of ethnic, cultural and spatial means (Narotzky 1997: 214). This is amply demonstrated by the development of tourism in ethnically diverse societies such as Fiji (see Samy 1980), as well as the occupational structure within the global cruise ship industry in which workers are clearly segmented by ethnicity and nationality (Wood 2000: 353–358).

Notwithstanding the worldwide dispersal and growth of transnational corporate tourism enterprises in key sectors, the degree to which wage-labour is generalized within a particular economy, and, indeed, the tourism industries, varies considerably according to the diverse political economies within which tourism operates (Harrison 2001: 29). However, the existence of a diversity of capitalisms together with an increasingly 'polyglot, feminized and internally differentiated' global workforce (Laffey and Dean 2002: 94) does not negate the centrality of wage-work (or lack of it) in the globalizing economy. If anything, processes of proletarianization have become even more pervasive, within both the capitalist heartlands, penetrating the previously socialized spheres of state employment and middle-class professions, as well as the new, albeit technologically less-advanced, enclaves of industrial capitalist production in China and elsewhere across the erstwhile 'periphery' (Walker and Buck 2007: 41–44). Accordingly it is estimated that the global workforce has grown from just under 1 billion in 1980 to close to 3 billion at the dawn of the twenty-first century (Anderson 2007: 29).

Capitalist wage-work and the appropriation of surpluses from the labour of the 'direct producers' thus remains 'the defining structural relation of capitalism' (Colás 2002: 193). The fact that tourism and hospitality are characterized by the simultaneity of production and consumption (in certain respects) as well as the exchange of a service rather than goods does not substantially alter the social relations of production that underpin the cash nexus in many parts of the global tourism industries:

> Wage-labour has if anything become a more pervasive feature of social expe-
> rience in the past half century, with the decline of peasant agriculture and the
> growing involvement of women in the labour-market. The fact that much of
> this labour now involves interacting with other people rather than producing
> goods does not change the social relations involved.
>
> (Callinicos 1989: 122)

Central to Marx's analysis of wage-labour is the concept of 'alienation' through which he explains how capitalism alienates workers from the products of their labour as well as themselves (Marx 1977e: 75–87). These products, or equally services such as hospitality, are produced for distant markets, that is, tourists, over which they have no control, through the appropriation of surplus value at the point of production, whether in the destination itself or within one of the many enterprises at different points in the global tourism commodity chain. Similarly, Hochschild (2003 [1983]) draws on Marx's notion of alienated labour to argue that workers who sell their 'emotional labour' under conditions of capitalist pro-duction, for example airline cabin crew, are not free to negotiate the terms of this exchange, or the conditions under which it takes place, and thus become detached from their own feelings. The alienation of work in capitalist societies and its relationship to tourism and related subsectors have also been forcefully demonstrated by Ritzer (1998: Chapter 10) in his analysis of 'McDonaldization' and the transformation of the labour process in advanced service-based econo-mies. Ritzer (1998: 62–65) draws from both Weberian and Marxist perspectives to demonstrate how the rationalization and routinization of service-based work involves not only structural constraints and forms of exploitation of nature but also changes of a wider cultural nature that incorporate both the workers as well as consumers

Nowhere perhaps has the intensification of the labour process been more apparent than in the globalized airline industries. In particular, staff working in once heavily regulated state airlines, with hitherto strong unions and levels of social protection, have been progressively exposed to the full force of competition and managerial control since the onset of successive waves of de-regulation and privatization in the late 1970s. As a consequence, pilots and cabin crew, particu-larly those working in the new low-cost airlines, have been subject to a range of cost-cutting strategies, from job cuts to the implementation of differential pay scales (for those working on the same shift) and terms and conditions within the same organization, whilst 'non-core' jobs such as in-flight catering and reservations have been outsourced (see Bennett 2003; Blyton *et al.* 1998; Whitelegg 2003). However, contrary to pessimistic claims that globalization has disempowered workers, the link between brand reputation, service quality and face-to-face interaction with airline workers has provided airline workers with some measure of bargaining power as the 'militancy' of BA cabin crew might suggest (Whitelegg 2003: 245). Additionally, the increasingly cosmopolitan character of cabin crew and pilots, who often live in countries other than the airlines' operational bases, has brought about new forms of transnational solidarity within the workforce that are akin to industrial labour (Whitelegg 2003: 245).

The exploitation of labour and the existence of poor working conditions in the tourism, hospitality and related industries worldwide does not inevitably translate into overt manifestations of labour unrest. This is partly explained by its heterogeneous and polyglot workforce, which is moreover spread throughout differentially capitalized firms. Nonetheless, there is ample evidence of antagonisms between workers and owners, particularly in transnational-owned hotel chains, airlines and other large-scale corporate-dominated sectors. Labour disputes have taken place in major resorts in Goa (Routledge 2001) and Hawaii (Schaefers 2006), whilst the luxury Asian-based Shangri-La hotel group was the focus of a protracted labour dispute in Jakarta between December 2000 and March 2003 involving hundreds of Indonesian hotel workers protesting over the unfair dismissal of 600 fellow workers (Liquor, Hospitality and Miscellaneous Union 2003). In addition to the infamous 1997 (and, indeed, 2010) strike by British Airways cabin crew (Whitelegg 2003), an unofficial strike by BA ground staff (mainly Punjabi women) at Heathrow airport in August 2005, in solidarity with 800 workers sacked by the American-owned in-flight catering company, Gate Gourmet (Arrowsmith 2005), served to shed light on corporate cost-cutting strategies within a relatively hidden yet crucial subsector of the globalized airline industry.

These struggles for better pay and conditions, against unlawful dismissal and in defence of trade union rights, can be seen against the growth of the structural power of capital in the global tourism and related industries, thus subjecting diverse elements of the 'tourism' workforce to the discipline of the global market. The fact that working class residents in tourism destinations are 'willing' to exchange their hospitality for cash (Arremberi 2001: 746) should hardly come as a surprise, particularly in the absence of alternatives to capitalist wage-labour. Nor does the (limited) scope for worker autonomy in tourism work emphasized by some analysts (e.g. Crang 1997), or the fact that resort workers may enjoy all or part of their work (Adler and Adler 2004: 217), contradict the profit-driven imperatives of capitalist enterprise and the associated tendency of capitalists to exploit workers through the reduction of wages and/or extension of the working day. As Marx makes clear in the preface to *Capital*, it is not a question of whether or not capitalists treat their workers 'fairly', but rather that individuals represent the 'embodiments of particular class-relations and class-interests' (Marx 1974:

20–21). Accordingly, beneath the veneer of the hospitality encounter, as in any other form of wage-labour, in a capitalist society, the only chance of survival for those with only their labour to sell is through the cash nexus in the form of wage-labour, as so brilliantly portrayed in the film *Cannibal Tours* by Dennis O'Rourke (1988).

What future for Marxist political economy and tourism?

This chapter has sought to reflect upon the relevance of Marxist thinking for the analysis of capitalist development and labour relations in the global tourism political economy. The relative absence of Marxist and/or Marxian analyses in the political economy of tourism represents a significant deficit of radical thinking, which is arguably derived from both the dominance of business-managerialist perspectives, and, more recently, 'culturalist' analyses of tourism, neither of which seeks to draw attention, much less challenge, the logics of exploitation and domination within the realm of the tourism political economy. Although those critical of the relevance of Marxist thought to tourism have perhaps been a little too eager to condemn Marx's apparent economic reductionism (see Ateljevic 2000), there is ample evidence to suggest that power and inequality within the globalizing political economy of tourism *are* closely tied to the realm of the economy. Moreover, the contemporary significance of Marx's historical materialism lies in its attempt to understand the ways in which humans organize the production and consumption of their material needs (and wants), and the class relations of power and inequality that flow from these. This neither implies determinism nor that non-economic factors such as ethnicity and gender should be ignored when analysing the organization and development of capitalist societies.

It can, however, be argued that Marx paid insufficient attention to the diversity of workers' experiences. In addition, Marxist political economy has to grapple with the fact that workers may benefit when capitalism 'works'. However, neither this, nor the fact that workers in the tourism industries may enjoy their work, undermines the core principles of Marxist political economy that have been outlined in this chapter, nor their relevance to the understanding of the globalizing tourism political economy. Nor should the fact that the 'performative' nature of much tourism and hospitality-related work may endow workers with a measure of power and autonomy as keepers of the 'brand' blind us to the realities of wage-work and the constant desire of capital to transgress (legislative, social) constraints on its pursuit of profit.

Although Marx may not have anticipated the degree to which capitalism has been able to sustain itself through various crises, been able to adapt to various socio-political contexts, and been marked by pluralized configurations of work and diverse labour relations, the centrality (or lack) of wage-work together with the tendency of capitalism to increase the rate and intensity of the exploitation of labour throughout diverse industries, including tourism, continues to lie at its core. Marxian enquiry clearly has not got all the answers. More and more there is scope to draw upon an increasingly diverse repertoire of radical political economy and social theory to interrogate the structural logics of power and inequality in twenty-first-century capitalist tourism development (see Therborn 2007). There is also little doubt that Marx underplayed the significance of consumption in the shaping of capitalist societies. The challenge is thus to reconcile the productivist emphasis of a Marxist political economy of tourism, which focuses on the relations between capitalists and workers in the tourism industries, with the rights of people (indeed, those self-same workers) to consume the pleasures of travel, in ways that, moreover, are commensurate with demands for distributive justice and economic democracy within destination societies.

Notes

1 Marx's notion of exploitation is not to be confused with the more commonly used notion of exploitation derived from the liberal tradition which denotes something that is morally wrong or unfair within the framework of capitalist social relations rather than challenging the underlying power structures and inequalities inherent in capitalist development (see Marx 1977d: 564–570). Liberal notions of 'fairness', which underpin both recent notions of 'ethical' and 'pro-poor tourism' as well as the guiding principles of campaigning non-governmental organizations and fair trade organizations, rely on making (subjective) ethico-moral judgements to determine what constitutes 'fair' in the context of remuneration, wages and employment conditions.
2 TUI AG encompasses three core business sectors, TUI Travel, TUI Hotels & Resorts and Cruises, which together comprise the World of TUI. This tourism giant grew out of the corporate restructuring of its predecessor, Preussag AG, through divestment of its industrial shareholdings and refocusing of its core economic activities on tourism, which in 2005 accounted for 85 per cent of its turnover. It subsequently expanded through the acquisition of major travel companies, including Hapag Lloyd AG in 1997 and the Thomson Travel Group in 2000, culminating in the merger with First Choice plc in 2007 (TUI 2010).

References

Adler, P. A. and Adler, P. (2004) *Paradise Laborers: Hotel work in the global economy*, Ithaca and London: Cornell University Press.

Amin, S. (1976) *Unequal Development*, Hassocks: Harvester.

Anderson, P. (2007) 'Jottings on the conjucture', *New Left Review*, 48: 5–37.

Arremberi, J. (2001) 'The host should get lost: Paradigms in the tourism theory', *Annals of Tourism Research*, 28: 738–761.

Arrowsmith, J. (2005) 'British Airways' Heathrow flights grounded by dispute at Gate Gourmet', *European Industrial Relations Observatory*. Online. Available at http://www.eurofound.europa.eu/eiro/2005/09/feature/uk0509106f.htm (accessed 9 March 2010).

Ateljevic, I. (2000) 'Circuits of tourism: Stepping beyond the "production/consumption" dichotomy', *Tourism Geographies*, 2: 369–388.

Baran, P. (1957) *The Political Economy of Growth*, New York: Monthly Review Press.

Baran, P. and Sweezy P. (1966) *Monopoly Capital*, New York: Monthly Review Press.

Barrett, M. and McIntosh M. (1980) 'The family wage', *Capital and Class*, 11: 51–72.

Baum, T. (1996) 'Unskilled work and the hospitality industry: Myth or reality?', *International Journal of Hospitality Management*, 15: 207–209.

Beauregard, R. (1998) 'Tourism and economic development policy in US urban areas', in D. Ioannides and K. Debbage (eds) *The Economic Geography of the Tourist Industry: A supply-side analysis*, London: Routledge.

Beddoe, C. (2004) *Labour Standards, Social Responsibility and Tourism*, London: Tourism Concern.

Bennett, S. A. (2003) 'Flight crew stress and fatigue in low-cost commercial operations: An appraisal', *International Journal of Risk Assessment and Management*, 4: 203–207.

Bianchi, R. V. (2002) 'Towards a new political economy of global tourism', in R. Sharpley and D. Telfer (eds) *Tourism and Development: Concepts and issues*, Clevedon: Channel View.

Bianchi, R. V. (2004) 'Tourism restructuring and the politics of sustainability: A critical view from the European periphery', *Journal of Sustainable Tourism*, 12: 495–529.

Bianchi, R. V. (2005) 'Euromed heritage: Culture, capital and trade liberalisation: Implications for the Mediterranean city', *Journal of Mediterranean Studies*, 15: 283–318.

Bianchi, R. V. (2009) 'The "critical turn" in tourism studies: A radical critique', *Tourism Geographies*, 11: 484–504.

Bianchi, R. V. and Santana Talavera A. (2004) 'Between the land and the sea: Exploring the social organisation of tourism development in a Gran Canaria fishing village', in J. Boissevain and T. Selwyn (eds) *Contesting the Foreshore: Tourism, society and politics on the coast*, Amsterdam: Amsterdam University Press.

Blyton, P., Martinez, L. M., McGurk, J. and Turnbull, P. (1998) *Contesting Globalisation: Airline restructuring, labour flexibility and trade union strategies*, London: International Transport Workers' Federation.

Booth, D. (1985) 'Marxism and development sociology: Interpreting the impasse', *World Development*, 13: 761–787.

Brennan, T. (2003) *Globalization and its Terrors*, London: Routledge.

Britton, S. G. (1980) 'The evolution of a colonial space-economy: The case of Fiji', *Journal of Historical Geography*, 6: 251–274.

Britton, S. G. (1982) 'The political economy of tourism in the Third World', *Annals of Tourism Research*, 9: 331–359.

Britton, S. G. (1991) 'Tourism, capital and place: Towards a critical geography of tourism', *Environment and Planning D: Society and Space*, 9: 451–478.

Bryden, J. (1973) *Tourism and Development: A case study of the Commonwealth Caribbean*, Cambridge: Cambridge University Press.

Buhalis, D. (1999) 'Tourism on the Greek Islands: Issues of peripherality, competitiveness and development', *International Journal of Tourism Research*, 1: 341–358.

Burns, P. (1993) 'Sustaining tourism employment', *Journal of Sustainable Tourism*, 1: 81–96.

Bywater, M. (1998) 'Who owns whom in the European travel industry?', *Travel and Tourism Analyst*, 3: 41–59.

Callinicos, A. (1989) *Against Post-Modernism: A Marxist critique*, Cambridge: Polity Press.

Chin, C. (2008) *Cruising in the Global Economy: Profits, pleasure, and work at sea*, Aldershot: Ashgate.

Church, A. and Frost, M. (2004) 'Tourism, the global city and the labour market in London', *Tourism Geographies*, 6: 208–228.

Cohen, E. (1982) 'Marginal paradises: Bungalow tourism on the Islands of Southern Thailand', *Annals of Tourism Research*, 9: 189–228.

Cohen, E. (1988) 'Authencity and commoditization in tourism', *Annals of Tourism Research*, 15: 371–386.

Colás, A. (2002) 'The class politics of globalisation', in M. Rupert and H. Smith (eds) *Historical Materialism and Globalization*, London and New York: Routledge.

Cox, R. (2002) *The Political Economy of a Plural World: Critical reflections on power, morals and civilization*, London: Routledge.

Crang, P. (1997) 'Performing the tourist product', in C. Rojek and J. Urry (eds) *Touring Cultures: Transformations of travel and theory*, London: Routledge.

Daher, R. F. (2007) 'Tourism, heritage and urban transformations in Jordan and Lebanon: Emerging actors and global-local juxtapositions', in R. F. Daher (ed.) *Tourism in the Middle East: Continuity, change and transformation*, Clevedon: Channel View.

Desai, M. (2004) *Marx's Revenge: The resurgence of capitalism and the demise of state socialism*, London: Verso.

Duffy, R. (2002) *A Trip Too Far: Ecotourism, politics and exploitation*, London: Earthscan.

Dunn, B. (2009) *Global Political Economy: A Marxist critique*, London: Pluto Press.

Edensor, T. (2001) 'Performing tourism, staging tourism: (Re)producing tourist space and practice', *Tourist Studies*, 1: 59–82.

Emmanuel, A. (1972) *Unequal Exchange*, London: New Left Books.

Frank, A. G. (1969) *Capitalism and Underdevelopment in Latin America*, New York: Monthly Review Press.

Fukuyama, F. (1989) 'The end of history', *The National Interest*, 16: 3–18.

Gill, S. (1995) 'Globalisation, market civilisation, and disciplinary neoliberalism', *Alternatives*, 24: 399–423.

Glyn, A. (2007) *Capitalism Unleashed: Finance, globalization and welfare*, Oxford: Oxford University Press.

Gorz, A. (1982) *Farewell to the Working Class: An essay on post-industrial socialism*, London and Sydney: Pluto Press.

Grugulis, I. and Wilkinson, A. (2002) 'Managing culture at British Airways: Hype, hope and reality', *Long Range Planning*, 35: 179–194.

Halford, S. and Strangleman, T. (2009) 'In search of the sociology of work: Past, present and future', *Sociology*, 43: 811–828.

Hall, C. M. (1994) *Tourism and Politics: Policy, power and place*, Chichester: John Wiley.

Harman, C. (1998) 'History, myth and Marxism', in J. Rees (ed.) *Essays on Historical Materialism*, London: Bookmarks.

Harrison, D. (2001) 'Tourism and less developed countries: Key issues', in D. Harrison (ed.) *Tourism and the Less Developed Countries: Issues and case studies*, Wallingford: CAB International.

Harvey, D. (1990) *The Condition of Postmodernity*, Cambridge, MA and Oxford, UK: Blackwell.

Harvey, D. (2005) *The New Imperialism*, Oxford: Oxford University Press.

Harvey, D. (2006) *Spaces of Global Capitalism: Towards a theory of uneven geographical development*, London: Verso.

Hickman, L. (2007) *The Final Call: In search of the true cost of our holidays*, London: Eden Project Books.

Hirst, P. and Thompson G. (1996) *Globalization in Question*, Cambridge: Polity Press

Hochschild, A. (2003 [1983]) *The Managed Heart: Commercialization of human feeling*, 2nd edn, Berkeley: University of California Press.

Husbands, W. (1981) 'Centres, peripheries and socio-spatial development', *Ontario Geography*, 17: 37–59.

International Labour Organization (2001) *Human Resources Development, Employment and Globalization in the Hotel, Catering and Tourism Sector*, Geneva: International Labour Organization.

Ioannides, D. and Debbage, K. (1998) 'Post-Fordism and flexibility: The travel industry polyglot', *Tourism Management*, 18: 229–241.

Jack, G. and Phipps, A. (2005) *Tourism and Intercultural Exchange: Why tourism matters*, Clevedon: Channel View.

Jamal, T. and Robinson M. (2009) *Handbook of Tourism Studies*, London: Sage.

Jurdao Arrones, F. (1990) *España en Venta*, Madrid: Ediciones Endymion.

Kiely, R. (1995) *Sociology and Development*, London: UCL Press.

Kousis, M. (1989) 'Tourism and the family in a rural Cretan community', *Annals of Tourism Research*, 16: 318–332.

Laffey, M. and Dean, K. (2002) 'A flexible Marxism for flexible times: Globalization and historical materialism', in M. Rupert and H. Smith (eds) *Historical Materialism and Globalization*, London: Routledge.

Latimer, H. (1985) 'Developing-island economies: Tourism vs agriculture', *Tourism Management*, 6: 32–42.

Lee, C-K. and Seyoung, K. (1998) 'Measuring earnings, inequality and median earnings in the tourism industry', *Tourism Management*, 19: 349–358.

Lenin, V. I. (1987) *Essential Works of Lenin*, edited by H. M. Christman, New York: Dover Publications.

Levy, A. and Scott-Clark, C. (2008) 'Country for sale', *The Guardian Weekend Magazine*, 26 April, pp. 30–41.

Liquor, Hospitality and Miscellaneous Union (2003) 'Long hotel dispute in Indonesia comes to an end', Press Release, 23 March. Online. Available at http://www.lhmu.org.au/lhmu/news/2003/1048872302_32503.html (accessed 24 October 2007).

MacCannell, D. (1992) *Empty Meeting Grounds: The tourist papers*, London and New York: Routledge.

MacCannell, D. (1999) *The Tourist: A new theory of the leisure class*, 2nd edn, Berkeley: University of California Press (first edition published 1976 by Shocken Books).

Madsen Camacho, M. E. (1996) 'Dissenting workers and social control: A case study of the hotel industry in Huatulco, Oaxaca', *Human Organization*, 55: 33–40.

Marx, K. (1973) *Grundrisse*, Harmondsworth: Penguin.

Marx, K. (1974) *Capital: A critical analysis of capitalist production*, Volume 1. London: Lawrence and Wishart (first English edition published 1887).

Marx, K. (1977a) 'Letter to Vera Sassoulitch', in D. McLellan (ed.) *Karl Marx: Selected writings*, Oxford: Oxford University Press.

Marx, K. (1977b) 'Speech on free trade', in D. McLellan (ed.) *Karl Marx: Selected writings*, Oxford: Oxford University Press.

Marx, K. (1977c) 'Journalism in the 1850s', in D. McLellan (ed.) *Karl Marx: Selected writings*, Oxford: Oxford University Press.

Marx, K. (1977d) 'Critique of the Gotha Programme', in D. McLellan (ed.) *Karl Marx: Selected writings*, Oxford: Oxford University Press.

Marx, K. (1977e) 'Economic and philosophical manuscripts', in D. McLellan (ed.) *Karl Marx: Selected writings*, Oxford: Oxford University Press.

Mason, P. (2008) *Live Working or Die Fighting: How the working class went global*, London: Vintage.

Meethan, K. (2001) *Tourism and Global Society: Place, culture, consumption*, Basingstoke: Palgrave.

Meiksins Wood, E. (2002) *The Origins of Capitalist Development: A longer view*, London: Verso

Michaud, J. (1991) 'A social anthropology of tourism in Ladakh (India)', *Annals of Tourism Research*, 18: 605–621.

Minton, A. (2009) *Ground Control: Fear and happiness in the twenty-first century*, London: Penguin.

Mosedale, J. (2006) 'Tourism commodity chains: Market entry and its effects on St. Lucia', *Current Issues in Tourism*, 9: 436–458.

Moya, E. (2009) 'Hedge funds are not for hedging says Spain's finance minister', *The Guardian*, 10 September. Online. Available at http://www.guardian.co.uk/business/2009/sep/10/hedge-funds-europe (accessed 10 September 2009).

Munck, R. (2000) *Marx@2000: Late Marxist perspectives*, London: Zed Books.

Narotzky, S. (1997) *New Directions in Economic Anthropology*, London: Pluto.

Negussie, E. (2006) 'Implications of neo-liberalism for built heritage management: Institutional and ownership structures in Ireland and Sweden', *Urban Studies*, 43: 1803–1824.

Oppermann, M. (1993) 'Tourism space in developing countries', *Annals of Tourism Research*, 20: 535–556.

O'Rourke, D. (1988) *Cannibal Tours*, Cairns, Australia: Camerawork Pty.

Pérez, L. A. (1980) 'Tourism underdevelops tropical islands', in I. Vogeler and A. de Souza (eds) *Dialectics of Third World Development*, Montclair, NJ: Allanheld, Osmun.

Perrons, D. (1999) 'Reintegrating production and consumption, or why political economy matters', in R. Munck and D. O'Hearn (eds) *Critical Development Theory: Contributions to a new paradigm*, London: Zed Books.

Radiven, N. and Lucas, R. (1997) 'Minimum wages and pay policy in the British hospitality industry: Past impact and future implications', *Progress in Tourism and Hospitality Research*, 3: 149–163.

Reid, D. G. (2003) *Tourism, Globalization and Development: Responsible tourism planning*, London: Pluto Books.

Ritzer, G. (1998) *The McDonaldization thesis,* London: Sage.

Routledge, P. (2001) ' "Selling the rain": Resisting the sale: Resistant identities and the conflict over tourism in Goa', *Social and Cultural Geography*, 2: 221–240.

Samy, J. (1980) 'Crumbs from the table? The workers' share in tourism', in F. Rajotte and R. Crocombe (eds) *Pacific Tourism as Islanders See It*, Fiji: South Pacific Social Sciences Association and Institute of Pacific.

Santana Turégano, M. A. (2003) 'Formas de Desarollo Turística, Redes y Situación de Empleo: El caso de Maspalomas (Gran Canaria)', unpublished thesis, Universidad Autónoma de Barcelona.Online. Available at http://www.tdx.cesca.es?TDX-0123104-173733/ (accessed 17 May 2007).

Schaefers, A. (2006) 'Turtle Bay and union settle dispute', *Honolulu Star Bulletin*, 21 July. Online. Available at http://starbulletin.com/2006/07/21/news/story01.html (accessed 19 October 2007).

Scott, J. E. (1997) 'Chances and choices: Women and tourism in Northern Cyprus', in T. M. Sinclair (ed.) *Gender, Work and Tourism*, London: Routledge.

Sharpley, R. (2009) *Tourism Development and the Environment: Beyond sustainability?* London: Earthscan.

Sinclair, M. T. (1991) 'Women, work and skill: Economic theories and feminist perspectives', in N. Redclift and M. T. Sinclar (eds) *Working Women: International perspectives on labour and gender ideology*, London: Routledge.

Sinclair, M. T. (1997) 'Issues and theories of gender and work in tourism', in M. T. Sinclair (ed.) *Gender, Work and Tourism*, London: Routledge.

Sklair, L. (2001) *The Transnational Capitalist Class*, Oxford: Blackwell.

Smeral, E. (1998) **'The impact of globalization on SMEs: New challenges for tourism policies in European countries'**, *Tourism Management*, 19: 371–380.

Smith, M. (2009) 'Development and its discontents: Ego-tripping without ethics or idea(l) s?', in J. Tribe (ed.) *Philosophical Issues in Tourism*, Bristol: Channel View.

Smith, V. L. (ed.) (1989) *Host and Guests: The anthropology of tourism*, 2nd edn, Philadelphia, PA: University of Pennsylvania Press.

Steiner, C. (2006) 'Tourism, poverty reduction and the political economy: Egyptian perspectives on tourism's economic benefits in a semi-*rentier* state', *Tourism and Hospitality Planning and Development*, 3: 161–177.

Sweezy, P. M. (1970) *The Theory of Capitalist Development*, New York: Monthly Review Press.

Therborn, G. (2001) 'Into the 21st century: The new parameters of global politics', *New Left Review*, 10: 87–110.

Therborn, G. (2007) 'After dialectics. Radical social theory in a post-communist world', *New Left Review*, 43: 63–114.

Timmo, N. (1993) 'Employment relations and labour markets in the tourism and hospitality industry', *International Journal of Employment Studies*, 1: 33–50.

Tribe, J. (2008) 'Tourism: A critical business', *Journal of Travel Research*, 46: 245–255.

Tucker, H. (2003) *Living with Difference: Negotiating identities in a Turkish village*, London: Routledge.

TUI (2010) 'Group profile'. Online. Available at http://www.tui-group.com/en/company/ profile (accessed 17 May 2010).

Turner, L. (1976) 'The international division of leisure: Tourism and the Third World', *World Development*, 4: 253–260.

van der Werff, P. E. (1980) 'Polarizing implications of the Pescaia tourist industry', *Annals of Tourism Research*, 7: 197–223.

Walker, R. and Buck, D. (2007) 'The Chinese road: Cities in the transition to capitalism', *New Left Review*, 46: 39–66.

Wallerstein, I. (1974) *The Modern World System*, Volume 1, New York: Academic Press.

Weaver, D. (1988) 'The evolution of a "plantation" tourism landscape on the Caribbean island of Antigua', *Tijdschrift voor Economische en Sociale Geografie*, 79: 319–331.

Whitelegg, D. (2003) 'Touching down: Globalisation, labour and the airline industry', *Antipode*, 3: 244–263.

Wood, R. C. (1992) *Working in Hotels and Catering*, London: Routledge.

Wood, R. E. (2000) 'Caribbean cruise tourism: Globalization at sea', *Annals of Tourism Research*, 27: 345–369.

Wood, R. E. (2004) 'Global currents: Cruise ships in the Caribbean sea', in Duval, D. T. (ed.) *Tourism in the Caribbean: Trends, development, prospects*, London and New York: Routledge.

Woolsey Biggart, N. (1994) 'Labor and leisure', in N. J. Smelser and R. Swedberg (eds) *The Handbook of Economic Sociology*, Princeton: Princeton University Press.

World Development Movement (2003) *Whose Development Agenda? An analysis of the European Union's GATS requests of developing countries*, London: WDM.

Worsley, P. (2002) *Marx and Marxism*, London and New York: Routledge.

Wright, E. O. (2009) 'Understanding class: Towards and integrated analytical approach', *New Left Review*, 60: 101–116.

3 Regulation theory and its evolution and limitations in tourism studies

Scarlett Cornelissen

The regulation school comprises a relatively wide-ranging body of scholarship that in the broadest of senses presents an analysis and critique of capitalism and its epochal transformations. The origins of the school date back to the late 1970s when, in the context of the general downturn in the world economy induced by the oil shocks of that decade, a number of French scholars tried to explain capitalism's apparent ability to stave off periods of crisis and to renew itself. Their explanation rested on a particular ontological basis, which, following the tradition of Marx and other critical socio-theoretic analyses, saw world capitalism as a system of inherent volatility that relied on the existence of specific political and economic institutions to ensure a return to equilibrium (see, for instance, Aglietta 1979, 1998; Boyer 1990).

If the peak and subsequent wane in the number of publications by regulationists is anything to go by, the school seems to have experienced its heyday in the decade leading up to the turn of the century. Nonetheless, the regulation school retains a position as one of the most comprehensive contemporary bodies of critical scholarship on both the inner workings of capitalism, as well as the overarching institutional frame that it comprises. The school's two core theoretical constructs – the regime of accumulation and the mode of regulation of economic interaction – have infused a significant volume of social science analyses, in this way providing a common language for very disparate intellectual branches.

Tourism scholarship is one such body of research, which draws from a diverse range of intellectual influences. However, reflective of the generally weak development of political economy perspectives in tourism (Bianchi 2002; Richter and Steiner 2008), the regulation school has, with some notable exceptions (e.g. Costa and Martinotti 2003; Hoffman 2003; Lafferty and Van Fossen 2001; Milne and Ateljevic 2001; Williams and Shaw 1998), found few representatives within tourism scholarship.

There are three general features of existing applications of the regulation approach in tourism. First, much of this application is to be found in the literature on Fordism and its different transmutations and variants in tourism production and consumption. Second, although using much of the same language and many of the constructs of the regulation school, tourism scholars tend to combine insights from cognate – but, to some extent, only tangentially related – bodies of scholarship.

These have included application of the flexible specialization approach (e.g. Hirst and Zeitlin 1992; Piore and Sabel 1984) and ideas about 'flexible accumulation' associated with the works of Harvey (1989) and others. These types of analyses have set the tone for what has become a significantly growing body of specialist analyses of tourism production, ranging, for example, from the dimensions of vertical integration in the airline industry and the effects of the international regime for civil aviation on tourism, to distribution and cooperation in the international tour operator industry and urban tourism development. Although fairly cohesive, this literature has tended to develop within the boundaries (and, as will be illustrated below, also the epistemological limitations) of select strands in tourism studies (and in particular economic geography).

The third feature of tourism's application of the regulation approach is therefore that it has been of a generally eclectic and partial nature, drawing on some, but not all, of the central concepts of the approach. On the whole, more attention has been given to the nature and dynamics of tourism as a regime of accumulation. There is considerably less theoretical development of tourism as a systemic mode of regulation (Milne and Ateljevic 2001; Williams 2004). Indeed, although the concept of regulation has become more prominent in tourism analysis, it is generally used in reference to processes of management, and, at that, is used to describe exchanges among a small number of actors. It has also tended to be developed in relation to notions of tourism sustainability. This differs from the conceptualization of *régulation* advanced by the founding French scholars, whose intention was to portray an institutionally embedded web of governance relations that undergird the regime of accumulation (see, for example, Boyer 2002).

This chapter provides an overview of the regulation approach in tourism, and explores some of the main contributions and deficiencies of this approach in contemporary tourism scholarship. The principal organizing question for the chapter is: 'What are the ways in which the regulation approach has been applied in tourism, and what have been the central epistemological and methodological values that this approach has yielded for tourism studies?' A primarily theoretical account will be provided of the evolution of the approach in tourism, as well as its main features, contributions and shortcomings. The chapter consists of three parts. The first provides an outline of regulation theory in its classical formulation. The second reviews the various ways in which this approach has been taken up in tourism scholarship. In the final part some conclusions are drawn on the insights that the regulation approach yields for understanding such aspects as development, power and governance in tourism, as well as what the implications are for a more satisfactory political economy of tourism.

Classical formulations of the regulation approach

Arising within the specific geo-institutional context of the 1970s, the regulation approach was led by a group of scholars who observed the weakening in the world economy at that time as not just a temporary, cyclical wane characteristic of capitalism's phases, but as a manifestation of a deeper crisis of the system. In its classical formulation, regulation theory reacted against descriptions of capitalism as the spontaneous outcome of economic exchange reflected in neoclassical theory, and did not regard capitalism as the result of accumulative technical progress as articulated in Joseph Schumpeter's work (see, for example, Altvater 1992; Boyer 1988; Jessop 2001). For Aglietta (1998: 54), one of the founding theorists:

> capitalism can only achieve progress for society if sets of mediation mechanisms, forming a mode of regulation, establish coherence among the imbalances inherent in the capitalist system. The cumulative effect of this coherence, once it has been achieved, is the establishment of a régime of growth.

Early regulationists thus set out to identify the nature and functioning of the various norms, rules, social practices and formal and informal codes that underlay what they perceived to be a mode of regulation – and the regime which it undergirds – in decline. Aglietta's (1979) analysis of capitalism in the United States pioneered an expanding body of research that rapidly grew in content and viewpoint. Two concepts are, however, central to the regulation approach: the 'regime of accumulation', referring to regularized practices that define the nature of the macro-economy (i.e. production and consumption) and can include norms and rules that govern relationships between economic agents or determine industrial organization; and the 'mode of regulation', which can be seen as 'an ensemble of norms, institutions, organizational forms, social networks and patterns of conduct which sustain and "guide" the . . . accumulation regime' (Jessop 1992: 48). From this, Fordism came to be identified as the regime of accumulation, which prevailed in the United States and had gained a position of hegemony in the postwar era. The apparent crisis of Fordism in the late 1970s provoked regulation scholars to explore the nature of the regime to emerge in Fordism's wake.

The theoretical prototype provided by the French scholars was quickly diffused and became modified in subsequent decades by scholars with varying disciplinary backgrounds and intentions. Jessop's (2001) comprehensive survey of the regulation school yielded seven distinct schools. And even though the use of the term Fordism has become 'vulgarized' (Jessop 1992: 46) in the process, what has remained central, however, has been the effort to delineate the content and underpinnings of the posited successor regime. Different scholars have given emphasis to different aspects.

In the assessment of classical regulationists, the features that most starkly defined Fordism were the system's reliance on Taylorist forms of labour use, marked by the extensive imposition of waged employment and clear divisions of labour, the mass production of standardized goods based on the assembly line model pioneered in the automotive industry, and the creation of mass markets driven by consumption (Esser and Hirsch 1992: 75). What sets regulationists' depiction of Fordism apart from other contending theoretical perspectives (see below) is their emphasis on the necessary fit between these micro-economic practices and macro-economic policies, which in postwar United States and Western Europe were typically based on Keynesian-inspired demand-side management and a focus on full employment. Distinctly, therefore, Fordism in the regulationist view was a system of totality derived from processes of 'intensive accumulation' at the micro level combined with appropriate macro-economic regulation to ensure the conditions for continuous expansion (Lipietz 1987). A structural crisis arose in the instance when institutions of regulation no longer served the regime of accumulation, unsettling the system's equilibrium and its capacity to adjust to smaller-scale disruptions.

Theoretical limitations and challengers of the classical regulation approach

Notwithstanding these basic ingredients, internal differentiation within the regulation school on the determinants of Fordism's strengths and weaknesses has been extensive (Boyer 1988). Importantly, there has in no sense been agreement among regulationists on whether Fordism has been eclipsed by a distinctly new, or a post-Fordist regime and what the primary components and drivers of the latter are. Scholars such as Esser and Hirsch (1992) and Jessop (1992) concur that new practices of regulation, forms of employment, corporate organization and patterns of consumption and lifestyles have been on the rise since the late 1970s. They note, however, that these, despite their coherent contribution to what may be termed new modes of accumulation, do not constitute 'a restabilized post-Fordist capitalism' but that 'there are tendencies towards it' (Esser and Hirsch 1992: 77). For many regulationists contemporary capitalism is reflective of both Fordist and posited neo-Fordist practices, which in different national settings may take on different hues. Regulationists are frustratingly less clear about the balance between older and variant forms of Fordism in a given context, or the factors that may determine the degree of crystallization of each, nor do they tend to provide satisfactory answers for why this should be the case.

Further complexity arises from the degree to which the Fordism/post-Fordism debate has become recast in theoretical bodies that, although cognate to the regulation approach and sharing many of its core tenets, also significantly differ from it in terms of the emphases they place on particular aspects of capitalism's processes, and the projections they make about Fordism's demise. Two of the theoretical bodies that have most prominently figured in the Fordism/post-Fordism debate are the neo-Schumpeterian perspective and the theory of flexible specialization (Amin 1994). It is perhaps the latter perspective that has most rivalled the regulation school.

The flexible specialization approach shares the regulation school's ambition to describe processes of economic exchange and production in relation to complex micro-level and industry-specific practices. Flexible specialization theorists, however, reject the claim to totalizing tendencies that underlies the regulationists' approach. In a detailed treatise, Hirst and Zeitlin (1992), two of the keenest advocates, outline the approach's key contentions around industrial characteristics, politics and policy. These commence with the identification of flexible specialization or craft production as an abstracted (ideal-type) form of technological production characterized by the 'manufacture of a wide and changing array of customized products using flexible, general-purpose machinery and skilled, adaptable workers' (Hirst and Zeitlin 1992: 71). Flexible/craft production is distinct from mass production, which is based on the use of generally unskilled labour and of machinery designed for limited and specialized purposes, the production of standardized goods in large quantities and the creation of economies of scale.

Rather than posing a patent break between these forms of production (thus declaring the transcendence of post-Fordism over Fordism), flexible specialization theorists contend that both craft and mass production mark contemporary industrial organization. As an economic paradigm, flexible specialization is characterized by specific micro- and macro-level regulatory practices. At the micro level these relate to the decentralization of production within a given firm, the use of adaptable production processes, subcontracting and the sharing of services among ancillary firms in a given geographical area (Piore and Sabel 1984). Expressed as an ideal, macro-level practices should create the conditions for firms to produce as efficiently as possible. This means the existence of institutions that enhance cooperation and coordination among firms while enabling them to compete against each other.

The flexible specialization approach has become very influential among scholars and policy-makers over the past two decades or so. Key elements of the flexible specialization thesis – particularly suppositions on the growth value of industrial districts (e.g. Storper and Christopherson 1987) – have found their way into the planning lexicon of many urban and regional authorities, particularly in Western Europe. Concepts closely related to the approach – such as vertical integration – can today be viewed both as analytical models and as descriptors for empirical processes unfolding in many of the world's major industries. In the academic sphere, the flexible specialization approach has aligned with other literature on competitiveness and flexible accumulation and they have consolidated into an eminent, if highly diverse, body of scholarship on economic regionalization. These approaches share assumptions regarding the expansion of the international sphere of production (or economic globalization); the generally reduced macro-regulatory capacities of national states; and the presumed rescaling of capitalist production. Strikingly, among the social science fields that have been most concerned with the implications of emergent capitalist trends, it is the arguments and language popularized by proponents of the flexible specialization approach that prevail in everyday intellectual deployment ahead of the more abstracted accounts offered by the regulation school.

Indeed, the extent to which the tenets of the regulation school are present in contemporary scholarship – particularly in the Anglo-Saxon context – seems considerably reduced. Although Boyer (2002) may protest that the regulation school has simplistically been equated with the Fordism/post-Fordism duality, and that regulationists' attempt to detail *régulation* as a compound process of capital accumulation has been semantically and analytically misunderstood in the Anglo-Saxon world, it is the case that the school's close association with the debate on Fordism has affected its position in the social sciences, where currently other conceptual strands seem to enjoy stronger development. For instance, economic geography, urban studies, critical sociology and critical political economy, for long the disciplinary habitats for the regulation approach in the Anglo-Saxon world, are today arguably more concerned with the scalar and socio-cultural effects of economic reorganization and the posited central role of consumption in capitalism's constitution than in detailing the micro- and macro-regulatory functioning of capitalism through what is perceived to be an overly mechanistic model.

The regulation school and tourism scholarship

Against this background, the line of research in tourism studies that explore the regulation approach's applicability to tourism processes is interesting. Assembled on a still slender number of contributions and comparatively recent in its emergence this line of research coheres around a general objective of developing a political economy agenda in tourism analysis that sufficiently acknowledges and theorizes the production, consumption and distributional aspects of tourism (e.g. Hoffmann *et al.* 2003; Milne and Ateljevic 2001; Shaw and Williams 2004). The building blocks of this research thus stem from earlier critical analyses of tourism as an essentially capitalist activity governed by the same rules of labour-wage exchange and relations and ownership of production as any other commodity. Britton's (1991) well-crafted essay set the tone for this.

However, if the broader development of political economy perspectives in tourism has tended to be tentative, selective (Williams 2004: 61) and generally peripheral, the application of insights from the regulation school has been even more so. In what follows, the manner in which the regulation approach has been applied in tourism studies is reviewed. This review is organized thematically, in accordance with the major slants and theoretical emphases. Predominant orientations in this regard relate to the emergence of new tourist regimes of accumulation, embodied in analyses of Fordist/post-Fordist forms of tourism production and consumption; and means of (national and subnational) regulation and how these affect tourism and its sustainability.

Tourism, post- (and neo-)Fordism and flexible specialization

It has been in the analysis of the impact on tourism of wider socio-economic and socio-political shifts, and specifically the posited transition from Fordist to post-Fordist economies, that the most extensive application of the regulation approach in tourism studies has occurred. Ioannides and Debbage (1997, 1998) collated much of the content of this body of tourism research in their overview of changing patterns of production and consumption in the travel industry, which they designated as pre-Fordist, Fordist and post-Fordist.

In the view of Ioannides and Debbage (1997) pre-Fordism was the dominant mode of production in tourism, characterizing the sector from its early emergence until about the 1960s. The most distinctive features of this mode are small-scale craft or artisanal production, marked by informality, low levels of employment and the limited presence of information technology. According to the authors this type of production persists in the micro-sized, family-owned and operated accommodation and tourism retail enterprises (such as souvenir stores) throughout the world. Graduation from pre-Fordist to Fordist tourism production occurred with the large-scale transformation of the sector from the 1960s onwards, mostly driven by overlapping shifts in the international economy. To tourism scholars, the sweeping changes in accumulation, employment and demand-side management documented by regulation theorists as part of the regime of Fordism/ Keynesianism had its counterpart in the advent of mass travel, mass consumption and mass tourism.

Industrially, tourism in the Fordist mode is marked by the creation of economies of scale and firms' continuous expansion into new markets riding on the adoption of dedicated information distribution systems (Milne and Gill 1998). There is little scope for consumer differentiation in this mode, in which the emphasis is on offering standardized products to presumably non-discerning tourists. Changes in the latter are instrumental in the transition to post-Fordist tourism, in which the combination of specific firm practices and more independently minded and demanding tourists leads to a mode of production and consumption defined by specialization, flexibility and customization. Post-Fordist tourist firms are smaller and more pliable in their operations than the large, industrially concentrated counterparts in the Fordist mode; location plays less of a determining role in their operations, and they readily make use of subcontracting and strategic alliances with other like firms (Shaw and Williams 2004).

Ioannides and Debbage (1997) are among those scholars who recognize elements of craft, mass and flexible production and consumption in contemporary tourism, and therefore refer to tourism's smorgasbord (or 'polyglot') of pre-Fordist, Fordist and neo-Fordist (rather than post-Fordist) characteristics. This distinction is theoretically advantageous for two reasons. First, it has served to overcome some of the obvious shortcomings of adopting a linear and non-transmutable Fordism/post-Fordism model to tourism development, in which empirical trends clearly indicate a more calibrated outcome. As a process, for instance, globalization has yielded many different effects on different tourism destinations, which also extends to how tourism firms manoeuvre and adapt their practices. Although multinational firms continue to dominate the international tourism economy, and persist in practices associated with Fordist accumulation (i.e. horizontal integration, oftentimes aggressively pursued, and the selling of routinized travel packages and products), these same firms would also enter into strategic networks or would use information technologies to lower their reliance on geographical fixity.

In general, analysts of industrial practices in tourism suggest that to reduce economic risk certain tourism industries show continuing forms of Fordist production such as horizontal integration and the development of economies of scale. This is particularly the case in the airline industry in which, according to Lafferty and Van Fossen (2001), factors such as airlines' close historical associations with national governments, the regimented nature of the international system of civil aviation regulation, and specific forms of profitability (which is generally of a more volatile nature) and employment (in the main quite inflexible) establish rigid conditions under which airlines seek to maintain economic viability. This has favoured the adoption of labour and production practices that are Fordist in nature. In contrast, in the accommodation and tour operator industries, firms may benefit from the use of more elastic techniques and collaborative relationships. Milne *et al.* (2004) suggest that computer information and distribution technologies have transformed industrial practices in the tour operator industry towards a more or less permanent adoption of practices that are generally associated with post-Fordism.

Finally, although many locations in the developing world are part of the Fordist production structure that arose during the era of mass industrial consolidation, there is today significant differentiation from the pattern of core–periphery exploitation depicted by prototype tourism political economists in the 1980s (such as Britton 1982, 1989). Instead, although multinational corporations that have their origins in the developed world still maintain an influential position in international tourism, many firms are originating within the developing world itself, which in industrial form and practice either act like traditional 'pre- or Fordist' firms or, largely through the use of technologies, are outwardly post-Fordist in nature (also see Bianchi 2002).

The second theoretical advantage of depicting tourism destinations or firms on a loosely arranged continuum of Fordism, neo- or post-Fordism, is that it helps to factor in tourism's industrial variability by demonstrating that destinations or firms my exhibit elements of one, two or all forms of Fordism, neo- or post-Fordism. Leiper (1979, 2008) has drawn attention to the fragmented nature of tourism and the difficulties this poses to the analyst. In contrast to manufacturing, for instance, to which Fordist/post-Fordism analysis has been extensively applied, the study of tourism's micro-level organization is made more complex by its varied institutional ensemble.

Tourism, regulation and sustainability

The way in which the concept of regulation has been applied in tourism has notably differed in substance from that of the regulation school. Regulation has been used in diverse senses in tourism analysis, but there have been four common features to its application. First, drawing on the expansion of regulation theory in urban studies, there has been a treatment of tourism regulation as a process defined by variable 'material and discursive practices' (Goodwin and Painter 1997: 21) rather than a distinct mode. The second feature has therefore been to view regulation as something that is not fixed to a specific temporal condition and regime of accumulation, but which fluctuates in time and space according to changing societal institutions. As such, the third feature has been a view of regulation as a meso-level process in which it performs a function not of overseeing epochal transition, but of inducing small-scale changes to enhance production and the social relations, rules and practices that sustain it. Even though somewhat more obscure, the fourth feature stems from the third and involves the way in which regulation has been theoretically advanced as a set of prescriptions for normatively valued tourism practices. This has particularly been the case in the application of regulation precepts to sustainability.

Gladstone and Fainstein's (2001) analysis of changing labour and spatial characteristics in the tourism sectors of New York and Los Angeles demonstrates the first three features described above. The authors combine the regulation approach and urban regime theory to explore the blend of economic factors, cultural dynamics, local politics and national institutions that shape tourism in the two metropolises. They describe the pro-growth urban regimes – made up of civic boosters, local businesses and politicians – that exist in each as a social mode of regulation, which although aligned with national policies display their own dynamics determined by the political setting in each city. Hence both cities exhibit a strong degree of income and occupational status polarization in their tourism labour markets, which are explained by the authors in terms of local regulatory relationships. The authors' analysis rests on an adapted application of the tenets of the regulation approach to explain tourism outcomes by way of middle-range social institutions and practices.

Hoffmann's (2003) appraisal of tourism development in the New York neighbourhood of Harlem pursues a similar line of analysis. She assesses growing patterns of tourism demand, particularly cultural tourism, as part of processes of change in the political economy of Harlem. Although these are largely in response to wider national and international forces of (post-Fordist) economic restructuring, they have spurred the advance of local tourism marketing and governing structures – a shifting local regulatory setting, in other words. Social alliances to foster economic rejuvenation, the creation of new local networks, and entrepreneurial activities represent civic-regulatory responses to post-Fordist transformations. Tourism, therefore, has generated both societal changes and institutional alterations in Harlem, engendering greater social and political inclusion. Hoffmann views tourism as a stabilizing force for the wider urban regime, distinctively treating tourism as a regulatory mode in and of itself, an analytical exposition she continues with co-workers elsewhere (see Hoffmann *et al.* 2003).

What stands out with this kind of analytical framing is the multiscalar approach to tourism regulation, with tourism seen to be embedded within multiple regulatory structures at different geographical levels. Hoffmann *et al.* (2003) use this kind of framework to appraise the regulation not only of tourism production or its industrial components, but also of the locations (cities and regions), labour markets and users (consumers) of tourism. There is an epistemological rationale to this, for such an approach enables an analysis of the dense relations of tourism agencies, structures and institutions at various scales of governance (Costa and Martinotti 2003). There is, however, also a strong normative undertone to this, for the attempt is not only to explore the interplay among different actors and identify the consequences, but also to envisage from this the way in which regulation can ameliorate tourism's negative effects and help improve the tourist sector.

This is no more visible than in some of the work that has sought to link regulation theory to tourism sustainability (e.g. D'Hauteserre 1999; Judd 2003; Mowforth and Munt 1998; Williams and Montanari 1999). D'Hauteserre (1999), for example, examines the environmental and social impacts of the establishment of Disneyland in Paris from the vantage of how the national mode of social regulation in France mediated – and by implication assuaged – potentially damaging effects. Williams and Montanari (1999) consider the relationship between flexible (post-Fordist) practices by small-scale, alternative tourism producers and sustainability. They contrast practices of self-regulation by firms – such as the establishment of and adherence to voluntary environmental codes in settings such as the Alps – with state-level intervention and examine which form of regulation produces greater sustainability. Their conclusion is that firm-level self-regulation should be supported by formal, legislated regulation by the national state in order to reach more sustainable outcomes. In a more extensive analysis Williams and Shaw (1998) juxtapose the production, distribution and management of resources in Fordist and post-Fordist tourism and examine how the restructuring of economies affects sustainability.

What is noteworthy in all of the above analyses is that regulation is treated not as an all-encompassing social structure to which all relations of production and consumption are subjected, but is variably interpreted, either as temporary forms of state policy or as modulating, spontaneous and fluctuating meso-level institutional practices arising in response to changing tourism conditions. There is much less emphasis in tourism studies, therefore, of regulation's totalizing character and on regulation as the main organizing frame for practices of production and accumulation, a significant theoretical variation from the classical regulation school perspective. Two exceptions exist in broader analyses from the field of political science. Hazbun (2004), for example, reviews tourism's changing political economy in the Middle East due to globalization, which he expresses in terms of the receding (de-territorialization) and reassertion (re-territorialization) of state authority. Contending that tourism is a driver of globalization, Hazbun (2004: 331) argues that political actors such as states and other agents such as transnational corporations and local communities generate rents (income) 'by asserting control over tourism spaces and the processes which convert places, cultures and experiences into territorially defined commodities'. This process of re-territorialization – or promotion of tourism destinations – in Hazbun's view allows more power for state, societal and transnational actors in their contention to control the flow of capital and spatial representation, but also raises these actors' regulatory influence.

In their investigation of economic reform, liberalization and structural adjustment in Egypt, Richter and Steiner (2008) explore the rise of tourism as a new form of economic rent deliberately exploited by the Egyptian state authorities. The authors contend that neo-patrimonialism – a distinctive type of state regulation – underpinned the growth of Egypt's tourism industry since the start of the new millennium, with tourism development regarded as a substitute for declining oil revenues. By promoting tourism through the use of policy and the regulation of private capital, therefore, Egypt's authorities supplanted one rentier economy with another. Although framed within the conventions of political science, Richter and Steiner's analysis places the same emphasis on the production of tourism spaces as a system of regulation constituted by an ensemble of public authority and private capital.

The regulation school and tourism: trends, merits and demerits

As noted by Jessop (2001) the early regulation theorists were not the only ones to investigate the causes of general patterns of instability and crises in the world economy. Indeed, the regulation school's attempts to theorize the nature, impetuses and implications of capitalism's transitions were part of a wider scholarly enterprise to examine the logic and weaknesses of capitalist production. They were, however, the first to develop a systematic critique of neoclassical economic approaches, demonstrating both the theoretical and the pragmatic shortcomings of the predominant economic doctrine of the time. To this effect – and their most lasting contribution – they introduced an account of capitalism that regarded it as both a system of medium- and micro-level institutions, norms and practices of accumulation and a macro-structure of organization (or mode of régulation) by which those practices were governed and maintained. In this regard the regulation school constituted one of the major bodies of thought within an evolving political economy perspective.

As suggested above, tourism scholarship drew conceptual inspiration from the regulation school, adopting many of its precepts to understand complex processes of change to tourism's industrial and organizational structures. This had some useful consequences for theoretical advances in tourism. For instance, of the variety of theoretical impulses that have animated tourism studies in recent years, three may be singled out: the cultural turn; the related advance of postmodernist insights on tourist lifestyles; and the general attempt to deepen understanding of both the production and consumption of tourism under conditions of societal change. By borrowing from the regulation school, and in particular how neo- or post-Fordist transmutations can be detected in the ways in which tourism activities are organized in the contemporary era, analysts have been able to develop accounts of how shifts in tourism supply are related to shifts in demand. This has enabled the study of processes such as vertical and horizontal integration, market segmentation and niche development in tourism, and their relationship to broader economic development. In sum, regulation theory has helped open the way for a greater understanding of the mutual (but also often dialectical) interplay between tourism production and consumption. Its application to tourism processes has also dovetailed neatly with newer developments in scholarship around tourism as a cultural phenomenon.

At the same time, however, tourism scholars have also been largely selective in their application of insights from the regulation school. Although much empirical depth has been given to the dimensions and effects of dominant regimes of accumulation in tourism, much less attention has been given to the various institutional arrangements – or modes of regulation – that exist within and across specific tourism sectors that sustain tourism regimes.

This has had some significant consequences for the degree to which tourism scholarship has been able to account for the connection between micro- and macro-level elements of tourism, and, in particular, how overarching structures of governance – or regulation – shape industrial processes. Specifically, the prevailing emphasis in tourism analysis that there is a mix between customization and standardization bears a closer resemblance to the constructs of flexible specialization theory than it does to the regulation approach. As noted above, the difference between the two schools lies in the extent to which they emphasize ruptures between different systems of accumulation and regulation.

Although they use much of the same language, proponents of the flexible specialization approach do not offer a perspective on post-Fordism *per se*; rather they seek to offer analytical and policy tools for what they observe to be changing forms of industrialization necessitated by the overall changed conditions of international capitalism. In this, emphasis is placed on evidently increased processes of vertical integration within firms, which, although it entails the breakdown of Fordist patterns of industrial organization, also consists of the re-agglomeration of economies based on more flexible practices of production and specialization.

Although adherents of flexible specialization would therefore agree to the empirical existence of different forms of industrial production and the regulatory practices that uphold them, they do not extend this to distinguish overarching and universalizing modes of regulation. Indeed, the emphasis on contingency, customization and variable deployment of existing technology, practices, resources and institutions, rather than the need to force homogenization across these, is what sets the flexible specialization approach most apart from the regulation school.

As such, the significance of the rise in recent years of tourism analyses that have sought to explain how and why destinations are restructured in accordance with Fordist/post-Fordist modifications (Torres 2002; also see Ioannides 2006), or those that have linked tourism to the development of agglomeration economies and industrial districts (e.g. Hjalager 2000), extends beyond the fact that they draw insights from the flexible specialization approach. It also implies a particular ontological positioning with regard to the way in which processes and the scale of industrial change are understood. Whereas in the regulation approach change is conceived as systemic and cumulative and with the general purpose of re-establishing macro-level equilibrium, in approaches such as flexible specialization it is conceptualized as aggregative, meso-level shifts in industrial practice determined by consensus among a limited group of private actors and public authorities.

This perspective has had some benefits in tourism analysis for understanding practices of regulation on the small scale, and, as illustrated, a number of scholars have made some innovative theoretical connections between tourism regulation and (ecological) sustainability. Yet comparatively few studies have approached tourism as a system of regulation in and of itself – for example systematically exploring the way in which competing sets of interests among a variety of stakeholders determine tourism processes in a given location – and how this is shaped by related economic processes (such as broader industrial change). More importantly, despite promising foundations laid by Britton (1991) and others, comparatively little analysis has been conducted of tourism as a capitalist activity, and we still have little understanding of tourism's place in wider capitalist structures. This is partly because of the way in which 'power' has been treated as a construct in tourism scholarship: in many newer critical analyses 'power' is generally accepted as a conceptual given, but is for the most part not problematized or fully scrutinized (see, for instance, Church and Coles 2007). The regulation approach's attention to the relationship between micro- and macro-structural processes may provide useful analytical beacons for tourism scholars in this regard.

As a final comment, most empirical accounts of tourism activities that are based on the regulation approach have drawn from a certain context – the forms of tourism production particular to the industrialized, Western world. The scholarship on tourism regulation has not been extensively tested on its degree of transferability – and hence validity – across different contexts.

Conclusion

The regulation approach has inspired a generation of critical scholarship on the nature, functioning and limitations of systemic capitalism. The school appears to have been marginalized in academic circles in recent years. Yet its core tenets constitute important intellectual undercurrents to the major empirical questions scholars continue to grapple with, most central of which concern future trends within capitalism and implications for world prosperity.

Thus far the regulation approach has seen limited extension in tourism scholarship. The reasons for this overlap with many of the reasons for the approach's relatively frailer position in the broader social sciences in recent years. These relate to a general dissatisfaction with the ostensible causal reductionism of the approach – something that according to Bianchi (2002) has tended to characterise traditional political economy analyses in tourism – and its apparent inability to provide an account for emergent sites of regulation beyond the national state in the era of globalization (e.g. Shaw and Williams 2004). However, it also has a lot to do with the sociological mechanisms of knowledge production, which in the field of tourism studies have both shaped trajectories of theory development and served to reinforce disciplinary dividing lines (for reviews of theoretical trends in tourism studies see Xiao and Smith 2008).

In a sense, therefore, the regulation approach's under-representation is also institutional in nature, relating to the way in which schools of thought have found footing in tourism research, and the disciplinary practices that have favoured certain theoretical bodies above others. Yet the approach has much to offer tourism studies, primary of which is its calling to attention aspects that have so far been neglected in tourism, such as power, the role of social institutions and the deep embedding of tourism production and consumption with other capitalist structures.

References

Aglietta, M. (1979) *A Theory of Capitalist Regulation: The U.S. Experience*, London: New Left Books.

Aglietta, M. (1998) 'Capitalism at the turn of the century: Regulation theory and the challenge of social change', *New Left Review*, 232: 41–90.

Altvater, E. (1992) 'Fordist and post-Fordist international division of labor and monetary regimes', in M. Storper and A. Scott (eds) *Pathways to Industrialization and Regional Development*, London: Routledge.

Amin, A. (1994) 'Post-Fordism: Models, fantasies and phantoms of transition', in A. Amin (ed.) *Post-Fordism: A reader*, Oxford: Blackwell.

Bianchi, R. (2002) 'Towards a new political economy of global tourism', in R. Sharpley and D. Telfer (eds) *Tourism and Development: Concepts and issues*, Clevedon: Channel View.

Boyer, R. (1988) 'Technical change and the theory of "regulation" ', in G. Dosi, C. Freeman, R. Nelson and L. Soete (eds) *Technical Change and Economic Theory*, London: Pinter Publishers.

Boyer, R. (1990) *Regulation Theory: A critical introduction*, New York: Columbia University Press.

Boyer, R. (2002) 'Introduction', in R. Boyer and Y. Saillard (eds) *Regulation Theory: The state of the art*, London: Routledge.

Britton, S. (1982) 'The political economy of tourism in the Third World', *Annals of Tourism Research*, 9: 331–58.

Britton, S. (1989) 'Tourism, dependency and development: A mode of analysis', in T. Singh, H. Theuns and F. Go (eds) *Towards Appropriate Tourism: The case of developing countries*, Frankfurt am Main: Peter Lang.

Britton, S. (1991) 'Tourism, capital, and place: Towards a critical geography of tourism', *Environment and Planning D: Society and Space*, 9: 451–478.

Church, A. and Coles, T. (eds) (2007) *Tourism, Power and Space*, London: Routledge.

Costa, N. and Martinotti, G. (2003) 'Sociological theories of tourism and regulation theory', in L. M. Hoffmann, S. S. Fainstein and D. R. Judd (eds) *Cities and Visitors: Regulating people, markets and city space*. Oxford: Blackwell.

D'Hauteserre, A. (1999) 'The French mode of social regulation and sustainable tourism development: The case of Disneyland Paris', *Tourism Geographies*, 1: 86–107.

Esser, J. and Hirsch, J. (1992) 'The crisis of Fordism and the dimensions of a post-Fordist regional and urban structure', in M. Storper and A. Scott (eds) *Pathways to Industrialization and Regional Development*, London: Routledge.

Gladstone, D. and Fainstein, S. (2001) 'Tourism in US global cities: A comparison of New York and Los Angeles', *Journal of Urban Affairs*, 23: 23–40.

Goodwin, M. and Painter, J. (1997) 'Concrete research, urban regimes and regulation theory', in M. Lauria (ed.) *Reconstructing Urban Regime Theory: Regulating urban politics in a global economy*, London: Sage.

Harvey, D. (1989) *The Condition of Postmodernity*, Oxford: Blackwell.

Hazbun, W. (2004) 'Globalisation, reterritorialisation and the political economy of tourism development in the Middle East', *Geopolitics*, 9: 310–341.

Hirst, P. and Zeitlin, J. (1992) 'Flexible specialisation versus post-Fordism: Theory, evidence and policy implications', in M. Storper and A. Scott (eds) *Pathways to Industrialization and Regional Development*, London: Routledge.

Hjalager, A. (2000) 'Tourism destinations and the concept of industrial districts', *Tourism and Hospitality Research*, 2: 199–213.

Hoffman, L. (2003) 'The marketing of diversity in the inner city: Tourism and regulation in Harlem', *International Journal of Urban and Regional Research*, 27: 286–299.

Hoffmann, L., Fainstein, S. and Judd, D. (eds) (2003) *Cities and Visitors: Regulating people, markets and city space*, Oxford: Blackwell.

Ioannides, D. (2006) 'Commentary: The economic geography of the tourist industry: Ten years of progress in research and an agenda for the future', *Tourism Geographies*, 8: 76–86.

Ioannides, D. and Debbage, K. (1997) 'Post-Fordism and flexibility: The travel industry polyglot', *Tourism Management*, 18: 229–241.

Ioannides, D. and Debbage, K. (1998) 'Neo-Fordism and flexible specialization in the travel industry: Dissecting the travel polyglot', in D. Ioannides and K. Debbage (eds) *The Economic Geography of the Tourist Industry: A supply-side analysis*, London: Routledge.

Jessop, B. (1992) 'Fordism and post-Fordism: A critical reformulation', in M. Storper and A. Scott (eds) *Pathways to Industrialization and Regional Development*, London: Routledge.

Jessop, B. (2001) *Regulation Theory and the Crisis of Capitalism, Volume 5, Development and Extensions*, Cheltenham: Elgar.

Judd, D. (2003) 'Visitors and the spatial ecology of the city', in L. Hoffmann, S. Fainstein and D. R. Judd (eds) *Cities and Visitors: Regulating people, markets and city space*, Oxford: Blackwell.

Lafferty, G. and Van Fossen, A. (2001) 'Integrating the tourism industry: Problems and strategies', *Tourism Management*, 22: 11–19.

Leiper, N. (1979) 'The framework of tourism', *Annals of Tourism Research*, 6: 390–407.

Leiper, N. (2008) 'Why "the tourism industry" is misleading as a generic expression: The case for plural variation, "tourism industries"', *Tourism Geographies*, 29: 237–251.

Lipietz, A. (1987) *Mirages and Miracles: The crises of global Fordism*. London: Verso.

Milne, S. and Gill, K. (1998) 'Distribution technologies and destination development: Myths and realities', in D. Ioannides and K. Debbage (eds) *The Economic Geography of the Tourist Industry: A supply-side analysis*, London: Routledge.

Milne, S. and Ateljevic, I. (2001) 'Tourism, economic development and the global–local nexus: Theory embracing complexity', *Tourism Geographies*, 3: 369–393.

Milne, S. Mason, D. and Hasse, J. (2004) 'Tourism, information technology, and development: revolution or reinforcement?', in A. A. Lew, C. M. Hall and A. M. Williams (eds) *A Companion to Tourism*, Oxford: Blackwell.

Mowforth, M. and Munt, I. (1998) *Tourism and Sustainability: New tourism in the Third World*, London: Routledge.

Piore, M. and Sabel, C. (1984) *The Second Industrial Divide: Possibilities for prosperity*, New York: Basic Books.

Richter, T. and Steiner, C. (2008) 'Politics, economics and tourism development in Egypt: Insights into the sectoral transformations of a neo-patrimonial rentier state', *Third World Quarterly*, 29: 939–959.

Shaw, G. and Williams, A. M. (2004) *Tourism and Tourism Spaces*. London: Sage.

Storper, M. and Christopherson, S. (1987) 'Flexibility, hierarchy and regional development: The changing structure of industrial production systems and their forms of governance in the 1980s', *Research Policy*, 20: 407–422.

Torres, R. (2002) 'Cancun's development from a Fordist spectrum of analysis', *Tourist Studies*, 2: 87–116.

Williams, A. M. (2004) 'Towards a political economy of tourism', in A. A. Lew, C. M. Hall and A. M. Williams (eds) *A Companion to Tourism*, Oxford: Blackwell.

Williams, A. M. and Shaw, G. (1998) 'Tourism and the environment: Sustainability and economic restructuring,' in C. M. Hall and A. A. Lew (eds) *Sustainable Tourism: A geographical perspective*, Harlow: Addison Wesley Longman.

Williams, A. M. and Montanari, A. (1999) 'Sustainability and self-regulation: critical perspectives', *Tourism Geographies*, 1: 26–40.

Xiao, H. and Smith, S. (2008) 'Knowledge impact and appraisal of tourism impact', *Annals of Tourism Research*, 35: 62–83.

4 The paradigms of political economy and tourism policy

National tourism organizations and state policy

Craig Webster, Stanislav Ivanov and Steven F. Illum

Many have written about tourism from the perspective of the social sciences and business. There is a great deal of interest in issues leading to the expansion of tourism industries, public investments to assist in the expansion of tourism, the environmental impact of tourism, and the externalities of tourism. However, few people have looked into the impact of economic paradigms on tourism marketing, planning and development. The intent of this chapter is to fully investigate the influence that models of political and economic thinking have in a state's management of tourism to determine whether its political response to tourism is an outgrowth of the dominant political and economic philosophy upon which a state is based.[1]

The chapter will explore the dominant paradigms of political economy and how they may impact a government's institutional response to tourism. Central to the study is the role that national tourism organizations (NTOs) play in developing tourism, an institution studied by others (Lennon *et al.* 2006; Adamczyk 2005; Tang and Xi 2005; King 2002).

The hypothesis is that regimes with more liberal approaches to political economy are associated with weak (or lack of) NTOs, whereas those with more mercantilist and social democratic approaches will have larger and more powerful NTOs. This chapter will also underscore that those regimes more fully infused with the ideology of social democracy have NTOs that are also qualitatively different from those of more mercantilist regimes. In general, the model of political economy that a state displays plays an influential role in the way that a state organizes itself to manage and promote tourism.

To explore how states organize themselves to respond to the challenge of tourism, two examples of each political economy in three different types of regime are considered. The result may seem somewhat superficial in terms of describing and analysing each state's paradigm. The chapter's purpose is not to give a full analytical and historical overview of each state's engagement in tourism but rather to discover if there is evidence showing that a state's response is consistent with its style of political economy.

The following section provides a review of the literature on the political economy of tourism, as well as looking into the various perspectives of political economy. This is followed by a discussion of how several states (the United

States, Canada, Sweden, Finland, South Korea and Japan) organize themselves in relation to tourism, and of the consistency of tourism's organization with the prevailing philosophy of political economy in each state. The chapter concludes with comments about the implications of how states respond to the tourism challenge.

Political economies and their paradigms

There is little written about the influence of political economy on tourism; the most notable attempts were by Britton (1982) and Williams (2004). Britton's (1982) seminal work on the issue in the Third World is useful and important for understanding the role of tourism and the international economy. In this work he elaborates upon how dependency theory can be applied to tourism development in less developed countries of the world. He explains how the structure of a political economy favours metropolitan centres of capital accumulation by reinforcing colonial relationships and ownership patterns, leaving local populations in a majority of less developed countries disadvantaged when 'locals can only participate in tourism through wage-labour employment or small, petty retail and artisan enterprises' (Britton 1982: 355). In this regard, free market economies keep peripheral economies underdeveloped. However, conspicuously absent from Britton's analysis is the role of the state, making one wonder what types of policies these states pursue to limit negative externalities of the structural inequalities of international tourist destinations.

Williams (2004) adds to the work of Britton and others to show how the academic field of political economy may provide insight into the effects of political economy on tourism, describing issues of commodification and market relationships. However, one of the chief concepts that Williams brings to the study of tourism is the introduction of the role of regulation theory to demonstrate the role of the state. Although Britton (1982) analyses how less developed countries are in a disadvantaged position, he fails to incorporate the political element. Williams (2004: 69) sheds light on the role of the state in the regulation of tourism; he argues that regulation theory provides a framework for a 'more holistic understanding of tourism'.

There are others trying to answer questions linked to the regulation of tourism (Hall 2004; Jeffries 2001; Page 2007). Some in the field of tourism research deal with comparisons of the regulation of tourism. For example, Palmer and Bejou (1995) compare the regulation of tourism in the United States and the United Kingdom. Vail and Heldt (2000) compare the approaches towards regulation in regions in the United States and Sweden. There are other works that deal with regulation and state responses to tourism in particular countries (e.g. Pearce 1996; Desforges 2000). No literature (to date) explains the variations in institutional responses to tourism across different countries. Instead, most of the literature either skirts the issue or implicitly suggests that each state's response to tourism is idiosyncratic.

Political science offers useful insights, dividing political regimes into three or four major categories of political economy. Unfortunately, much of the literature on the topic is related to international political economy concerned with issues that cross nation-state borders rather than comparing political economies. The most common texts in international political economy (Balaam and Veseth 2007; Caporaso and Levine 1992; Frieden and Lake 1999; Gilpin 1987, 2001; Lairson and Skidmore 2002; Pearson and Payaslian 1999) target issues that cross boundaries. However, these authors do offer insights into different paradigms of political economy. The study of Gilpin (1987), perhaps the most influential work on international political economy, notes that there are generally three different paradigms: realism, liberalism and Marxism. Each of these is linked with a different understanding of the relationship between the market, state and society. In his *realist* paradigm, he explains how the state plays an important role in the economy. His *liberal* approach is more closely linked with a *laissez faire* approach to the economy. In stark contrast, the *Marxist* paradigm stresses the importance of equity, based upon an understanding of the nature and logic of capitalism touted by Marx. This trichotomy introduced by Gilpin has been adopted and modified by others in comparing political economies.

The comparative political economy approach to social science involves the study of how political systems shape economic interactions in states. One of the key aspects of such an approach is the notion that there is a philosophical foundation to political choices that are made and that these political choices create institutions that regulate economic and social interactions. So it is critical to understand that each of these approaches is based upon a different value system and very different understanding of what the role of the state is in terms of regulating the economy.

In O'Neil's (2007) view, there are four fundamental types of political economy (see Table 4.1), each based upon a different assumption of the relationship between the market and the state, although countries often have policies and programs that may not be entirely consistent with the basic philosophical approach of the paradigm. Some of the language used is inherited from Gilpin (1987). This approach with four major models has been adopted by others in the field, for example Draper and Ramsay (2007). O'Neil notes that one general model for how states may design their political economies is to make the market paramount and, thus, is a liberal economy. Liberal political economies reflect limited welfare and minimal state involvement in the economy and permit high levels of social and economic inequality. The liberal model is based upon the notion that the free market is the best in terms of organizing the production and distribution of wealth in a society. Thus, liberal regimes put a premium on market forces, allowing market forces the greatest freedom possible, in order to produce and distribute wealth. Of course, the downside of such a liberal approach is that economic outcomes will enable certain individuals to attain more wealth than others, meaning that in terms of outcome there will not be an equal distribution of wealth. The philosophical defence of such a system is that it is the best at producing wealth (even if there are inequalities in terms of distribution) and that all have an equal opportunity to compete in the market. This argument posits that the productive capacity of free markets more than makes up for its shortcomings in terms of distributing wealth.

Table 4.1 Political economic systems

	Liberalism	Social democracy	Communism	Mercantilism
Role of the state in the economy	Little; minimal welfare state	Some state ownership, regulation; large welfare state	Total state ownership; extensive welfare state	Much state ownership or direction; small welfare state
Role of the market	Paramount	Important but not sacrosanct	None	Limited
State capacity and autonomy	Low	Moderate	Very high	High
Importance of equality	Low	High	High	Low
How is policy made?	Pluralism	Corporatism	State/party	State
Possible flaws	Inequality, monopolies	Expense of the welfare state, inefficiency	Authoritarianism and inefficiency	Can tend toward authoritarianism; can distort market
Examples	United States, United Kingdom, former British colonies	Western Europe (Germany, Sweden)	Cuba, Soviet Union, China	Japan, South Korea, India

Source: O'Neil (2007: 97). From Essentials of Comparative Politics, second edition by Patrick O'Neil. Copyright © 2007, 2004 by W. W. Norton & Company, Inc. Used by permission of W. W. Norton & Company, Inc.

In stark contrast to the liberal model are the most statist political economies—the communist and mercantilist models. These approaches involve a state that plays a key role in setting economic policy for the country. However, there are major differences. The communist model is based on Marxist principles that lead to the marginalization of market forces and an emphasis on social and economic equality, as Marxist principles indicate that markets are tools that enable the bourgeoisie to dominate the society, politically as well as economically. As a result, communist states marginalize markets and minimize private ownership to allow for greater equality. In addition, communist political economies tend to have extensive welfare states (much more so than is found in other political economies) as private goods and services are mostly marginalized and in order to ensure equality in social and economic outcomes.

Mercantilist political economies are somewhat different, allowing for private ownership and markets, but with a great deal of state intervention in the markets. In such political economies, the state works in such ways to manage and direct markets in ways that are desired by the political leadership. It frequently does this through a mixture of cooperative arrangements and planning with the leadership of major industries and outright ownership of the means of production in industries. The focus of the political leadership in such a political economy is to ensure that the country is strong (economically and militarily), and mercantilists view markets with suspicion, seeing that they are a necessary element to produce and distribute wealth, but that, unchecked, they undermine the economic and military capabilities of the country. As mercantilists tend to focus on the longer-term economic and military strength of the country they are willing to overlook some aspects of the population's welfare. Thus, in mercantilist states, although the state plays a key role in terms of organizing and leading the economy, such economies generally tend to have weaker welfare state institutions than other states, with the possible exception of the liberal ones.

The social democratic model is a mixture of the liberal and more statist approaches. In social democratic political economies, the state plays an important role in regulating the economy and is involved in the economy as an owner of some industries. However, the state retains markets and permits market forces to function in order to supply many goods and services. The major difference between the social democratic model and the communist model of political economy is this stress on the retention of market forces in order to supply many private goods. However, as they are both descended from Marxist philosophy, social democratic approaches use regulation of the economy to ensure more equitable economic outcomes in the society. When market forces leave the society lacking in critical provisions for the citizens, the social democratic state steps in to offer goods to the population by way of an extensive welfare state. Thus, because of the similarities between social democratic and communist philosophies, both political economies minimise inequalities through strong welfare state institutions..

These four different ways of organizing a political economy are archetypes and few political economies would fit completely into any one category. For example, there were and are communist regimes that have varying levels of permissiveness of markets. Indeed, even within any one category of political economy there is a great deal of variation. For example, in his 2007 documentary film, *Sicko*, Michael Moore denigrated the medical system in the United States by visiting hospitals in Canada and the United Kingdom to ask doctors, employees and patients how much particular services cost. His intention was to highlight that, in the United States, medical care is not a public but a private good. This is an interesting example of how political economies may be broadly described as 'liberal' by their variations of (1) how political systems function, (2) the extensiveness of welfare states and (3) what is considered a public good.

One major subfield of comparative political economy is the study of comparative welfare regimes. The first major stride here was made by Esping-Andersen (1990) who defined three different welfare regimes in capitalist countries: conservative (re-enforcing the political and social order), socialist (building an egalitarian social order by creating an extensive welfare state with equal access to all and no user fees) and liberal (the state correcting for market failures, supporting the market, and providing basic needs as a last resort).

This literature is interesting for several reasons. Most notably, it shows that while there are three broad classifications of welfare states, they are sophisticated and may have different programs, each based upon very different logic. For example, while Canada has an almost entirely liberal welfare state, its state-sponsored healthcare adds a socialist element. In addition, this indicates welfare states are largely in sync with predominating political and economic philosophies. Thus, while welfare states may have programs with a mixture of conservative, socialist and liberal elements, their programs are largely consistent with their dominant political philosophy.

States' political regimes and their responses to tourism

In review, there are three major 'styles' of economy in *capitalist* countries—liberal, social democratic and mercantilist. States' political institutions should be an outgrowth of their inherent basic principles upon which the polity has understood that the economy will be managed politically. Organizational responses to tourism are inherently political decisions dealing with the quantity and quality of regulation that the state will have upon the tourism industry. Do states respond to tourism in accordance with the principles of political economy on which they are based?

We may expect liberal regimes to have weak institutions to deal with the tourism sector. In such regimes a state has determined that the market will simply take care of tourism-related issues as tourism-related things are inherently private goods and the market is the best mechanism for the provision of such goods. In fact, in liberal regimes, a state may not actually have strong institutions to manage or organize tourism, favouring instead free market responses. It is expected that social democratic and mercantilist states may build stronger public agencies to deal with the tourism challenge, as both of these regimes of political economy place the state in a central role in the economy. There may be qualitative differences in social democratic and mercantilist states' approaches to tourism. Mercantilist states will likely have stronger tendencies towards privatization whereas social democratic states will stress how tourism is intended to benefit the welfare of the members of the host society.

We now turn to a few examples of states with very different political economies to determine whether these expectations hold true. We begin with a look at two liberal states and then move to two examples each of social democratic and mercantilist states. It is expected that the structure and quality of the states' responses to the tourism challenge will be different because the political economies of the states rest on very different philosophies—the liberal stressing the primacy of the market, the social democratic stressing social and economic equality among citizens, and the mercantilist stressing the importance of the state working to manage its economy.

C. Michael Hall (2004) discusses seven functions of government in relation to tourism: coordination, planning, legislation and regulation, entrepreneurship, stimulation, social tourism and public interest protection roles. These are quite vast areas, each deserving special attention. This chapter will focus only on the promotion function performed by NTOs, analysing their structure, goals, responsibilities and activities in the six countries representing the three types of regimes.

Liberal state: the United States

It is noteworthy that the United States does not have an NTO *per se*. The government institution responsible for tourism development and management at the federal level is a unit in the Department of Commerce, the Office of Travel and Tourism Industries (OTTI), largely a 'think tank' that performs research, collects data and recommends policy. According to the OTTI website:

> The primary functions of the OTTI are:
> * management of the travel and tourism statistical system for assessing the economic contribution of the industry and providing the sole source for characteristic statistics on international travel to and from the United States;
> * design and administration of export expansion activities;
> * development and management of tourism policy, strategy and advocacy; and
> * technical assistance for expanding this key export (international tourism) and assisting in domestic economic development.
>
> (Office of Travel and Tourism Industries 2010)

Although the US response to the tourism challenge is present, the OTTI has a rather limited scope. First, the function of the OTTI is collecting data to support research. In some respects, the production of free-of-charge data is considered a public good, to be used by researchers in academia and business.[2]

OTTI claims to be involved with promotion yet it is rather vague about how this is carried out. It would appear that the OTTI perceives itself to be the guardian of US tourism interests with a Secretary for Tourism and interagency committee to make sure that US tourism interests are represented in the federal government. According to the OTTI, the major way it represents US tourism internationally is through participation in the Asia-Pacific Economic Cooperation (APEC) Tourism Working Group and the Organisation for Economic Co-operation and Development (OECD) Tourism Committee.

OTTI notes that it subsidizes tourism promotion:

> On February 20, 2003, President George W. Bush signed the Omnibus Appropriation Act into law for FY 2003. Included in this appropriation was Sec. 210, authorising the Secretary of Commerce to award grants and make lump sum payments in support of an international advertising and promotion campaign encouraging people to travel to the United States. The Omnibus Appropriation authorised and appropriated $50M for this campaign. The Act requires the Secretary to appoint the US Travel and Tourism Advisory Board to recommend appropriate coordinated activities to the Secretary for funding. The Board comprises CEOs of tourism-related entities. The Secretary consults with the Board on the disbursement of funds.
>
> (OTTI 2010)

Thus, the OTTI not only collects data and advises (and incidentally sells analytical reports), but also plays a role in terms of influencing the allocation of resources to support private sector initiatives for the promotion of the US's tourism product. This rather recent approach is completed in conjunction with CEOs in the private sector. Conservative critics of this suggest it is a form of corporate welfare, a response following the terrorist attacks on the United States in 2001, seen as important to encourage tourists to visit the country.

What can be said of the US government's response to the challenge of tourism? First, there is no strong state organization to guide tourism in the United States; instead, the Department of Commerce is charged with the duty of guarding the country's tourism interests. Second, the range of OTTI's duties seems to be limited, largely stressing data collection and giving advice. The OTTI has recently expanded its responsibilities, dispersing subsidies to encourage international tourism in the United States. These are made in conjunction with CEOs of major tourism companies.

The US government's response to the tourism challenge is largely consistent with a liberal ideology and political economy. The state does not take the lead in encouraging tourism. Instead, a group embedded in a larger government agency is charged with the responsibility of representing the interests of the United States in tourism. In addition, it is largely a think tank, gathering data and serving as a centre for the analysis and dissemination of data. Only in recent years has it granted subsidies to non-profit organizations to promote US tourism. As expected in a liberal political economy, participating members of the private sector lead in determining which applying local organizations (Convention and Visitors Bureau and Chambers of Commerce) should be given subsidies to encourage destination product growth. The OTTI does not have administrative authority to participate in categorizing accommodation establishments or licensing tourism companies, unlike other NTOs (e.g. the Bulgarian State Agency for Tourism). The United State's approach is very liberal. Now we turn to its liberal neighbour to the north to question whether Canada is equally as liberal in its approach towards tourism.

Liberal state: Canada

At the federal level, the Canadian Tourism Commission (CTC) is a Crown corporation wholly owned by the Government of Canada that performs research and advertising for Canada in ten other countries. Whereas the US government's tourism arm is largely a 'think tank', the Canadian government's analogue has 'think tank' elements but also actively markets and promotes Canada internationally.

Article 5 of the Canadian Tourism Commission Act (2000, c. 28) states that the objectives of the Commission are to:

(a) sustain a vibrant and profitable tourism industry
(b) market Canada as a desirable destination
(c) support a cooperative relationship between the private sector and provincial/territorial governments of Canada
(d) provide information about Canadian tourism to the private sector and to the governments of Canada (provinces and territories).

(Canadian Tourism Commission 2008)

Furthermore, CTC's website states that:

With our partners in the tourism industry and all levels of government, we:
• advertise and market Canada in ten countries around the world
• conduct industry research and studies
• promote product and industry development

(Canadian Tourism Commission 2008)

There is ample evidence that the CTC is active in the promotion of tourism. In fact, the website shows that there are a large number of employees working abroad to promote Canada's tourism product. The CTC has offices in nine countries besides those of Canada (the United States, France, Germany, the United Kingdom, Mexico, Australia, South Korea, Japan and China). Not surprisingly, there are several offices in the United States (fifteen locations spread across such cities such as Chicago, New York City, Seattle, Los Angeles and Boston), with only one office per country in the other countries. This says a great deal about the importance of the United States for Canada's tourism industry. Proximity to the largest economy in the world seems to impact upon the CTC's allocation of resources. Whereas only three people work in the Chinese office, five in Japan, three in South Korea, one in Australia, four in Mexico, six in the United Kingdom, five in Germany and five in France, twenty-five work for the CTC in the fifteen US locations. As opposed to the US government's efforts, Canadian authorities play an important and direct role in promoting Canada's tourism product, as demonstrated by extensive allocation of human resources.

Private–public cooperation is the basis for managing the CTC. Its board of directors may consist of up to twenty-six directors, up to sixteen of whom are appointed from the private sector (Canadian Tourism Commission Act, Articles 7 and 11). No more than seven of the sixteen private sector representatives are tour operators representing provinces and territories, and up to nine represent other sectors of the industry. The structure and large number of elected tour operators illustrate that Canada focuses on active promotion of the country as a destination.

Similar to the OTTI, the CTC does not categorise accommodation establishments or license travel companies. Instead, it concentrates on marketing the destination. This also puts the CTC into the liberal category of government involvement, an organization with limited responsibilities but one that establishes that much of the guidance and support for the institution leading the regulation and promotion of tourism should come from the private sector.

Social democratic state: Finland

The Finnish Tourist Board (MEK) was created in 1973 under the auspices of the Ministry of Employment and the Economy. According to MEK, its core functions are marketing communications for Finnish tourism, collecting market data and making them available to the industry, and promoting high-quality product development and commercialization (Finnish Tourist Board 2008).

MEK has undergone drastic changes in the very recent past (Lehtonen 2008). In previous years, MEK acted much like a typical NTO. Its 2006 annual report stated that MEK had fifteen offices abroad; however, by 2008, it eliminated these by developing a partnership with Finpro (Lehtonen 2008), a private agency now charged with marketing Finnish tourism abroad. This reorganization resulted in a massive reduction in manpower at MEK. Director General Jaakko Lehtonen (2008) reported in June 2008 that fewer than twenty-eight employees remained; a year earlier, there were over 100 employees. Marketing Finland, according to MEK, now engages the private sector, as 'the share of campaign costs covered by industry operators must be at least 50 per cent' (Finnish Tourist Board 2008).

The Finnish response has changed radically in the past few years from a very statist one to one more linked with the private sector. Until 2006, the state was the major tool promoting Finland abroad. Since then the state's manpower has been drastically downsized and responsibilities have been shifted to a private firm. In essence, it seems that the Finnish authorities have moved towards a much more liberal approach of managing tourism, downsizing the state's own institution and outsourcing much of the work carried out traditionally by the state's institution to a private firm.

Social democratic state: Sweden

The Kingdom of Sweden engages in tourism through its two major institutions, NUTEK[3] (the Swedish Agency for Economic and Regional Growth, a state organ reporting to the Ministry of Enterprise, Energy and Communications) and VisitSweden, a private communication company equally owned by the Swedish state and tourism industry. NUTEK, as the state's tourism authority, is charged with the task of collecting tourism data, promoting the cooperation of tourism affairs within Sweden and abroad, and marketing and market development (Ministry of Industry Employment and Communications 2005: 19).

The Swedish state has taken an interesting route, with a state organ responsible for various aspects of tourism, including gathering tourism statistics and planning, with at the same time private sector involvement in the promotion of tourism abroad.

NUTEK's 2008 annual report quite explicitly spells out the goal of Sweden's tourism policy: 'Sweden is to be a highly attractive tourist destination and tourism is to be competitive in the long term, contributing to sustainable growth and increased employment throughout the country' (NUTEK 2008: 5 and Ministry of Industry Employment and Communications 2005: 17). Thus, the state's role seems to be not only to encourage tourism but also to support increased employment, consistent with socialist values.

Reasons for the state to become involved in Swedish tourism and its development include:

- The tourist industry has major socio-economic and growth policy importance, both as an export industry and as a domestic business activity.
- A significant part of the infrastructure that is of major importance to the tourist industry, such as transport, sights of interest, nature, culture, etc. are owned by the state or are public enterprises.
- The tourist industry is important from the perspectives of growth and employment policies, particularly in sparsely-populated areas and in areas where conditions for other business activities to develop are less positive.
- The tourist industry is subject to state involvement in most countries. The world's largest industry, with few exceptions, receives public sector support through national tourist organization.

  (Ministry of Industry Employment and Communications 2005: 17)

This highlight the fact that one of the major reasons for state involvement is that many other countries do the same. Swedish authorities argue that, as other countries subsidize tourism, Sweden should as well. One of the major reasons for state involvement in tourism is the stimulation of employment, especially in areas that are depressed or have few other occupational resources to develop.

International marketing is performed by VisitSweden, promoting Sweden as a business and leisure travel destination (VisitSweden 2008). This organization has offices in eleven key markets – China, Denmark, Finland, France, Germany, Italy, Japan, Spain, the Netherlands, the United Kingdom and the United States. Currently it has a ten-member board of directors, with four appointed by the state and four by the tourism industry; two are deputy members. Its website provides for online booking in only nine cities as of 2008. Therefore, VisitSweden performs not only pure promotional activities but also intends to stimulate sales by providing an online sales platform.

From the discussion above we may conclude that the management of Swedish tourism is divided into two parts: (1) developing domestic tourism (controlled by the state Swedish Agency for Economic and Regional Growth) and (2) promoting tourism abroad (implemented by the public–private joint venture VisitSweden). All in all, the Swedish response to the tourism challenge is largely centred upon the state's involvement in Sweden's economy. In Sweden, the state is the major actor assisting in developing its tourism. One state institution engages in tourism issues while the other is mutually owned by state and private interests. Certainly, this is a very different approach from that in the United States and Canada; however, Swedish authorities allow for private sector participation, consistent with a social democratic outlook.

Concern has been expressed about the policies of Swedish authorities with regard to equality in outcomes of marketing actions. For example, some regions lack employment opportunities and the state has responded to create such opportunities in less populated or less developed areas of the country. Although there is no sign that the Swedish state attempts to redistribute wealth from the wealthy to the poor (at least from the information gleaned from the official state information on the regulation of tourism), the government seems more concerned with the unemployed than with the owners of the means of production, something consistent with a Marxist approach towards economic regulation.

Mercantilist state: Japan

The Japanese government's response to the tourism challenge is the Japan National Tourist Organization (JNTO), under the auspices of the Ministry of Land, Infrastructure, Transport and Tourism. JNTO is, according to the Japanese government, an independent administrative institution. These are responsible for administrative rather than planning functions. Tourism planning is the responsibility of the Tourism Planning Division of the Ministry of Land, Infrastructure, Transport and Tourism, which concentrates on the international promotion of Japan as a destination. It has thirteen offices in eleven countries and participates actively at travel trade shows worldwide, in concert with the mercantilist philosophy. In addition, JNTO operates a tourist information centre in Tokyo and cooperates with local government and regional tourism associations, thus supporting local tourism offices, providing them with information and promotional materials and hospitality training courses.

In contrast to other NTOs covered by this chapter, JNTO is involved in licensing and regulating tourism services, although on a very small scale. It also conducts the National Examination for Licensed Guide-Interpreters for the Ministry of Land, Infrastructure, Transport and Tourism. JNTO is a public agency financed by the Japanese state; however, the organization participates in the Visit Japan Campaign (VJC): 'JNTO overseas offices perform key roles in overseas VJC Promotion Meetings that have been set up via strategic alliances between the government and the private sector, involving Japanese diplomatic entities, local opinion leaders and travel agents, among others' (Japanese National Tourism Organization 2008).

Marketing and selling the Japanese tourism product is the major goal of JNTO, in complete concert with the mercantilist regime of its government, with the state institution playing a major role in coordinating and planning in conjunction with the private sector.

Mercantilist state: South Korea

The Republic of Korea's organizational response to the tourism challenge is currently the Korean Tourism Organization (KTO), responsible to the Ministry of Culture and Tourism. The International Tourism Corporation, the precursor to the current state institution, was renamed the Korean Tourism Organization in 1982. The KTO currently operates twenty-six offices in fourteen foreign countries (Korean Tourism Organisation 2008). The KTO is involved in marketing South Korea and is engaged in developing resorts, infrastructure, tourism technology and tour packages. The KTO's website provides opportunities to download discount coupons for accommodation and other travel services, and to make online bookings for tourist services. The KTO's involvement in tourism marketing is much greater than that of the NTOs discussed previously.

In addition to the KTO, tourism in South Korea is promoted by the Korea Convention Bureau (KCB). This other state agency operates under the auspices of the KTO. It aims to 'establish Korea as a premier destination for tourists, convention delegates and business travelers' (Korean Tourism Organisation 2008). The KCB helps international meeting planners in their selection, organization and implementation of conference events in South Korea by facilitating site inspection tours, and coordination services. Furthermore, the Convention Promotion Division Team at the KCB carries out promotion and marketing activities for Korea's convention industry as follows:

- annual hosting of the Korea Convention Fair
- promotion of Korea as a convention destination through advertisements and overseas exhibitions
- publicity for upcoming meetings in Korea
- conducting convention market surveys
- operating the Korea Convention Council

(Korean Tourism Organisation 2008)

In South Korea, the state plays a major role in tourism development through the KTO. A separate state agency, the KCB, deals with the meetings, incentives, conferences and events (MICE) market. This further supports the position that South Korea has a strong mercantilist orientation towards selling its destination in the international travel market. The state has made a point of having state institutions involved in regulating and marketing tourism for the country.

Regimes and their responses to tourism

This chapter's major comparative information about different countries and their organizational responses to the challenge of tourism is summarized in Table 4.2. What is noteworthy is that all six countries considered provide an organizational response to the economic challenge of tourism, with the liberal states providing the weakest institutional responses to tourism. Indeed, we have seen that the United States, the world's major economy and one of the world's prominent tourist destinations, does not have an NTO. Instead, some of the responsibilities of an NTO are relegated to an office within the Department of Commerce, and the responsibilities of the office are largely linked with data gathering. Canada's institutional response is modest, not doing what many NTOs do and having offices in only nine countries, although the response is more significant than that of the United States. However, the Canadian response, consistent with a liberal approach, includeds significant involvement by the private sector, meaning that the state's influence in terms of the regulation and promotion of tourism is shared with actors from the market.

Of the countries considered for this analysis, only the United States lacks an NTO, a state organization actively involved in selling its national product. By contrast, governments of all of the other countries considered in this chapter seem to be more actively involved in selling their national tourism product. Such efforts to sell the tourism product are largely publicly funded in Sweden, South Korea and Japan, while only recently has Finland moved to involve the private sector in the promotion of Finland abroad.

In all six countries considered, data gathering, market research and destination marketing are considered important roles for state authorities, commonly linked with major contributors to economies. Gathering tourism data is important to all countries considered in this comparative work. It seems that in all of the countries considered the gathering of tourism data is considered the state's responsibility and there seems to be no indication that such a responsibility will be taken away from the state.

Conclusions: the paradigms and future studies

States express organizational differences in their responses to the tourism challenge. Liberal political economies tend to have limited state responses to the challenge of tourism, although, from what we have seen, there is some variation in the involvement that the state has in terms of engaging in tourism. Non-liberal states tend to have a history of more state involvement in organizing tourism, whether they are mercantilist or social democratic political economies. There are also notable differences between how social democratic and mercantilist governments respond to the tourism challenge. Social democracies traditionally had strong state institutions to deal with the challenge of tourism, although in recent years it seems that they have been involving more private actors. Finland is perhaps an extreme case, slashing government authorities' manpower and

Table 4.2 Summary of results on national tourism organizations (NTOs)

	USA	Canada	Finland	Sweden	South Korea	Japan
Type of regime	Liberal	Liberal	Social democracy	Social democracy	Mercantile	Mercantile
Presence of NTO	No	Yes	Yes	Yes	Yes	Yes
Activities of NTO:						
Information gathering	Yes	Yes	Yes	Yes	Yes	Yes
Market research	Yes	Yes	Yes	Yes	Yes	Yes
Destination marketing activities (publication of brochures, destination website, participation in travel fairs)	No	Yes	Yes	Yes	Yes	Yes
Online bookings	No	No; only offers and links to websites of partner companies	No; only offers and links to websites of partner companies	Yes	Yes	Yes
Categorization/licensing	No	No	No	No	No	Partial; tour guides
NTO offices abroad	No	9 countries	15 till 2006; no offices since then	11 offices of VisitSweden	26 offices in 14 countries	13 offices in 11 countries
Funding	Public/private	Public/private	Public/private	Public for NUTEK; public/private for VisitSweden	Public	Public for the JNTO; public/private for Visit Japan Campaign

shifting responsibilities to a private firm. Mercantilist regimes tend to maintain the state's pre-eminence in terms of tourism planning, marketing and data gathering. Responses to tourism challenges are largely consistent with the style of each country's political economy. Prevailing paradigms of political economy influence how strongly states respond to the tourism challenge. Paradigms may create barriers to action as well as prescribe responses.

A country's tourist regime can be referred to as 'liberal' when it appears to play a minimal role in regulating tourism with a modest organizational response. Other countries have tourist regimes that are 'mercantilist' or 'social democratic' in nature. Indeed, there is evidence that these descriptors could be used effectively to illustrate how countries respond to the tourism challenge with a deep philosophical understanding of relationships between state, society and the market.

There are other considerations that should have ramifications for the future study of the topic. Two of the liberal states (Canada and the United States) examined in this chapter have federal governments. Future study may examine whether federal countries differ from non-federal countries in their responses to the tourism challenge. It seems that federal states may take over tourism responsibilities, building strong NTOs and playing an important role in organizing and planning tourism. The US government lacks an NTO but the 'elastic clause'[4] of its Constitution grants authorities the leeway to do things 'necessary and proper'. Apparently, organizing tourism has not yet been considered absolutely necessary for more federal government involvement; the current prevailing paradigm in the United States leaves the work to the private sector, with minimal governmental interference. For other countries, constitutional impediments to more active state participation in tourism organization and planning are likely minor relative to the attachment to a particular political and economic philosophy, as in the United States.

Looking further into the question of statist and non-statist responses to the tourism challenge, it may be that there are few or no differences between how social democratic and mercantilist states respond to the tourism challenge. Instead, it may make more sense to further examine the dichotomy of statist and non-statist responses. However, as the regimes of social democracies differ from those of mercantilist states, future study may highlight how social democratic government responses are more likely to address the issue of job creation. Mercantilist approaches are more likely to address the need to feed commerce on the assumption that there will be a trickle-down effect with a positive impact on the welfare of a nation's total population.

It is intriguing that the two social democratic states (Finland and Sweden) in this analysis have gone through a radical restructuring in recent years. Sweden eliminated its autonomous state tourism agency (the Swedish Tourist Authority) in 2005, giving the responsibility to a regional development agency. This may illustrate something about the role of tourism; that it may be conceived as a regional development proposition. Finland has sharply downsized its state's organization dealing and outsourced a large portion of responsibility to a private firm, Finpro. In this case it seems that the state has leaned towards a more liberal direction, assuming the private sector can oversee tourism development and manage tourism promotion.

Future research may show that transitioning states have responded well to the tourism challenge. Free from communist command-driven economies, they adopted different approaches to tourism. Some of them adopted a more free market approach and then later shifted to a more state-oriented approach. For example, Poland transitioned out of a communist regime in 1989 and did not create an NTO until 2000. It may have chosen a more market-based approach to engage in tourism. Was such a shift because of the failure of a more liberal approach of the regime? Was it because the government had shifted directions? Was it because the weaknesses of the liberal model of the United States had become apparent? An investigation into the changes in approaches of the former communist states in terms of the process of creating or choosing not to create NTOs would be informative. For example, is the reason that Bulgaria does not have an NTO because its elites have adopted a more liberal approach in terms of steering the economy in general or is it because of an oversight of some sort?

Future research should also look into how regimes in countries evolve over time. The analysis here is mostly ahistorical and does not deal very much with this question. Such research may be helpful in determining which factors seem to influence a shift in approaches to how the state deals in institutional ways with the challenges of tourism. It would seem that the political ideology of governmental administrations in power would play a role in changing the way that states organize themselves to deal with tourism issues, although other factors such as economic trends, war, and other political factors and trends could play a role in shaping tourism regimes of countries. Indeed, when describing tourism at the level of the regime, much specific and useful information is lost, although the label of a particular regime may have some analytical value in it.

In closing, this chapter has perhaps opened the way for some discussion. It will hopefully assist others in studying a link between economic and political thinking and a state's political response to tourism. Liberal/free market thinking seems to lead states to take a more *laissez faire* approach to tourism; what we can refer to as a 'liberal regime' (or perhaps a '*laissez faire* regime' or 'free market regime') with regard to tourism. Non-liberal thinking creates a condition in which states seem to take a strong role in organizing tourism and these can be categorized as either 'mercantilist' or 'social democratic' tourism regimes. Indeed there is already literature that conceptualizes policies as being either '*laissez faire*' or 'liberal' (see, for example, Desforges 2000; Palmer and Bejou 1995). However, it seems that the conceptualization of a state having a tourism regime that can be described as belonging to one of the archetypes of political economy seems to have no precedent in the tourism literature.

The prevailing regimes/paradigms of tourism ought to be more thoroughly investigated. The discussion here certainly reinforces Paul Kennedy's (1994) notion that the United States is following a *laissez faire*/liberal approach to organizing its economy, and it seems that this also applies to the management of tourism. 'Muddling through' may have its merits. *Laissez faire* approaches to managing tourism seem to be largely the focus of Anglophone countries. It will be interesting to see which approaches are most successful in decades to come and, more importantly, which approaches will be increasingly embraced by states serious about competing for international tourists.

Notes

1 The research was undertaken in July 2008 and the findings were valid at the time of the research.
2 Esping-Andersen (1990) notes that US officials were by far the most helpful in assisting with gathering data for his research. Apparently, federal authorities in the United States have a highly evolved research culture relative to that in many other countries.
3 The Swedish Tourist Authority, the governmental office charged with tourism responsibilities, was phased out in 2005 and its responsibilities were shifted over to NUTEK.
4 Article 1 of the United States Constitution, section 8, clause 18, states that 'The Congress shall have Power – To make all Laws which shall be necessary and proper for carrying into Execution the foregoing Powers, and all other Powers vested by this Constitution in the government of the United States, or in any Department or Officer thereof'.

References

Adamczyk, B. (2005) 'The National Tourism Organisations of Poland, the Czech Republic, Slovakia and Hungary – the organisation and activities', *Tourism: An International Interdisciplinary Journal*, 53: 247–258.

Balaam, D. and Veseth, M. (2007) *Introduction to International Political Economy*, 4th edn, Upper Saddle River, NJ: Pearson-Prentice Hall.

Britton, S. G. (1982) 'The political economy of tourism in the third world', *Annals of Tourism Research*, 9: 331–358.

Canadian Tourism Commission (2008) 'The official corporate website of the Canadian Tourism Commission'. Online. Available at http://www.corporate.canada.travel/en/ca/ (accessed 1 July 2008).

Caporaso, J. and Levine, D. (1992) *Theories of Political Economy*, Cambridge: Cambridge University Press.

Desforges, L. (2000) 'State tourism institutions and neo-liberal development: A case study of Peru', *Tourism Geographies*, 2: 177–192.

Draper, A. and Ramsay, A. (2007) *The Good Society: An introduction to comparative politics*, New York: Pearson Longman.

Esping-Andersen, G. (1990) *The Three Worlds of Welfare Capitalism*, Cambridge: Polity Press.

Finnish Tourist Board (2008) 'MEK – Matkailun edistämiskeskus'. Online. Available at http://www.mek.fi (accessed 1 July 2008).

Frieden, J. A. and Lake, D. A. (1999) *International Political Economy: Perspectives on global power and wealth*, London: Routledge.

Gilpin, R. (1987) *The Political Economy of International Relations*, Princeton: Princeton University Press.

Gilpin, R. (2001) *Global Political Economy: Understanding the international economic order*, Princeton: Princeton University Press.

Hall, C. M. (2004) 'The role of government in the management of tourism: The public sector and tourism policies', in L. Pender and R. Sharpley (eds) *The Management of Tourism*, Thousand Oaks, CA: Sage Publications.

Japanese National Tourism Organization (2008) Online. Available at http://www.jnto.go.jp (accessed 1 July 2008).

Jeffries, D. (2001) *Governments and Tourism*, Oxford: Butterworth-Heinemann.

Kennedy, P. (1994) *Preparing for the Twenty-First Century*, New York: Vintage.

King, J. (2002) 'Destination marketing organisations – connecting the experience rather than promoting the place', *Journal of Vacation Marketing*, 8: 105–108.

Korean Tourism Organization (2008) Online. Available at http://kto.visitkorea.or.kr/enu/index.jsp (accessed 1 July 2008).

Lairson, T. D. and Skidmore, D. (2002) *International Political Economy: The struggle for power and wealth*, 3rd edn, Fort Worth: Harcourt, Brace.

Lehtonen, J. (2008) 'New MEK', presentation by the MEK Director General, 2 June. Online. Available at http://www.mek.fi/W5/mekfi/index.nsf/730493a8cd104eacc22570 ac00411b4b/b9499338950fd79ac2257466003c793e/$FILE/JL_Mek_Market_020608. pdf (accessed 19 June 2008).

Lennon, J., Smith, H., Cockerell, N. and Trew, J. (2006) *Benchmarking National Tourism Organisations and Agencies: Understanding best performance*. Oxford: Elsevier.

Ministry of Industry, Employment and Communications (2005) 'A policy for long-term competitive Swedish tourism'. Online. Available at http://www.sweden.gov.se/content/1/c6/10/61/41/4ea8a59c.pdf (accessed 19 June 2008).

NUTEK (2008) 'Tourism and the travel tourist industry in Sweden'. Online. Available at http://fm.nutek.se/forlaget/pdf/info_048–2008.pdf (accessed 19 June 2008).

Office of Travel and Tourism Industries (OTTI) (2010) 'Welcome to tourism industries'. Online. Available at http://tinet.ita.doc.gov (accessed 10 May 2010).

O'Neil, P. (2007) *Essentials of Comparative Politics*, 2nd edn, New York: Norton.

Page, S. J. (2007) *Tourism Management. Managing for Change*. Oxford: Butterworth-Heinemann.

Palmer, A. and Bejou, D. (1995) 'Tourism destination marketing alliances', *Annals of Tourism Research*, 22: 616–629.

Pearce, D. G. (1996) 'Tourist organizations in Sweden', *Tourism Management*, 17: 413–424.

Pearson, F. and Payaslian, S. (1999) *International Political Economy*, Boston: McGraw-Hill.

Tang, F.-F. and Xi, Y. (2005) 'Lessons from Hong Kong: The role of tourism boards', *Cornell Hotel and Restaurant Administration Quarterly*, 46: 461–466.

Vail, D. and Heldt, T. (2000) 'Institutional factors influencing the size and structure of tourism: Comparing Darlarna (Sweden) and Main (USA)', *Current Issues in Tourism*, 3: 283–324.

VisitSweden (2008) 'Visit Sweden – the official travel guide to your holiday in Sweden'. Online. Available at http://www.visitsweden.com (accessed 19 June 2008).

Williams, A. M. (2004) 'Toward a political economy of tourism', in A. A. Lew, C. M. Hall and A. M. Williams (eds) *A Companion to Tourism*, Oxford: Blackwell.

5 Global commodity chains and tourism

Past research and future directions

Michael Clancy

Although political economy approaches have widely been applied to the study of global tourism, the reverse cannot be claimed. Judd (2006), among others, notes that the broad literature on economic geography, globalization and political economy all ignore tourism, despite the importance of the activity to the world economy and even more so to many national and regional economies. Brown and Hall (2008: 841) make similar claims, suggesting that tourism 'has been all but ignored by political scientists and international relations scholars'. Although attention to tourism appears to come in and out of vogue – witness that two journals, *Third World Quarterly* (2008) and *Latin American Perspectives* (2008), have devoted recent special issues to tourism – the activity has been largely neglected in the literatures of international political economy (IPE), development studies and globalization. This despite Harrison's (2004) point that tourism has been a global activity for centuries, and the packaging of tourism products as commodities has been around since at least the mid-nineteenth century. In addition, tourism studies share many concerns basic to IPE and development studies; fundamental to each has been the twin questions of power and the distribution of economic benefits. Tourism is undoubtedly lucrative as an economic activity, but its overlapping and multifaceted nature makes it difficult to trace exactly *who* it is lucrative for. In this sense tourism may be studied much like other industries, and this opens tourism up to the empirical, theoretical and methodological questions of broader IPE.

The significance of tourism as an economic activity is clear enough. In 2008 some 924 million international tourism arrivals were recorded, up 2 per cent from the previous year when spending was estimated at $856 billion by the United Nations World Tourism Organization (UNWTO 2008, 2009). This represents some 30 per cent of global service exports. Although defining developing countries is always a minefield, most analysts agree that a growing proportion of international tourism arrivals and expenditure takes place in the global South (Brown and Hall 2008). Harrison (2004: 11), using UNWTO statistics, reports that 21 per cent of arrivals and 26 per cent of receipts went to less developed countries (LDCs) in 1989, with corresponding percentages growing to 30.5 per cent and 30 per cent by 1997. This excludes former Soviet bloc countries in Eastern Europe. Today it is safe to estimate that at least one-third of international tourism spending takes place in the global South, making tourism a central issue for development studies.

This chapter investigates one contemporary approach to IPE, global commodity chains (GCC), and discusses its promise for tourism studies. The global commodity chains approach is particularly relevant in understanding the dynamics of two key areas of political economy: globalization and development. As Bair (2005, 2009) points out, GCC research originated out of critical approaches to IPE, specifically world systems theory, but more recent work has come from literature on globalization or network literature, along with transaction cost theory drawn from economics. Because of its diverse roots there exists division between those who utilize the approach as a critical analytical framework and those interested in policy prescriptions. Nonetheless, commodity chains research directly addresses the core issues at the heart of political economy: the distribution of economic surplus and power.

The primary unit of analysis for GCC research is the industry, and most previous GCC studies have focused on manufacturing industries or agriculture. Little attention has been devoted to services and especially tourism. One enduring debate within the literature on the political economy of tourism has been over who precisely benefits from global tourism. Because GCC research examines suppliers, backwards and forwards linkages, evolving networks and industrial upgrading, and relates them all to the distribution of economic surplus coming from tourist expenditure, it is particularly adept at providing answers. The remainder of the paper proceeds as follows: the next section discusses the GCC approach, including its evolution and some criticisms; a following section examines how commodity chains have been applied to tourism; and a final concluding section discusses future directions for research.

Development, globalization and global commodity chains

The GCC approach originated in the 1990s as an approach aimed at better understanding development in the Global South under changing patterns of globalization, most notably the decentralization of global production and changing patterns of trade. In the past development was often operationalized as countries moving up the international division of labour: late developers looked to make transitions in their production profile from primary products to moving into increasingly complex manufacturing and high-end services. At the industrial level, this was done holistically. Global sourcing, however, changed all that. Now the more relevant question for late developers is not *whether* a country makes computers or automobiles, but rather *which* production processes take place locally within the globalized computer or automobile industries.

Global commodity chains research directly investigates this set of processes by examining globalization and development at the industry or sector level. Industry studies in general have grown in popularity in recent years (Shapiro 1994; Gereffi 1999; Bair and Gereffi 2003; Breznitz 2007; Ó Riain 2004), but many do not directly utilize the GCC approach. Hopkins and Wallerstein (1986: 159) define a commodity chain as 'a network of labor and production processes whose end result is a finished commodity'. Studies using the commodity chains framework follow the temporal and spatial life of products, from extraction of natural resources to production processes, transport, wholesaling, retailing, marketing and consumption. By examining organizational principles, capital, labour and technological requirements behind stages along the way, the research uncovers which links in the chain are most lucrative and powerful, and why. In other words, at the heart of the research agenda is the question, '[w]here does the global commodity chain touch down geographically, why, and with what implications for the extraction or realization of an economic surplus?' (Appelbaum and Gereffi 1994: 43).

The primary unit of analysis for the global commodity chains framework is the industry. It then identifies three main elements: (1) an input–output structure, detailing the temporal life of a product, (2) a spatial structure, summarizing where in the world various nodes of the life cycle take place and (3) a governance structure. Gereffi (1995) soon added a fourth, the 'rules of the game', referring to the regulatory context in which the industry operates, although this element has been neglected in most subsequent GCC research. Early GCC studies initially identified two archetypal governance structures: a producer-driven chain (PDC) and a buyer-driven chain (BDC). Producer-driven chains have been found in traditionally organized industries dominated by large manufacturers. These companies typically internalise activities along the chain, therefore controlling most if not all production processes as well as distribution and marketing. As a result, they garner a greater share of the economic surplus. Found most commonly among capital-intensive industries with high entry barriers and economies of scale, ownership and control by transnational corporations (TNCs) are present at most, if not all, links along the chain. Typical industries are the aircraft, automobile and, until recently, computer industries. Globally integrated firms dominate in buyer-driven chains as well, but they are more commonly marketers, wholesalers and retailers who maintain an arms-length relationship with producers. Here organization is horizontal rather than vertical. Through reliance on global sourcing strategies, much or all production in the industry is carried out in poor regions of the world, and dominant firms act primarily as 'big buyers' of the product. Global buyers concentrate on design and marketing within the industry. Meanwhile suppliers are frequently captive to the big traders and retailers, and, with competition fierce, are under constant pressure to reduce costs. Technology and capital requirements in BDCs tend to be low and few barriers to entry exist. Profit margins at many production nodes of the chain tend to be quite low and downwards pressures on high proportionate labour costs predominate. Typical buyer-driven chains are found in apparel and footwear, electronics and toys.

More recent research within the GCC framework has uncovered alternative governance structures beyond PDCs and BDCs. Writing about the global computer software industry, for example, Ó Riain (2004) argues that neither archetype applies. He identifies a technology-driven commodity chain (TDC), in which creating the standards and platforms results in commanding a very high proportion of the value added across the industry as well as power in shaping the nature of the chain itself. Recently Gereffi *et al.* (2005) identified five separate governance typologies: hierarchy, captive, relational, modular and market.

Implicit in the GCC framework is that development is the result of not only gaining entry into global commodity chains but also industrial upgrading or moving from less lucrative links in the chain to more lucrative links. Industrial upgrading is particularly important as leading global firms decentralize production not only geographically, but also organizationally. Originally popular with firms working in labour-intensive industries such as apparel, footwear and simple electronics, this practice of externalizing many production processes has moved more recently into higher value added activities such as automobile and computer hardware production. For potential suppliers, the key is first to break into the commodity chain, and subsequently to upgrade to more lucrative links. Bair (2005: 165) summarises four types of industrial upgrading strategies, ranging from functional upgrading to product upgrading, process upgrading and inter-chain upgrading.

Although the GCC approach has its roots in world systems theory, GCC analysis departs from that approach in several ways. Rather than focusing on the world economy, GCC approaches utilize the industry as the primary unit of analysis. In addition, the GCC framework is more open-ended and less structural and does not discount the importance of policy or strategies of firm upgrading (Bair 2009; Smith and Mahutga 2009). This has led some to criticize the approach for ignoring the importance of unequal exchange, among other sins (Dunaway and Clelland 1995). More recently, some branches of the GCC approach have embraced a parallel framework, known as global value chains (GVC), (Sturgeon 2001; Bair 2005, 2009; Gereffi *et al.* 2005).[1] There is no consensus, however, on the relationship between the GCC and GVC approaches. Both start by examining industries from the standpoint of global production systems and the new organization of the global firm. Each also assumes that a necessary, though not sufficient, condition for improving many aspects of development – employment opportunities, a better standard of living, improvements in public health, welfare, infrastructure, education, etc. – is capturing and maintaining increased material benefits from the global economy.

The early GCC research program emphasized critical examination of these processes and the related development possibilities for various sites in the global South. Many studies showed, for instance, that, even as states and firms in poor countries sought integration into global markets, the benefits accruing to them remained quite limited because of the manner in which the relevant global industries were governed. Yet as Bair (2009: 10–11) points out, the GCC framework parted from traditional world systems approaches by, first, giving greater focus to the role of the firm and power of lead firms in governing industrial chains and, second, hinting at the possibility of industrial upgrading in order to foster more attractive development outcomes. This latter focus has become even more pronounced with the GVC turn, as much of the research is more policy relevant, suggesting ways in which governments and local firms might upgrade within industries. Separately, Bair (2005) and Dussel Peters (2008) have suggested this focus has limited theory building at the expense of developing empirical research with policy-relevant conclusions. Moreover, the GVC turn has often come at the expense of a more critical approach of early GCC research, which included greater focus on surplus extraction, working conditions and broader development outcomes. For this reason Dussel Peters (2008) points to the need to go beyond industrial upgrading in GCC/GVC research. In many cases upgrading constitutes a necessary but not sufficient condition for broader and more beneficial development outcomes. One task for researchers is to examine the *basis* for upgrading among local firms. Do firms upgrade as the result of some form of innovation or learning, or do they upgrade through 'efficiencies' that often come off the backs of workers?

Global commodity chains and tourism

Mapping the tourist commodity chain immediately leads to a challenge: What exactly is the tourist commodity? Tourism is a service, or more accurately a package of consumer goods and services that includes access and local transport, accommodation, food and drink, shopping and souvenirs, guides and local attractions and entertainment. Together these are difficult to measure given that tourists differentiate their consumption. Moreover, not all consumption of these goods and services is done by tourists. As the World Travel and Tourism Council (WTTC) has suggested, '[T]he industry does not produce or supply a homogeneous product or service like traditional industries (agriculture, electronics, steel, etc)' (cited in Judd 2006: 326). Others agree, suggesting that tourism is 'not an industry in the conventional sense as there is no single production process, no homogeneous product and no locationally confined market' (Tucker and Sundberg 1988, cited in Smith 1998: 31). This has contributed to ongoing debate over (1) exactly what constitutes the tourism industry and (2) whether tourism is in fact the world's largest industry, as is often claimed (Theobald 2005).[2] As Davidson (2005: 26) points out, even those who adopt an industry perspective on tourism disagree on which activities or subindustries make up the tourism industry. The UN, for instance, counts seven such subindustries whereas the US Travel Data Center includes fourteen. Many backers have argued that tourism is largely invisible and constitutes, in fact, a much larger economic activity than is frequently measured. In an effort to more fully and accurately capture the scope of the activity economically the World Tourism Organization, after working with the Organisation for Economic Co-operation and Development (OECD), adopted the Tourism Satellite Account (TSA) method of measurement in 2000 (Judd 2006), but the methodology remains somewhat controversial.

Despite these problems Judd (2006) argues for treating tourism as an industry comparable to other industries within the study of political economy, arguing that the problem is more methodological than conceptual. In one of the few studies that explicitly adopts a commodity chains approach to tourism, he shares the concern that the activity remains separate from many studies and debates regarding political economy. Despite claims to the contrary, however, his approach suggests that the problem *is* in fact conceptual. He contends that the central problem lies in the failure to identify exactly *what* constitutes the tourist product and offers that the 'tourist experience should be understood as a product consciously produced and marketed, and that its value is determined by the costs of the inputs necessary for its construction' (Judd 2006: 324). Using this definition he identifies the primary links of tourism within a global commodity chains framework as (1) marketing and image of a destination, (2) place infrastructure and (3) tourist providers and some service industry labour. In other words, tourism should not be reduced to simply the provision of basic goods and services to tourists, but should also include place marketing as well as the often publicly financed built environment.

Such an approach goes beyond most industry approaches to tourism, which focus on firms that are clearly selling to or serving tourists (Davidson 2005). Most commonly these are transport firms, firms involved in accommodation and attractions, and firms that package tourism products (Britton 1981). Judd (2006) prefers a broader conceptualization of the tourism commodity but this is problematic on at least two counts: First, in claiming that tourism must be defined based on its production costs rather than on consumption or market prices, Judd ignores the materialist foundation of the GCC approach. At its heart the GCC framework begins with the finished commodity and works backwards to examine how and where profits are distributed. Value is determined not solely by the costs of inputs, but by prices paid and the subsequent distribution of economic surplus. Second, Judd's (2006) tourism commodity chain components are overarching to the point of being totalizing. Those interested in the automobile commodity chain do not examine necessary infrastructure such as roads, bridges and tunnels, gas stations, auto body shops and car washes. Moreover, much of the place infrastructure for tourism is simultaneously built for non-tourists. How does one disaggregate these linkages? Under such a definition, mapping the chain becomes next to impossible.

Judd (2006) contends that the central problem is that scholars do not treat tourism as a single product or industry. Yet the reality is that there is no single tourism product and therefore levels of commoditization and organization vary considerably (Shaw and Williams 2004). Moreover, tourism is made up of several subindustries, the largest and most organized of which account for the bulk of tourist expenditure in most cases. Of course, the tourist product varies considerably, and tourism markets have become increasingly fragmented organizationally and spatially, but over the period since the end of World War II, as global tourism has expanded, a clear organization has taken shape in these lucrative subindustries. Mosedale (2006) distinguishes between, on the one hand, tourism as a provision of a series of goods and services and, on the other hand, a larger experiential commodity that goes beyond the tangible. Drawing from Urry's (1990) work, as well as others on late capitalism, he suggests that ultimately the tourist commodity is intangible and involves symbolic value as well as exchange value. Although this is undoubtedly the case, two caveats should be made. First, this hardly makes tourism unique. Many goods and services share an intangible value for consumers – a Porsche is much more than transportation, as an iPhone is more than a smartphone. Second, much of this symbolic value is reflected in the exchange value of the commodity, and it is this that is of paramount interest to commodity chains researchers.[3]

Tourism is also different from other economic activities in other ways, most notably in that it does not possess the same temporal or spatial differentiation as many other industries. First, as is the case with most consumer services, production and consumption take place simultaneously. The product cannot be stored. Second is the requirement of localization. In its purest form, national tourism requires a physical visit to the nation in question. One cannot outsource the essence of Parisian tourism to China. This isn't to deny that in the postmodern age of simulacra and imitation this hasn't been tried, and with considerable success – Irish pubs in Singapore, New York-New York casino on the Las Vegas Strip, Disney's Small World, company-owned Caribbean islands for cruise ship passengers, to name a few – yet more than most industries, tourism contains a relatively coherent and localized package of goods and services. Conversely, tourism has always been much more fragmented than old, vertically integrated products. The tourist product itself is the result of multiple producers, suppliers and labour processes. Finally, under the umbrella of global tourism there are ever-growing forms of niche tourism ranging from ecotourism, roots tourism, heritage tourism, medical tourism, adventure tourism and so on. Although countries may specialise in one or more of these niches, it is still the material aspect of tourism that is of interest here.

Tourism is therefore best thought of not as a singular industry but instead as several subindustries. Tourism spending contains at least five major categories: access transport (generally not included in aggregate tourism statistics), accommodation, food and drink, shopping and attractions. To this add other miscellaneous spending and internal transportation. Depending on the sending and receiving market, these goods and services are packaged together or sold separately with varying frequency, although overall packaging appears to be decreasing. Again, unlike other industries, in which various countries might specialise in one or two particular links of the global chain, virtually all links will be found in each country. The governance structure, however, may still be global because of international supplying and foreign ownership and control, each of which has a profound impact on the distribution of benefits derived from the industry. What may be done is to break tourism down by subindustry and to map the respective governance structures of each commodity chain globally and locally in order to highlight developmental possibilities over time.

Hotel commodity chains

Cooper *et al.* (1998) among others argue that, globally, accommodation constitutes by far the greatest share of overall tourism expenditure. Although the range of accommodation varies widely, most tourists rent accommodation by the night, week or month. Sharpley (2004) makes three initial observations regarding the accommodation sector that are important taking off points. First, it is made up a many different subsectors, including hotels and motels, all-inclusive resorts, bed and breakfasts (B&Bs), hostels, camping, self-catering apartments and homes, private renters and home exchange. Second, the accommodation sector is part of the international hospitality industry. It therefore possesses international linkages such as ownership, marketing, licensing and supply chains. Finally, accommodation, like other areas in tourism, involves not simply the provision of a *product*, but also the provision of an *experience*. Understanding the local development trajectory of any industry requires paying attention to its global organization, the corresponding local organization and the role of state policy. At the global level, the commodity chains framework calls for first uncovering the governance structure of the industry in question. Gereffi (1999) argues that the leading firms within the chain tend to influence the governance structure that follows. Within the accommodation sector, the dominant and most organized area is that of hotels. Although many hotels remain independent, since the 1950s and beyond the global trend has been the emergence of hotel chains. Regionally, however, great variation exists, with one study estimating that 70 per cent of hotel rooms in the United States were affiliated with corporate chains, whereas only 15 per cent of European hotels belonged to chains (Sharpley 2004). Chains are attractive because they provide economies of scale and synergies in management, marketing and advertising and technology. By the year 2000, four companies had hotels in at least eighty different countries, while fifteen chains had hotels in at least twenty countries (Shaw and Williams 2004: 44). Many chains have been parts of larger TNCs and at times have been linked with other areas of tourism, including joint ownership with airlines or tour operators, although most airlines have divested themselves of hotels. Table 5.1 summarises the world's largest hotel chains.

As I have argued elsewhere (Clancy 1998), a notable feature of the international hotel commodity chain is the manner in which leading firms have entered markets. Much like other buyer-driven models, hotel chains enter markets primarily through non-equity means. Many pursue various contractual agreements such as branding, franchising, management contracts and leasing agreements with the owners of properties. Yet although many lead firms in BDCs spread contractually through sourcing of various production processes to firms elsewhere in the world,

Table 5.1 World's largest hotel chains, 2007 (by number of rooms)

Rank	Company	Country	Rooms	Properties
1	IHG (InterContinental)	UK	585,094	3,949
2	Wyndham Hotel Group	USA	550,576	6,544
3	Marriott International	USA	537,249	2,999
4	Hilton Hotels Corp.	USA	502,116	3,000
5	Accor	France	461,698	3,871
6	Choice Hotels International	USA	452,027	5,570
7	Best Western International	USA	308,636	4,035
8	Starwood	USA	274,535	897
9	Carlson Hotels Worldwide	USA	146,600	969
10	Global Hyatt Corp.	USA	135,001	721

Source: *Hotels* (2008).

hotel firms spread contractually in order to serve new consumer markets. As a result, many hotels are owned by one firm, operated by another and franchised to a third, although many big chains operate hotels through their own franchises.

Because the product itself is experiential, chains are able to attract customers through advertising and reputation. The latter aids consumers in containing risk, a factor especially important when travelling abroad. Chains concentrate on hotel operating, marketing and design while much of the actual accommodation 'production' is carried out by others. Through control of computer reservation systems and, more recently, proprietary websites, along with favoured positioning in global distribution systems, chains are able to capture a disproportionate share of room night reservations. Together, chains have come to inhabit the most lucrative links of the accommodation commodity chain in that the fees from reservations and contractual terms constitute a major centre of surplus and most large chains have come to operate under multiple brands. Global chains act much like big buyers in BDCs through determining specifications of properties, setting standards, remodelling and redecorating, and determining the terms of management contracts and leases. Hotel owners are much like captive suppliers who provide rooms and other physical structures to chains. The typical terms of a management contract between an operator and owner are for ten to twenty-five years and include a 2–3 per cent commission on net turnover and 1–2.5 per cent sales and marketing fees in addition to an initial flat fee, along with an incentive fee of anything from 5–10 per cent of gross operating profit after reaching a certain level of turnover. As an alternative to the commission on net turnover, some contracts stipulate an annual flat fee. For those hotel owners who hire one firm to operate a hotel but franchise with a global brand there is an additional royalty fee of as much as 4 per cent of room turnover. As one long-time actor in the international and Irish hotel sector put it,

> It is essentially risk free for operators. Many companies are getting themselves a percentage and they don't have to put anything in. They may provide a general manager and a couple of others, but other than that they don't even employ anyone.
>
> (Clancy 2009: 102)

This does not mean that hotel owners cannot prosper as well in such circumstances. Yet the capital requirements for hotels are high and it is the owners who are saddled with high fixed costs and usually substantial debt.

Spatially, the governance structure tends to reproduce global inequality because the most lucrative links of the chain, franchising and hotel operations, are centred in the global North. This is not to suggest that firms in the global South see no benefits. Hotel ownership as real estate investment is frequently lucrative, but the high capital costs close off such investment to many. In addition, firms in the global South have in some cases upgraded by moving from hotel ownership into their own franchising, branding and hotel operations. Yet this tends to be the rare exception.

Airline commodity chains

Transport is the lifeblood of international tourism, and since the end of World War II air travel has increasingly become the most important mode of transport. Tourism statistics, however, frequently omit transport, even though, from a consumer standpoint, transport tends to make up the first or second highest component of a tourist trip. The air transport commodity chain is marked by three features that differentiate it from other industries. First is regulation or 'the rules of the game'. International air transport is governed outside of the General Agreement on Tariffs and Trade (GATT)/World Trade Organization (WTO) regulatory framework and instead is the product of the 1944 Chicago Convention on air transport. Among the most important norms arising from that convention was that of regulating international scheduled air service through bilateral air services agreements (ASAs) between governments and cabotage rules (see also Chapter 14, this volume, by Duval and Macilree). Bilaterals refer to government-to-government negotiations over air services between any two nations. Most bilaterals have historically been highly restrictive, dictating carriers, routes and frequencies, and in many cases stipulating that revenues be equally distributed among participating carriers. Today tens of thousands of such ASAs govern international air travel. Cabotage refers to the right to operate air service between two points in a domestic market by a foreign-owned carrier. The Chicago Convention allows governments to restrict or ban the practice and most have effectively banned it. As a result, with a few exceptions, the global air market has really been two markets: one heavily regulated international market for country-to-country travel, and multiple separate domestic markets served only by respective domestic carriers.

Second is a related 'national champion' system that characterises the global airline industry. With few exceptions, most global airlines emerging after World War II were wholly or partially government owned. Scheduled international air carriers served as a means to show the flag (as a result such carriers are known as flag carriers). Third has been an erosion of these first two factors over the past twenty-five years. Following domestic deregulation in 1978, the United States and later Great Britain began pursuing liberalized ASAs. Meanwhile the European Union instituted a series of packages that effectively created a single European air transport market by 1997. Liberalization continued and was recently marked by a transatlantic 'open skies' agreement between the United States and the EU that went into effect in 2008. Coinciding with partial deregulation has been the widespread privatization of publicly owned carriers during this period as well as the rise in low-cost carriers (LCCs). Between 1985 and 2002 at least 130 governments announced plans to fully or partially privatize state-owned carriers (Hanlon 2007: 15). Although the LCCs were originally confined to domestic markets, regional integration and more liberal ASAs have recently made LCCs major competitors in some international markets. Operating through a lean business model, these new entrants have put increased pressure on the flag carriers. By 2004, for example, some sixty new carriers had entered service in Europe, accounting for 24 per cent of scheduled intra-European air traffic. In the United States, LCCs made up 25 per cent of the domestic market that same year (European Low Fare Airlines Association 2004).

International air transport operates in a more liberal environment than ever before, but outside of the EU there remains little opportunity for cabotage. In addition, foreign investment limitations have made it difficult for global airlines to operate like other TNCs. One response has been the emergence of airline alliances in recent years. In many ways these alliances have been in response to the highly regulated global markets as well as national laws that strictly curtail foreign ownership and limit cross investment. Today three global alliances (Star, SkyTeam, OneWorld) dominate the industry, with carriers cooperating with each other through frequent flier programs, code sharing, marketing and other means (Wheatcroft 1998; Dennis 2005; Hanlon 2007). In addition, some international legacy carriers have established alliances with domestic and regional LCCs.

Airline size is measured in different ways, from passengers carried to revenues, revenue passenger kilometres and passenger kilometres. Table 5.2 shows the world's largest passenger air carriers, as determined by passenger kilometres flown. It reveals that six of the top ten passenger air carriers are based in the United States and nine of ten are US or European carriers. Just one, Southwest, is a low-cost carrier.

The GCC governance structure of the industry reflects the features noted above. Traditionally airlines formed a classic PDC in which large producers (airlines) occupied the more lucrative rungs of the chain, often internalizing additional rungs and occupying a powerful position as a buyer of inputs (Clancy 1998). Yet as Doganis (2001: 4) points out, the paradox of the global airline business is that, although the industry has been characterized by at least fifty years of rapid growth, profit margins continue to be extremely thin, frequently as low as 2 per cent of revenues during even the best years. Profits tend to flow in a

Table 5.2 World's largest airlines, 2007 (passenger kilometres flown)

Rank	Airline	Passenger kilometres flown (millions)
1	American Airlines	222,761
2	United Airlines	191,933
3	Delta Air Lines	166,209
4	Continental Airlines	130,965
5	Air France	128,914
6	Lufthansa	122,091
7	Northwest Airlines	117,357
8	Southwest Airlines	116,385
9	British Airways	113,275
10	Singapore Airlines	90,901

Source: IATA (2007).

highly cyclical manner, and the industry is characterized by very high fixed costs. The industry also suffers from the relative inability to distinguish the product (air travel) combined with often brutal price competition between providers on specific routes.

In fact, if air transport is thought of as its own commodity chain, airlines have traditionally been among the poorest performers of any of the firms operating within that chain, while related businesses such as airports, air catering, aircraft manufacturing and leasing, and global distribution systems have been much more profitable (Spinetta 2000, reported in Doganis 2001: 6). In the past, air carriers have compensated for the lack of profitability in providing air services through various strategies, including vertical integration into other transportation or tourism services (owning computer reservation or global distribution systems, catering services, hotel chains and tour operators) or, more commonly, securing subsidies from governments. This latter strategy has become increasingly untenable in recent years. As governments have privatized national airlines, they have also become more reluctant to provide subsidies. Government financial support has also come under fire during bilateral and multilateral airline negotiations. In addition, most air carriers have shed off their most lucrative subsidiaries in recent years, primarily as a means to raise capital and satisfy shareholders. As a result, the organization of the airline commodity chain has become more fluid. Carriers have sought to source many of their activities through contractual agreements with regional carriers. Carriers have also reduced costs through a range of strategies including equipment leasing and outsourcing of maintenance and, in some cases, crews.

Today the airline commodity chain is in flux, but it looks less and less like a classic PDC. Low-cost European carrier Ryanair may offer hints of the future of the chain. Over the past fifteen years the carrier has become one of the largest operating in Europe, and has used its size and market power to negotiate and renegotiate the terms with many of its suppliers. These include landing fees in airports, to new planes from Boeing, to marketing deals with car rental agencies and hotels that it advertises on its website and on flights. Not least, it has set a new standard in the industry for terms with its customers. Now customer tickets promise transport only. Additional fees must be paid for food, drink, luggage, check-in, preferred seats and many other features once included in the price of a ticket. In addition, the carrier markets constantly to its captive audience during flights, selling hotel, car and transportation vouchers and other merchandise. As a result, for fiscal 2008, Ryanair ancillary revenues grew by 35 per cent to €488 million and made up almost 20 per cent of overall income (Ryanair 2008). Overall, the company recorded after-tax profit margins of 18 per cent, thet highest in the industry. Ryanair has behaved much like a big buyer in BDCs, moving away from less lucrative rungs on the chain while driving down costs of inputs through its market power (Clancy 2009). Whether other carriers are able to successfully follow similar strategies remains to be seen. What is expected is a significant shakeout of the industry in coming years, the product of changing regulatory frameworks combined with the ongoing global economic crisis.

Other tourism commodity chains

Although hotels and air transport make up major subindustries within the larger tourism commodity chain, tourism remains diverse and multifaceted. This is true in terms of both the product offered to various tourists, as well as spatial differentiation. Mosedale (2006) demonstrates this in his study of one aspect of the tourism commodity chain in St Lucia. By focusing on package tourism between the United Kingdom and the Caribbean island, he uncovers the governance structure of the package tour industry as it applies to that market. He shows that the market power of large, vertically integrated tour operators within the UK sending market, along with the importance of that market to St Lucia, translates into bargaining strength and favourable entry conditions in the local market. Because tour operators occupy the most powerful rung of this particular chain by effectively controlling access to UK tourists, they are able to negotiate very low rates with local hotels and other service providers. The implications for development are clear: local actors, especially smaller less capitalized producers, are confined to the less lucrative rungs of the commodity chain where they face continual downwards price pressures. Meanwhile outside tour companies gain a greater share of profits from the chain.

Another promising area for GCC research is the global cruise ship industry, one of the fastest growing areas of world tourism. Over the past ten to fifteen years this segment has grown by close to 10 per cent annually. Chin (2008) shows that global cruise companies have increasingly integrated horizontally and vertically. Horizontally, a series of buyouts and mergers have left just three major companies controlling the overwhelming portion of the cruise market (Dowling 2006; Chin 2008). The deployment of mega-ships, accommodating from 3000 to 5000 passengers, has achieved greater economies of scale while growing demand has allowed companies to maintain extremely high occupancy rates compared with those of hotels. Much like traditional PDCs, these firms have entered into related activities through acquisitions of hotels and other accommodation, luxury rail cars, motor coaches and vans. In addition, they have also acted as big buyers, contracting out with firms offering services at shore stops, such as excursions, (Chin 2008: 60–1; Clancy 2008; Kroll 2004). Although many cruises are marketed as 'all inclusive', cruise ships have also been very successful in increasing their ancillary revenues, much like successful airline LCCs (Klein 2002). Some of this comes from successfully substituting sales on board for those that were previously made on shore excursions (shopping, entertainment). Cruise companies frequently contract out with a range of outside service firms (photographers, shopping, art auction companies) to provide these services aboard the ship. Their buying power also allows them to negotiate rates in ports of call, often driving down arrival fees (Chin 2008). One of the consequences of this tight organization is that many of the ports served by cruise ships contribute little to the operation of the ships, and in turn gain little from their operations. Patterson and Rodriguez (2003: 77), for example, report that cruise lines making port in Dominica in the Caribbean purchase nothing other than potable water.

GCCs and global tourism: conclusions and future prospects

As the discussion above demonstrates, the commodity chains approach applied to tourism sheds light on key questions associated with political economy and development. Most important among these are where power lies and who benefits. Although debate continues on exactly what constitutes tourism and whether a particular 'industry' can be identified, identifying subindustries or specific economic activities that are part of the tourist project has produced useful findings. Finally, utilizing commodity chains studies in examining the political economy of tourism aids in bringing tourism back into the larger fold of political economy rather than treating it as somehow outside the real economy. That said, one caveat is warranted. Because tourism is not just organizationally differentiated but also *spatially* differentiated, our findings may not be completely generalisable. For example, organizational differences on the supply or demand side of tourism vary greatly. The UK and German outbound travel markets, for instance, have traditionally been much more controlled by outbound tour operators than, say, the US market. That organization is felt in both the Gambia and St Lucia, two destinations with heavy UK demand for their services, while other destinations may have very different experiences.

In the future, there will be many avenues to further utilize GCC research on tourism. The bourgeoning ecotourism segment is one such area, as is gap year tourism or religious tourism. One of the most promising areas for the application of the GCC framework is in aiding in pro-poor tourism research. The term 'pro-poor tourism', which originated in the UK Department for International Development (DFID) report in 1999 (DFID 1999), is defined as a partnership that 'generates net benefits for the poor' (Ashley *et al.* 2001: 2; cited in Harrison and Schipani 2007: 196). Proponents of pro-poor tourism argue that in many cases tourism in the global South directly or indirectly benefits the poorest segments of the population. This claim, of course, is contentious and returns us to many of the debates over tourism that took place in the 1960s and 1970s. A number of case studies examining whether and how tourism benefits the poor have been carried out since then, mainly under the auspices of the Overseas Development Institute and/or the International Centre for Responsible Tourism (ICRT) at Leeds Metropolitan University.

It should be noted at the outset that the pro-poor tourism approach is policy oriented rather than explanatory in nature, yet in its own manner it is concerned with industrial upgrading (or more often market entry), which requires analysis of the industries as they touch down locally. As Harrison (2008) among others has pointed out, pro-poor tourism is not without its problems, most plain of which is a general orientation among its proponents towards merely 'tweaking' existing North–South tourism. Rather than considering the larger sources of structural inequalities, the approach generally accepts the market orientation of the global tourism industry while looking for ways to expand local linkages. In many ways the research on pro-poor tourism is rather damning in that it demonstrates the harsh inequalities in many poor areas where international tourism is the predominant economic activity. Research shows that many of the gains made under the pro-poor promotion come at the margins, mainly in the informal sector, such as local transportation, handicrafts and serving as informal tour guides.

Empirically, however, several pro-poor studies are instructive for just that reason. They may serve as a bottom-up examination of the tourism global commodity chain(s). Pro-poor studies tend to offer the most in demonstrating which value chains are most accessible to the poor, also identifying which ones are less accessible or even inaccessible. Ashley (2006) and Mitchell and Faal (2006), for instance, each adopt a pro-poor stance towards their respective studies of Luang Prabang in Laos and the Gambia, and both studies utilize value chains analysis in order to uncover where tourist dollars go. Ashley shows that the value chain most accessible to the poor is in the food and drink sector, with some secondary earnings going to textile weavers, raw material suppliers and local transport owners. Similarly, Mitchell and Faal (2006: 2) offer the sobering conclusion that 'the holiday package part of the tourist value chain (flights, plus bed and breakfast accommodation) largely by-passes the poor' in a country where the bulk of international tourists came via package holidays. Instead, the gains from international tourism mainly come from 'discretionary' spending by tourists, including in the informal sector. This is consistent with Mosedale's (2006) findings in which package tourism dominates elsewhere.

Ultimately, GCC approaches to tourism map how various activities within the myriad of goods and services that make up the activity are organized, identifying which links on the various chains are most lucrative, and ultimately highlighting the distribution of benefits within these industries. In this sense they contribute to critical approaches to tourism studies while aiding in bringing tourism into larger debates over globalization, political economy and development.

Notes

1 For a detailed genealogy of the global commodity chains and global value chains approaches see Bair (2005, 2009).
2 Tourism researcher Alan Lew has been at the forefront of those arguing that the scope of tourism is often exaggerated by academics, practitioners and the media. He led a 2008 discussion/debate on the issue through the listserv TRINET and his blog, http://tourismplace.blogspot.com/.
3 GCC models share the world systems conception of exploitation through unequal exchange through trade and sourcing. This recalls criticisms of the theory from the traditional Marxist left, replacing surplus extraction from production with surplus extraction through exchange. The classic statement remains that by Brenner (1977).

References

Appelbaum, R. and Gereffi, G. (1994) 'Power and profits in the apparel commodity chain', in E. Bonacich, L. Cheng, N. Chinchilla, N. Hamilton and P. Ong (eds) *Global Production: The apparel industry in the Pacific Rim*, Philadelphia: Temple University Press.

Ashley, C. (2006) *Participation by the Poor in Luang Prabang Tourism Economy: Current earnings and opportunities for expansion*, Overseas Development Institute Working Paper 273, London: ODI.

Ashley, C., Dilys R. and Goodwin, H. (2001) *Pro-Poor Tourism Strategies: Making tourism work for the poor*, PPT Report No. 1, Nottingham: ODI, IIED and CRT.

Bair, J. (2005) 'Global capitalism and commodity chains: Looking back, going forward', *Competition and Change*, 9: 153–180.

Bair, J. (2009) 'Global commodity chains: Genealogy and review', in J. Bair (ed.) *Frontiers of Global Commodity Chains Research*, Stanford: Stanford University Press.

Bair, J. and Gereffi, G. (2003) 'Upgrading, uneven development, and jobs in the North American apparel industry', *Global Networks*, 3: 143–169.

Brenner, R. (1977) 'The origins of capitalist development: A critique of neo-Smithian marxism', *New Left Review*, 104: 25–92.

Breznitz, D. (2007) *Innovation and the State: Political choice and strategies for growth in Israel, Taiwan, and Ireland*, New Haven: Yale University Press.

Britton, S. (1981) *Tourism, Dependency and Development: A mode of analysis*, Occasional Paper 23, Canberra: Development Studies Centre, Australian National University.

Brown, F. and Hall, D. (2008) 'Tourism and development in the global South: The issues', *Third World Quarterly*, 29: 839–849.

Chin, C. (2008) *Cruising in the Global Economy: Profits, pleasure and work at sea*, Aldershot: Ashgate.

Clancy, M. (1998) 'Commodity chains, services and development: Theory and preliminary evidence from the tourism industry', *Review of International Political Economy*, 5: 122–148.

Clancy, M. (2008) 'Cruisin' to exclusion: Commodity chains, the cruise industry and development in the Caribbean', *Globalizations*, 5: 405–418.

Clancy, M. (2009) *Brand New Ireland*, Aldershot: Ashgate

Cooper, C., Fletcher, J., Wanhill, S., Gilbert, D. and Shepard, R. (1998) *Tourism: Principles and practices*, 3rd edn, New York: Prentice Hall.

Davidson, T. L. (2005) 'What are travel and tourism? Are they really an industry?', in W. Theobald (ed.) *Global Tourism*, 3rd edn, Oxford: Butterworth-Heinemann.

Dennis, N. (2005) 'Industry consolidation and future network structures in Europe', *Journal of Air Transport Management*, 11: 175–183.

DFID (1999) *Tourism and Poverty Elimination: Untapped potential*, London: DFID.

Doganis, R. (2001) *Flying off Course: The economics of international airlines*, 3rd edn, London: Routledge.

Dowling, R. K. (2006) 'The cruising industry', in R. K. Dowling (ed.) *Cruise Ship Tourism*, Wallingford: CABI.

Dunaway, W. and Clelland, D. (1995) 'Review of Gary Gereffi and Miguel Korzeniewicz (eds) *Commodity Chains and Global Capitalism*,Westport: Praeger, 1994', *Journal of World-Systems Research*, 1 Book Review #5.

Dussel Peters, E. (2008) 'GCCs and development: A conceptual and empirical review', *Competition and Change*, 12: 11–27.

European Low Fare Airlines Association (2004) 'Liberalisation of European air transport: The benefits of low fares airlines to consumers, airports, regions and the environment', Brussels: ELFAA. Online. Available at http://www.elfaa.com/documents/ELFAABenefitsofLFAs2004.pdf (accessed 10 May 2010).

Gereffi, G. (1995) 'Global production systems and third world development', in B. Stallings (ed.) *Global Change and Regional Response: The new international context for development*, New York: Cambridge University Press.

Gereffi, G. (1999) 'International trade and industrial upgrading in the apparel commodity chain', *Journal of International Economics*, 48: 37–70.

Gereffi, G., Humphrey, J. and Sturgeon, T. (2005) 'The governance of global value chains', *Review of International Political Economy*, 12: 78–104.

Hanlon, P. (2007) *Global Airlines: Competition in a transnational industry*, 3rd edn, London: Butterworth-Heinemann.

Harrison, D. (ed.) (2004) *Tourism and the Less Developed World: Issues and case studies*, Oxford: Oxford University Press.

Harrison, D. (2008) 'Pro-poor tourism: A critique', *Third World Quarterly*, 29: 851–868.

Harrison, D. and Schipani, S. (2007) 'Lao tourism and poverty alleviation: Community-based tourism and the private sector', *Current Issues in Tourism*, 10: 194–230.

Hopkins, T. and Wallerstein, I. (1986) 'Commodity chains in the world economy prior to 1800', *Review*, 10: 157–170.

Hotels (2008) 'Hotels 325'. Online. Available at http://www.hotelsmag.com/article/CA6575623.html (accessed 13 July 2008).

IATA (2007) *World Air Transport Statistics*, 52nd edn, Geneva: IATA.

Judd, D. K. (2006) 'Commentary: Tracing the commodity chains of global tourism', *Tourism Geographies*, 8: 323–336.

Klein, R. (2002) *Cruise Ship Blues: The underside of the cruise industry*, Gabriola Island, BC: New Society Publishers.

Kroll, L. (2004) 'Cruise control', *Forbes*, 6 September. Online. Available at http://www.forbest.com/forbes/2004/0906/096 (accessed 4 January 2005).

Latin American Perspectives (2008) Special issue on tourism, 25 (3) (May).

Mitchell, J. and Faal, J. (2006) *The Gambian Tourist Value Chain and Prospects for Pro-Poor Tourism*, Draft Report, London: ODI.

Mosedale, J. (2006) 'Tourism commodity chains: Market entry and their effects on St. Lucia', *Current Issues in Tourism*, 9: 436–458.

Ó Riain, S. (2004) *The Politics of High Tech Growth: Development network states in the global economy*, Cambridge: Cambridge University Press.

Patterson, T. and Rodriguez, L. (2003) 'The political ecology of tourism in the commonwealth of Dominica', in S. Gossling (ed.) *Tourism and Development in Tropical Islands*, Cheltenham: Edward Elgar.

Ryanair (2008) 'Annual Report'. Online. Available at http://www.ryanair.com/site/about/invest/docs/2008/Annual%20report%202008%20web.pdf (accessed 13 August 2008).

Shapiro, H. (1994) *Engines of Growth*, Cambridge: Cambridge University Press.

Sharpley, R. (2004) 'The accommodation sector: Managing for quality', in L. Pender and R. Sharpley (eds) *The Management of Tourism*, London: Sage.

Shaw, G. and Williams, A. (2004) *Tourism and Tourism Spaces*, London: Sage Publications.

Smith, D. and Mahutga, M. (2009) 'Trading up the commodity chain? The Impact of extractive and labor intensive manufacturing trade on world-system inequalities', in J., Bair (ed.) *Frontiers of Commodity Chains Research*, Stanford: Stanford University Press.

Smith. S. L. J. (1998) 'Tourism as an industry: Debates and concepts', in D. Ioannides, and K. Debbage (eds) *The Economic Geography of the Tourism Industry: A supply side analysis*, New York: Routledge.

Spinetta, J. C. (2000) 'The new economies', Air Transport: Global Economics Require Global Regulatory Perspectives round table, Brussels IATA-AEA, Brussels, November, unpublished.

Sturgeon, T. (2001) 'How do we define value chains and production networks?', *IDS Bulletin*, 32: 9–18.

Theobald, W. (2005) 'The meaning, scope and measurement of travel and tourism', in W. Theobald (ed.) *Global Tourism*, 3rd edn, London: Butterworth-Heinemann.

Third World Quarterly (2008) Special issue on tourism and development in the global south, 29 (5).

Tucker, K. A. and Sundberg, M. (1988) *International Trade in Services*, London: Routledge.

UNWTO (2008) *World Tourism Barometer*, 6 (2) (June), Madrid: UNWTO.

UNWTO (2009) *World Tourism Barometer*, Interim Update (April), Madrid: UNWTO.

Urry, J. (1990) *The Tourist Gaze*, London: Sage.

Wheatcroft, S. (1998) 'The airline industry and tourism', in D. Ioannides and K. Debbage (eds) *The Economic Geography of the Tourist Industry*, London: Routledge.

6 Thinking outside the box

Alternative political economies in tourism

Jan Mosedale

> Individuals are dealt with here only in so far as they are personifications of economic categories, the bearers of particular class-relations and interests.
>
> (Marx 1972: 92)

> Today's capitalist economic order is a monstrous cosmos, into which the individual is born and which in practice is for him, at least as an individual, simply a given, an immutable shell, in which he is obliged to live.
>
> (Weber 2002: 13)

As the first quote by Marx demonstrates (although arguably handpicked to fit the purpose of this chapter and not necessarily indicative of Marx's wider writing), structure takes centre stage in historical materialism and individuals are often reduced to being influenced by social structures such as class. Similarly, Weber likens the capitalist order (or structure) to a fixed outer shell (sometimes referred to as an iron cage) within which individuals are confined. For political economists, structures and the resulting asymmetries of power are the key factors that determine social life. As succinctly outlined by Bianchi in Chapter 2, historical materialism is primarily concerned with the transformation of natural materials by labour, the mode of production (social relationships and organization that frame production) and the structures that ensure the continued stability of capitalism. Historical materialism therefore involves a combination of the following ingredients: material resources, a particular arrangement of social relations, and economic and political institutions that are set in a specific historical context.

Extreme structural determinism (as used by Marx in the quote above) would theoretically reduce individuals who continually conform to the patterned structures of their lives. Although this is obviously an extreme position, structures are often represented as existing separate from agency, yet nonetheless with the ability to determine practices and transactions in social life. Yet both agents and structures are important in shaping social outcomes, as they are mutually constituted (see Giddens 1984 for his structuration theory or Bourdieu 1977 for his concept of habitus), as the reflection of Thompson (1978: 297–298) about class demonstrates:

> Classes arise because men and women, in determinative productive relations, identify their antagonistic interests, and come to struggle, to think and to value in class ways: thus the process of class formation is a process of self-making, although under conditions which are "given".

Structure is therefore not an impersonal force that is inherent in capitalism, but rather the outcome of agency as fashioned and circulated by a dominant mass of individuals. This suggests a multilayered relationship between agency and structure that needs exploring.

The debate concerning structure and agency is not one that is easily resolved as it depends on differing ontologies of our complex social world rather than epistemological certainties. Researchers differ in terms of the relative importance they assign to structure and agency and their inter-relationships in determining social life: 'structural theories privilege structural forces, whereas individualist theories reverse this prioritization and favour individual forces' (Wight 1999: 115). I am not attempting to solve the 'problem' of agency and structure in this chapter; instead, I want to think outside the box and take a look beyond the 'immutable shell' or iron cage towards alternative political economies. My motivation stems not from a rejection of historical-materialist political economy or a denial of the influence of structure on agency and everyday life, but rather from a recognition that a conversation across theoretical approaches (e.g. political economy, cultural studies, feminism, poststructuralism and postcolonialism) can only be helpful in representing the frictions of the capitalist economy, recognizing the discursive elements that create 'the economy', acknowledging the social practices through which it is (re)produced and highlighting the alternatives to dominant structures.

The cultural turn

Critics of Marxian political economy concentrate on two key points: the over-emphasis on the superstructure, thus further bolstering the dominant discourse ordering social life, and the focus on materiality and resulting neglect of cultural factors. With the cultural turn, Marxian political economy has had to face its critics. The cultural turn encompasses a multitude of different approaches to research, which are all based on the realization that the cultural dimension has been neglected in the political economy approach to the study of social, economic and political processes. The cultural turn has its roots in the emergence of cultural studies and the realization that culture is an integral part of everyday life as it transcends all social processes, including – but not limited to – the economic. The following quote illustrates the complex relationship between what is deemed to be economic and what is considered cultural:

> economic and symbolic processes are more than ever interlaced and inter-articulated; that is, . . . the economy is increasingly culturally inflected and . . . culture is more and more economically inflected. Thus the boundaries between the two become more and more blurred and the economy and culture no longer function in regard to one another as system and environment.
>
> (Lash and Urry 1994: 64).

Thus, the cultural turn has confronted previous conceptions of the economy and what constitutes the economic as the incorporation of cultural viewpoints offers multiple and fluctuating understandings. Following the cultural turn, researchers have been compelled to reconsider the artificial boundaries of 'the economic', thus opening up new avenues for research: 'Then a whole new world moves into view' (Thrift and Olds 1996: 311). I briefly want to address two ways in which 'the cultural' has been framed in political economy following the cultural turn: cultural materials and their production, circulation and consumption, and the embeddedness of 'the economic' within the cultural fabric of society.

Production, circulation and consumption of cultural materials

In the classical political economy approach to economic geography, production and distribution were the main focus of attention, with consumption taking a lesser role. With the cultural turn, consumption has become more prominent within the 'new' economic geography and especially sociology. Tourism research has also been quick in realizing the importance of the links between production and consumption, because of their spatial and temporal fixity (Urry 1990). Consumption has been one of the areas in which the cultural turn has managed to influence tourism research because of the close links (spatial and temporal) with production (for reviews see Aitchison 1999; Ateljevic 2000; Shaw *et al.* 2000; Shaw and Williams 2002, 2004). Why, what and how tourists consume now seem to be an important part of explaining and analysing economic processes.

The main criticism that Urry (1994) levies against the sociology of consumption is its focus on the material as the object of consumption. Instead he focuses his attention on the analysis of the consumption of services and more specifically tourism, as these are gaining importance in Western economies and raise challenging questions of 'interpretation and explanation'. Lash and Urry (1994) build on Marx's (1971) circuits of capital (Marx identifies four types of capital: money, commodities, the means of production and labour), but contend that the objects involved in these circuits of capital are increasingly becoming immaterial as signs and symbols gain importance in consumption. Although they recognize that material objects are still in circulation, these objects possess an 'increasing component of sign-value or image embodied *in* material objects' (Lash and Urry 1994: 4, emphasis original). For instance, MacCannell (1976) suggests that the tourism product attains significance beyond the importance of labour by embodying a symbol, lifestyle or other symbolic significance to the consumer. The tourist (consumer) turns the services and experiences into signs 'by doing semiotic work of transformation' (Lash and Urry 1994: 15).

The economic then becomes the production and circulation of signs, which are closely linked to the cultural. Sign-value is usually conferred to material objects by way of 'branding'; however, the successful act of infusing an object with sign-value does not merely involve yet another production process, but the participation of producer and consumer (Lash and Urry 1994). This represents a point of contact between production and consumption, thus reducing the dichotomy between the two processes. Instead, production and consumption are seen as counterparts that are being reworked in a circuit of culture, which covers stages of production, representation and consumption (Johnson 1986). There is a need for feedback or implicit dialogue between production and consumption in order for material objects and, in the case of tourism, services (experiences) to represent the desired sign-value. To analyse the changing cultural meaning of texts, objects, ideas, products, etc., and in the sense of Appadurai's (1986) concept of the 'social life of things', one needs to take the cultural processes into account that influence the abstract significance society attributes to them (Du Gay *et al.* 1997), such as identity and the social regulation of these relationships.

Ateljevic and Doorne (2003) have applied the circuit of culture in tourism and combined it with commodity chain analysis in order to follow a commodity through its production and subsequent consumption processes. By tracing the journey of Chinese tie-dye fabrics purchased by a tourist from New Zealand, from production and initial consumption in China to the recipients of the gifts in New Zealand, Ateljevic and Doorne (2003) demonstrate the social relations of production and consumption as they follow the path of the fabric and unveil the recreation of meaning set on the object and thus the importance of the cultural context in consumption.

Economy is embedded in the cultural

This point of view situates the economic squarely in the context of cultural place at various scales such as the individual, firm, region, nation-state, etc. and analyses the embeddedness of economic practice and of its organizations. This is a research avenue that still needs to be examined in tourism research as it will provide an indication of the relationships between economic organizations and the political, social and economic fabric of the societies they operate in (Yeung and Li 2000; Riley 2000; Pavlinek and Smith 1998) and vice versa.

The essence of this theory is the embeddedness of firms within networks of social relations that are subject to the social context. Because embeddedness is based on the social context, Zukin and DiMaggio (1990) argue that economic action needs to be contextualized within cultural, social and political contexts. These types of embeddedness form the following discussion.

Cultural embeddedness refers to the embeddedness of institutions in collective understandings and values that influence economic action and strategy. Cultural/ religious values, for instance, set limits to the commodification of sacred spaces. This is well documented in tourism research on contested sites, where access is claimed for different purposes (recreation, sightseeing or religious rituals) by different social groups (locals, tourists and pilgrims respectively). Digance (2003: 150), for instance, uses the example of Uluru (or Ayers Rock) as a site that is contested by mass tourists/commercial operators, the Aboriginal people, who view Uluru as a sacred site, and what she describes as 'more secular pilgrims', for example new age 'hippies'. Kolås (2004: 274) analyses the process of place-making in Tibet, or more specifically the Diqing Tibetan Autonomous Prefecture in Yunnan Province, which has been (re)-discovered as the mystical Shangri-La, and the resulting tensions between culturally different social groups:

people not only engage with landscape, they re-work, appropriate and contest it . . . a critical investigation should also ask . . . who has the power to create, reinvent and contest places and what is at stake for those who engage in these practices.

In terms of cultural embeddedness, an important question would also be: Who (which social group) has the power to engage in market exchanges over the contested site of Shangri-La?

The cultural influence on economic actions and social relations is of increased importance when these cross national as well as cultural boundaries. Scherle (2004) has demonstrated this in his analysis of the cultural influence on bilateral business relationships between German and Moroccan small- and medium-sized tourism businesses. However, it is indicative of the importance of personal social relations that both cultural groups 'reverted to the long-term social capital they had developed with their co-operators' (Scherle 2004: 248) in order to resolve these cultural conflicts.

Cultural norms and rules help guarantee a stable environment for market exchanges and the resolution of conflict, but can at the same time restrict free market exchange: 'culture has a dual effect on economic institutions. On the one hand, it constitutes the structures in which economic self-interest is played out; on the other, it constrains the free play of market forces' (Zukin and DiMaggio 1990: 17). In contrast to cultural embeddedness, *structural embeddedness* places economic exchange in the context of social relations and the patterns of these dyadic relationships. In fact, it analyses the structural processes of interactions within social relations of economic action. As Granovetter (1985: 495) states, 'the anonymous market of neoclassical models is virtually nonexistent in economic life and . . . transactions of all kinds are rife with . . . social connections'. Networks of social relations are key to the concept of structural embeddedness as they 'serve as templates that channel market exchange and . . . facilitate collective action both within and outside market contexts' (Zukin and DiMaggio 1990: 20). Pavlovich (2003), for instance, uses network theory to examine the structural embeddedness of the Waitomo Caves in New Zealand. She encourages the use of 'relational' network analysis in tourism research, as it

is particularly relevant in the tourism industry, as groupings of organisations cluster together to form a destination context. Complementary products of activities, accommodation, transport and food co-exist alongside support activities and infrastructure to form a complex system of connections and interrelationships.

(Pavlovich 2003: 203)

Finally, *political embeddedness* is concerned with power relations between economic actors and non-market institutions and how these in turn shape economic institutions and influence their decisions. In short, economic action is dependent on the non-market regulatory institutions and frameworks at various spatial scales (international, national, regional, local), which ultimately shape the structure of markets. However, this is a rather simplistic, explanatory view as 'the political context of economic action is made up of a complex web of interrelations and expectations' (Zukin and DiMaggio 1990: 20).

Although political embeddedness seems akin to the structural approach of political economy, dichotomies such as capitalist and working class or economy and culture are not the focus of attention. Rather, political embeddedness 'explores historically contingent asymmetries of power' (Zukin and DiMaggio 1990: 20). Socio-economic approaches are concerned with the adaptations of institutions to the historical sum of actions and view capital as embedded in the socio-cultural economy. These approaches do not reject the structuralist concept of historical materialism but recognize that, although economic actors operate within macro-economic, cultural and social frameworks, these actors still have the capacity to cause different results.

Cultural political economy

Clearly a changing understanding of the economy from an asocial space of economic transactions to a dynamic, socio-spatial and differentiated economic landscape embedded in place-specific cultural contexts and social relations has repercussion for the historical materialism of Marxian political economy (Thrift and Olds 1996; Crang 1997; Lee and Wills 1997; Amin and Thrift 2000). This shift from a Marxian-dominated political economy approach (one meta-narrative) towards a research agenda embracing the cultural dimensions of the economy and politics and emphasizing agency and social relations over structural determination (thus discovering multiple coexisting narratives of the same, economic and cultural story) has important implications for political economy approaches. Thrift and Olds (1996: 319) call this 'the fall of the singular'. With such a dramatic change in viewing the research 'object' comes a strong obligation to 'contextualize rather than to undermine the economic, by locating it within the cultural, social and political relations through which it takes on meaning and direction' (Lee and Wills 1997: xvii).

The cultural turn has resulted in a number of debates within geography on whether and how best to incorporate aspects of culture while keeping the achievements of Marxian political economy: 'There is no doubt that a Cultural Turn has been needed to counter the previous extraordinary neglect of culture. The question is, what kind of Cultural Turn is most insightful?' (Sayer 2001: 705). There are two main approaches to political economy that are trying to tackle the challenge of culture and agency: cultural political economy (CPE) and poststructural political economy.

The first approach, CPE, developed out of the engagement of economic geography with the cultural turn (see, for instance, Thrift and Olds 1996; Lee and Wills 1997; Ray and Sayer 1999). At the forefront of CPE is the wider and more complex conception of 'economy' gained from the cultural turn, the complicated nexus between 'economy' and 'culture' (although see Castree 2004 for a critique of such a nexus) and how best to integrate cultural aspects without falling prey to an oversocialized explanation of economies at the expense of possible structural causes [what Jessop and Oosterlynck (2008: 1155) call 'soft economic sociology']. Clearly, the aim is not to swap economic determinism with cultural determinism.

CPE is not anti-Marxian political economy, but is seen as 're-invigorating' or 'rounding out' Marxism (Jessop and Sum 2001: 93, 97; Hudson 2006). CPE aims to extend Marxian political economy by focusing on three themes: (1) the boundaries between what is considered to be economic and what is deemed cultural, (2) discourse and the subjectivities of knowledge creation and (3) the material transformations and associated meanings. Although CPE as an approach in itself has not gained any traction in tourism research to date, the three themes that form the root of the CPE concept have been addressed (at various levels of engagement) without explicitly incorporating them into a CPE.

Dismantling the boundaries between 'the economic' and 'the cultural'

Because the concepts of what constitutes 'the economic' and 'the cultural' and the distinctions made between them are socially constructed, they have some bearing on the configuration and articulation of the relationships between the market, state and society and the ensuing systems of reproduction and regulation. Although the cultural turn has led to less debate in critical tourism literature than, for instance, in geography, it has not been ignored following Britton's (1991) initial 'call to action'.

Ateljevic (2000), as well as Ateljevic and Doorne (2003), equate the contested ground between 'the economic' and 'the cultural' with the dichotomy between production and consumption. This reduces culture and agency to consumptive practices and dismisses the effects of cultural aspects within production systems, processes and relationships. However, Ateljevic (2000: 377) puts forward a neo-Gramscian view of negotiated (re)production in which 'tourism production and consumption operate in a form of continuing circular processes'. At the heart of this view are continuously changing meanings of tourist experiences along the circuits of production and consumption depending on individual interpretations of tangible and intangible products.

The representation of the product in society, for example in advertising and media, is an important influence on the construction of social identities that are associated with the particular product. Production and consumption frame the commodification of the product and are also integral to the construction of identities within the processes of production and consumption (e.g. host–guest). Because some products have an impact on cultural life beyond the consumer, social regulations are in place to limit negative impacts of consumption and production: 'A cultural artefact . . . has impact upon the regulation of social life, through the ways in which it is represented, the identities associated with it and the articulation of its production and consumption' (Woodward 1997: 2–3). This view of the circuit of culture (Johnson 1986) acknowledges the importance of the consumer in the attribution of sign-values and goes beyond the dichotomy of production and consumption. It realises that, through the constant renegotiation of representation at different levels, there are a multitude of meanings of tourist experiences, which depend on the cultural interpretation of the tourist (Ateljevic 2000).

Examining subjects and subjectivities

Semiotics and discourse create and confirm differences between subjects, objects, experiences and meanings. Especially feminist scholars challenge the conveying of unmediated aspects of 'reality' through the discursive framing of artificial boundaries. In their view, the subjects, objects and experiences only acquire meaning through discourses, which confer – through meaning – the dominant form of social norms to everyday practices:

> Through discourse we come to understand where things fit in the world, literally and figuratively. We also come to comprehend the relationships among categories that have been established. And, discourses tell us a great deal about what is appropriate and what is inappropriate, what is valued and what is devalued, and what is possible and what is impossible.
>
> (Dixon and Jones 2006: 49)

This includes communication and agreement between various discursive actors, as Ateljevic and Doorne (2002: 651) observe: 'producers and consumers communicate and negotiate between each other in the economic, social, political, and cultural (con)texts they create, constitute and (re)produce, which themselves construct a common sense hegemonic understanding'.

Ateljevic and Doorne (2002) demonstrate in their analysis of images used in the tourism marketing of New Zealand that its visual representations in the early 1900s were used to reinforce notions of a colonial nation, to differentiate colonial identities and to reflect the dominant discourse amongst the tourists from the home nation. Representations in the 1990s further a new vision of New Zealand as a postcolonial nation consisting of multiple identities, yet continue 'to reinforce, reproduce, and maintain inequities in global structures of wealth and power that were established in the 19th century' (Ateljevic and Doorne 2002: 662). Yet the dominant discourse (both popular and academic) on tourism often portrays tourism as an objective and neutral development practice: 'the dominant tourism culture is essentialised and marked as a neutral activity, hardly ever questioned, yet assumes a distinct set of values and expectations' (Ateljevic and Doorne 2002: 663). CPE utilizes discourse analysis in order to understand how discourses become accepted and incorporated into everyday life and the implications of these discourses for economies and their regulation.

For example, Mowforth and Munt (2003) discuss the implications of various discourses for carrying capacity and sustainability in respect to sustainable tourism development. Their discussions illustrate the importance of disciplinary discourses for knowledge creation and practice. Lanfant (1980: 18) also criticizes the traditional discourse within tourism research as simplifying production–consumption relationships: 'The discourse about international tourism . . . is based on a set of antipositions between originating and receiving societies, industrial and underdeveloped societies, arrivals and departures of tourists, etc.'.

Materiality

However, although recognizing the significance of social construction, pluralities and discourse, material objects, their transformations and associated meanings remain significant in CPE. Despite the importance of discourse and representation, one should not lose sight of the role that material objects and their use-value play in social life. There is a danger of dematerializing culture by merely ascribing sign-value to objects, yet 'things' are an integral part of social life: '"nonhumans" such as objects and technologies enable human agency and are crucial in making leisure and tourism geographies happen-able and perform-able' (Haldrup and Larsen 2006: 276). In economic activity, nature is transformed through the input of labour (see Bianchi, Chapter 2) into objects that are deemed to be useful and are valued by society. This transformation into material goods invariably entails the use of materials, tools, machines, etc. as well as human and non-human practices (Hudson 2008). At the same time, value is determined by social relationships leading to a dominant discourse about which material goods are valuable in a particular context: 'Economics is only a system of values' (Steinem 1997: 84). Economies are therefore mutually constituted by discourse, material goods, social practices and political economic structures (Peterson 2006): 'Discourses, sensuous bodies, machines, objects, animals and places are choreographed together and build heterogeneous cultural orders that have the capacity to act, to have effects and affects' (Haldrup and Larsen 2006: 278).

The work by Ateljevic and Doorne (2002) has highlighted the need to interpret the 'hidden' discursive ideologies of past and current tourism representations and has thus offered a critical reading of national representations. Although representation is important, it is also necessary to illuminate the practices that lead to certain representations. This involves a look at the materiality behind representations of touristic landscapes. On the one hand the materiality of what is captured in photographs is important as signs that point to touristic sights have become more important than the actual sight (Lash and Urry 1994): 'The signifier slips free from the signified and it is the markers that create the experience' (Crang 1997: 361). On the other hand, pictorial representations are mediated through technologies and their development. Crang (1997: 363), for instance, attributes the simplification of photographic practices through the development of easy 'point–press–shoot' cameras by the photography industry for 'on the one hand democratizing aesthetic production and, on the other, colonizing an ever-expanding range of spaces and experiences'. These experiences are formed in a series of performances (in themselves mediated by way of the material camera) that ascribe meanings to the material objects that are photographed. For the tourist photographer this interaction with the material creates an experience in the moment rather than a mere reflection of the moment (Scarles 2009). As Haldrup and Larsen (2006: 282) emphasize, representation is therefore not just a discursive order, but also a combination of discourse (past and present), technology and practices: 'Neither the camera nor the photographer makes pictures: it is the hybrid of the camera–tourist'. And of course, access to a camera and a holiday may be affected by structural forces such as class (see Hall's discussion on class in Chapter 8), and the production of a camera or holiday experience also involves divisions of labour, social relationships in production and, more generally, the regulation of capitalism. In short, Marxian political economy still has a role to play in CPE.

Alternative political economies

Whereas Marxian political economy analyses the structural conditions (class, race, gender, etc.) that influence and shape capital production and, more recently, reproduction, poststructuralist scholars aim to demonstrate and unveil the discourses that lead to the formation and institutionalization of these structures. One area of poststructuralist feminist research is the deconstruction of binary, dialectic, discursive categories such as male/female and heterosexual/homosexual and how these categories are employed at specific times and in specific places to create spaces of exclusion or inclusion. The point that poststructuralists are making is that the discourses, which bestow meaning to terms, are subject to the dominant social value and power. Once a structure is being seen as 'normal' – patriarchy or capitalism in the case of Northern societies – this dominant structure creates the social norms that influence discourses and give meaning to terms, hence reproducing its dominance as it has 'the ability to construct and maintain difference through language and practice' (Dixon and Jones 2006: 49). Poststructural feminism perceives the binary relationship between certain dialectic terms as being too simplistic and aims to 'reveal intricate webs of material and discursive power relations' (Aitchison 2000: 134).

The aim of poststructural political economists such as Gibson-Graham (1996) is to unveil the patriarchal hierarchy of the dominant capitalist system and its reproduction through discursive practices. She argues that it is incorrect to refer to countries as being capitalist just as it is incorrect to refer to countries as being Christian or heterosexual. Instead, communities are constituted of a number of different discourses, which do not all follow the dominant discourse and may in fact contradict the dominant discourse even though it may be represented widely as the only valid discourse (O'Neill and Gibson-Graham 1999). Therefore, Gibson-Graham (1996: 2) employs discourse analysis to examine the discursive reproduction of capitalism and to challenge the notion 'that capitalism is the hegemonic, or even the only, present form of economy and that it will continue to be so in the proximate future'. This poststructural feminist approach extends the Marxian focus on the capitalist production system to widen the research possibilities and challenge the represented hegemony of capitalism by including non-capitalist processes and spaces: 'If we were to dissolve [deconstruct] the image that looms in the economic foreground [capitalism], what shadowy economic forms might come forward?' (Gibson-Graham 1996: 3). Gibson-Graham (1996) addresses the capitalism/non-capitalism binary to highlight the economic differences between different strands of the pluralist economy in order to diffuse the myth of an economic sameness, a *grand narrative* of capitalism.

> As the black boxes of the formal, informal, alternative, and domestic economies are opened up for scrutiny, 'the economy' emerges as a complex interdependency of different economic relations within the variously constituted household, volunteer, self-employed, family business, prison, and illegal, as well as industrial market, sectors.
>
> (Gibson-Graham 2000: 102)

Pavlovskaya (2004), for instance, challenges the assumption/myth of the post-Soviet transition towards a market-based, capitalist economy through an analysis of households in Moscow during the 1990s. She contends that 'The dominant discourse of transition fails to see the many "other transitions" that accompany the restructuring of industries and regions' (Pavlovskaya 2004: 330). Indeed, these households were engaged in various economic activities linked to multiple economies in order to survive, at least during the transitional period. By undermining the patriarchal discourse of capitalism, Gibson-Graham (1996) aspires to prepare the ground for a multifaceted, flexible and open-ended economy of non-capitalist practices that is able to take over from the current thinking and representation of the capitalist economy. This example of poststructuralist feminism demonstrates that the poststructuralist approach not only constitutes a theoretical paradigm, but also is seen by proponents to be a form of political intervention: 'Poststructural knowledge actively shapes "reality" rather than passively reflecting it. The production of new knowledges is a world-changing activity, repositioning other knowledges and validating new subjects, practices, policies, and institutions' (Gibson-Graham 2000: 101). Within the project of postcapitalist politics, Gibson-Graham (2006: xxxvi) moves beyond analysing and deconstructing the capitalist discourse (see Gibson-Graham 1996) and towards a politics of 'a new kind of economic reality'. She endeavours to transform the dominance of capitalist political economy, 'to displace the familiar mode of being of the anticapitalist subject, with its negative and stymied positioning', by offering interventions that generate new economic languages, identities, communities and social relations (Gibson-Graham 2000, 2006: xxxv).

Although the themes raised by CPE have received some interest within tourism research, tourism scholars have to date not discovered poststructural political economy. This lack of interest in alternatives to capitalism within tourism and mobility may be due to the continued dominance of so-called alternative types of tourism. Despite continued calls for a more critical analysis, broad generalizations bestowing the moral high ground to adjectives and prefixes such as eco, green, soft, appropriate, alternative and responsible continue to abound in tourism research (Wheeler 1992, 2003; Butler 1990). As Wheeler (2003: 232) emphasizes, alternative tourism 'must be treated with caution, indeed scepticism, scrutinised and critically analysed from a realistic, practical perspective'. Do alternative forms of tourism occupy different spaces between the market and state or do they merely reproduce dominant relationships in a different form? It is time that tourism research considers possible alterities of tourism and mobility.

Conclusion: alternative political economies

> There is no alternative.
>
> (Margaret Thatcher)

The cultural turn has forced political economists to take cultural meanings and discourses into consideration. The approaches towards integrating immaterial aspects within political economy have differed. This chapter has first described the CPE approach, which firmly incorporates the cultural within a structuralist Marxian political economy, before turning to an account of poststructural political economy. Both are similar in that they reconsider the artificial boundaries of 'the economic', yet they differ greatly in their interpretation of the structure and agency debate. On the one side, CPE is firmly grounded within the dominant structures of capitalism and identifies culture as one strategy to provide a link between the macro-narratives or superstructures of Marxian political economy and the micro-narratives of cultural studies. One the other side, poststructural political economy aims to break down the dominant structures by deconstructing discourses (as structure is merely a dominant discourse) and creating alternative discourses to provide space for agency.

As stated previously, the intent here is neither to denounce Marxian political economy nor to advocate for agency as the sole determinant force. Instead, I posit that political economy can benefit from an engagement with poststructural theory. Marxian political economy has contributed and continues to contribute greatly to tourism research (the contributions to this volume demonstrate this). In fact, 'Outside every "text" there continues to be an objective yet contested world of exploitative production relations, however remote geographically' (Gotham 2002: 1753). Societies continue to be influenced by material processes and inherent inequalities, yet the representation of these processes and inequalities and the associated discursive practices also have an effect.

The value of Marxian political economy clearly lies in an analysis of capitalism:

> At the end of the day, then, the key point is that Marxian political economy is still needed to provide answers to the 'why' questions about capitalist economies, to reveal the inner mechanisms that drive the accumulation process that lies at the heart of the spatial and temporal dynamics of the economy and that delineate the limits to capital.
>
> (Hudson 2006: 385)

Yet what is also needed is to go beyond analysing the representations of the dominant discourse (capitalism) and to include alternative discourses and practices. Alternative economic practices create spaces in which the principles of the capitalist market system are transformed into alternative forms of production by way of employing different exchange mechanisms and valuing labour differently from conventional wage-based labour. Considering mobile alternative economic practices enables a wider view on what is often considered a singular 'economy' and highlights multiple forms of economic practices.

Exchange spaces situated at the margins of contemporary mobility, such as WWOOFing – willingly working on organic farms (Mosedale 2009, 2010) – house exchanges (De Groote and Nicasi 1994) and couch surfing (Germann Molz 2007), just to name a few, produce spaces in which the rules, conventions and norms of the capitalist marketplace do not always apply. Issues of concern in conventional market transactions, such as pricing, commodity exchanges, brands and marketing, are quite different from those apparent in alternative economic spaces. These distinct features give insight into contemporary practices in mobility, most notably in respect to multiple/diverse economies and notions of value in economic exchanges. Marginal mobile practices are also of interest with reference to empowerment, activism and resistance to the hegemony of the dominant capitalist economy.

Poststructural approaches in conjunction with Marxian political economy and CPE (for a similar argument see Larner and Le Heron 2002; Phillips 2002; Le Heron 2007) can provide a useful avenue to balance structure and agency and analyse the multiple capitalist and non-capitalist economies that interact to shape our everyday practices.

References

Aitchison, C. (1999) 'New cultural geographies: The spatiality of leisure, gender and sexuality', *Leisure Studies*, 18: 19–39.

Aitchison, C. (2000) 'Poststructural feminist theories of representing Others: A response to the "crisis" in leisure studies' discourse', *Leisure Studies*, 19: 127–144.

Amin, A. and Thrift, N. (2000) 'What kind of economic theory for what kind of economic geography', *Antipode*, 32: 4–9.

Appadurai, A. (ed.) (1986) *The Social Life of Things: Commodities in cultural perspective*, Cambridge: Cambridge University Press.

Ateljevic, I. (2000) 'Circuits of tourism: Stepping beyond the "production/consumption" dichotomy', *Tourism Geographies*, 2: 369–388.

Ateljevic, I. and Doorne, S. (2002) 'Representing New Zealand: Tourism imagery and ideology', *Annals of Tourism Research*, 29: 648–667.

Ateljevic, I. and Doorne, S. (2003) 'Culture, economy and tourism commodities: Social relations of production and consumption', *Tourist Studies*, 3: 123–141.

Bourdieu, P. (1977) *Outline of a Theory of Practice*, Cambridge: Cambridge University Press.

Britton, S. G. (1991) 'Tourism, capital and place: Towards a critical geography of tourism', *Environment and Planning D*, 9: 451–478.

Butler, R. (1990) 'Alternative tourism: Pious hope or Trojan horse?', *Journal of Travel Research*, 28: 40–45.

Castree, N. (2004) 'Economy and culture are dead! Long live economy and culture!', *Progress in Human Geography*, 28: 204–226.

Crang, P. (1997) 'Cultural turns and the (re)constitution of economic geography: Introduction to section one', in: R. Lee and J. Wills (eds) *Geographies of Economies*, London: Edward Arnold.

De Groote, P. and Nicasi, M. (1994) 'Home exchange: An alternative form of tourism and case study of the Belgian market', *Tourism Review*, 49: 22–26.

Digance, J. (2003) 'Pilgrimage at contested sites', *Annals of Tourism Research*, 30: 143–159.

Dixon, D. P. and Jones, J. P., III (2006) 'Feminist geographies of difference, relation and construction', in S. Aitken and G. Valentine (eds) *Approaches to Human Geography*, London: Sage.

Du Gay, P., Hall, S., Janes, L., Mackay, H. and Negus, K. (1997) *Doing Cultural Studies: The story of the Sony Walkman*, London: Sage/Open University.

Germann Molz, J. (2007) 'Cosmopolitans on the couch: Mobile hospitality and the internet', in J. Germann Molz and S. Gibson (eds) *Mobilizing Hospitality: The ethics of social relations in a mobile world*, Aldershot: Ashgate.

Gibson-Graham, J. K. (1996) *The End of Capitalism (as We Knew It): A feminist critique of political economy*, Oxford: Blackwell.

Gibson-Graham, J. K. (2000) 'Poststructural interventions', in E. Sheppard and T. J. Barnes (eds) *A Companion to Economic Geography*, Oxford: Blackwell.

Gibson-Graham, J. K. (2006) *Postcapitalist Politics*, Minneapolis: University of Minnesota Press.

Giddens, A. (1984) *The Constitution of Society: Outline of a theory of structuration*, Cambridge: Polity Press.

Gotham, K. F. (2002) 'Marketing Mardi Gras: Commodification, spectacle and the political economy of tourism in New Orleans', *Urban Studies*, 39: 1735–1756.

Granovetter, M. (1985) 'Economic action and social structure: The problem of embeddedness', *American Journal of Sociology*, 91: 481–510.

Haldrup, M. and Larsen, J. (2006) 'Material cultures of tourism', *Leisure Studies*, 25: 275–289.

Hudson, R. (2006) 'On what's right and keeping left: Or why geography still needs Marxian political economy', *Antipode*, 38: 374–395.

Hudson, R. (2008) 'Cultural political economy meets global production networks: A productive meeting?', *Journal of Economic Geography*, 8: 421–440.

Jessop, B. and Oosterlynck, S. (2008) 'Cultural political economy: On making the cultural turn without falling into soft economic sociology', *Geoforum*, 39: 1155–1169.

Jessop, B. and Sum, N. L. (2001) 'Pre-disciplinary and post-disciplinary perspectives', *New Political Economy*, 6: 89–101.

Johnson, R. (1986) 'The story so far: And further transformations?', in D. Punter (ed.) *Introduction to Contemporary Cultural Studies*, London: Longman.

Kolås, Å. (2004) 'Tourism and the making of place in Shangri-La', *Tourism Geographies*, 6: 262–278.

Lanfant, M. F. (1980) 'Introduction: Tourism in the process of internationalization', *International Social Science Journal*, 32: 14–43.

Larner, W. and Le Heron, R. (2002) 'From economic globalisation to globalising economic processes: Towards post-structural political economies', *Geoforum*, 33: 415–419.

Lash, S. and Urry, J. (1994) *Economies of Signs and Space*, London: Sage.

Lee, R. and Wills, J. (eds) (1997) *Geographies of Economies*, London: Edward Arnold.

Le Heron, R. (2007) 'Globalisation, governance and post-structural political economy: Perspectives from Australasia', *Asia Pacific Viewpoint*, 48: 26–40.

MacCannell, D. (1976) *The Tourist: A new theory of the leisure class*, New York: Schoken Books.

Marx, K. (1971) *Capital: A critique of political economy, Volume 2, The process of circulation of capital*, London: Lawrence and Wishart.

Marx, K. (1972 [1852]) 'The eighteenth Brumaire of Louis Bonaparte', in K. Marx, F. Engels and V. Lenin (eds) *On Historical Materialism*, Moscow: Progress Publishers.

Mosedale, J. (2009) 'Wwoofing in New Zealand as alternative mobility and lifestyle', *Pacific News*, 32: 25–27.

Mosedale, J. (2010) 'Being mobile off the grid: Experiencing mobility and alternative economic practices', paper presented at the Annual Meeting of the Association of American Geographers, Washington DC, April.

Mowforth, M. and Munt, I. (2003) *Tourism and Sustainability: Development and new tourism in the Third World*, 2nd edn, Abingdon: Routledge.

O'Neill, P. and Gibson-Graham, J. K. (1999) 'Enterprise discourse and executive talk: Stories that destabilize the company', *Transactions of the Institute of British Geographers*, 24: 11–22.

Pavlinek, P. and Smith, A. (1998) 'Internationalization and embeddedness in east-central European transition: The contrasting geographies of inward investment in the Czech and Slovak Republics', *Regional Studies*, 32: 619–638.

Pavlovich, K. (2003) 'The evolution and transformation of a tourism destination network: The Waitomo Caves, New Zealand', *Tourism Management*, 24: 203–216.

Pavlovskaya, M. (2004) 'Other transitions: Multiple economies of Moscow households in the 1990s', *Annals of the Association of American Geographers*, 94: 329–351.

Peterson, V. S. (2006) 'Getting real: The necessity of critical poststructuralism in global political economy', in M. de Goede (ed.) *International Political Economy and Poststructural Politics*, New York: Palgrave Macmillan.

Phillips, M. (2002) 'Distant bodies? Rural studies, political-economy and poststructuralism', *Sociologia Ruralis*, 42: 81–105.

Ray, L. and Sayer, A. (1999) *Culture and Economy After the Cultural Turn*, London: Sage.

Riley, R. (2000) 'Embeddedness and the tourism industry in the Polish southern uplands: Social processes as an explanatory framework', *European Urban and Regional Studies*, 7: 195–210.

Sayer, A. (2001) 'For a critical cultural political economy', *Antipode*, 33: 687–708.

Scarles, C. (2009) 'Becoming tourist: Renegotiating the visual in the tourist experience', *Environment and Planning D: Society and Space*, 27: 465–488.

Scherle, N. (2004) 'International bilateral business in the tourism industry: Perspectives from German–Morrocan co-operations', *Tourism Geographies*, 6: 229–256.

Shaw, G. and Williams, A. M. (2002) *Critical Issues in Tourism: A geographical perspective*, 2nd edn, Oxford: Blackwell.

Shaw, G. and Williams, A. M. (2004) *Tourism and Tourism Spaces*, London: Sage.

Shaw, G., Agarwal, S. and Bull, P. (2000) 'Tourism consumption and tourist behaviour: A British perspective', *Tourism Geographies*, 2: 264–289.

Steinem, G. (1997) 'Revving up for the next 25 years', *Ms. Magazine*, 8: 82–84.

Thompson, E. P. (1978) *The Poverty of Theory and Other Essays*, London: Merlin Press.

Thrift, N. and Olds, K. (1996) 'Refiguring the economic in economic geography', *Progress in Human Geography*, 20: 311–337.

Urry, J. (1990) *The Tourist Gaze: Leisure and travel in contemporary societies*, London: Sage.

Urry, J. (1994) *Consuming Places*, London: Routledge.

Weber, M. (2002) *The Protestant Ethics and the 'Spirit' of Capitalism*, London: Penguin.

Wheeler, B. (1992) 'Alternative tourism – a deceptive ploy', *Progress in Tourism, Recreation and Hospitality Management*, 4: 140–145.

Wheeler, B. (2003) 'Alternative tourism – a deceptive ploy', in C. Cooper (ed.) *Classic Reviews in Tourism*, Clevedon: Channel View.

Wight, C. (1999) 'They shoot dead horses don't they?: Locating agency in the agent–structure problematique', *European Journal of International Relations*, 5: 109–142.

Woodward, K. (1997) 'Introduction', in K. Woodward (ed.) *Identity and Difference*, London: Sage/ Open University.

Yeung, Y. M. and Li, X. (2000) 'Transnational corporations and local embeddedness: Company case studies from Shanghai, China', *Professional Geographer*, 52: 624–635.

Zukin, S. and DiMaggio, P. (1990) *Structures of Capital: The social organization of the economy*, New York: Cambridge University Press.

Part II

Tourism and key themes in political economy

7 Yes, Virginia, there is a tourism class
Why class still matters in tourism analysis

C. Michael Hall

To understand a subject such as tourism in depth requires more than an account of travel or 'what I did on my holidays'. It demands an analysis of politics, of the structure of business, of the places in which it occurs, of the nature of industrial production and private life. In particular, it demands a way of accounting for the relationships among these things. Most significantly for such a venture it also means 'grasping the fact that tourism is an important avenue of capitalist accumulation' (Britton 1991: 451). Unfortunately, most students of tourism have not grasped this fact, or, if they have, they keep very quiet about it. Instead, with some relatively limited exceptions in the literature (e.g. Church and Coles 2007), the political-economic positioning of tourism is treated as a taken-for-granted and unquestioned fact. Nevertheless, following the observation of Britton (1991) it seems apparent that in order to understand how tourism is involved in creating the social meaning and materiality of space and place, and how these representations of place are explicitly incorporated into the accumulation process, 'we need a theorization that recognises, and unveils, tourism as a capitalistically organised activity driven by the inherent and defining social dynamics of that system, with its attendant production, social, and ideological relations' (Britton 1991: 451).

For some authors, notably Connell (1977), this is essentially what class analysis attempts to do. Therefore the subject of class analysis is power, 'how it is organised, on the largest possible scale; how it is won and used, stabilised and overthrown; what its effects are in everyday life' (Connell and Irving 1980a: 1). Class analysis is therefore concerned with the political nature of the entire socio-economic structure. And, like the analysis of power itself, it is therefore inherently political in terms of both subject and its undertaking.

The notion of class existed well before the work of Marx and Engels (Wolf 1999). However, their texts remain fundamental to anyone interested in the theory of classes and capitalist development. Yet looking at the work of Marx also presents substantial difficulties, most critically because, although the concepts of class and class conflict are integral to his work, Marx never managed to complete a comprehensive formulation of the concepts and many of his major works, including *Capital*, remain unfinished. This means that there are substantial debates over the different interpretations that can exist of Marx's work, meaning that, as Giddens and Held (1982: 3) noted, 'it is probably no longer possible to provide even a summary description of Marx's views of class and class conflict which would command the agreement of everyone'. That said let us at least try and outline some key features that have influenced how ideas of class may be relevant for tourism studies.

First, Marx believed that class divisions only arise when a surplus is generated, so that it is possible for a class of non-producers to live off the productive activity of others. Those who gain control of the means of production become an economically and politically dominant ruling class. Such class divisions are inherently conflictual and lead to class struggle, which to Marx was the 'engine' of historical development (Giddens and Held 1982: 3–4). In tourism this division has usually been associated with heritage tourism and the politics of memory, rather than with attitudes to tourism and tourism development per se (Johnson 1999; Markwell *et al.* 2004; Edelheim 2007).

Second, one of the consequences of the capitalist class system was worker alienation, by which Marx means the loss of control a worker has over the labour process by virtue of that labour being sold to a capitalist employer. For Marx this process led to a situation in which workers were employed in dull, non-creative and unrewarding tasks. In this context the leisure holiday can therefore be interpreted not only as a means of temporary escape (real or imagined) from alienation but also as a way of keeping the labour force under control (Langman 1991).

Third is the relationship between ideology and class, with Marx and Engels suggesting in *The German Ideology* that 'the ideas of the ruling class are in every epoch the ruling ideas: i.e. the class which is the ruling material force of society is at the same time its ruling intellectual force' (in Sayer 1989: 6). The relationship being ideology and class has been important for the development of the ruling class equals ruling culture idea (Connell 1977) and has influenced more critical accounts of tourism (Frow 1991; Ateljevic 2000; Tribe 2008), although nowhere does it have the degree of significance that it has had in the cognate field of leisure studies (Rojek 2005).

Fourth, capitalism is an inherently unstable system of production, which is prone to boom and depression cycles. At times of depression or economic crisis larger firms tend to expand at the expense of smaller ones, leading to an increased concentration of economic life that goes hand-in-hand with the growing centralization of economies in which the activities of banks and other financial institutions are expanded in conjunction with the state to coordinate economic life (Giddens and Held 1982). Although there is substantial writing on the effects of economic and financial crisis on tourism there is surprisingly little research on the way that tourism, as a major factor in contemporary globalization, may actually contribute to the instability of capitalism (Lakshmanan and Chatterjee 2006). Similarly, there is little attempt to draw tourism into discussions of class struggle and labour struggle as a manifestation of class conflict with the notable exception of Britton (1991). Indeed, class and labour struggles are usually regarded as political risks to be minimized in the process of tourism development (e.g. Brown 2000). Nevertheless, tourism is political and is often the subject of conflict (Hall 1994, 2007).

This chapter outlines some of the ways in which theorizations of class are inextricable from a full understanding of the political economy of tourism. It first discusses issues associated with the conceptualization of power before examining 'varieties' of class analysis: categories, structural determination, representative groupings and structure and agency. The chapter finishes by emphasizing the continued importance and relevance of class as a construct in tourism studies.

Power

For Connell and Irving (1980a: 17) 'the main subject of class analysis is power, its institutionalization, use, and effects'. Yet conceptualizing power (and as we shall see the concept of class), presents substantial difficulties. It has been characterized as an 'essentially contested concept' (Gallie 1955–56). For Wolf (1999: 4)

> Power is often spoken of as if it were a unitary and independent force, sometime incarnated in the image of a giant monster such as Leviathan or Behemoth, or else as a machine that grows in capacity and ferocity by accumulating and generating more powers, more entities like itself. Yet it is best understood neither as an anthropomorphic force nor a giant machine but as an aspect of all relations among people.

The power structure debate is grounded in broader questions as to how power is conceptualized and how it can be studied. Key questions with respect to power structure research include (1) what organization, group or class in the social structure under study receives the most of what people seek for and value (*who benefits*)?; (2) what organization, group or class is over-represented in key decision-making positions (*who sits*)?; (3) what organization, group or class wins in the decisional arena (*who wins*)?; and (4) who is thought to be powerful by knowledgeable observers and peers (*who has a reputation for power*)? (Domhoff 2007). Other questions reflect Lasswell's (1936) comment about politics: politics is about power, who gets what, where, how and why. Unfortunately, in tourism studies such questions are only rarely asked (Hall 1994, 2007, 2010a; Bianchi 2002; Church and Coles 2007; Macleod and Carrier 2010).

Much writing on tourism decision-making, whether realized or not, has been heavily influenced by the pluralist interpretation of power in the United States, in which power is often perceived as being pluralistic in fashion because of a range of interest groups being visible in the policy-making process as well as the right to assemble, freedom of speech, elections, competitive political parties and the existence of a market economy (Domhoff 2007). The emphasis by writers such as Dahl (1961) on overt preferences of interest groups and the exercise of political power, and who argued that power was intentional and active and related to several, separate, single issues and bound to the local context of its exercise, served to strengthen the pluralistic conception of power that 'since different actors and different interest groups prevail in different issue-areas, there is no overall "ruling elite"' (Lukes 2005: 5). Such an overt interest group model of power structures has long been influential within tourism, especially in the early work of Murphy (1985), and such a 'participatory' model of how destination communities operated has dominated tourism planning literature since the 1980s, although now with a strong emphasis on collaboration, networks and public–private partnerships, with only little criticism of the underlying assumptions with respect to how power may be used to exclude other interests from decision-making.

Considering power in relational terms highlights the manner in which power works differently in interpersonal and institutional relations as well as in society as a whole. Wolf (1999) distinguished between four different modalities with respect to the relationship between power and social relations. First is the capability of an individual in a Nietzschean sense. Second is power manifested in interactions between people as refers to the Weberian notion of the ability of an ego to impose its will in social action upon an alter. Third is the power, referred to by Wolf (1999) as tactical or organizational power, that controls the contexts or instrumentalities by which individuals or groups direct or circumscribe the actions of others. Fourth is the role of structural power, which is the power manifest in relationships that not only operates within settings and domains but also organizes the settings themselves. This last mode of power is akin to what Foucault (1984) described as 'governance', the exercise of 'action upon action' in which he sought to determine those relations that structured consciousness, an area also significant to Marxist analysis of the structural relations of power (Hall 2010a).

Although Wolf's (1999) different modalities of power are not shared by all power theorists they do share some significant common ground. In particular they highlight that the pluralist conception of power was 'too narrowly drawn' (Bachrach 1967: 87). Bachrach and Baratz (1962) argued that power had a 'second face' that was not perceived or understood by pluralists nor detectable by their modes of inquiry. Instead, 'power was not solely reflected in concrete decisions; the researcher must also consider the chance that some person or association could limit decision-making to relatively non-controversial values, by influencing community values and political procedures and rituals, notwithstanding that there are in the community serious but latent power conflicts' (Lukes 2005: 6). Including, those associated with class.

Categories of class

Class is a concept around which considerable confusion reigns. 'Arguing about classes is like going for a swim in a country dam. As soon as you put your foot in, you are up to your neck in mud' (Connell and Irving 1980b: 78). At its most basic a class is simply a category. This conception of class 'underlies most of the modern sociology of stratification' (Connell 1977: 4) and has led to the development of a substantial literature on social stratification in various forms, including relative access to or ownership of housing, wealth, power and even mobility (Gössling *et al.* 2009; Hall 2010b). For example, it is estimated that the percentage of the world's population participating in international air travel is in the order of just

2–3 per cent (Peeters *et al.* 2006). With respect to the African context, Pirie (2009: 22) noted that,

> The mobility gap may match the wide differentials of income and life chances on the continent; it is surely rooted in and expresses gaps in privilege and plenty. The condition presupposes what might be termed a 'mobility morality'. Super-mobile people are at one end of the mobility scale. At the other extreme are Africans stranded in rural villages where mobility deprivation is acute. They are the kinetic underclass.

Pirie (2009: 21) also concludes that the 'way we act on, and the way we think, talk and write about, geographical mobility needs reconceptualizing in terms of fairness, equity, environmental justice, and human rights'. Yet issues of those who do not travel and why receives only passing interest in most mainstream tourism research (Hall 2010b), leading Hall (2005) to claim that tourism studies as it is currently constituted is probably the only discipline to study the rich – as you have to be relatively wealthy in time and money to be able to travel for leisure. But leaving such sanguine aside, the dominant discourse in tourism focuses on the 'given' of mobility and movement rather than immobility, and issues of social and economic exclusion are more likely to be dealt with in relation to destination communities under the umbrella of pro-poor tourism than the exclusion of potential consumers from tourism opportunities, consideration of constraints or seeking to understand the roles 'of economic and other structural and regulative mechanisms such as class, race, gender, and religion that affect the economic and social capital of individuals in society and therefore their life chances' (Hall 2010b).

Statistics on the impacts of particular income categories on travel and mobility are available. Table 7.1 indicates that there is a clear relationship between household income and the number of trips taken as well as the distance travelled. In the United Kingdom in 2008, on average, people in the highest income quintile group made 24 per cent more trips than those in the lowest income quintile group and travelled two and a half times further (10,290 miles versus 4,112 miles per person) (Department for Transport 2009). Table 7.2 indicates the percentage of European households that cannot afford a personal car and a one-week annual holiday because of household income levels (below 60 per cent of median equivalized income). Within the EU-27, almost two-thirds of those at risk of poverty were unable to afford a one-week annual holiday (65 per cent). By type of household, single parents with dependent children had the highest relative incapacity to afford a one-week holiday (76 per cent) (Eurostat European Commission 2010b). Possession of a personal car and capacity to afford a one-week annual holiday have been adopted as indicators of the material deprivation rate by the Indicators Sub-Group of the Social Protection Committee at the European Commission, to complement monetary measures of living standards with some non-monetary measures in monitoring poverty and social exclusion at EU level (Hall 2010b).

Table 7.1 Travel by household income quintile by number of trips and distance travelled in Great Britain, 2008

	Lowest real income	Second level	Third level	Fourth level	Highest real income	All income levels
Trips per person per year by main mode						
Walk	271	230	228	200	181	221
Bicycle	15	16	15	17	16	16
Car driver	225	334	438	497	536	410
Car passenger	199	219	252	240	218	227
Other private transport	11	14	15	13	10	13
Bus and coach	107	88	55	48	35	66
Rail	15	14	17	29	59	27
Taxi and minicab	13	14	9	9	11	11
Other public transport	2	2	1	2	2	2
All modes	860	931	1,032	1,054	1,069	992
Distance per person per year by mode						
Walk	204	186	200	186	191	193
Bicycle	34	36	40	49	51	42
Car driver	1,469	2,277	3,297	4,432	5,845	3,494
Car passenger	1,466	1,783	2,023	2,275	2,268	1,974
Other private transport	90	138	182	187	137	149
Bus and coach	537	454	327	334	199	367
Rail	223	290	370	626	1,348	570
Taxi and minicab	55	52	40	45	79	54
Other public transport	34	26	40	127	172	80
All modes	4,112	5,241	6,519	8,261	10,290	6,923

Source: Adapted from Department for Transport (2009).

Such analyses of economic categories may be useful in identifying the relative gaps between the haves and the have-nots in society but, by themselves, such data do not explain the how and why of such disparity. However, if classes are simply taken to be a bounded set of people, the difficulties of defining boundaries unambiguously will constantly appear to be an objection to class analysis (Connell and Irving 1980a).

Class and structural determination

One response is to utilize theoretical analysis of the modes of production that make a society in conjunction with or even with priority over empirical observation of that society. As Poulantzas (1975: 17) observed: 'Social classes are not empirical groups of individuals, social groups that are "composed" by simple addition; the relations of these agents among themselves are not inter-personal relations. The class membership of the various agents depends on the class places that they occupy.' An analysis of the modes of production, the abstract structure of relations that can be identified in the analysis of societies, their involvement in a given social formation and their interaction allows for definition of 'certain objective places occupied by the social agents in the social division of labour . . . It may thus be said that a social class is defined by its place in the ensemble of social practices, i.e. by its place in the social division of labour as a whole' (Poulantzas 1975: 14). The core of Poulantzas' approach is the idea of class 'place' or, as he describes it, 'the structural determination of class'. Yet the notion that classes are structurally determined not only at the economic level, but also at the political and ideological level, is 'the most distinctive and problematic of Poulantzas' analysis' (Wright 1976: 346), given that 'the whole analysis hangs on the comprehensiveness and precision of the original model of the mode of production' (Connell and Irving 1980b: 6). This means therefore that structural determination is regarded as having priority over personal agency, thereby separating the concept of class from the process of class formation (Mukonoweshuro 2008). As Connell and Irving (1980b: 7) argue,

> the conception of class as a place in a structure of theoretically-defined relations fails because it yields only an abstract, top-down approach to the politics of class. Classes are real groups of flesh-and-blood people, formed under particular stars at particular times and places, who work out their fate together – and whose fate is what politics is all about.

Classes as representative groupings

One response to the excesses of structural determination, without falling into the trap of defining class merely as a category without politics, is to understand class as a set of people, what may also be described as a 'quasi-group' (Dahrendorf 1959), who become aware of their common position in the social structure,

Table 7.2 Enforced lack of a personal car and capacity to afford a one-week annual holiday in the European Union (% of population below 60% of median equivalized income)

Geographical area	Enforced lack of a personal car					Capacity to afford a one-week annual holiday
	2004	2005	2006	2007	2008	2007
European Union (27 countries)	NA	NA	NA	22	20	65
European Union (25 countries)	NA	20	18	17	17	–
European Union (15 countries)	NA	16	14	14	14	–
New member states	NA	38	38	35	30	–
Euro area	NA	16	14	14	14	
Belgium	25	27	25	25	23	58
Bulgaria	NA	NA	NA	67	48	98
Czech Republic	NA	44	45	43	37	73
Denmark	30	27	28	24	23	23
Germany	NA	26	17	17	18	55
Estonia	46	48	37	39	34	87
Ireland	25	26	26	24	21	42
Greece	20	19	16	19	16	76
Spain	12	12	10	10	11	58
France	14	13	13	11	15	63

Country						
Italy	9	8	8	8	8	71
Cyprus	NA	9	8	8	5	82
Latvia	NA	55	52	47	43	91
Lithuania	NA	51	43	29	26	89
Luxembourg	7	9	7	9	10	39
Hungary	NA	41	44	42	37	90
Malta	NA	8	8	9	6	83
Netherlands	NA	17	18	20	19	35
Austria	16	14	15	20	24	58
Poland	NA	36	35	33	28	89
Portugal	25	24	25	28	20	89
Romania	NA	NA	NA	75	64	97
Slovenia	NA	13	14	16	14	64
Slovakia	NA	38	47	48	38	84
Finland	25	29	30	28	27	47
Sweden	14	14	15	14	11	35
United Kingdom	NA	14	13	14	14	43
Iceland	8	8	5	6	6	28
Norway	24	25	17	20	21	18

Source: Eurostat European Commission (2010a,b).
NA, not available.

develop common ideas and organizations to represent and promote their interests, and enter into conflict with other groups (Connell and Irving 1980b). As described by Krauss (1967: 134–135),

> Classes are formed when an aggregate of persons defines their interests as similar to those of the other persons in their aggregate, and as different from and opposed to the interests of another aggregate of persons . . . The big difference between social stratification and social class is communalisation.

Communalization can also be understood as the historical process of class formation that includes actual events and transformations. The issue as to how individuals and social organizations came to be in certain social roles was also important in the influential work of Thompson (1968: 212–213):

> The making of the working class is a fact of political and cultural, as much as of economic, history. It was not the spontaneous generation of the factory system . . . The factory hand or stockinger was also the inheritor of Bunyan, of remembered village rights, of notions of equality before the law, of craft traditions. He was the object of massive religious indoctrination and the creator of political traditions. The working class made itself as much as it was made.

Structure and agency in class formation and reproduction

Thompson's approach clearly incorporated the role of agency into class formation. Agency refers to the active capacity of individuals to pursue goals of their own choosing, in contrast to the class structure, which constrains the actor by limiting access to resources (Rojek 2005). The interplay between structure and agency in class formation came to be described by Giddens (1973) as 'class structuration'; he noted that 'one of the specific aims of class analysis in relation to empirical societies must necessarily be that of determining how strongly, in any given case, the "class principle" has become established as a mode of structuration' (Giddens 1973: 110). The further development of the concept of structuration by Giddens (1987) to identify the interplay between spatial and social structures had considerable impacts in tourism and the social sciences in the 1980s and early 1990s and arguably influenced the development of interest in mobility. Nevertheless, considerable tensions exist in the implications of structuration theory given that the production of a structure cannot be logically separated from the actual events that make up the process of class interaction, making 'class well-nigh undefinable' (Connell and Irving 1980a: 10). Connell and Irving's (1980a: 12–13) solution was to overcome the tendency of some approaches towards class analysis to

> separate concepts of structure from concepts of situation or the real existence of groups of people . . . 'Structures' can of course be found in almost everything; but we are interested only in those, which have some generality and have some relation to the determination of historical change, which express

the constraints and potentials discoverable in a situation. What is often referred to as 'structure' in the theoretical literature that separates it from situation and process is basically the persisting order in relationships that links a series of situations. The analysis of such structures is not mysterious; it is a matter of accounting for the reproduction of this order in relationships through real historical time.

Yet this approach takes us straight back to Marx's *Capital*. According to Marx (2007 [1867]: 633),

> Capitalist production, therefore, under its aspect of a continuous connected process, of a process of reproduction, produces not only commodities, not only surplus-value, but it also produces and reproduces the capitalist relation; on the one side the capitalist, on the other the wage-labourer.

Reproduction of class occurs in both tangible and intangible ways, through both commodities and culture. In *Capital*, for example, Marx was interested in the 'fetishism' of commodities that occurred because of the social reality of capitalism. Wolf (1999: 35) suggests rephrasing the issue of fetishism in cultural terms and 'ask which entities come to be selected for this process, under what circumstances, and why. Of special interest would be to ascertain how fetishes, already raised to a position of superiority, model relations of asymmetrical power in society'. Arguably, one response to this question can be found in Bourdieu's (1984) concept of cultural capital whereby, in addition to material distinctions such as the ownership and control of economic property, non-material types of wealth such as networks of influence, cultural taste, knowledge access and leisure and travel choices also reflect class distinctions (Rojek 2005). Bourdieu's notion of cultural capital has been extremely influential in considering the role of distinction and taste in tourism (e.g. Urry 1990; Britton 1991; Munt 1994; Perkins and Thorns 2001; Hall 2005). However, curious in the adoption of the significance of taste and gazing in tourism has been the loss of the class element, particularly given that the potential reproduction of and resistance to taste cultures are bound up with issues of power. Perhaps even more damning is the seemingly endless fascination with experiences, the experience economy and supposed co-creative agency while seemingly ignoring (or forgetting) the role of structure (Hall 2010a).

Arguably the most effective use of power is the power to shape preferences to believe a situation of inequality and the primacy of 'the market' and 'competition' to be 'normal' and to act otherwise as being 'idealistic' or 'unrealistic'. This situation recalls Bourdieu's (2000 [1997]) ideas with respect to how the maintenance of 'habitus' appeal to the workings of power (Hall 2010a), 'leading those subject to it to see their condition as "natural" and even to value it, and to fail to recognize the sources of their desires and beliefs' (Lukes 2005: 13). Such domination is, according to Bourdieu (2000 [1997]: 37),

> exerted not in the pure logic of knowing consciousness but through the schemes of perception, appreciation and action that are constitutive of habitus

and which, below the level of the decisions of consciousness and the controls of the will, set up a cognitive relationship that is profoundly obscure to itself.

In such circumstances power is therefore the imposition of internal constraints with those subject to such constraints being 'led to acquire beliefs and form desires that result in their consenting or adapting to being dominated, in coercive or non-coercive settings' (Lukes 2005: 13). But such power does not emerge from thin air. It arises from agents who benefit from the exertion of such power. Therefore, in considering issues of class and power in tourism, a fundamental question that all students of tourism should be asking is: Who benefits?

Conclusions

This chapter has indicated a number of different ways in which class is conceptualized. It has linked class with issues of inequality and, more fundamentally, with power. Class is not a presently fashionable concept in tourism studies although it is an important part of the intellectual legacy of the more critical traditions in the subject. Current concerns with individual agency as part of poststructural theorizing in tourism arguably downplay the role of structure and of class formation and reproduction even though notions of 'taste' and 'distinction' are recognized as significant. For a number of students of tourism, along with some social theorists, class is dead [along perhaps with history (Fukuyama 1989), ideology (Bell 2000) and politics (Boggs 2000)]. Pakulski and Waters's (1996: 7) book confirmed 'the good news that class has collapsed and is decomposing, leaving only the merest traces of its effects. If it ever was real and salient, and we are certainly prepared to admit that class was a sturdy historical reality, it is no longer.' Unfortunately, such a statement finds considerable reinforcement in some versions of how tourism is considered, especially in business schools in which tourism is taught, where ethical issues are usually understood at a micro level, that is, personal decision, if they are considered at all, and broader issues of tourism's contribution to inequality (yes, there is such a thing) are ignored. After all, tourism has to be good for you doesn't it?

This chapter was titled the way it was because of the influential work by Connell and Irving (1980b) in which they noted the relationships between the ruling class and the ruling culture in an Australian context. The title is based on the story from 1897 of a little girl called Virginia O'Hanlon who lived in New York. Concerned at being told by her friends that Santa did not really exist she asked her father as to the truth of the matter. Her father's response was to suggest that she write to the *New York Sun*, then a prominent city newspaper, assuring her that if the *Sun* reported it, it must be so. The paper, in reply, ran a famous editorial noting that her friends had been affected by the scepticism of a sceptical age and stating, 'Yes, Virginia, there is a Santa Claus'. So, yes, dear reader, there is still such a thing as class in relation to tourism. Even at a superficial level it is apparent that substantial inequality exists with respect to holiday-taking and leisure mobility (Tables 7.1 and 7.2), let alone differences in pay and conditions for workers.

However, a more substantial analysis also suggests that 'Yes, Virginia, there is also a ruling class'. And as they said of the architect of St Paul's in London: '*Si monumentum requires, circumspice*' – If you seek [his] monument, look around you' (Connell and Irving 1980b: 88). In the case of tourism it can also be found all around you, at destinations and also in universities, the textbook and the classroom. The ruling class have a ruling culture and it goes by the name of neoliberalism; as Harvey (2005: 119) writes, 'a benevolent mask of wonderful-sounding words like freedom, liberty, choice, and rights, to hide the grim realities of the restoration or reconstitution of naked class power, locally as well as transnationally, but most particularly in the main financial centers of global capitalism'. According to Harvey (2005: 203), the financial, corporate and political elite have used neoliberalism to implement policies that have restored their 'ruling-class power' by increasing their political power and wealth. In tourism this plays out most strongly with respect to the focus on competitiveness, free trade, free markets, the replacement of union labour with 'individual entrepreneurial freedom', and if there are areas where markets do not exist, such as water, the environment, or education, then they must be created. But then that's another story . . . .

References

Ateljevic, I. (2000) 'Circuits of tourism: Stepping beyond the "production/consumption" dichotomy', *Tourism Geographies*, 2: 369–388.

Bachrach, P. (1967) *The Theory of Democratic Elitism: A critique*, Boston: Little, Brown.

Bachrach, P. and Baratz, M. S. (1962) 'Two faces of power', *American Political Science Review*, 56: 947–952.

Bell, D. (2000) *The End of Ideology: On the exhaustion of political ideas in the fifties*, revised edn, Cambridge: Harvard University Press.

Bianchi, R. V. (2002) 'Towards a new political economy of global tourism', in R. Sharpley and D. J. Telfer (eds) *Tourism and Development: Concepts and issues*, Clevedon: Channel View.

Boggs, C. (2000) *The End of Politics: Corporate power and the decline of the public sphere*, New York: Guilford Press.

Bourdieu, P. (1984) *Distinction*, London: Routledge.

Bourdieu, P. (2000 [1997]) *Pascalian Meditations*, trans. R. Nice, Stanford: Stanford University Press.

Britton, S. G. (1991) 'Tourism. Capital and Place: Towards a critical geography of tourism', *Environment and Planning D: Society and Space*, 9: 451–478.

Brown, D. O. (2000) 'Political risk and other barriers to tourism promotion in Africa: Perceptions of US-based travel intermediaries', *Journal of Vacation Marketing*, 6: 197–210.

Church, A. and Coles, T. (eds) (2007) *Tourism, Power and Space*, London: Routledge.

Connell, R. W. (1977) *Ruling Class, Ruling Culture: Studies of conflict, power and hegemony in Australian life*, Cambridge: Cambridge University Press.

Connell, R. W. and Irving, T. H. (1980a) *Class Structure in Australian History: Documents, narrative and argument*, Melbourne: Longman Cheshire.

Connell, R. W. and Irving, T. H. (1980b) 'Yes, Virginia, There Is a Ruling Class', in H. Mayer and H. Nelson (eds) *Australian Politics 5*, Melbourne: Longman Cheshire.

Dahl, R. A. (1961) *Who Governs? Democracy and power in an American city.* New Haven: Yale University Press.

Dahrendorf, R. (1959) *Class and Class Conflict in Industrial Society*, Stanford: Stanford University Press.

Department for Transport (2009) *Transport Statistics Bulletin, National Travel Survey: 2008*, National Statistics Publication produced by Transport Statistics, Department for Transport, London: Department for Transport.

Domhoff, G. W. (2007) 'C. Wright Mills, Floyd Hunter, and 50 years of power structure research', *Michigan Sociological Review*, 21: 1–54.

Edelheim, J. R. (2007) 'Hidden messages: A polysemic reading of tourist brochures', *Journal of Vacation Marketing*, 13: 5–17.

Eurostat European Commission (2010a) 'Enforced lack of a personal car' (last updated 17 February 2010). Online. Available at http://nui.epp.eurostat.ec.europa.eu/nui/show.do?dataset=ilc_mddu05&lang=en (accessed 27 February 2010).

Eurostat European Commission (2010b) *Combating Poverty and Social Exclusion. A statistical portrait of the European Union 2010*, Luxembourg: Eurostat European Commission.

Foucault, M. (1984) 'The subject and power', in B. Wallis (ed.) *Art After Modernism: Rethinking representation*, New York: New York Museum of Contemporary Art.

Frow, J. (1991) 'Tourism and the semiotics of nostalgia', *October*, 57: 123–151.

Fukuyama, F. (1989) 'The end of history?' *The National Interest*, 16. Reprinted in Foreign Affairs Agenda (1997) *The New Shape of World Politics: Contending paradigms in international relations*, New York: W. W. Norton.

Gallie, W. B. (1955–1956) 'Essentially contested concepts', *Proceedings of Aristotelian Society*, 56: 167–198.

Giddens, A. (1973) *The Class Structure of the Advanced Societies*, London: Hutchinson.

Giddens, A. (1987) *Social Theory and Modern Society*, Oxford: Blackwell.

Giddens, A. and Held, D. (eds) (1982) *Classes, Power and Conflict: Classical and contemporary debates*, Berkeley: University of California Press.

Gössling, S., Ceron, J-P., Dubios, G. and Hall, C. M. (2009) 'Hypermobile travelers', in S. Gössling and P. Upham (eds) *Climate Change and Aviation*, London: Earthscan.

Hall, C. M. (1994) *Tourism and Politics: Power, policy and place*, London: John Wiley.

Hall, C. M. (2005) *Tourism: Rethinking the social science of mobility*, Harlow: Pearson.

Hall, C. M. (2007) 'Tourism, governance and the (mis-)location of power', in A. Church and T. Coles (eds) *Tourism, Power and Space*, London: Routledge.

Hall, C. M. (2010a) 'Power in tourism: Tourism in power', in D. Macleod and J. Carrier (eds) *Tourism, Power and Culture: Anthropological insights*, Bristol: Channel View.

Hall, C. M. (2010b) 'Equal access for all? Regulative mechanisms, inequality and tourism mobility', in S. Cole and N. Morgan (eds) *Tourism and Inequality: Problems and prospects*, Wallingford: CABI, in press.

Harvey, D. (2005) *A Brief History of Neoliberalism*, Oxford: Oxford University Press.

Johnson, N. (1999) 'Framing the past: Time, space and the politics of heritage tourism in Ireland', *Political Geography*, 18: 187–207.

Krauss, I. (1967) 'Some perspectives on social stratification and social class', *Sociological Review*, 15: 129–140.

Lakshmanan, T. R. and Chatterjee, L. (2006) 'The entrepreneurial city in the global marketplace', *International Journal of Entrepreneurship and Innovation Management*, 6: 155–172.

Langman, L. (1991) 'Alienation and everyday life: Goffman meets Marx at the shopping mall', *International Journal of Sociology and Social Policy*, 11: 107–124.

Lasswell, H. D. (1936) *Politics: Who gets, what, when, how?*, New York: McGraw-Hill.

Lukes, S. (2005) *Power: A radical view*, 2nd edn, Basingstoke: Palgrave Macmillan.

Macleod, D. and Carrier, J. (eds) (2010) *Tourism, Power and Culture: Anthropological insights*, Bristol: Channel View.

Markwell, K., Stevenson, D. and Rowe, D. (2004) 'Footsteps and memories: Interpreting an Australian urban landscape through thematic walking tours', *International Journal of Heritage Studies*, 10: 457–473.

Marx, K. (2007 [1867]) *Capital: A critique of political economy – Volume I–Part II: The process of capitalist production*, New York: Cosimo Classics.

Mukonoweshuro, E. G. (2008) 'Problems of the structural determination of class: A critical methodological review', *Australian Journal of Politics & History*, 36: 23–38.

Munt, I. (1994) 'The "other" postmodern tourism: Culture, travel and the new middle classes', *Theory, Culture & Society*, 11: 101–123.

Murphy, P. (1985) *Tourism: A community approach*, New York: Methuen.

Pakulski, J. and Waters, M. (1996) *The Death of Class*, London: Sage.

Peeters, P., Gössling, S. and Becken, S. (2006) 'Innovation towards tourism sustainability: Climate change and aviation', *International Journal of Innovation and Sustainable Development*, 1: 184–200.

Perkins, H. C. and Thorns, D. C. (2001) 'Gazing or performing? Reflections on Urry's tourist gaze in the context of contemporary experience in the antipodes', *International Sociology*, 16: 185–204.

Pirie, G. H. (2009) 'Virtuous mobility: Moralising vs measuring geographical mobility in Africa', *Afrika Focus*, 22: 21–35.

Poulantzas, N. (1975) *Classes in Contemporary Capitalism*, London: New Left Books.

Rojek, C. (2005) *Leisure Theory: Principles and practice*, London: Palgrave.

Sayer, D. (ed.) (1989) *Readings from Karl Marx*, London: Routledge.

Thompson, E. P. (1968) *The Making of the English Working Class*, revised edn, Harmondsworth: Penguin.

Tribe, L. (2008) 'Tourism: A critical business', *Journal of Travel Research*, 46: 245–255.

Urry, J. (1990) *The Tourist Gaze: Leisure and travel in contemporary societies*. London: Sage.

Wolf, E. R. (1999) *Envisioning Power: Ideologies of dominance and crisis*, Berkeley: University of California Press.

Wright, E. O. (1976) 'Class boundaries in advanced capitalist societies', *New Left Review*, 98: 3–41, reprinted in Scott, J. (ed.) (1996) *Class: Critical concepts*, Volume 4, London: Taylor and Francis.

8 Gender and tourism

Gender, age and mountain tourism in Japan

Janet Momsen and Michihiko Nakata

Processes of tourism development can be seen as important identifiers of social change of which interest in gender is an important aspect (Kinnaird and Hall 1994; Swain and Momsen 2002; Hall *et al.* 2003; Swain 1995; Pritchard *et al.* 2007). Tourism has followed the theoretical trajectory of other social sciences over the last half century, from materialist and structural approaches to the cultural and poststructural (Aitchison 2005). Within this broad trend lie the changing discourses of feminist and gender approaches in tourism studies that Aitchison (2005) suggests may have fractured the coherence of gender and tourism studies as a subdiscipline. At the same time tourism is increasingly seen as an important element in the economic development of less globally accessible nations and regions (Torres and Momsen 2004, 2005; Gunasekara and Momsen 2007; Momsen 2010). Thus tourism and gender has also been influenced by attitudes to development (Momsen 2009). This chapter looks at the influence of both general social science and development studies on changing approaches to gender and tourism and illustrates this with a case study from Japan.

Kinnaird and Hall (1994) were among the first to look at gender and tourism specifically. They suggested that 'tourism processes are gendered in their construction, presentation and consumption, and the form of this gendering is configured in different and diverse ways which are both temporally and spatially specific' (Kinnaird and Hall 1994: 2). Tourism influences economic, social, environmental, political and cultural life and gender relations are embodied in all these aspects. Gendered impacts will also differ according to an individual's role as host or guest in the industry.

In economic terms tourism often exploits under-employment and a reserve army of female labour in rural areas and poor countries. At the end of the twentieth century, using data from seventy-three countries, women working in the formal tourism sector, including restaurant, catering and hotel sectors, made up 46 per cent of the world tourism workforce (Michael *et al.* 1999). The proportion of men and women tourism workers was roughly equal in countries where tourism is a more mature industry such as in Italy, Germany, New Zealand and Thailand. A UNED-UK (1999) report suggests that tourism is a particularly important sector for women as in most countries female employment in tourism was higher than that in the labour market in general. The proportion of women tourism workers varied widely, from 77 per cent in Bolivia and 75 per cent in Peru, Botswana and Estonia to under 5 per cent in some Muslim countries (UNED-UK 1999). The participation of women in the industry increased steadily throughout the 1990s, especially in those countries with the most rapid expansion of tourism, and probably reflects the influence of visitors and external tourist business partners. However, most women's jobs are in the lowest paid sectors of the tourism industry and are seasonal and insecure. Although tourism has grown worldwide in the last decade, the formal employment position of women has changed little. However, they remain important in the informal sector, producing and selling souvenirs and providing services from hair braiding to prostitution (Kempadoo 1999). Gender equality in this sector is now appearing as local men offer their services as gigolos to female tourists, especially in the Caribbean and Thailand (Dahles 2002).

The employment of women is often seen in terms of their caring skills, the 'managed heart', which was thought to make them superior for hospitality work that involves, more than in most industries, face-to-face interaction (Momsen 2009). Although women often hold the least well-paid jobs in tourism, they have been able to gain some economic independence in parts of the world where few other jobs are available to them. At the same time, interaction with tourist strangers brings new ideas to individuals and communities and these contacts are important in expanding social capital in isolated areas (Canoves and Villarino 2002).

Tourism can be a gendered social catalyst. Bringing hosts and guests together at a single location introduces a cross-cultural exposure that may induce changes in perceptions and behaviours on both sides. These cultural border zones within which the interactions between tourist and local take place form new spaces of modernization that may be exploited to mutual benefit but in some cases may just create confusion and misunderstanding on both sides (Momsen 2002a). Individual women travellers may cause problems because of their 'otherness' and their alien behaviour, as Hottola (2002) notes in his study of the misconceptions of local men in India when faced with Western women backpackers.

Women are often seen as the preservers of traditional cultures and tourism may benefit poor communities by encouraging the survival of traditional crafts because of increased demand. It has been argued that these traditional crafts provide the authenticity sought by tourists. Production of souvenirs is flexible work in the informal economy, which is often undertaken by women. However, greater financial returns for craftwork may encourage change in gender roles, with men becoming dominant in production as in Peru or taking over the lucrative marketing of crafts as in Malta or Indonesia (Momsen 2009). On the other hand, women may be able to exploit the photogenic appearance of their traditional costumes to obtain economic benefits from visitors.

The tourist gaze may also be gendered. Women and men experience holidays differently with women often being more influenced by relations with vacation companions and their responsibility for family members than are men (Selänniemi 2002). Small (2002), in a study of holiday memories, shows that age also influences the tourist gaze, especially for children.

Tourism on the development agenda

Participation, empowerment and inclusion have become new key words in the field of development studies but they do not always improve gender balance, especially when participation is aimed at household heads, usually men (Momsen 2003). Many practitioners see tourism as a way to improve livelihoods among hosts as tourism expands into poorer countries. Pro-poor tourism (Torres and Momsen 2004; Scheyvens and Momsen 2008) looks at specific aspects of tourism as a wealth creator but rarely considers the importance of gender balance in tourism-related changes. More often it is seen in terms of sustainability of both tourism and the environment.

Tourism may be seen as the key to development in resource-poor areas and among minority groups. In a study of the gender impact of a tourism project on a Mayan community in Quintana Roo, Mexico, it was found that, despite the non-governmental organization (NGO) being led by a woman, participation was considered only at the household level (Momsen 2003). Husbands, as household heads, committed wives to work on the project although the women did not have the spare time. The benefits were considered only in terms of male needs such as feeder roads. When we held a women's focus group they told us that what they wanted was a clinic and a secondary school in the village rather than improvements to roads but these views had never been presented to the NGO (Momsen 2003). A study aimed at improving the economy of a Miwok-Maidu Native American community in California's Sierra Nevada through tourism was also led by a woman economist but again ignored gendered views at the grassroots (Momsen 2002b). In both cases the NGOs involved expected women community members to provide cultural performances and crafts for sale to visitors but the communities themselves saw the tourism activity as a reclamation and reaffirmation of a culture that had been almost lost, rather than an exercise in local economic development. The Miwok-Maidu Foundation in California, like the Maya in Mexico, did not see earning money by commoditizing their culture as of major importance, and the women in particular did not wish to interact directly with tourists on the ecotourism tours being developed in both countries (Momsen 2002b).

The cultural turn and poststructural ideas of embodiment and sexuality bring new approaches to the study of gender and tourism (Pritchard *et al.* 2007). However, Aitchison (2005) argues that these should not allow for a rejection of the previous materialist analyses. She suggests that a social–cultural nexus should be the basis of a new conceptual framework within which to explore 'the mutually informing nature of the social and the cultural in shaping both materialities and relations of gender and tourism' (Aitchison 2005: 207). Within this a third-wave feminism that considers intersections of race, class, age, sexuality, nationality, ability, etc. as challenging the primacy of gender among social inequalities is leading to an awareness of the need for an embodied and ethical tourism. Pritchard *et al.* (2007: 9) see the tourism industry as potentially offering 'opportunities for a global revolution in the economic, social and political condition of women. Yet at the same time it can be a force for ghettoization, oppression and inequality – shoring up exploitative practices, objectifying indigenous women and female employees as part of the tourism "package".' Whether dealing with women as hosts or guests, touristic activities will have gendered impacts and gender stereotypes must be challenged.

Mountain tourism in Japan

A new form of tourism is sweeping Japan that brings to the fore many aspects of gender stereotypes and of intersectionality, especially age and gender, as discussed above. Middle-aged women, mostly aged between fifty and seventy years, are 'collecting' mountain summits. They hike up mountains in organized groups on one- to four-day expeditions. It is not unusual in Japan for men and women to undertake leisure activities separately, but hiking in the mountains, in contrast to mountaineering, is definitely a hobby of women. The number of middle- aged couples who hike mountains together is increasing, although they are still not a majority. However, in the case of organized mountain tours, which involve more dangerous and higher mountains, usually above 3,000 metres, couples rarely go together. We hypothesise that Japanese women of this older generation are fitter and live longer than previous generations and have reached an age when they have both the time and the money to undertake these activities. Reaching the summit is often celebrated by relaxing in baths fed by hot springs.

In this chapter we look at the development of Japanese mountain tourism from its roots in eighteenth-century pilgrimages to sacred sites, often associated with mountains, to its spread in the last two decades through popularization in the mass media. The reasons why middle-aged women, often in a single-sex group, are so attracted to this form of tourism are also examined.

The population of Japan today is distinctive because of its longevity. In 2005 one-fifth of Japan's population was over sixty-five years of age, the highest proportion in the world. Current life expectancy at eighty-six years for Japanese women and seventy-nine years for men is also the highest in the world. It means that 76 per cent of women but only 54 per cent of men live to be eighty years old (Ministry of Health, Labor and Welfare, Japan 2010). There are more elderly women than men and the government is considering improving general health care for the elderly (Komatsu 2003). In Japan, women have an 'M' shaped pattern of labour force participation Thirty years ago women married straight out of college and did not work after marriage. Today they give up work outside the home when the first child is born and may go back to work part-time when the children are grown. Of the group aged from fifty-five to fifty-nine years, most men are still working but only 23 per cent of women are in employment (Komatsu 2003). Among those over sixty-five years, 83 per cent of men are married but only 46 per cent of women. On the whole women have smaller pensions and do most of the caring for the elderly (Komatsu 2003). However, despite having less money than men from pensions in their own right and being responsible for elder care, many of these women have inherited money from their husbands. Their children are grown and they now have time and income to get involved in new leisure activities. In addition, longevity is accompanied by a high level of physical fitness into the third age. This demographic situation is the underlying reason for the growth of tourism to the mountains by older women in Japan.

Women mountain tourists

Most of the women involved in this type of tourism are *Sengyo Shufu* or full-time housewives with husbands who are salaried workers. The group of *Sengyo Shufu* emerged during the unprecedented expansion of the Japanese economy in the 1960s (Suzuki 2000: 105). To accomplish a rapid economic expansion, men were expected to wholeheartedly devote all of their time to their paid work. In turn, the role of women was to take over all of the responsibilities at home, as full-time housewives, in order to support their husbands' contributions to the growth of the national economy. The *Sengyo Shufu* had to undertake childcare, oversee their children's education, carry out the housekeeping and care for their parents-in-law. The proportion of *Sengyo Shufu* reached its peak in 1975 when the baby boomers (born in the years 1947–1949) began to marry, and declined with the slowdown of the economy in the 1980s (Suzuki 2000: 110). The typical profile of the *Sengyo Shufu* is that of a big city urban dweller, highly educated, affluent because her husband's income is above the national average, and with fewer children than the Japanese norm (Suzuki 2000: 104–105). *Sengyo Shufu* live in small houses that are well equipped with many labour-saving devices that help to reduce the time spent on housework. Most *Sengyo Shufu* now have control of the household finances (Suzuki 2000: 103). These women are also healthier than their mothers and in their middle-age have time for leisure activities as their children are grown up. These characteristics explain the numerical dominance of such middle-aged housewives among tourists climbing Japan's mountains today. In Japanese culture it is not unusual for married couples to take separate vacations (Creighton 1995) and men and women usually climb mountains in separate groups.

Mountain tourism in Japan

Japan is a country of mountains and there are many poems and artistic portrayals of mountains in the classical literature (Fukada 1964). The major summits of Japan became accessible through the founder of Shugendo, a mountain religion linked to both Buddhism and Shinto, and his followers. The founder of Shugendo climbed Mt Fuji in 633 A.D. Modern mountain climbing (alpinism) was invented by the British in the late eighteenth century and introduced to Japan in the late nineteenth century when a few British mountaineers came to climb Japan's high peaks. The first Japanese Alpine Club was founded in 1905.

In the 1980s there was a remarkable change in both the age structure of Japanese mountaineers and the style of mountaineering in Japan. Middle-aged people have replaced the young and the majority of these new mountaineers are female. This is an unprecedented situation not only in Japan but also worldwide

(Fujita 1997: 4, 201). The new style of mountaineering is sometimes called *Junrei Tozan* (pilgrimage mountaineering) (Kikuchi 2001: 3).

Junrei Tozan has its roots in the tradition of pilgrimages in Japan. There were three main types of pilgrimage: those to Shinto shrines; those to sacred mountains for Shugendo; and those to a circuit of Buddhist temples. It was stimulated by the 1964 publication of a book *Nihon Hyaku Meizan (One Hundred Famous Mountains in Japan)* by Fukada Kyuya. He selected these mountains after climbing more than 200 and deciding that a famous mountain should be distinctive and have a history that made it revered. Leading mass media in Japan endorsed the book as a kind of textbook for the general public to re-discover Japan through the climbing of Fukada's 100 mountains as a pleasurable pursuit. Fukada (1964) had begun to write about these mountains in 1959 in the form of a series published in a small magazine, and later it was made into a television programme and became very popular. Most of the sacred mountains of the Shugendo religion are included in Fukada's 100 mountains. The way in which tourism to the mountains has diffused is analogous to the pattern seen two to three hundred years ago in the circuit of Buddhist temples. Carrying a stick as a symbol was one of the rites of pilgrims doing the circuit of Buddhist temples. Contemporary mountain tourists also usually carry a stick. Just as with the Buddhist temples, the list of 100 mountains to be climbed has been developed at various scales, from national to district.

In the past women had not been allowed to climb the sacred mountains above a certain height. In 1872 the Meiji Government abolished this restriction under government decree No. 98 (Sakakura and Umeno 1992: 14). Although women were allowed to join the Japanese Alpine Club very few did so. In Japan mountaineering was regarded as a male activity and it was difficult for women to become involved. This impediment is still in existence to some degree, largely because women do not like to be associated with a male-dominated club. There appears to be no link between women's participation in organized alpine climbing and the current dominance of middle-aged women in *Junrei Tozan*.

After Fukada's sudden death in 1971, a Fukada Club was founded by his supporters. In addition to climbing mountains, the activities of the club included the exchange between members of information on the mountains and advocating for the conservation of mountain environments (Fujita 1997: 85). The Fukada Club selected an additional 100 famous mountains according to the criteria laid down by Fukada. This second set of famous mountains became targets for more advanced mountaineers. In 1978 the Japanese Alpine Club, of which Fukada had been vice-president in the 1960s, selected a further group of 100 mountains that became the targets for the most advanced climbers. Thus a hierarchy of mountains was developed on the basis of the difficulty of their ascent.

In 1980 a different list of 100 famous mountains was introduced, called 'One Hundred Mountains Famous for their Wild Flowers'. This list was based on a bestselling book by a woman playwright Tanaka Sumie (1908–2000). Many middle-aged women began to climb the mountains listed in the Tanaka book (1980), attracted by the search for wild flowers. Some thirty-five of Tanaka's mountains were included in Fukada's 100 mountains. In the 1990s many local areas identified their own 100 mountains and published books about these. In 1994 the Japanese Broadcasting Corporation (NHK), a non-commercial and semi-government corporation whose networks cover the country, broadcast programmes on Fukada's 100 famous mountains on its educational TV channel. This programme was broadcast on weekday afternoons and so appeared to be aimed at housewives who could watch at that time. The series of programmes continued for a year and was followed by a series on Tanaka's mountains with wild flowers. These television programmes seem to have triggered the boom in mountain tourism among middle-aged women. The number of mountaineers over forty years of age increased from 1.32 million (36.4 per cent) in 1976 to 2.03 million (53.8 per cent) in 1988 and 3.06 million (64.4 per cent) in 2000, while the number of younger mountaineers has declined. According to a survey of wardens of mountain huts in 2002, women made up the majority of this older group (see Table 8.1) (Nagano-ken Sanngaku Sogo Center 2002).

The expansion of *Junrei Tozan* was helped by the growth of tour operators specializing in tours to the 100 famous mountains. Most of the applicants for guided tours are middle-aged, and 70–80 per cent of participants are over fifty. They are generally inexperienced in mountain walking but are mountain lovers. They tend to use guided mountain tours when the targeted mountains are a little bit too difficult for them to tackle by themselves. For these tours participants have to be less than seventy years of age. The guided mountain tours usually have between ten and twenty participants, and participants usually sign up individually or in a group of two or three. These tours are often combined with visits to hot springs, which are one of the biggest tourist attractions in Japan. There is no information on the total number of mountain tour operators but an association founded in 2003 has sixty-five operators as members. Estimates of the number of participants in guided mountain tours annually range from 200,000 to 500,000 (Kurokawa 2003; Kikuchi 2001). These tours vary in difficulty. Some involve two or three days' climbing with a night or two in a mountain hut. The distance walked can be as much as 40 kilometres and it can cover several thousand metres in altitude. Compared with the difficulty rating applied to the hiking in the California Sierra

Table 8.1 Mountain hikers (%) in Japan by gender and age group

Age group	Male (n = 828)	Female (n = 264)
Under 30 years	4	6
30–39 years	11	17
40–49 years	23	17
50–59 years	34	46
60–69 years	23	13
70–79 years	5	1
Total	100	100

Source: Adapted from *Gakujin* (2003).

Nevada, most of the Japanese mountain tours would be classified as being of very high difficulty (Nakata 2004). It is clear that participants have to be very fit to undertake such strenuous hikes.

A growing number of accidents among mountain hikers in recent years has become an issue of public concern. Table 8.2 shows the steady increase in these accidents, with a very high proportion of those injured being between the ages of fifty and seventy years (80 per cent in 1999, 78 per cent in 2003 and 81 per cent in 2008).

Among those killed or missing in accidents on Japanese mountains, the middle-aged made up 87 per cent in 1999, 93 per cent in 2003 and 91 per cent in 2008. Two accidents occurred on 13 and 14 July 2009 in the mountains of Hokkaido Island because of bad weather. Ten people, aged from fifty to sixty-nine years, of whom eight were female and two male, froze to death in the central highlands of Hokkaido. They were participants on two separate guided mountain tours. One tour involved three women participants of whom one died. The other tour involved thirteen participants (ten female and three male) of whom nine died, seven women and two men. This is the worst disaster in the history of guided mountain tours in Japan.

Infrastructure development has also helped to support the growth of this type of tourism. The spread of motorway networks and convenience stores throughout the country has encouraged domestic tourism. The building of mountain huts where people can sleep overnight has also facilitated such tourism. At the same time mountain tourism is relatively cheap and environmentally friendly and so it appeals to a wide range of tourists, especially, perhaps, urban women looking for the wild alpine flowers.

This new type of tourism has its roots in Japanese cultural traditions of pilgrim-ages to temples and shrines, usually associated with mountains. It has also built on the long tradition of bathing in hot springs. There are currently about 3,000 hot springs used for bathing in Japan (Yamamoto 1999:102) and the tours take advantage of these with a relaxing bathe after the climb being included in most tours. The 100 mountains of special touristic interest are distributed throughout Japan but eighty-three of them are located in Honshu, the largest and most densely populated island. This contiguity of people and mountains has encouraged moun-tain tourism.

This case study of Japanese mountain tourism has illustrated the importance of age, class and gender in characterizing a particular form of tourism. It reflects the importance of Japanese cultural traditions linked to pilgrimages, brought up to date through the mass media, and the existence of a society with a considerable number of relatively wealthy, healthy, older women with plenty of leisure time. How far the growing levels of employment among Japanese women of all ages and the social crisis of the increasing numbers of accidents among older mountain climbers will change the nature of this form of tourism is yet to be seen.

Table 8.2 Accidents among mountain hikers

	1999	2003	2008
Number of accidents	1,195	1,358	1,631
Total number injured	1,444	1,666	1,933
Middle-aged injured (50–70 years)	1,158	1,298	1,567
Total dead or missing	271	230	281
Middle-aged dead or missing (50–70 years)	235	213	256

Source: Japanese Police Agency (2009).

References

Aitchison, C. (2005) 'Feminist and gender perspectives in tourism studies: The socio–cultural nexus of critical and cultural theories', *Tourist Studies*, 5: 207–224.

Canoves, G. and Villarino M. (2002) 'Rural tourism, gender, and cultural conservation in Spain and Portugal', in M. B. Swain and J. H. Momsen (eds) *Gender/Tourism/Fun?*, New York: Cognizant Communication Corporation.

Creighton, R. M. (1995) 'Japanese craft tourism: Liberating the crane wife', *Annals of Tourism Research*, 22: 463–476.

Dahles, H. (2002) 'Gigolos and rastamen: Tourism, sex, and changing gender identities', in M. B. Swain and J. H. Momsen (eds) *Gender/Tourism/Fun?*, New York: Cognizant Communication Corporation.

Fujita, K. (1997) *Chuukonen Yama to deau: Tozan Buumu o Kogengaku* (*Study of the Mountaineering Boom in Japan*), Tokyo: Yama to Keikoku-sha.

Fukada, K. (1964) *Nihon Hyaku Meizan* (*One Hundred Famous Mountains in Japan*), Tokyo: Shinchosha.

Gakujin (2003) A leading monthly magazine for mountaineers in Japan, October, Tokyo: Tokyo Shimbun Shuppan.

Gunasekara, R. B. and Momsen, J. H. (2007) 'Amidst the misty mountains: The role of tea tourism in Sri Lanka's turbulent tourist industry', in L. Jolliffe (ed.) *Tea and Tourism: Tourists, traditions and transformations*, Clevedon, UK: Channel View.

Hall, D., Swain, M. B. and Kinnaird, V. (2003) 'Tourism and gender: An evolving agenda', *Tourism Recreation Research*, 28: 7–11.

Hottola, P. (2002) 'Amoral and available? Western women travelers in South Asia', in M. B. Swain and J. H. Momsen (eds) *Gender/Tourism/Fun?*, New York: Cognizant Communication Corporation.

Japanese Police Agency (2009) Online. Available at http://www.npa.go.jp/safetylife/chiiki28/h20_sangakusounan.pdf (accessed 16 May 2010).

Kempadoo, K. (ed.) (1999) *Sun, Sex and Gold: Tourism and sex work in the Caribbean*, Lanham, MD: Rowman and Littlefield.

Kikuchi, T. (2001) *Yama no shakai Gaku* (*Sociology of Mountains in Japan*), Tokyo: Bungei-shunjyu.

Kinnaird, V. and Hall, D. (eds) (1994) *Tourism: A gender analysis*, Chichester: Wiley.

Komatsu, M. (2003) 'Japan's aged society from a gender viewpoint: Reading the White Paper on Aged Society', *Dawn Newsletter*, December, pp. 10–11.

Kurokawa, S. (2003) 'Alpine tour', newsletter, August. Online. Available at http://www.alpine-tour.com/ (accessed 29 March 2010).

Michael, C., Gardiner, R., Prowse, M. and Hemmati, M. (1999) 'Women's employment in tourism worldwide: Data and statistics', in UNED-UK (ed.) 'Gender and tourism: Women's employment and participation in tourism', Report for the United Nations Commission on Sustainable Development, 7th Session, London: DFiD.

Ministry of Health, Labor and Welfare, Japan (2010) 'Abridged life tables', 11 July. Available at http://www.mhlw.go.jp/english/database/lifetab03/index.html (accessed 2 November 2010).

Nagano-ken Sanngaku Sogo Center (Nagano Pref. Comprehensive Mountaineering Center) (2002) 'Survey of wardens of mountain huts in Japan Alps', March, National Institute for Training Mountaineers. Available at http://www.pref.nagano.lg.jp/xkyouiku/sance (accessed October 2010).

Momsen, J. H. (2002a) 'Conclusion', in M. B. Swain and J. H. Momsen (eds) *Gender/Tourism/Fun?*, New York: Cognizant Communication Corporation.

Momsen, J. H. (2002b) 'NGOs, gender and indigenous grassroots development', *Journal of International Development*, 14: 859–867.

Momsen, J. H. (2003) 'Participatory development and indigenous communities in the Mexican Caribbean', in J. Pugh and R. B. Potter (eds) *Participatory Planning in the Caribbean: Lessons from practice*, Aldershot: Ashgate.

Momsen, J. H. (2010) *Gender and Development*, London and New York: Routledge.

Nakata, M. (2004) 'Junei Tozan (*pilgrimage mountaineering*): Mountaineering of middle aged people in Japan', unpublished MA thesis, University of California, Davis.

Pritchard, A., Morgan, N., Ateljevic, I. and Harris, C. (eds) (2007) *Tourism and Gender: Embodiment, sensuality and experience*, Wallingford: CABI.

Sakakura, T. and Umeno, T. (1992) *Nihon Jyosei Tozanshi (History of Women Mountaineers in Japan)*, Tokyo: Otsuki Shoten.

Scheyvens, R. and Momsen, J. H. (2008) 'Tourism and poverty-reduction: Issues for small island states', *Tourism Geographies*, 10: 22–41.

Selänniemi, T. (2002) 'Couples on holiday: (En)gendered or endangered experiences?', in M. B. Swain and J. H. Momsen (eds) *Gender/Tourism/Fun?*, New York: Cognizant Communication Corporation.

Small, J. (2002) 'Good and bad holiday experiences: Women's and girls' perspectives', in M. B. Swain and J. H. Momsen (eds) *Gender/Tourism/Fun?*, New York: Cognizant Communication Corporation.

Suzuki, R. (2000) *Cho Shoshika Kiki ni tatsu Nihon (Rapidly Decreasing Child Population in Japan)*, Tokyo: Shuei-sha.

Swain, M. B. (1995) 'Gender in tourism', *Annals of Tourism Research*, 22: 247–266.

Swain, M. B. and Momsen, J. H. (eds) (2002) *Gender/Tourism/Fun?*, New York: Cognizant Communication Corporation.

Tanaka, S. (1980) *Hana no Hyaku Meizan (One Hundred Mountains Famous for the Wild Flowers)*, Tokyo: Bungeishunjyu-sha.

Torres, R. M. and Momsen, J. H. (2004) 'Challenges and potential for linking tourism and agriculture to achieve PPT Objectives', *Progress in Development Studies*, 4: 294–318.

Torres, R. M. and Momsen, J. H. (2005) 'Gringolandia: The construction of a new tourist space in Mexico', *Annals of the Association of American Geographers*, 95: 314–335.

UNED-UK (1999) 'Gender and tourism: Women's employment and participation in tourism', Report for the United Nations Commission on Sustainable Development, 7th session, London: DFiD.

Yamamoto, K. (1999) *Chirigaku ga wakaru* (*Introduction to Geography*), Tokyo: Asahi Shimbun-sha.

9 The political economy of temporary migration

Seasonal workers, tourists and sustaining New Zealand's labour force

Kirsten Lovelock and Teresa Leopold

Global migration has become a defining phenomenon of the twenty-first century and is receiving increased attention from researchers from a variety of disciplinary backgrounds. Migration was once the preserve and experience of only select populations, and, with the exception of a minority that could afford to tour, the intention and outcome for most twentieth-century migrants was permanent settlement. In contrast, contemporary migration increasingly embraces many categories of people, from the skilled to the unskilled, the permanent and the temporary, family members, refugees, legal and illegal migrants and those who are in the process of becoming one of those categories. Now, more than ever before, migration encompasses not only a wider range of people but also a wider range of countries of origin and destination (Castles and Miller 2003; Birrell *et al.* 2006; Bedford 2006; Bedford and Ho 2006).

This wider nexus of people also includes tourists who are increasingly indistinguishable from some categories of migrants, especially when they cross borders as temporary labour. These tourists, referred to commonly as working holidaymakers, challenge historic conceptualizations of what constitutes a tourist by becoming at once producers and consumers in destination societies (Bianchi 2000; Hall and Williams 2002). Just as tourists and workers have been conceptualized as separate entities, tourism and migration have historically been considered different forms of mobility (Williams and Hall 2000). It is only recently that researchers have focused on the migration–tourism nexus (Bell and Ward 2000; Bianchi 2000; Gustafson 2002; Williams and Hall 2000; Truly 2002; Coles and Timothy 2004; Heuman 2005; Illés and Michalkó 2008). The connections between migration and tourism (and vice versa) have become increasingly important because of significant shifts in the role that migration plays in the international political and economic order and the consequent shifting definitions of what constitutes a migrant (and tourist) in the twenty-first century. However, although increasingly attracting research attention there are aspects that remain poorly investigated.

As others have observed, economic globalization does not just involve the movement of capital and commodities; it also involves the movement of people and labour (Williams and Hall 2000; Castles and Miller 2003). The dramatic increase in the number of temporary migrants in the last thirty years is an outcome of economic globalization, the internationalization of labour markets, and emergent transnationalism. Countries increasingly compete with one another to attract capital and labour to meet changing domestic production labour needs (Hugo 2006a; Iredale 2000; Birrell 2000; Spoonley 2006; Bedford 2006; Bedford and Ho 2006). To stay (or become) competitive, countries depending on immigration have had to respond to the increased mobility of and competition for skilled workers with more flexible migration policies and with the development of recruitment policies for semi-skilled labour in occupations not desirable for locals, whilst also maintaining some control over migratory flows (Birrell *et al.* 2006; Iredale 2000; Martin 2006, 2008; Bedford 2006; Lovelock and Leopold 2009).

The most significant change in countries of immigration has been an increasing shift from the dominant emphasis on permanent migration and settlement towards offering temporary residence and temporary work permits so that labour market shortages can be addressed (Spoonley and Bedford 2008; Hugo 2006a; Birrell *et al.* 2006; Martin 2006). Both permanent and temporary migration, however, not only address immediate labour market needs but can also facilitate the development of strong networks [social, cultural, economic (including tourist) and political] that link and facilitate relations between the destination and origin countries (Hugo 2006a; Birrell *et al.* 2006; Castles and Miller 2003; Williams and Hall 2000). The increase in temporary migration in the twenty-first century has been facilitated by the internationalization of labour markets, multinational companies placing people internationally, cheaper international travel and more sophisticated telecommunications technologies that allow migrants to stay in contact with their countries of origin (Hugo 2006a). In addition, the emergence of mass tourism has facilitated greater mobility globally, and migration and tourism share a symbiotic relationship, as migration can stimulate tourist flows and tourism may facilitate both permanent and temporary migration and labour market needs in the destination country (Williams and Hall 2000; Hall and Williams 2002; Gössling and Schulz 2005; Hugo 2006a; Bedford and Ho 2006; Illés and Michalkó 2008).

Temporary and permanent migrant groups are not homogeneous entities and nor is labour migration a homogeneous process. The selection of migrants is shaped by the nature of political and economic relations between countries over time and the nature of the segmented labour market that migrant groups will be incorporated into. Skill, gender, race and ethnicity shape the migratory process and the migratory experience. Immigration policy criteria are shaped by how migration might impact socially and culturally on the host society, the skills the migrant will bring (especially in relation to the skills required by the host society), their economic contribution, whether they will be a burden on or present a risk to the state (criminality, political threat, threat to security). That is, immigration policy is by its very nature formulated along lines of national interest and is integral to how a nation seeks to reproduce and sustain itself.

Migration plays a major role in the international economic and political order (Castles and Miller 2003; Hugo 2004; Gustafson 2002; Williams and Hall 2000). The competition for both skilled and semi-skilled migrants takes place in a context of changing international political economy. Significant changes in international trading relationships, evidenced by an increasing number of free trade agreements and the establishment of common markets, mean that migratory labour relationships can serve many purposes within this wider context of neoliberalism, including the potential for economic leverage, economic development, the management of political relationships and the ability to address security through closer economic, social and political relations (Hugo 2004; Castles and Miller 2003; Hall 2005). Thus, we see the emergence of a range of policies regulating temporary migration and an increasing number of bilateral and multilateral policies/programmes that attempt to address a multitude of issues, including labour needs, economic development and sustainability and political stability between and across regions, under the guise of temporary migration programmes. This chapter analyses the nexus between temporary labour migration and tourism in the context of the New Zealand political economy.

The political economy of labour migration to New Zealand

New Zealand has been a country of permanent migration since the time of colonization and immigration has been central to New Zealand's economic and social development. The government's focus has therefore, at least until very recently, been dominated by a concern to attract and retain permanent settlers. Migratory flows since the time of colonial settlement have shaped immigration policy and the selection of dominant source countries. But although colonial ties continue to be important in the postcolonial era, increasingly shifts and changes in trading relationships, exclusion from some common markets, the need to establish new markets and the transition towards a knowledge-based economy have led to an increased awareness of the role that mobility can play in sustaining and developing New Zealand's economy in the twenty-first century. New Zealand has one of the highest per capita inflows of migrants and one of the highest outflows of citizens per capital out of the Organisation for Economic Co-operation and Development (OECD) countries (Department of Labour 2008).

New Zealand's colonial-derived connections to the Pacific shaped the earliest labour migration and work permit schemes (Spoonley 2006). Labour recruitment from the Polynesian Pacific (Samoa, the Cook Islands, Niue and Tokelau) in the post-WWII period and from Tonga and Fiji in the 1960s met both labour needs in the manufacturing sectors of the growing urban centres and also rural labour needs that emerged as a consequence of significant domestic rural–urban migration (Spoonley 2006; Levick and Bedford 1988; Gibson 1983; McPherson 1981). Various schemes involved recruiting semi-skilled or low-skilled workers from the Pacific. However, migration from the Pacific was vulnerable to economic downturn, changes in the nature of the domestic economy and political unrest in source countries and/or political expediency in New Zealand during a recession (Gibson 1983; McPherson 1981; Levick and Bedford 1988; Spoonley 2006). For instance, the South Pacific Work Permit scheme and the Pacific Islands Industrial Development scheme (both introduced in 1976) were measures taken by the state to curtail and formally regulate the movement of temporary labour from the

Pacific in a time of rising unemployment domestically (Gibson 1983). By 1987, a separate temporary work scheme with Fiji was terminated, in part as a reaction to domestic unemployment but also as a political sanction for the political unrest in Fiji at this time (Gibson 1983).

Early research focusing on the political economy of labour migration in New Zealand highlighted the nature of capitalist demand for certain kinds of workers in the post-World War II period (Spoonley 2006) and how immigrants (such as those from the Pacific providing low-cost labour) represented a more controllable labour force than domestic labour. The presence of migrants in the secondary labour market, undertaking low-paid work that is insecure, in which there is no progression and in which the work is often menial, contribute to the racialization of these workers (and also the end to those schemes that supported their entry once unemployment increased).

Local responses to global economic change

Changes in the global political economy and a global recession impacted on New Zealand's economy resulting in a period of significant social and economic change in the 1980s. The neoliberal centre-left (Labour) government responded by embarking on a course of radical social and economic restructuring that resulted in welfare reform, a transformation of the labour market and significant changes to immigration policy in this period (Spoonley 2006). The neoliberal policies ensured that many state functions were privatized in this period and that measures that had once offered protection of domestic industry and/or ownership of industry were reduced or removed (Spoonley 2006). Increasing emphasis was placed on reducing production costs, in particular labour costs, and on the necessity for New Zealand industry to become internationally competitive. By mid-1985, unemployment had risen to 6 per cent with significant job losses occurring in manufacturing, and temporary migrant worker schemes with the Pacific were cancelled. Neoliberalization continued under a conservative (National) government in the period 1990–1999. Workers experienced increasing insecurity with respect to paid employment and fundamental changes occurred to workplace agreements. The state had previously taken a central role in regulating the labour market, ensuring that workers were both represented by and party to collective national agreements. The introduction of the Employment Contracts Act 1991 substantially undermined national worker representation and the workforce union membership fell from 42.3 per cent in 1991 to 17.7 per cent in 2001. Consequently, employers gained greater control over the cost of labour (Spoonley 2006). Flexibility became a central concern of employers vulnerable to shifts in domestic and international demand and with this came an increase in 'non-standard' work, that is, casual, part-time, temporary, fixed-term, multiple job holders and own-account self-employed (Spoonley 2006). These changes ensured that by the 2000s the New Zealand labour market was more receptive not only to engaging temporary workers, but also to meeting skill shortages through temporary migration. Accordingly, the distinction between temporary and permanent migration is being applied increasingly less rigorously by policy-makers as they acknowledge that permanent migration can be facilitated by temporary migration (Bedford and Ho 2006; Bedford 2006; Spoonley and Bedford 2008).

Whilst the labour market was undergoing significant change in the 1980s and 1990s, the new economic conditions led to significant revisions of immigration policy in 1986 and in 1991. In 1986, preferential source countries were removed and selection criteria changed to facilitate the transition to a knowledge-based economy with an increased focus on the need for skilled labour (Bedford and Ho 2006; Spoonley 2006). The removal of preferred source countries was also in part a move to allow for developing relationships with potentially significant trading partners in Asia (Spoonley 2006). In this period, immigration addressed labour market demand for skilled labour, shortages driven by an ageing population and inadequate levels of skill and capital for investment, and helped to establish relations with a number of Asian states.

The labour market outcomes for immigrants in this period were problematic; many skilled migrants encountered problems gaining entry into the labour market and experienced gatekeeping over the recognition of qualifications and there is evidence that immigrants were earning lower incomes than New Zealanders in all age brackets (Boyd 2003). A growing body of research revealed that many skilled migrants were experiencing unemployment and under-employment and in some cases this led to return migration (Henderson *et al.* 2001; Fletcher 1999). More generally, there were significant settlement issues for these new migrants (Ho *et al.* 1997, 2000). One of the principal difficulties that New Zealand faced was securing skilled migrants with strong English language communication skills and the qualifications and experience necessary for the local labour market. However, it should also be noted that there were problems with respect to how New Zealand was responding as a host society to skilled migrants from a range of source countries. At this time insufficient attention was paid to how structural inequities in the host society shape migrant experiences and labour market outcomes (Lovelock and Trlin 2007; Spoonley 2006).

In response to some of these outcomes, a human capital model of skilled migration was introduced in 1991, and New Zealand joined what Hugo (2006a) has called the 'global quest for talent'. A national points system served as a regulator of national labour and capital requirements (Spoonley and Bedford 2008). Employability, age and settlement factors, including a minimum standard of English, served as selection criteria and further revisions in 1995 granted points for New Zealand work experience. These changes ensured that a symbiotic relationship between temporary and permanent migration was established in policy, with previous work experience in New Zealand facilitated through a range of temporary work permit provisions, including the Working Holiday Maker (WHM) scheme.

Policy development in New Zealand in the 2000s has continued to be demand-focused, in which local labour market considerations are at the forefront and temporary migrants are increasingly meeting skill shortages in a number of sectors and regions (Spoonley and Bedford 2008). In 2002 a number of specific 'talent' visas were introduced and, in 2007, policy revisions continued to emphasize the need for skills and securing 'talent' and labour, whilst maintaining border security, as the primary objectives of contemporary immigration policy (Department of Labour 2008). Temporary and permanent migration address skill shortages that constrain economic growth. No longer considered dichotomous, temporary migration is now an acknowledged important precursor for permanent migration, allowing both the state and the migrant to assess migration suitability, to meet labour market demand, especially demand generated seasonally, and to undertake the necessary New Zealand-based work experience that will facilitate continued employability in the New Zealand labour market should the temporary migrant seek permanency.

Temporary migration schemes

In the last twenty years, countries of immigration have been seeking a range of skills to address specific labour market needs and there has been an increasing shift towards using temporary migrant schemes and/or temporary work permits. Arguably, temporary migrant schemes have until recently been the preserve of the semi-skilled, labelled variously as seasonal work schemes, guest worker schemes and/or foreign worker schemes and therefore intended to target workers from developing countries. Increasingly, we now find the emergence of temporary migrant worker schemes that target skilled, young workers (aged eighteen to thirty years) from developed nations and/or those from countries with which significant trading relationships exist or are being developed, co-existing with temporary migrant schemes that target business migrants with capital to invest.

Temporary migration and temporary work permits have always been a feature of immigration policy in New Zealand (Bedford 2006), as most movements into and out of New Zealand are short term. In 2008/2009, for instance, 1.4 million people were granted temporary visas to visit, study or work in New Zealand (Department of Labour 2009). The Working Holiday Maker scheme is relatively recent, but it nonetheless sits amongst a range of other temporary migration and work permit provisions that have aimed to address various labour market shortages over time. As is the case internationally, temporary migration has become an increasingly important component of the immigration programme in New Zealand and a range of programmes are currently addressing a range of labour market needs and other contemporary social, economic and political objectives (Bedford 2006; Bedford and Ho 2006; Birrell *et al.* 2006; Lovelock and Leopold 2009).

Tourism, agriculture and seasonal labour demands

Both the tourism and agricultural sectors have experienced significant labour shortages over the last two decades. Tourism and agriculture are significant industries in New Zealand and both sectors represent a powerful lobby for labour shortages to be addressed through immigration.

The aforementioned global changes in migratory flows and their relation to the internationalization of labour markets and shifts in immigration policy have been accompanied by a growth in tourism, the internationalization of tourist markets and the emergence of mass tourism as a significant global and local industry (Williams and Hall 2000; Hall and Williams 2002). In New Zealand, the tourism industry has generated demand for labour and has also facilitated migratory flows, both temporary and permanent. The interdependencies between tourism and migration are not new, but there have been significant shifts in both the scope and the scale of relations between the two forms of mobility. Tourism has increasingly become an important component of economic and regional unions and underpins and often invites formal economic relations (Hall and Williams 2002). For example, reducing barriers to tourism has been identified as a priority for Asia-Pacific Economic Cooperation (APEC) since the 1990s. Changes in both local and international labour markets has had implications for the tourism migration nexus (Williams and Hall 2000). The tourism industry itself offers careers (both skilled and semi-skilled) that are transnational and, in turn, these labour migrations can facilitate visits from family and friends, thus stimulating further tourism (VFR tourism) and the potential for permanent settlement.

The rise of tourism has impacted differentially on regional economies in New Zealand and increasingly local authorities engage in migrant labour recruitment to address regional economic development (Spoonley and Bedford 2008). As an industry, tourism has been influential in lobbying the state over labour shortages and the need to facilitate labour migration on a temporary and seasonal basis (Newlands 2006).

Agriculture remains New Zealand's most important primary industry, contributing 60 per cent of export earnings and employing approximately 9 per cent of the labour force (Statistics New Zealand 2009). Changes in the agricultural sector over the last two decades have seen conversion of pastoral land into horticultural and viticultural production. The introduction of labour-intensive crops such as grapes, avocados, kiwi fruit and asparagus has generated increasing demands for seasonal labour (Lovelock and Leopold 2009; Ramasamy *et al.* 2008). Rural New Zealand has been experiencing significant depopulation over the last thirty years and, as is the case generally, the local labour pool is ageing. These demographic drivers have contributed to the current labour shortage in rural New Zealand.

New Zealand's export economy has been growing over the last two decades, with the strongest growth period being between 1999 and 2008, enhanced by the agricultural sector and market conditions, including a stable labour market and well-priced export commodities (Treasury 2009). Agriculture, manufacturing and the service sectors – within which the tourism industry is a significant player – form the foundation of New Zealand's economy. The value of export crops from horticulture is approximately NZ$3.0 billion per annum and the total gross value from agriculture in 2008 was NZ$23 billion (MAF 2009).

New Zealand's economy is, however, vulnerable to changes in international commodity prices and global economic conditions and trends. Thus, although New Zealand has experienced a period of growth and stability, the current global recession is having an impact on the local economy and labour market (Department of Labour 2009). Unemployment has risen to 4.7 per cent and many of the temporary migrant schemes in New Zealand are subject to the proviso that New Zealanders will be given employment preference in times of unemployment (Department of Labour 2009). However, until very recently there has been a sustained expansion in provisions for temporary migration and work permits and a growth in the number of bilateral agreements facilitating the movement of temporary labour required to address the seasonal demands from both the agricultural and the tourism sectors in New Zealand. This labour migration is significant not only in that it reduces labour market shortages, but also because bringing in human capital can arrest wage inflation pressures that arise from shortages and ultimately reduce the cost of labour for employers (Hall and Williams 2002). Further, labour migration also assists in the reproduction of tourism capital, through its circular relation with migration – in which intergenerational VFR tourism invariably follows labour migration and can also potentially facilitate permanent migration (Hall and Williams 2002) or return migration (Illés and Michalkó 2008).

More recent temporary labour migration schemes

The most recent scheme targeting low or semi-skilled workers is the Recognized Seasonal Employer (RSE) Work Policy, which was introduced in 2007. The RSE is a temporary migration policy that specifically addresses labour shortages in agriculture, horticulture and viticulture and targets workers from Pacific Forum states. The policy initially included five countries, Kiribati, Tuvalu, Vanuatu, Samoa and Tonga, and most recently also includes the Solomon Islands (Ramasamy *et al.* 2008; Lovelock and Leopold 2009). This policy is not solely about recruiting labour from the Pacific to address labour shortages in New Zealand; it is also about addressing development issues in the region – attempting to assist in the alleviation of poverty in the Pacific – and is illustrative of a trend towards policies that, although pivoting on migration, address demographic and development issues regionally. The Pacific has historically been a source of semi- or low-skilled labour for New Zealand and New Zealand has been and continues to be engaged in a number of development initiatives and the provision of aid in the Pacific. Pacific Forum states have comparatively high fertility rates and a surplus of labour in addition to development needs. This policy facilitates remittance transfer back to those states that participate, and labour opportunities for young workers from the Pacific (Ramasamy *et al.* 2008; Lovelock and Leopold 2009). The RSE policy is an example of a policy that attempts to address the alleviation of regional poverty via cooperation and collaboration whilst also addressing seasonal labour needs in New Zealand (Lovelock and Leopold 2009).

The RSE scheme facilitates the transfer of labour and capital between rural New Zealand and rural communities in the Pacific, but importantly there is no intention on the part of the state to encourage permanent settlement for these migrants in New Zealand. The workers are semi-skilled and are remitting income home to alleviate rural poverty (Ramasamy *et al.* 2008; Lovelock and Leopold 2009). In this respect, both the level of skill and the fixed temporary nature of this migration ensures that the RSE policy differs markedly from the Working Holiday Maker scheme and its various programmes, which also facilitates the entry of temporary labour to address seasonal demands in New Zealand but in which the door to residency or permanency remains open, the workers are often skilled but taking up semi-skilled work, and remittance of income is not a feature of this form of mobility.

The Working Holiday Maker scheme

The Working Holiday Maker scheme provides entry and the ability to temporarily work in New Zealand. The WHM targets young tourists (aged eighteen to thirty years of age) from a wide range of countries who are invariably skilled and who will take up work in unskilled or low-skilled occupations on a temporary basis (not usually more than twelve months) while travelling in New Zealand (Department of Labour 2008). WHMs must have sufficient funds to support themselves while in New Zealand and have a return ticket. Under this scheme working is secondary to learning about New Zealand culture (hence the requirement for sufficient funds) and nearly all of the programmes are bilateral, allowing young New Zealanders to also be WHMs whilst abroad.

Amidst the reforms of the mid- to late 1980s, the first Working Holiday Maker scheme was initiated with Japan in 1985. In 1997 the programme with Japan involved the provision of 4,000 entry permits. In June 2000 the WHM quota was increased from 10,000 to 20,000 places per annum and included nine programmes. From 2000 regular increases in quotas ensured that by 2008 there were WHM programmes with twenty-seven countries and up to 50,000 places available (Department of Labour 2008). The regional scope includes North America, Latin America, Western Europe, the transitional economies of Eastern Europe, South-East Asia and Asia. In the 2007/2008 period, the largest numbers of WHMs came from the United Kingdom (27 per cent) and Germany (17 per cent). During 2007/2008, 34,890 WHMs were approved entry through the various programmes and 52 per cent of the permits issued were to women.

In 2003, the Department of Labour conducted a review of the WHM scheme. The review concluded that in a time of full employment the scheme had had little negative impact on local labour markets and that the WHMs had made a positive contribution to the communities they had worked in, taking up employment that could not be filled locally and meeting seasonal need (Department of Labour 2004).

In 2005, the tuberculosis screening policy was extended to include WHMs who intended to stay in New Zealand for 6 months or longer. Medical screenings for all categories of migrants were also introduced in late 2005. The health screening requirements evidence the challenge to welfarism that international migration can provoke when health care is primarily provided for by the state.

Most of the WHM programmes are bilateral and have time restrictions on the length of stay, usually twelve months. There is some variance between individual programmes and the programme with the United States is the only unilateral programme (Department of Labour 2008). There are no caps on the programmes with Germany, the Netherlands, Sweden and the United Kingdom, and those from the

United Kingdom are able to stay for up to two years. Some of the work restrictions were also eased in 2005, which allowed holidaymakers from Belgium, the Netherlands, Sweden and the United States to work for up to twelve months with the same employer.

A number of the more recent programmes have included mutual voting rights, in both local and national elections. This is a significant and interesting provision as it addresses one of the central concerns that many have had over temporary migration and the lack of rights that are characteristic of many guest worker schemes (Martin 2006). Such an inclusion suggests that for these temporary migrants the state is open to embracing them as potential (or actual) citizens, when foreign worker schemes exclude participation in those areas typically the preserve of citizens or permanent residents, for example political processes and positions and/or access to state welfarism (Freeman 1998). Although all temporary workers in New Zealand have access to health care and are protected under national labour legislation, not all temporary workers in New Zealand have voting rights.

The intention behind the WHM has changed little over the last two decades. The functional emphasis of the scheme is to mutually assist young tourists to work while holidaying abroad. The main objective is to strengthen links internationally, foster cultural understanding and goodwill and address short-term labour shortages in New Zealand. More recently, provisions have been made to allow for WHMs to study for up to six months while they reside in New Zealand (Newlands 2006; Tucker 2003). There is also widespread acknowledgement that this scheme, as with other temporary labour schemes, can facilitate the permanent migration of skilled workers (Department of Labour 2005, 2006, 2007, 2008; Bedford 2006; Birrell *et al.* 2006). Compared with other temporary permit holders however, only 2 per cent of those who choose to become permanent residents in New Zealand have entered the country through the WHM scheme (Department of Labour 2008). Nonetheless, policy-makers have responded to this potentiality by facilitating the transition between a temporary permit status and a permanent resident status (Department of Labour 2008, Bedford 2006).

The changes in the WHM scheme over the last two decades have primarily involved expanding the number of programmes and agreements with an increasingly wide range of participant countries and a dramatic increase in the quotas. With respect to the latter, this was largely achieved by significant pressure being applied by tourism, agriculture and horticulture industry lobby groups (Newlands 2006). Although these tourists meet labour shortages in tourism, agriculture, horticulture and viticulture they also contribute to the local economy. Newlands' (2006) research revealed that WHMs travel extensively while they are in New Zealand and visit not only the main centres but also the regions. They usually arrive in New Zealand with more money than they are required to and spend all or more than they have. This research found that the social effects were positive for both the WHM and the communities that they resided in and that there were specific benefits including immediate and potentially long-term VFR tourism. Most of the WHMs earned very modest incomes, tended to work in lower-paid occupations and, in some instances, were being paid less than the minimum wage

(Newlands 2006). WHMs also contribute to New Zealand through individual income tax and Goods and Services Tax paid on goods and services purchased while they are here.

A critical appraisal of the WHM policy formation process by Newlands (2006) revealed that it was driven largely by government institutions (Ministry of Tourism, Ministry of Foreign Affairs and Trade and Development, Ministry of Labour) and mostly negotiated by the Ministry of Foreign Affairs and Trade, behind closed doors. In most cases it took several years to reach agreement over the nature of the bilateral agreement. In addition to this, industry lobby groups (from tourism, agriculture, horticulture and viticulture) had considerable impact on the extension of quotas and the expansion of WHM scheme programmes, but beyond these entities there was no systematic consultation with other stakeholder groups. There has also been little in the way of measuring the social and economic contribution made by WHMs and, with the exception of Newlands' (2006) research, no policy review or account of outcomes has been undertaken for these migrants.

The WHMs in New Zealand are often well educated and are prepared to take work that requires a low level of skill. In New Zealand they are not predominantly English speaking (as a first language), they have usually travelled extensively and most are primarily motivated by the desire to live and understand the culture and society more fully. Although some would like to earn more while in New Zealand so they can meet the high costs of accommodation in the areas where they work, for most making money is not their first priority (Newlands 2006; Harding and Webster 2002).

Of course, these WHMs are not only meeting labour shortages in tourism, agriculture, horticulture and viticulture in a number of regions throughout New Zealand, and are prepared to take on low- or semi-skilled work for modest remuneration or at times less than the minimum wage, they are also potentially permanent residents, can also potentially become students and are also young tourists. All of these characteristics ensure that a particular kind of political economy is operating with respect to these temporary migrants; both with respect to immigration objectives but also with respect to two of New Zealand's largest industries: agriculture and tourism.

Conclusion

The WHM scheme illustrates that immigration is not an autonomous process unrelated to other international processes (Hugo 2006a: 126). Indeed, pre-existing trade and migratory flows and the desire to establish new trade and migratory flows are precursors to these programmes and ensure a flow of people that not only assist with labour but also contribute to the productive and consumptive requirements of advanced capitalism in the twenty-first century. It is no accident that the bilateral programmes that New Zealand is party to are with significant countries of migration, significant source countries for tourism, significant destination countries for our agricultural products and/or investment in agriculture and potentially significant source countries for permanent migration and future markets for our agricultural products.

New Zealand is committed to facilitating the liberalization of trade through a number of regional, bilateral and multilateral trade agreements (Ministry of Foreign Affairs and Trade 2009). The WHM programmes complement such agreements and are often a part of establishing explicit 'people'-related interactions or cultural exchanges. Thus, since the 1980s, New Zealand has entered into the following trade agreements: Closer Economic Relations with Australia (1983); New Zealand and Singapore Closer Economic Partnership (2001); Trans-Pacific Strategic Economic Partnership (Trans-Pacific SEP) (2005); New Zealand–China Free Trade Agreement (NZ-China FTA) (2008); and ASEAN – Australia/New Zealand Free Trade Area (currently signed but not yet in force) (New Zealand Foreign Affairs and Trade 2009). In 2000, New Zealand also introduced the Latin American Strategy, which has involved various trade agreements with countries in Latin America and the establishment of 'people links' both through export education and various programmes under the WHM scheme. New Zealand has also become a significant investor in the agricultural sectors of both Brazil and Argentina. There are a range of agreements currently under negotiation with Malaysia, the Gulf Co-operation Council and Hong Kong; a proposed expansion of the Trans-Pacific Strategic Economic Partnership; an agreement with Korea; and the commencement of negotiations with India and Japan.

Further, the bilateral nature of the vast majority of WHM programmes demonstrates considerable commonality between countries in terms of labour needs and productive and consumptive practices in an increasingly globalized world. This said, it is important not to suggest that the interests of capital are all determining, as the motivations and actions of individuals and groups must also be factored into any consideration of the political economy of this form of mobility. Newlands' (2006) research suggests considerable parity between the policy objectives and what working holidaymakers seek and expect while holidaying and working in New Zealand.

The WHMs are young tourists who are generally well educated and middle class (or aspiring middle class). Uriely's (2001) research demonstrates that taking up unskilled work, extra-ordinary work and/or unpaid work is part of the tourist experience for the young, largely middle-class, well-educated tourist. These labour migrants are not working to remit back home or to alleviate poverty in their country of origin. Although the work is low paid it allows them to meet certain kinds of touristic objectives, in which experiencing a different society is paramount and an 'authentic' experience is sought. The 'authentic experience' is defined as not being treated like a tourist, but as a friend or equal, and is one in which engagement with locals in their locales is central (Pearce 1982). Similarly, seasonal retirement migrants have claimed that their access and knowledge of the authentic makes them unlike tourists and enables them to differentiate themselves from such (Gustafson 2002). It is possible that work facilitates an authentic experience (Clarke 2004), as once engaged in the productive process, as well as the consumptive, these labour migrants in some sense cease to be pure tourists, or at least the boundaries become blurred. Instead they embark on a transition towards being members of the society that they are now in, and where, through working, they are simultaneously engaged in generating a product that they will metaphorically consume – 'experience' – or at least embody.

Interestingly, the tourism sector in New Zealand, although facing labour shortages, does not want large numbers of foreigners working in service delivery (Newlands 2006). This is primarily because it can undermine the tourist experience; many tourists want to have a 'Kiwi' experience and to meet and/or encounter New Zealanders while they consume New Zealand (Newlands 2006; Hall and Williams 2002). For this reason, there is a greater emphasis placed on the role that WHMs can play with respect to seasonal shortages in agriculture, which in turn stimulates regional development and tourism in these areas.

WHM schemes appear to provide a more authentic tourist experience, allow young tourists to gain work experience in New Zealand, facilitate VFR tourism and also meet seasonal labour shortages in primary industry. In addition they offer the possibility of export education revenue and/or permanent migration or residence and an ongoing contribution to the New Zealand economy. Furthermore, WHMs, as educated and predominantly middle-class temporary migrants, do not present a threat to border security and/or unwanted long-term illegal migration; indeed they are the class of migrant that New Zealand is seeking to recruit through its various policies. Although their rates of pay are low and their presence protects against wage inflation and reduces production costs, it is difficult to maintain an argument that they are exploited in quite the same way as other classes of temporary migrants engaged in semi-skilled work. Comparatively they occupy a privileged niche.

It might, however, be argued that WHM schemes allow developed nations and developing nations with significant market potential to secure skill and to reproduce and perpetuate advantage and, thus, in some ways, such schemes can potentially contribute to the uneven distribution of resources (especially human capital) and uneven development globally. That is, although we do live in an age of increased mobility, the vast majority of the world's inhabitants do not travel or migrate internationally (Hall and Williams 2002). Furthermore, not all tourists or migrants travel the same pathways or experience the same outcomes.

The future of WHM schemes, the recession and rising unemployment in New Zealand

The growth of programmes under the WHM scheme has occurred during a time of economic prosperity in which New Zealand's economy has been strong and unemployment low. The global economic downturn since 2008 has affected the New Zealand economy and the local labour market. There are constraints on credit, falling house prices, decreases in consumption, decreases in commodity prices and a falling exchange rate (Department of Labour 2009). This has had a number of implications for the labour market, with job growth stalling and unemployment rising to a five-year high at 4.7 per cent (Statistics New Zealand 2009).

There have been decreases in employment opportunities in the café and restaurant industry and also in the accommodation sector. Employment losses in agriculture in the first six months of 2009 have also been significant. The labour market is expected to weaken further throughout 2009. In addition there has been a decline in the number of tourists coming to New Zealand, with visitor arrivals down by 3 per cent in the period from October 2007 to October 2008. This has had implications for temporary workers, with a slowing in the rate of applications for visas for temporary work. If unemployment continues to increase there will be a return to the employment of New Zealanders in those sectors that have until recently employed temporary migrant labour. Yet despite these changes, it has also been predicted that there will remain a demand for labour in a number of sectors (Department of Labour 2008).

It is clearly in New Zealand's long-term interest to maintain a flow of WHMs and other classes of skilled/young tourist–student–labour migrants in as much as they simultaneously address and arguably serve a number of political and economic objectives and priorities for New Zealand. Nonetheless, it remains to be seen whether the historic precedent of ending such schemes in times of rising and high unemployment will be repeated with the WHM scheme and whether all programmes will be affected in the same way.

References

Bedford, R. (2006) 'Skilled migration in and out of New Zealand: Immigrants, workers, students and emigrants', in B. Birrell, L. Hawthorne and S. Richardson (eds) *Evaluation of the General Skilled Migration Categories*, Canberra: Commonwealth of Australia.

Bedford, R. and Ho, E. (2006) 'Immigration futures: New Zealand in a global context', *New Zealand Population Review*, 32: 49–63.

Bell, M. and Ward, G. (2000) 'Comparing temporary mobility with permanent migration', *Tourism Geographies*, 2: 87–107.

Bianchi, R. V. (2000) 'Migrant tourist-workers: Exploring the "contact zones" of post-industrial tourism', *Current Issues in Tourism*, 3: 107–137.

Birrell, B. (2000) 'Information technology and Australia's immigration program: Is Australia doing enough?', *People and Place*, 8: 77–84.

Birrell, B., Hawthorne, L. and Richardson, S. (2006) 'International approaches to skilled migration', in B. Birrell, L. Hawthorne and S. Richardson (eds) *Evaluation of the General Skilled Migration Categories*, Canberra: Commonwealth of Australia.

Boyd, C. (2003). 'Migrants in New Zealand: An analysis of labour market outcomes for working-aged migrants using 1996 and 2001 census data'. Online. Available at http://www.dol.govt.nz/publication-view.asp?ID=140 (accessed 7 March 2010).

Castles, S. and Miller, M. J. (2003) *The Age of Migration: International population movements in the modern world*, New York: Guilford Press.

Clarke, N. (2004) 'Free independent travelers? British working holiday makers in Australia', *Transactions of the Institute of British Geographers*, 29: 499–509.

Coles, T. and Timothy D. J. (2004) 'My field is the world': Conceptualising diasporas, travel and tourism', in T. Coles and D. J. Timothy (eds) *Tourism, Diasporas and Space*, Abingdon: Routledge.

Department of Labour (2004) 'Working holidaymakers in New Zealand'. Online. Available at http://www.immigration.govt.nz/NR/rdonlyres/74371547-318C-4F35-9FF9-BA5619BDF719/0/WorkingHolidaymakersinNewZealand.pdf (accessed 7 March 2010).

Department of Labour (2005) 'Migration trends/outlook 2004/2005'. Online. Available at http://www.immigration.govt.nz/migrant/general/generalinformation/research/migtrendsoutlookarchive.htm (accessed 7 March 2010).

Department of Labour (2006) 'Migration trends/outlook 2005/06'. Online. Available at http://www.immigration.govt.nz/migrant/general/generalinformation/research/migtrendsoutlookarchive.htm (accessed 7 March 2010).

Department of Labour (2007) 'Migration trends/outlook 2006/07'. Online. Available at http://www.immigration.govt.nz/migrant/general/generalinformation/research/migtrendsoutlookarchive.htm (accessed 7 March 2010).

Department of Labour (2008) 'Migration trends/outlook 2007/08'. Online. Available at http://www.immigration.govt.nz/migrant/general/generalinformation/research/migtrendsoutlookarchive.htm (accessed 7 March 2010).

Department of Labour (2009) 'Migration trends/outlook 2008/2009'. Online. Available at http://www.immigration.govt.nz/research (accessed 7 March 2010).

Fletcher, M. (1999) *Migrant Settlement: A review of the literature and its relevance to New Zealand*, Wellington: New Zealand Immigration Service.

Freeman, G. P. (1998) 'Migration and the political economy of the welfare state', *Annals of the American Academy of Political and Social Science*, 485: 51–63.

Gibson, K. D. (1983) 'Political economy and international labour migration: The case of Polynesians in New Zealand', *New Zealand Geographer*, April, pp. 29–42.

Gössling, S. and Schulz, U. (2005) 'Tourism-related migration in Zansibar, Tanzania', *Tourism Geographies*, 7: 43–62.

Gustafson, P. (2002) 'Tourism and seasonal retirement migration', *Annals of Tourism Research*, 29: 899–918.

Hall, C. M. (2005) *Tourism: Rethinking the social science of mobility*, Harlow: Pearson Education.

Hall, C. M. and Williams, A. M. (2002) *Tourism and Migration: New relationships between production and consumption*, Dordrecht: Kluwer Academic Publishers.

Harding, G. and Webster, E. (2002) *The Working Holiday Maker Scheme and the Australian Labour Market*, Melbourne: Melbourne Institute of Applied Economic and Social Research, University of Melbourne.

Henderson, A., Trlin, A. and Watts, N. (2001) 'Squandered skills? The employment problems of skilled Chinese immigrants in New Zealand', in R. Starr (ed.) *Asian Nationalism in an Age of Globalization*, Richmond: Curzon Press.

Heuman, D. (2005) 'Hospitality and reciprocity: Working tourists in Dominica', *Annals of Tourism Research*, 32: 407–418.

Ho, E., Bedford, R. and Goodwin, J. (1997) 'Astronaut families: A contemporary migration phenomenon', in W. Friesen and M. Ip (eds) *East Asian New Zealanders: Research on new migrants*, Aotearoa/New Zealand Migration Research Network Research Paper, Auckland: Massey University, Albany Campus.

Ho, E., Cheung, E., Bedford, C. and Leung, P. (2000) *Settlement Assistance Needs of Recent Migrants*, Wellingtion: New Zealand Immigration Service.

Hugo, G. (2004) 'Future immigration policy development in Australia and New Zealand', *New Zealand Population Review*, 30: 23–42.

Hugo, G. (2006a) 'Globalization and changes in Australian international migration', *Journal of Population Research*, 23: 107–133.

Hugo, G. (2006b) 'Temporary migration and the labour market in Australia', Australian Geographer, 37: 211–231.

Illés, S. and Michalkó, G. (2008) 'Relationships between international tourism and migration in Hungary: Tourism flows and foreign property ownership', *Tourism Geographies*, 10: 98–118.

Iredale, R. (2000) 'Migration policies for the highly skilled in the Asia-Pacific Region', *International Migration Review*, 34: 882–906.

Levick, W. and Bedford, R. (1988) 'Fiji labour migration to New Zealand in the 1980s', *New Zealand Geographer*, April, pp. 14–21.

Lovelock, K. and Trlin, A. (2007) *Voluntary Associations and Immigrants: A survey of host society associations in Auckland and Wellington*, Palmerston North: New Settlers Programme, Massey University.

Lovelock, K. and Leopold, T. (2009) 'Labour force shortages in rural New Zealand: Temporary migration and the Recognised Seasonal Employer (RSE) Work Policy', *New Zealand Population Review*, 33/34: 213–234.

McPherson, C. (1981) 'Guest-worker movements and their consequences for donor and recipient countries: A case study', in G. W. Jones and H. V. Richter (eds) *Population Mobility and Development: Southeast Asia and the Pacific*, Canberra: Development Studies Centre, Australian National University.

Martin, P. (2006) 'Managing labor migration: Temporary worker programmes For the 21st Century', paper presented at International Symposium on International Migration and Development, Turin, September.

Martin, P. (2008) 'Low and semi-skilled workers abroad', in International Organisation of Migration (ed.) *World Migration 2008, Managing Labour Mobility in the Evolving Global Economy*, Geneva: International Organisation of Migration.

Ministry of Agriculture and Fisheries (MAF) (2009) 'MAF statistics: International trade'. Online. Available at http://www.maf.govt.nz/statistics/international-trade/ (accessed 29 March 2010).

Ministry of Foreign Affairs and Trade (2009) 'Trade and economic relations'. Online. Available at http://www.mfat.govt.nz/Trade-and-Economic-Relations/index.php (accessed 7 March 2010).

Newlands, K. J. (2006) 'The modern nomad in New Zealand: A study of the effects of the Working Holiday Schemes on free independent travelers and their host communities', unpublished thesis, Auckland University.

Pearce, P. (1982) *The Social Psychology of Tourist Behaviour*, Oxford: Pergamon.

Ramasamy, S., Krishnana, V., Bedford, R. and Bedford, C. (2008) 'The Recognised Seasonal Employer Policy: Seeking the elusive triple wins for development through international migration', *Pacific Economic Bulletin*, 23: 171–186.

Spoonley, P. (2006) 'A contemporary political economy of labour migration in New Zealand', *Tijdschrift voor Economische en Sociale Geografie*, 97: 17–25.

Spoonley, P. and Bedford, R. (2008) 'Responding to regional labour demand: International migration and labour markets in New Zealand's regions', *International Migration and Integration*, 9: 203–223.

Statistics New Zealand (2009) 'Agricultural production statistics: June 2009 (provisional)'. Online. Available at http://www.stats.govt.nz/browse_for_stats/industry_sectors/agriculture/agriculturalproduction_hotpjun09prov.aspx (accessed 29 March 2010).

The Treasury (2009) 'New Zealand – Economic and Financial Overview'. Online. Available at http://www.nzdmo.govt.nz/publications/nzefo (accessed 7 March 2010).

Truly, D. (2002) 'International retirement migration and tourism along the Lake Chapala Riviera: Developing a matrix of retirement migration behavior', *Tourism Geographies*, 4: 261–281.

Tucker, E. (2003) 'Maximising outcomes from the Working Holiday Schemes', Cabinet Policy Committee Paper POL (03) 353. Unpublished.

Uriely, N. (2001) ' "Travelling workers" and "Working tourists": Variations across the interaction between work and tourism', *International Journal of Tourism Research*, 3: 1–8.

Williams, A. M. and Hall, C. M. (2000) 'Tourism and migration: New relationships between production and consumption', *Tourism Geographies*, 2: 5–27.

10 Changing power relations

Foreign direct investment in Zanzibar

Dorothea Meyer

The traditional Marxist-inspired political economy approach to tourism offers a critical debate related to the role of international capital and power, and in particular the control of the 'North' over the 'South'. Tourism is often viewed as exemplifying these political and economic structures whereby Northern-based corporations influence the tourism development in the South with little if no power given to destinations to steer their own development (e.g. Britton 1982).

However, an increasingly complex geography of tourism production, distribution and consumption has emerged that seems to question the seemingly straightforward North–South polarity. Within the discussion of international power structures and dependency debates, foreign direct investment (FDI) is frequently viewed as a key culprit in developing and maintaining dependency relationships, which are said to be detrimental to development aspirations of developing countries. A common focus is on so-called 'leakages' and it is often argued that these leakages are considerably higher when foreign-owned companies are involved; similarly, it is often claimed that the percentage of expatriate labour is considerably higher in Northern-owned enterprises operating in the South.

The analysis of power has been at the heart of the political economy used in tourism. Bianchi (2002: 265) stresses the importance of the 'systemic sources of power which serve to reproduce and condition different modes of tourism development'. According to Bianchi capital restructuring and economic globalization have resulted in a changing configuration within the tourism production system, thus requiring a detailed examination of relationships between all of the actors in the system in order to unveil the impacts of the transnationalization of the tourism system.

This chapter will use a multidisciplinary approach that borrows ideas from Wallerstein (1979) by focusing on power relationships within the world capitalist system, and in particular on how 'centres of power' emerge and change over time and influence tourism development in developing countries. This chapter aims to revitalise discussions related to FDI in tourism by focusing in on the macro and meso levels impacting on tourism development in Zanzibar (Tanzania) by emphasizing an apparent power shift and the role of South–South investment.

The political economy of foreign direct investment (FDI) in tourism

Since the 1960s, international tourism has been promoted as a major component of economic development for many economically less developed countries (OECD 1967; WTO 2004) and is seen as a 'passport to development' (De Kadt 1979). Tourism is commonly used as a tool to stimulate marginal economies and to act as a catalyst for national and regional development, bringing employment, foreign exchange earnings, balance of payments advantages and important infrastructure developments (Roche 1992; Pearce 1989; Coccossis and Parpairis 1995; Wahab and Pigram 1997). Indeed, most countries are now tourist destinations and many 'regard tourism as an important and integral aspect of their development policies' (Jenkins 1991: 61). More cynically, perhaps, for some countries tourism represents the only realistic development option and foreign exchange generator (Brown 1998).

Much of the tourism literature in the 1980s identified the terms of international trade and the power of foreign investors as structures and agents of dependency, which were viewed as inhibiting national development or at least threatening national control over the development process (e.g. Bryden 1973; Turner and Ash 1975; Britton 1982). Clancy (1999) argues that early calls for encouraging tourism exports were based on modernization assumptions. The economic benefits associated with tourism, that is, employment creation, foreign exchange earnings, government revenues, the establishment of forwards and backwards linkages, and income and employment multipliers, were emphasized by policy-makers as well as by academics (Lea 1988; Matthews 1978; Pearce 1989). However, Britton (1982) maintains that tourism's economic benefits were often overstated and he contends that destinations are frequently dependent on Northern-based transnational corporations (TNCs), which control much of transport, accommodation and the packaged tourism products.

The dependency paradigm gained prominence when it became apparent that tourism did not necessarily act as the development agent it promised to be (Oppermann and Chon 1997). The multiplier effects of tourism in developing countries were considerably less than expected, while the international orientation and organization of mass tourism required high investment costs and led to a high dependency on foreign capital, skills and management personnel (Bryden 1973; Müller 1984; Östreich 1977; Pavaskar 1982; Oppermann and Chon 1997). It is estimated that leakages are increased with the involvement of TNCs based in the generating countries and a very general estimate for developing countries puts the amount of leakages as high as 40 per cent (Diaz Benevides 2001).

The political economy approach to the study of tourism development in economically less developed countries traditionally focuses on the systemic sources of power that serve to reproduce and condition tourism development. The aim is to understand the structure and dynamics of tourism development with an emphasis on power relations resulting in uneven bargaining powers and unequal material interests of different classes, or, as Bianchi (2002: 266) put it, 'on the antagonistic relationships between capital and labour'. For the study of tourism in economically less developed countries, the emphasis has been on the systemic causes of poverty and inequality within destinations and between the 'core' and the 'periphery' (Cox 1987; Sherman 1987; Strange 1994). Freitag (1994) sees correlations between traditional agricultural production and the tourism industry, both supporting an 'enclave pattern of development', while Finney and Watson (1975) term tourism the 'new kind of sugar'. According to Britton (1982: 336) this enclave development pattern is supported by the organizational structure of the international tourism industry itself, that is, the monopolistic control over each of the very diverse elements that are combined as a tourism product by 'Northern'-based TNCs who control capital resources, possess managerial expertise and, because of their direct access to markets, are able to dictate consumer demand through marketing and promotion.

Although the neocolonial model did highlight many of the major structural inequalities between generating and receiving countries, it often failed to investigate the crucial aspects of local and regional economic development structures. It seems that most critics of tourism development in economically less developed nations accept the seemingly causal link between high levels of foreign ownership and the leakage of economic surpluses back to the metropolitan core, that is, destination countries in the South becoming progressively subordinated to meeting the needs of foreign tourists in return for limited economic benefits (Turner and Ash 1975). Bianchi (2002) argues that the neocolonial model was fixated on an excessively deterministic relationship between the North and the South, and destinations in the South were portrayed as inert objects or 'subsystems' (Hills and Lundgren 1977: 255), unable to resist the hegemonic power of metropolitan tourist capital. However, in very few cases were attempts made to theorize the concrete situations of dependency in their historical geographical contexts, and limited research has analysed the emergence and role of the semi-periphery.

Although the idea of core–periphery relations derives in large part from the dependency theorists discussed above, the notion of 'semi-periphery' is original to Wallerstein's (1979) approach. Wallerstein argues that the world system is characterized by a single division of labour and multiple cultural systems and that the world economy can be divided into three zones: the core, the periphery and the semi-periphery. These zones are based on relational qualities and form and develop in relation to one another as the results of the actions of individuals and groups living in these places. Agnew (1982: 162) argues that these zones are neither homogeneous nor are they themselves actors in the capitalist world system – they are a result of local–global action. World systems theory suggests that the capitalist world system does not operate uniformly but rather produces uneven development.

The contemporary usage of world systems theory thus places much less emphasis on global divisions of cores and peripheries, and much more emphasis on Wallerstein's original view of core–periphery relationships as processes (Wallerstein 1979), operating at all scales in the capitalist world system. The central relation of the world systems perspective is that of core and periphery, geographically and culturally distinct regions specializing in capital-intensive (core) and labour-intensive (periphery) production. The semi-periphery is described as combining both economic and political elements that are highly intertwined. Related to the political elements it is argued that semi-peripheral states can aid in stabilizing the world system through deflecting and absorbing some of the peripheral opposition to the core. Economically, the semi-periphery is seen as *intermediate* between core and periphery in terms of the capital intensity, and skill and wage levels of their production processes. A key concept for Wallerstein is that core–periphery relations are not fixed and deterministic but that movement into and out of a semi-peripheral status is possible, both from above and from below; however, upward movement of some states is largely at the expense of the downward movement of others, and the semi-periphery thus serves both as core to the periphery and as periphery to the core.

This chapter aims to provide a brief *story* of these resource-exchange relationships and go beyond the simple North (core)–South (periphery) dichotomy by focusing in on a variety of core–periphery relationships and processes that exist within the structures of international tourism related to the Zanzibar archipelago. Special emphasis is given to the changing trends in tourism-related FDI and the consequences that these relationships have on the developmental impacts of tourism for Zanzibar. The key questions that will be posed are: Who actually controls tourism development in Zanzibar? How important is the semi-periphery in these power relationships? And does it actually matter who has invested in and controls much of the tourism infrastructure?

Methodology

The main fieldwork for this study was conducted between October 2007 and February 2008, with additional interviews and site visits undertaken until April 2010. The study population consisted of senior hotel management in selected hotels, employees, suppliers and tourists (see Table 10.1).

Data were collected using semi-structured interviews, informal conversations and participatory field observation. Hotels were selected to represent a mix of locally and foreign-owned hotels, and those that were catering to both the package market and the independent traveller market. In total, twenty-eight hotels on Unguja (twenty-four) and Pemba (four) were visited, ranging from 'unclassified' to five-star. Relevant government officials, representatives of international and local non-governmental organizations (NGOs) and community-based organizations (CBOs), suppliers and tourists were interviewed. These data were supplemented by secondary data and participatory observations (i.e. 'being a tourist' and staying in fourteen of these twenty-eight hotels).

The case study: Zanzibar

The Zanzibar archipelago is part of the United Republic of Tanzania, located approximately 35 kilometres off the coast from Tanzania's economic capital Dar Es Salaam. The Zanzibar archipelago consists of two main islands, Unguja (frequently referred to as Zanzibar Island) and Pemba, plus approximately fifty islets.

Table 10.1 Number of participants – interviews and informal conversations

	Hotel management	Employees	Suppliers	Public and private sector organizations	(I)NGOs	Tourists	Local community groups	Total
Semi-structured interviews	28	9	11	7	7	–	3	65
Informal conversations	9	38	15	5	3	27	9	106
Total	37	47	26	12	10	27	12	171

The Revolutionary Government of Zanzibar enjoys a high degree of autonomy within the United Republic of Tanzania, complete with its own president, cabinet, legislature and judicial system. The population of Zanzibar is roughly 1 million, with around two-thirds of the people living on Unguja, and about 97 per cent of Zanzibar's population follow the laws of Islam. In 2004 the average annual income was US$327, but this hides the fact that about half of the population lives below the poverty line (RGOZ 2005).

Zanzibar was traditionally highly dependent on the spice trade (cloves in particular); however, annual clove sales have plummeted by 80 per cent since the 1970s. Today, Zanzibar exports spices, seaweed and fine raffia, while tourism is the main foreign currency earner. The service sector, which is dominated by tourism, is the main driver of economic development in Zanzibar and its share of gross domestic product (GDP) was 51 per cent in 2007 (RGOZ 2009). Official tourist arrivals for 2007 were just under 150,000, with Italy being by far the most significant source market (around 30 per cent), followed by the United Kingdom (10 per cent), other European markets and South Africa. Data on receipts from tourism are scarce but the Commission for Tourism (2007) estimates that annual tourism revenues could reach US$116 million by 2012, while direct employment figures for 2005 were estimated to stand at 7,500 with indirect employment estimated at 36,000. Gössling (2003: 197) argues that 'tourism may thus be important in terms of foreign exchange earnings, but it contributes little to the livelihoods of most of the local population'.

Foreign direct investment in Zanzibar

After independence and the subsequent establishment of the United Republic of Tanzania, the country adopted socialist policies that created a highly protective economic regime – foreign investment was not encouraged and international tourism was not promoted. Between 1985 and 2000, the government started liberalizing economic activity with a major focus on private-sector management of economic activity, aided by an increasingly open foreign investment policy. As a result, FDI in tourism began to grow and between 1986 and 2002 Zanzibar received total FDI inflows of US$440 million, mainly from Britain, Bahrain, Germany, Italy, Kenya, South Africa, Mauritius and the United Arab Emirates. Most of these investments went into tourism, business services, sea transport and manufacturing (RGOZ n.d.; MIGA 2006).

The Zanzibari investment policy provides for openness to domestic and foreign investment, the right to private ownership and establishment of business ventures, full protection of property rights, a liberalized foreign exchange market, favourable repatriation conditions, a stable and predictable regulatory framework, simplification of investment establishment procedures and the right to national and international impartial arbitration in the event of an investment dispute. Although the Zanzibar Investment Promotion Authority's (ZIPA) policies do not distinguish between domestic and foreign investors, in order to benefit and be registered under ZIPA, the minimum levels of investment to establish a hotel in Zanzibar are US$300,000 for local investors and US$4 million for foreign investors (ZIPA 2007), leading to the development of large-scale foreign-owned properties, particularly on the east coast.

Between 2004 and 2007 alone, 298 projects were approved by ZIPA of which 67 per cent were tourism projects – 30 per cent locally owned and 70 per cent foreign owned; European projects accounted for roughly 40 per cent and African projects for 13 per cent (Nassor 2007). However, the statistics provided by ZIPA show only the number of projects rather than the far more important bed capacity. Foreign-owned hotels catering mainly for the package tour mass market are considerably larger than locally owned businesses. Although it is estimated that locally owned accommodation providers offer on average rarely more than ten rooms (twenty beds), foreign-owned package tour accommodation often comprises 100 rooms or more – examples of these are the Kenyan-owned Blue Bay resort (112 rooms), the UAE-owned Zamani Kempinski (117 rooms) and the Italian/Swiss-owned Neptune Pwani (154 rooms) and Gemma Dell Est (150 rooms). Thus, the actual bed stock in Zanzibar is in the majority foreign-owned, and not only Northern-owned but with a considerable percentage of South–South investment. Based on secondary data from the Commission for Tourism, ZIPA and the Zanzibar Association of Tourism Investors (ZATI), supplemented by primary data collected in 2007–2008, the accommodation providers that were found in Zanzibar can be roughly divided into six categories (see Table 10.2).

The very high level of FDI is not surprising given the growth in tourism arrivals and the favourable investment policy developed as a consequence of the lack of local investment capital and the particular non-affiliation to the tourism industry based on the religious and cultural background of the Zanzibari population. What seems peculiar at first glance is the considerably high level of South–South investment. The prevailing pattern of tourism FDI in East Africa (when looking at the early tourism developments in Kenya in the 1980s for example) was the high level of investment from traditional generating regions such as Europe (the United Kingdom, Germany, Switzerland and Italy in particular) and the United States. Although Italian/Swiss investment still constitutes a high percentage in Zanzibar today, a considerable shift towards South–South investment (Kenya and South Africa in particular) and also increased investment volumes from the Arab world seems to have taken place. Although Arab investments focus on top-end hotels, Kenyan and South African investments, similar to Italian investments, seem to concentrate on mid-range mass-marked package tour accommodation mediated by tour operators based in generating regions. Kenyan and South African investment probably stands out slightly as these properties are strongly linked to European tour operators, but, unlike the Italian properties, are not owned by Northern-based TNCs – as such these properties come to symbolise the semi-periphery in that they depend on core European TNCs for tourists while they themselves are investors in the periphery.

Do these ownership patterns matter?

South–South investment is frequently seen as essential to complement North–South cooperation in order to achieve the internationally agreed development goals

Table 10.2 Types of accommodation providers in Zanzibar in 2007/2008

Type	Mass-market hotels	Reserved for Italians	The locals	Tourists who lost their return tickets	Luxury hotels	The jewels
Examples	Ras Nungwi, Zanzibar Beach Hotel, Blue Bay, Breezes	Vera Club, Venta Club, Bravo Club	Amaan Bungalows, Mnarani Beach, Tembo House	Matemwe Bungalows, Pongwe Beach, Fumba Beach Lodge	Kempinski, Serena, Gemma Dell Est	Mnemba Island, Chumbe Island
Star rating	3–4 star	3 star	1–3 star	2–3 star	4–5 star	3–5 star
Customers	Package tourists from Europe and South Africa	All-inclusive, mainly Italian customers	Independent and specialized, small-scale package tourists (Europe)	Independent and specialized small-scale package tourists (Europe)	High-end package tours and individual travellers, Europe, United States	High-end and eco-tourism Europe, United States, South Africa
Estimated bed capacity	36%	25%	19%	11%	8%	1%
Ownership	Mixed but large proportion from Kenya and South Africa	Italian, Swiss	Local and joint ventures	European	Arab, European	European, South African

and to overcome some of the most pressing development challenges (G-77, 2004). Levy-Yeyati *et al.* (2002), for example, argue that South–South FDI represents an opportunity for economically less developed countries needing investment capital when most Northern TNCs are more risk averse. Southern corporations tend to invest in neighbouring economically less developed countries and, as such, South–South FDI flows, however small, are significant for many poor countries. In many economically less developed countries, South–South flows account for more than half of the total FDI (UNCTAD 2007). UNCTAD (2004) argues that the development impact of South–South FDI is particularly important for poverty reduction efforts as it is able to offset the significant decline in FDI flows from the North. This enlargement and diversification of the pool of countries that are sources of FDI may reduce fluctuations, contributing to the economic development of recipient countries. Furthermore, Southern investors often have greater familiarity with technology and business practices suitable for economically less developed countries, which allows them to use more appropriate production processes and locally available inputs given that a country's absorption capacity is greater with a smaller technological gap between a foreign firm and the domestic firms (Durham 2004). Furthermore, because of the long value chain in tourism there is theoretically much room for spillovers into the community, and evidence from East and Southern Africa shows that the tourism industry is benefiting from FDI inflows, including the transfer of technology, skills acquisition and linkages to other economic sectors. UNCTAD (2007) confirms that tourism FDI in Botswana, Kenya, Mauritius, Uganda and Tanzania has improved the service delivery and the supply capacity of these countries.

The current high level of South–South investment in Zanzibar is directly related to the cultural and geographical proximity to source countries. Kantarci (2006) confirms that FDI is largely influenced by the earlier trade relations and by the geographical and cultural proximity to host countries (Culpan and Akcaoglu 2003). The degree of cultural proximity between the host country and the home country is seen as a key factor, as similarities in culture and language tend to facilitate the process of planning, development, managing and controlling hotels, resorts and tourist facilities located abroad (Go *et al.* 1990).

The cultural, historical and geographical proximity, coupled with the downturn in tourism in Kenya in the late 1990s, were said to have been key influences motivating British–Kenyan and Asian–Kenyan investors to move to Zanzibar. Furthermore, Kenyan entrepreneurs possess extensive experience in managing resorts and negotiating with European tour operators, whereas their Zanzibari counterparts often lacked this knowledge.

A Kenyan investor operating a mass-market beach resort commented on his decision to invest in Zanzibar that

> it was an easy decision for me. While I had nearly two decades of excellent business in Mombasa, the political and also economic situation in the late 1990s made it very difficult to make a profit. European tour-operators were driving the prices down while we received more and more low-paying

tourists making it impossible to invest in resources and staff. A downward spiral. Zanzibar seemed an ideal opportunity which I decided to grab with both hands. I am Swahili and it is easy for me to understand, communicate and negotiate with Zanzibaris. I know the product very well – it is the same as in Kenya – but of course far better – thus an easy decision.

This is mirrored by a South African investor who claims that the strong link between Tanzania and South Africa allowed him relatively easy access to approval for his investment in the early 2000s. It seems that another important advantage of South–South investments is that they embody business models that are less corporatized and more informal than Western models, and which are often more appropriate to the host country context. As a result, learning and spillovers to the domestic economy seem to be possible. More generally, investors from developing countries, including some of the South African corporations moving into Africa, tend to be less risk-averse and more willing to deal with the informal governance arrangements and processes found in many African economies in relation to the procurement of goods and services, bureaucracy and security issues. Another South African investor argued that his 'African heritage' enabled him to attract and train personnel, which was of the utmost importance given the labour shortages in Zanzibar. He had already invested in a property on the Mozambican coast and it was a short step to move further up the coast given the increased demand for tropical beach holidays in Southern Africa. It is perhaps interesting to note that these South–South investors are by and large of British-Kenyan, Asian-Kenyan or white South African origin – thus frequently combining Northern and Southern characteristics.

To provide an insight into how these changed investment patterns and power relations influence the developmental impacts of tourism development in Zanzibar, two issues will be discussed in detail here: procurement and labour relations.

Procurement and linkages

Yeung (1994: 299) states that 'developing country TNCs are a special species of the capitalist beast – they are more beneficial to the host economy than other TNCs from developed countries'. Analysing the manufacturing sector Gelb (2005) found that South–South investors are more likely to provide accessible goods and services to domestic firms and households. South–South investment is also more likely to make use of distribution/procurement and business network models that will not only lead to more successful entry for the foreign firm, but also more effectively promote backwards and forwards linkages within the domestic economy and therefore support domestic enterprise development. However, do the findings from the manufacturing sector also apply to the tourism industry in Zanzibar? And do operating practices differ between Northern and Southern investors?

One of the key problems in Zanzibar is the lack of local supplies. At the moment the tourism industry can only purchase some meat (poultry), fish and fruit and vegetables locally – 80 per cent of all vegetables and 20 per cent of all fruits used by the tourism industry are imported from mainland Tanzania, Kenya and beyond (Steck *et al.* 2010). Local meat including poultry is largely unsuitable for high-end hotels and restaurants, and, although fish is caught locally, the market price for high-value fish favoured by the tourism industry is said to have doubled (RGOZ 2004). Dry, tinned and bottled goods all need to be imported – some are sourced from Dar Es Salaam, but to avoid double taxation most of these goods are imported directly from Dubai.

The procurement patterns among the different hotel categories vary considerably. This study found that on average over 60 per cent was sourced either nationally (i.e. from mainland Tanzania) or internationally. Generally, 'mass-market hotels', hotels 'reserved for Italians' and 'luxury hotels' imported more than locally or foreign-owned small-scale hotels. Imports by 'mass-market hotels' and hotels 'reserved for Italians' were rather high when it came to furniture, fixtures, fittings and equipment (over 90 per cent compared with just under 80 per cent for 'luxury hotels' and 65 per cent for locally and foreign-owned small-scale hotels). Key source markets were Kenya, Dubai and Europe. One manager explained that in order to satisfy European tour operators it was necessary to adopt uniform standards across the chain rather than to procure local produce.

Both the 'mass-market hotels' (South–South investment) and the hotels 'reserved for Italians' (Italian and Swiss investment) operated buffet menus because of their all-inclusive nature. As such the quality of the food was not as important as it was for the 'luxury hotels' and a slightly higher amount of fruit and poultry was sourced locally. Because of their all-inclusive policy these hotels also generally used a higher amount of Tanzanian beverages including fruit juice, spirits and beers compared with the 'luxury hotels'.

However, there were also marked differences based on nationality of owner and clientele. As could maybe have been expected, many of the South African hotels sourced their processed foods and beverages from South Africa, whereas the Kenyan-owned hotels over-proportionally used Mombasa given the proximity to Zanzibar. The Italian-owned hotels had a rather different pattern of procurement based on their clientele (mainly Italians), their high seasonality (December–January and July–August were the key months) and their link to other hotels within the same chain located along the Swahili coast. The general manager of an Italian-owned all-inclusive explains:

> We try to buy as much as we can locally – by locally I mean within Tanzania or Kenya. We need to be extremely careful about the costs of our supplies, and imports from further afield are of course expensive. However, we operate on a very seasonal basis and our high season is over the Christmas period. Our customers expect to see the traditional Italian Christmas feast which means we bring most of it in either from Dubai or Italy. Our Italians love salami and Parma ham and of course they need Italian pasta, pizza, Prosecco, Panettone and Torrone – so all that is imported for the main season – we have a big containership coming into Mombasa and Zanzibar for our whole group . . . it is very impressive . . . and we can also use our charters [flights].

The 'luxury hotels' aimed to use local produce such as high-quality fish, fruits and vegetables but mentioned that they were often prohibited from buying locally because of the lack of quality and quantity (for a general discussion of constraints/opportunities to develop inter-sectoral linkages see Meyer 2008). The highest percentage of local sourcing was undertaken by hotels owned by 'locals' and 'tourists who lost their return tickets'; given their smaller scale they felt that it was more feasible and less expensive to source locally, and quality was not of such utmost importance.

These findings are confirmed by a recent study by Steck *et al.* (2010) who found that high-end hotels tend to use a high proportion of raw ingredients rather than processed food, which seems to be preferred by the mass-market and club hotels. Although some meat is available locally the quality is often not high and consistent enough, leading to roughly 60 per cent of meat being imported to Zanzibar by the top-end hotels. Budget hotels on the other hand use a higher amount of local meat produce but at the same time a higher amount of imported ingredients as they mainly have simple menus such as pasta and pizza.

Contrary to Yeung's (1994) and Gelb's (2005) findings a study of investments in sub-Saharan Africa discovered that developing country firms were actually less integrated in terms of local sourcing (UNIDO 2006). Distance, agreements and the duration of the investment, among other factors, affect the share of intermediate inputs sourced by multinationals from a host country, which is likely to increase with the distance between the host and the source economy. This was confirmed in this study in which Kenyan businesses relied largely on nearby Mombasa whereas South African businesses procured mainly in South Africa and Dubai. As such, South–South FDI may in some cases have less positive vertical linkages than North–South flows, as in the case of accommodation owned by 'tourists who lost their return tickets'.

Employment and labour relations

Gelb (2005) argues that South–South investment can increase the supply of entrepreneurs for the host country through immigration. He found that Asian firms in particular tend to use large numbers of expatriate managers and supervisors in their foreign investments, and these individuals often leave their employers to set up their own firms in the host economies and as such contribute to increased knowledge transfer between source and host countries.

However, with regard to employment and labour relations, the international non-governmental organization Save the Children (2005) argues that South–South FDI is not always more beneficial than North–South FDI. The increased transparency of Northern TNC's foreign operations related to environmental and labour standards has improved thanks to corporate social responsibility (CSR) initiatives. Such initiatives, however, are less common among Southern companies, which may have comparably low environmental and labour standards.

As discussed in the introduction to this chapter it is frequently argued that Northern-based tourism TNCs rely heavily on expatriate labour and as such it will be interesting to see if this is the case in Zanzibar and if there are differences in operating practices between Northern and Southern investors.

The tourism industry in Zanzibar is characterized by a serious lack of skilled personnel due to the absence (until recently) of relevant training institutes, the Muslim tradition, adversarial attitudes towards the tourism industry, and generally low levels of entrepreneurial initiative. This situation has led to the influx of large numbers of migrant workers from mainland Tanzania and Kenya.

The majority of hotels undertake in-house training ranging from rather basic training by the locally owned hotels to very elaborate training by the upmarket hotels including scholarships and international exposure in other hotels that are part of the Serena or Kempinski chain. A further main concern for many hotels is related to the poaching of staff by other hotels once they have been trained in-house.

Although Steck *et al.* (2010) estimate that the total number of direct employees in tourism accommodation in Zanzibar in 2009 was 9,848 (of which 70 per cent were Zanzibaris born and raised), these figures are highly debated, and Honey (2008) mentions that most foreign hotels bring with them their own middle management and Zanzibari are only employed in low-paid jobs with limited opportunities for growth, if at all.

This study found that the level of migrant labourers, in particular Kenyans, is considerably higher than is officially portrayed. In official interviews with hotel managers it was generally confirmed that the level of expatriates is relatively low (around 5 per cent). Informal conversations with employees away from their place of work painted a very different picture. For some hotels – in particular Kenyan-owned hotels and hotels 'reserved for Italians' – it was mentioned that the number of Kenyans employed was very high – even up to 50 per cent. A Kenyan waitress in a hotel in Nungwi commented:

> I was trained in Nairobi but there are no jobs in Kenya. I heard Tanzania is looking for people like me – I went to Arusha for a while but they are very tough on illegals – someone told me that Zanzibar is a good place. I am Kenyan . . . I have worked here for six month – no bother at all . . . about half here are from Kenya – you are free here – no checks – I'd like to stay as long as I can.

This was confirmed in an interview with senior researchers at the International Labour Organisation based in Dar Es Salaam who mentioned

> yes, the number of Kenyans working in Zanzibar is very high. We do not have any official figures but we are very aware of this. Zanzibar does not have sufficient labour inspectors to actually check and it is not a Union Affair. But I would agree that the numbers can be up to 50 per cent of employees for some hotels.

This is confirmed by an Action Aid Study (La Cour Madsen 2003:4) that quotes a senior official in the Ministry of Youth, Employment and Development of

Women and Children as saying that 'if they [foreign workers] were removed a lot of vacancies would emerge but when they are first here it is difficult to find them'.

Businesses are permitted to employ a certain number of expatriates (5 per cent); should they require additional expatriates they need to apply annually and pay a certain amount per labourer, although it is highly likely that this practice is not always adhered to given that employers are rarely checked. The Italian and Swiss hotels employed a considerable number of seasonal staff from Italy to provide the 'all-inclusive Italian entertainment' for their guests.

Comparing the employment practices of the different categories of hotels it is estimated that the use of Kenyan staff is considerably higher when skilled staff are needed (i.e. in the 'mass-market beach hotels', hotels 'reserved for Italians' and 'luxury hotels') and also when the property is Kenyan owned and managed. Several Kenyan managers confirmed that they regularly bring over Kenyan workers from related Kenyan properties to 'assist in staff training'.

Salaries paid to employees in the accommodation sector in Zanzibar also varied considerably between the different categories of hotels. This was mainly related to star rating and clientele rather than ownership. Local companies' minimum monthly basic pay was roughly US$50 whereas high-end foreign-owned hotels paid on average US$120. Employment benefits offered by high-end foreign companies included health services, bonuses for exemplary work, training, motivational awards, family support, free meals, free transportation to and from work, uniforms and at times free accommodation or a housing allowance that averaged 15 per cent of the basic pay. In the more upmarket hotels and those that did not rely on an all-inclusive service extra benefits such as tips and service charges could easily add another 50 per cent plus to the monthly wage package.

This was confirmed by Steck *et al.* (2010) who argued that the average wage for Zanzibari in the tourism accommodation sector was 135,000 TZS per month, while the current minimum salary is 80,000 TZS per month. They found that the majority of hotels, in particular the more upmarket hotels, were paying well above this, with salaries generally starting at 100,000 TZS. The ownership and clientele seem to make a difference to employment patterns whereby hotels with a strong dependency on a particular customer segment tend to employ European personnel able to converse in the language of their guests, in this case Italian. Furthermore, hotels with strong links to a better-skilled labour market tend to use these connections extensively. Remunerations were generally considerably higher in foreign-owned hotels than in local hotels, while additional benefits in the form of tips and service charges were generally low in all-inclusive 'mass-market hotels' and hotels 'reserved for Italians'.

Conclusion

The aim of this chapter was to provide a brief insight into tourism-related power structures by focusing on FDI, its sources and impacts on development in Zanzibar. By illustrating the emergences of new 'power centres' in the form of South–South investment it was hoped to add to the political economy debates.

As shown in the case of Zanzibar, South–South FDI in tourism is important and growing considerably; as with all FDI, some of it is beneficial for economically less developed neighbours, some is not. It has hopefully been demonstrated that the 'semi-periphery' in terms of Kenyan and South African investment has emerged as a powerful player within these Zanzibari power relations and that Southern investors can provide an important link between peripheral host regions and Northern-based tour operators. Their procurement and labour relations impact on development in Zanzibar. Kenyan investors, for example, seem to be located within the 'semi-periphery of power' by being in control of capital, procurement as well as labour, while also being highly dependent on tour operators in the North bringing in their clientele. This complex relationship between different 'power centres' has direct impacts on the periphery and it was shown that the origin of ownership matters to some degree.

However, it was also shown that possibly more important than ownership are the clientele catered for and consequently the product sold. The least beneficial development impacts in terms of procurement and employment seem to be related to accommodation providers selling a mid-range, all-inclusive mass market product mediated by Northern-based tour operators – in the case of Zanzibar these properties were both Southern and Northern owned.

As such, rather than focusing purely on the geographical location of ownership to interpret the tourism-related world system, it is probably even more important to refocus the discussion on the political and cultural processes that create and maintain the tourism system.

Agnew and Corbridge (1995: 205), for example, argue that

> economic, cultural and geopolitical power is embedded in a network of dominant but internally divided countries, regional groupings like the EU and city-regions in the so-called Second and Third Worlds, international institutions including the World Bank, the IMF, GATT and the United Nations, and the main circuits and institutions of international production and financial capital.

These actors and regions are tied together in a complex market economy-based ideology and the increased recognition that territoriality alone is not a secure basis for economic or geopolitical power. Although the power of Northern TNCs over peripheral tourism destinations based on capital investment seems to be fading because of increasingly strong South–South investment, the control over some parts of the tourism system seems to remain firmly rooted within well-established Northern-controlled networks. The members of these networks might differ considerably from those of only a decade ago, but ultimately tourism development in Zanzibar seems to be controlled by companies able to sell a relatively inexpensive product to the mass market, that is, generating country-based tour operators. This is related to processes rather than geographical location in the discussion of core and peripheries and the ideas that the 'core' of the world system exists as a network of interconnected, physically dispersed territories with a shared understanding of how to produce and distribute tourism products that make the 'tourism world system' work for them – whether they are Kenyan, Italian or even Zanzibari members of this network.

It seems that with the increasing inter-linkages between the 'global and the local', territorial outcomes are *never* likely to be the only important consideration; rather, the processes that shape the formation of these inter-linkages will be of increasing interest. The rise in South–South investment into sub-Saharan Africa will not automatically change the terms of the relationship between Africa and the 'North' but it can contribute to the creation of a strong Southern business class and over the long run it may contribute to changing the power balance.

References

Agnew, J. (1982) 'Sociologizing the geographic imagination: Spatial concepts in the worldsystem perspective', *Political Geography Quarterly*, 1: 159–166.

Agnew, J. and Corbridge, S. (1995) *Mastering Space*, London: Routledge.

Bianchi, R. V. (2002) 'Towards a political economy of global tourism', in R. Sharpley and D. J. Telfer (eds) *Tourism and Development: Concepts and issues*, Clevedon: Channel View.

Britton, S. (1982) 'The political economy of tourism in the Third World', *Annals of Tourism Research*, 9: 331–357.

Brown, D. O. (1998) 'In search of an appropriate form of tourism for Africa: Lessons from the past and suggestions for the future', *Tourism Management*, 19: 237–245.

Bryden, J. M. (1973) *Tourism and Development: A case study of the commonwealth Carribbean*, Cambridge: Cambridge University Press.

Clancy, M. J. (1999) 'Tourism and development: Evidence from Mexico', *Annals of Tourism Research*, 26: 1–20.

Coccossis, H. and Parpairis, A. (1995) 'Assessing the interaction between heritage, environment and tourism: Mykonos', in H. Coccossis and P. Nijkamp (eds) *Sustainable Tourism Development*, Hong Kong: Avebury.

Cox, R. (1987) *Production, Power and World Order: Social forces in the making of history*, New York: Columbia University Press.

Culpan, E. and Akcaoglu, E. (2003) 'An examination of Turkish direct investments in Central and Eastern Europe and the Commonwealth of Independent States', in S. T. Marinova and M. A. Marinov (eds) *Foreign Direct Investment in Central and Eastern Europe*, Farnham: Ashgate.

De Kadt, E. (1979) *Tourism, Passport to Development?*, Oxford: Oxford University Press.

Diaz Benevides, D. (2001) 'Tourism policy and economic growth', seminar presented at the Internationale Tourismus Börse, Berlin, March.

Durham, B. J. (2004) 'Absorptive capacity and the effects of foreign direct investment and equity foreign portfolio investment on economic growth', *European Economic Review*, 48: 285–306.

Finney, B. and Watson, A. (1975) *A New Kind of Sugar: Tourism in the Pacific*, Honolulu: East West Culture Learning Institute.

Freitag, T. (1994) 'Enclave tourism development: For whom the benefits roll', *Annals of Tourism Research*, 21: 538–554.

G-77 (Group of 77) (2004) 'Marrakech Declaration on South–South Cooperation', December. Available at http://www.g77.org/doc/docs/Marrakech%20Final%20 Docs%20(E).pdf (accessed October 2010).

Gelb, S. (2005) 'South–South investment: The case of Africa', in J. Joost Teunissen and A. Akkerman (eds) *Africa in the World Economy: The national, regional and international challenges*, The Hague: Fondad.

Go, F., Pyo, S. S., Uysal, M. and Mihalik, B. J. (1990) 'Decision criteria for transnational hotel expansion', *Tourism Management*, 11: 297–314.

Gössling, S. (2003) 'The political ecology of tourism in Zanzibar', in S. Gössling (ed.) *Tourism and Development in Tropical Islands: Political ecology perspectives*, Cheltenham: Edward Elgar.

Hills, T. L. and Lundgren, J. (1977) 'The impact of tourism in the Caribbean', *Annals of Tourism Research*, 4: 248–267.

Honey, M. (2008) *Ecotourism and Sustainable Development: Who owns paradise*, Washington DC: Island Press.

Jenkins, C. (1991) 'Tourism development strategies', in L. Lickorish, A. Jefferson, J. Bodlender and C. Jenkins (eds) *Developing Tourism Destinations*, Harlow: Longman.

Kantarci, K. (2006) 'Perceptions of foreign investors on the tourism market in Central Asia including Kyrgyzstan, Kazakhstan, Uzbekistan, Turkmenistan', *Tourism Management*, 28: 820–29.

La Cour Madsen, B. (2003) *Islands of Development: What do poor women in Zanzibar get out of tourism liberalisation?*, London: ActionAid, UK Media Department.

Lea, J. (1988) 'Tourism and development ethics in the Third World', *Annals of Tourism Research*, 20: 701–715.

Levy-Yeyati, E., Panizza, U. and Stein, E. (2002) 'The cyclical nature of North–South FDI flow', IADB Research Department Working paper 479, Buenos Aires: Universidad Torcuato di Tella Business School.

Matthews, H. (1978) *International Tourism: A political and social analysis*, Cambridge: Schenkman.

Meyer, D. (2008) 'Pro-poor tourism: From leakages to linkages. A conceptual framework for creating linkages between the accommodation sector and 'poor' neighbouring communities', *Current Issues in Tourism*, 10: 558–583.

MIGA (2006) *Attracting Investment in Tourism. Tanzania's Investor Outreach Programme*, Investing in Development Series, Washington DC: World Bank.

Müller, B. (1984) 'Fremdenverkehr, Dezentralisierung und regionale Partizipation in Mexiko', *Geographische Rundschau*, 36: 20–24.

Nassor, S. (2007) 'Tourism development in Zanzibar-Tanzania', paper presented at the Swiss Investment Forum, Zurich, Switzerland, June.

OECD (1967) *Tourism Development and Economic Growth*, Paris: Organisation for Economic Co-operation and Development.

Oppermann, M. and Chon, K. S. (1997) *Tourism in Developing Countries*, London: International Thomson Business Press.

Östreich, H. (1977) 'Gambia: Zur sozio-ökonomischen Problematik des Ferntourismus in einem westafrikanischen Entwicklungsland', *Geographische Zeitschrift*, 65: 302–308.

Pavaskar, M. (1982) 'Employment effects of tourism and the Indian experience', *Journal of Tourism Research*, 21: 32–38.

Pearce, D. (1989) *Tourism Development*, 2nd edn, Harlow: Longman.

RGOZ (n.d.) 'Zanzibar investment policy', Revolutionary Government of Zanzibar. Online. Available at http://www.zanzibarinvest.org/investment_policy.pdf (accessed 10 April 2010).

RGOZ (2004) 'Report of the Sustainable Management of Land and Environment (SMOLE) Programme, Revolutionary Government of Zanzibar', Zanzibar: Zanzibar Ministry of Water, Energy, Construction, Lands and Environment.

RGOZ (2005) 'Strategic Framework for the Zanzibar Poverty Reduction Plan (ZPRP) Review', Zanzibar: Revolutionary Government of Zanzibar.

RGOZ (2009) 'Zanzibar economic bulletin (January–March 2009)', *A Quarterly Review of the Economy*, 2.

Roche, M. (1992) 'Mega-events and micro-modernisation: On the sociology of new urban tourism', *British Journal of Sociology*, 43: 563–600.

Save the Children (2005) 'Beyond the rhetoric: Measuring revenue transparency in the oil and gas industries'. Online. Available at http://www.savethechildren.org.uk/en/54_5101.htm (accessed 14 May 2010).

Sherman, H. L. (1987) *Foundations of Radical Political Economy*, Armonk, NY: M. E. Sharpe.

Steck, B., Wood, K. and Bishop, J. (2010) 'Tourism more value for Zanzibar: Value chain analysis', Final Report, February 2010. Zanzibar: VSO, SNV and ZATI.

Strange, S. (1994) *States and Markets*, 2nd edn, London: Pinter.

Turner, L. and Ash, J. (1975) *The Golden Hordes. International tourism and the pleasure periphery*, London: Constable.

UNCTAD (2004) *World Investment Report 2004: The shift towards services*, New York: United Nations Conference on Trade and Development.

UNCTAD (2007) *FDI in Tourism: The development dimension*, New York: United Nations Conference on Trade and Development.

UNIDO (2006) *Understanding the Contributions of Different Investor Categories to Development: Implications for targeting strategies*, Africa Foreign Investor Survey 2005, Vienna: United Nations Industrial Development Organization.

Wahab, S. and Pigram, J. J. (eds) (1997) *Tourism, Development and Growth: The challenge of sustainability*, London: Routledge.

Wallerstein, I. (1979) *The Capitalist World Economy*, Cambridge: Cambridge University Press.

WTO (2004) 'African governments told tourism can combat poverty if they provide the right conditions', World Tourism Organization News Releases, 18 May. Online. Available at http://www.hospitalitynet.org/news/4019575.search?query=wto+ (accessed 16 September 2010).

Yeung, H. (1994) 'Third World multinationals revisited: A research critique and future agenda', *Third World Quarterly*, 15: 297–317.

ZIPA (2007) 'Investment eligibility'. Online. Available at http://www.zanzibarinvest.org/eligibility.htm (accessed 1 May 2010).

11 Dubai

'An exotic destination with a cosmopolitan lifestyle'

Kevin Meethan

On the 24 September 2008, the Atlantis Hotel in Dubai was formally opened with a lavish party that *The Times* (21 November 2008) described in the following way:

> In the lobby of the Atlantis about 2,000 guests sipped Dom Pérignon. Outside, A-list celebrities from Robert De Niro to Lindsay Lohan walked the red carpet. After the pop singer Kylie Minogue performed on stage the sky lit up with the world's largest fireworks display, seven times greater than this year's Olympic Games opening ceremony in Beijing and extravagant enough to be seen from outer space.

The total cost of this party ran to £13.5 million. The hotel, which cost £1 billion, was built on the Palm Jumeirah, one of three artificial palm-shaped islands that have to rank as one of the most unusual civil engineering projects ever undertaken, but then, as Hazbun (2006: 214) writes, this is but one of many 'spectacular headline grabbing tourist related projects' that now characterise Dubai. Such excesses of conspicuous consumption are perhaps more commonly associated with other cities such as Las Vegas that have an established reputation for reckless extravagance and an equal penchant for eye-catching architecture (Hannigan 1998), but Dubai catches the eyes for other reasons too. How is it that a small city-state with a population of 59,000 in 1968 can have so quickly become a city housing 1.6 million people (Department of Tourism and Commerce Marketing 2009), the majority of whom are expatriate workers? And why, out of all the Gulf states, has Dubai managed to project itself so spectacularly into the global luxury tourist market? Rapid urbanization is not in itself a new phenomena, but Dubai's pattern has a number of unique characteristics (Bagaeen 2007, Pacione 2005, Shihab 2001). To begin to address such questions and to examine the particular nature of its political, social and economic characteristics, we first need to set the global and regional context.

Contemporary tourism

What I term contemporary tourism, which developed from the last three decades of the twentieth century onwards, is significantly different from modern tourism that preceded it in a number of respects. Modern tourism was characterized by mass consumption with little choice and product differentiation, with very sharp conceptual and spatial divisions between work and leisure, and was mostly confined to national markets (Meethan 2001, Urry 2000). Contemporary tourism by contrast can generally be characterized as post-Fordist. It is more differentiated and diverse in what it offers and where it is located, and, although domestic markets are still important, the expectation in most developed economies is that holidays involve travel to another country, with the result that markets are now inter-regional and global, even though strong regional trends are discernible, and we also see the emergence of new flows and networks in and between regions such as the Middle East, India, South-East Asia and China (see, for example, Ghimire 2001 and Singh 2009).

In part this is a consequence of increasing globalization, itself rooted in the phase of neoliberal deregulation that began in the 1980s. Among other effects, this caused the role of the state to be redefined – in many cases the involvement of national government was reduced in favour of the privatization of state assets – and the introduction of market mechanisms into the provision of public services (Dicken 2003: 165) so that economic development was to be facilitated by the extension of entrepreneurship and the free market. Of course, the notion of a 'free market' is often no more than a rhetorical device or ideological aspiration; all markets are governed by rules of some description and, as Dicken (2003) points out, although this has often been referred to as a process of deregulation, it is more accurately described as one of re-regulation (see also Glenn 2007). That aside, there is no dispute that the net result has been the emergence of global networks of production and consumption that in turn reordered the spatial hierarchy of modernity and capital accumulation through the processes of de-territorialization and re-territorialization. Such processes are often seen to signify a shift in power away from the nation-state and into the hands of the multinational corporations (MNCs). However, as Hazbun (2004) has noted, the fact that capital is now more footloose may increase the capacity of the state to act in order to produce the kinds of places that can attract inward investment, and, similarly, Woods (2000: 6) claims that globalization provides new opportunities for state action through access to wider markets for, as Biersteker (2000: 153) points out, control over flows of both people and finance are equally as important as control over territory.

However, tourism is distinct from other areas of economic activity in one key aspect: it is not mobile. For example, the choice of a site for a factory depends on the availability of a workforce, good transport linkages and adequate infrastructure. Usually, such locations are often found on industrial estates, or near road, rail and port interchanges, or in urban clusters where other forms of advantage may be found such as intellectual capital, particular skills or cheaper labour (Porter 1998). For many areas of economic activity choosing a location may have nothing to do with the aesthetics of the environment or the cultural significance of place,[1] whereas most forms of tourism and their associated services place a high value on such matters. This is most apparent in urban locations where regeneration strategies are often linked to the aestheticization of the urban fabric and its role in developing tourism. Some enclave developments aside, tourism cannot relocate in the same way that factory production or some service sector activities can; rather it involves the temporary import of people as opposed to the export of goods, and as such supports a wide range of ancillary employment in hotels, catering and hospitality, transport, retail and entertainment – in other words what we have is an economy of leisure consumption that is rooted in the specificity of place.

One of the key arguments in the globalization literature has focused on the apparent decline of the nation-state (see, for example, Glenn 2007; Woods 2000). My own position on this is close to that described as 'transformationalist',[2] which is to say that, although global relations are inevitably changing the role of the state, in certain circumstances it may be reinforced, and in others diminished. For example, the recent global financial crisis and subsequent dramatic moves to take parts of the private banking system in both the United Kingdom and the United States into state ownership show the power of state regulation being reasserted. However, the collapse of an entire national economy, as happened in Iceland, also shows the limitations of state power in the face of global financial markets. Another factor we need to take account of is the way in which tourism is used as a means to integrate states into the broader global economy, a trend that has been particularly noticeable in the Middle East and South-East Asia, and Hazbun's (2004) study of tourism in the former sums up the issues quite neatly. Between 1980 and 2000, he writes, international tourism grew rapidly across the region as many states saw tourism as a means not only to generate income, but also a way to integrate their economies into the global system, while at the same time exerting control over the process (Hazbun 2004: 320; see also Gray 1997). For many years dependent on oil revenues, certain member states have more recently invested heavily in building up foreign trade and tourism as alternative economic growth strategies (Henderson 2006a,b; Herb 2008).

In part, such developments have been achieved through state-led policies such as tax breaks and other incentives to attract investors (Hazbun 2004: 325). Hazbun also adds that such developments, being less capital intensive than other forms of development, offered relatively high returns for relatively low investment (see also Harrison 2001; Mansfield and Winckler 2007). Until the recent economic downturn, tourism in the Middle East had grown at a faster rate than in any other region, and growth in the first half of 2008 was estimated to have increased by 17 per cent over the previous year (United Nations World Tourism Organization 2009).

Economic development in the United Arab Emirates and Dubai

Until 1971 Dubai was one of a number of gulf emirates that had been linked to the British Empire since the nineteenth century through a series of treaties, and which were collectively known as the Trucial States. Before the exploitation of oil reserves, which began in the 1960s, the economies of the states relied on subsistence agriculture, nomadic animal husbandry, the pearl trade, fishing and seafaring (Shihab 2001: 249) and, in the case of Dubai, entrepôt (tax free import– export) trade. When Britain withdrew from east of the Suez Canal, six of the emirates

– Abu Dhabi, Dubai, Sharjah, Ajman, Umm al Quwain and Fujairah – formed the United Arab Emirates (UAE), later joined by Ras al Kaimah in 1972; Abu Dhabi is the largest emirate and is also the de facto capital (Davidson 2006).

Oil wealth began to make its impact in the early 1970s, but, with smaller oil reserves than some of the other emirates, Dubai also continued to develop its entrepôt trade, which had been well established for some years. Most notably this was accomplished by the expansion of the Jebel Ali Port, which is now the largest port in the Middle East (Matly and Dillon 2007) and which takes full advantage of its strategic location as a transport hub, as does the new development of Dubai airport (see Vesperman *et al.* 2008). In itself this is part of a larger strategy, implemented from the 1990s onwards, to develop tourism (Sharpley 2008), as, situated midway between Asia and Europe, Dubai has a potential market of 2 billion people within four hours flying time of the city.

According to Hvidt (2007), Dubai is also exceptional among Middle Eastern states in implementing outward-looking policies that have enabled it to become a significant player in the global economy (see also Hazbun 2006; Davidson 2007), and of particular importance is the form of governance within the emirate. Like many of the other Gulf states, Dubai exhibits many of the characteristics of a rentier state, defined as one in which profits, or rents, are derived from the exploitation of natural resources, in this case oil and natural gas. In addition, such rents are external to the domestic economy and the government is the recipient of the income (Shambayati 1994; Beblawi 1990). In addition, although the UAE as a whole is governed by a legislative body composed of the hereditary rulers of each emirate, each has enough power to 'ensure that a ruler continues to be the absolute authority within his emirate' (Al Abed 2001: 14). Dubai has been ruled by the Maktoum family since it was first founded in the nineteenth century, and according to Hvidt (2007: 557) the current government of Dubai can be characterized as one of 'soft' authoritarianism, while Davidson (2006: 42) describes it as being 'one of the purest autocracies in the world'.

There are a number of consequences that follow from such arrangements. First, wealth creation is centred round a small element of society while the rest tend to be engaged in the utilization of such wealth, and, second, the state becomes the major employer and distributor of the earnings. Typically, and Dubai is no exception here, this is accomplished through the provision of free education and health care, no taxation and subsidized state sector employment. However, as has often been pointed out, rentier state economics can in effect be used to 'buy off' political opposition through a system of patronage in which people seek to establish patron–client relations with individuals in the state structure (see, for example, Mansfield and Winckler 2007). This allows the government to pursue long-term strategic planning without political opposition or the need to negotiate planning permission through independent monitoring bodies (Henderson 2006a,b), a factor that has been significant in the slower and less dramatic diversification policies pursued by Kuwait for example (Herb 2008). With few independent checks and balances to contend with, Dubai has also been able to ensure long-term political stability, a crucial factor in attracting both investors as well as tourists. As Al Sageh (2004: 109) has pointed out, in Dubai the ruling elite have continued to derive their authority by traditional means while at the same time pursuing economic and social modernization. There is of course an inherent danger in a rentier system that other economic sectors may be ignored or under-developed, and there is also a great deal of variation in the general characteristics of such states. As Okruhlik (1999) cautions, discussions concerning rentier states often fall into an assumed economic determinism, whereas the important point is not so much how rents are extracted, but how they are deployed. In addition, economic and political structures that rely on individual patron–client relations can also be found in non-rentier states and, arguably in the case of Dubai and other Gulf states, existed prior to the petrochemical boom, and, although Dubai exhibits strategies of wealth distribution that distinguish such a state, it has never entirely relied on that income alone.

For many years the Dubai government has taken an active and pragmatic role in development (Hvidt 2007) and also in attracting foreign investment through the establishment of entrepôt tax free export-processing zones (Davidson 2007). Dubai began to invest in tourism infrastructure from the 1980s onwards as 'a catalyst for direct foreign investment and wider business development' (Sharpley 2008: 21). By the mid-1990s the focus had shifted towards developing tourism as a sector in its own right (Sharpley 2008), driven by the need to generate new income once the oil and gas reserves were exhausted (Hazbun 2004; Henderson 2006a,b; Gray 1997). By 2002 the share of gross domestic product (GDP) derived from tourism stood at 18 per cent and that from oil and gas revenues at 17 per cent (Henderson 2006a); in fact 90 per cent of GDP is now derived from the non-oil sectors (Henderson 2006a), while at the same time Dubai has become one of the fastest-growing tourist destinations (Henderson 2006b).

More recently there has also been a shift into the speculative property, hotel and leisure development market based on public–private partnerships, with the government prepared to grant land to developers and provide the infrastructure. The absence of capital gains and property tax all act as strong incentives for capital investment. To further boost this sector, in recent years the property market has been opened up for overseas buyers, for until 2005 expatriates were not allowed to own the freehold for property. In this respect Dubai most closely resembles what Glenn (2007: 128–129) has termed a 'competition state', that is, one that creates conditions favourable to the investment of transnational capital. Relations between the public and private sectors still rely on personal contact and patronage, as the private sector is not formally included in the decision-making process. Instead, the governing elite pursue an 'open door' policy that encourages leaders to be accessible and responsive to the needs of business elite. Such an arrangement, together with the fact that a relatively small number of the ruling elite hold multiple offices, allows the ruler to have an exceptional degree of control (Hvidt 2007: 569–571).

Workforce and population

In addition, the redistribution of wealth by the state, another aspect of rentierism that can be found in Dubai, is that of a dual labour market. As I pointed out in my opening remarks, the majority of Dubai's population are expatriates, estimated to be 75.8 per cent of the population (UAEinteract 2008), who in turn occupy an estimated 90 per cent of jobs (Shihab 2001: 251). Another figure worth noting is the high ratio of men to women – slightly over 3:1 – which indicates that the majority of migrants are single (UAEinteract 2007). As Sassen (2008: 480) notes, the growth of Dubai required a large migrant workforce at both top-level and bottom-level occupations, and, although some migrants will be employed in skilled occupations, the majority are employed in either services or the construction industry while the indigenous population of Dubai tend to seek employment in the public sector. In classic rentier fashion, public sector salaries tend to be higher with work hours following the eight-hour five-day-week pattern compared with the private sector in which the ten-hour six-day working week is the norm (Nelson 2004: 14). As Herb (2008: 11) points out, the wages paid to expatriate workers in the private sector are 'well below rates paid to citizens in the public sector' with the net result that as little as 5 per cent of Emiratis are employed in the private sector. This is despite a number of policy directives aimed at reducing dependency on an expatriate workforce by restricting unskilled labour and repatriating illegal migrants (Pacione 2005: 257). The wage disparity is a disincentive for the indigenous population, but this is also matched by the unwillingness of many in the private sector to employ nationals because of a lack of skills (Al Ali 2008). More recently efforts have been made to encourage more women to enter the workforce (see Gallant and Pounder 2008); the Dubai Women Establishment, for example, states that it 'will adopt best international practices to accord women their position in the workplace and the family, while preserving the traditional and cultural values of the UAE' (http://dwe.gov.ae/arb). This statement neatly encapsulates the balancing act that Dubai is attempting to achieve between globalization on the one hand and regional, traditional cultural values on the other. For example, Nelson (2004: 7) points out that many Emiratis shun employment in personal services such as hotel work, waiting at tables and hairdressing and nursing, which, in turn, given the strategic shift into tourism, creates the need for migrant workers, for, as Sassen (2008: 480) notes, 'High price restaurants, luxury housing, luxury hotels, gourmet shops, boutiques . . . are all more labour intensive than their lower price equivalents'.

However, the majority of migrants are employed in the construction industry. Of those, the biggest share of the workforce is from the Indian subcontinent, in particular the state of Kerala. As many as 20 per cent of all migrants from that state make the journey to Dubai, and, of those, 40.8 per cent are employed in the private sector and 47.5 per cent as non-agricultural workers (Willoughby 2005: 15). To enter, those travelling from India need to have a work permit, or a 'no objection certificate' and an exit permit, issued by the Indian Government if proof of employment can be shown. Such bilateral attempts to regulate the flow of workers have not been entirely successful (Willoughby 2005) and have actually created an additional market for agents who are able to purchase the necessary documentation and then recruit the workforce (Willoughby 2005: 19). An alternative strategy for those seeking work is to enter Dubai as a tourist and then search for a job, but, as Willoughby argues, it is more often brokers who provide the necessary paperwork for which the workers pay a fee and their airfare, which, he estimates, costs an average of US$1,664 (Willoughby 2005: 22–23). This is a considerable sum of money for someone from a low-wage economy such as Kerala, who often has to rely on loans from family or money lenders that can take years to repay.

Clearly such a system is open to corruption and can be exacerbated by the custom, which is actually illegal in the UAE, of employers holding their workers' passports so that they cannot leave. In many ways this resembles a form of indentured servitude with workers living on low wages in overcrowded and squalid accommodation (Human Rights Watch 2006). Despite such factors, there is no shortage of people willing to borrow the money to buy the permits, as even the low wages on offer are better than what many can hope to earn in their homeland.

In common with many migrant workers, a proportion of income is sent back to Kerala in the form of remittances, which have a significant impact on the local economy (Gopinathan Nair 1999; Prakash 1998; Sassen 2008; Zachariah and Irudaya Rajan 2007; Zachariah *et al.* 2002, 2003). Residency permits are dependent on work, and length of residence does not confer any right to stay. Once a contract ends, so too does the right to remain in Dubai. Low wages also contributes to the gender imbalance of the workforce as the government will only issue residency permits to wives and children of those earning in excess of 3,000 dirhams per month if accommodation is provided, and 4,000 dirhams if not. With many in the construction sector earning as little as 643 dirhams per month (Human Rights Watch 2006: 7)[3] the lower-paid workers are effectively excluded from bringing their families over.

With a closely regulated labour market and a centralized political economy, Dubai was able to rapidly acquire all of the trappings of a world city, initially financed by oil but looking, as in the post-industrial areas of the developed world, to support the long-term security of its economy by investing in tourism and trading in the import and export of leisure seekers. But what kind of tourism space is being constructed, and who does it serve?

Tourism development in Dubai

In its own terms, Dubai sells itself as 'An exotic destination with a cosmopolitan lifestyle' (http://www.dubaitourism.ae/Incentive/default.asp) that is also 'safe' (Henderson 2006b: 92). Here the tourist is offered not only the exotic orientalism of the souks, the old city, the desert landscape and the warm waters of the Gulf, but also a choice of malls, as both import duties and sales tax are low and so too are the prices, particularly for gold. The city also hosts the Dubai Shopping Festival, held in January–February, when tourism numbers elsewhere in the Northern hemisphere, at least, are at their lowest. In some respects the developments are similar to other resorts and enclaves elsewhere, offering a purpose-built environment wholly given over to the pursuit of leisure, but the scale of the development is unique, which is most apparent in the creation of the three Palm Islands of Jumeirah, Jebel Ali and Deira to house hotels and upmarket villas and apartments, and the building of iconic high-quality hotels such as the Jumeirah Beach and Atlantis. Although some aspects of Arabic culture such as the old souks and other historic buildings are protected, and tourists can experience a 'desert adventure' or camel racing, or perhaps visit the heritage village, the basic activities offered are those you would expect to find in most developed states. The planned Dubai Opera House (if built, considering the present economic slump) would add another prestigious icon to the city and appeal to the rich cosmopolitan elite that the city wishes to attract.

The urban landscape that Dubai offers is unashamedly modern; although the old city still remains it is dwarfed by the scale of the new. The provision of iconic and spectacular architecture also serves an economic function by providing both high-quality urban spaces for work and leisure and contributing to the wider global branding and marketing of the city, so that, although the souks provide the exotic, the cosmopolitan appeal lies in more 'Westernized' attractions. One such is Dubailand, which unabashedly claims to be 'the world's most ambitious tourism, leisure and entertainment project, designed to catalyse the position of Dubai as an international hub of family tourism' (http://www.dubailand.ae/facts_figures.html). Begun in 2003, Dubailand will eventually occupy 278 square kilometres, although, like many other developments, at the time of writing it is by no means certain that this target will be met. To date, four projects have been completed: the Al Sahra Resort; a spectacular stage show that celebrates Arabic culture, 'Jumana Secret of the Desert'; the Dubai Autodrome; and Dubai Sports City. The last includes a golf course, soccer school and tennis, cricket and rugby academies at various stages of development. Perhaps the most unlikeliest of attractions is Dubai's indoor ski slope, Ski Dubai, with 22,500 square metres of 'real snow'. In addition there is also a Global Village where goods and cultural artefacts from around the world can be bought, and the Universal Studios 'Ride The Movies' theme park is scheduled to open in 2010. Sport is an important component of the tourist product, and the emirate hosts a number of highly prestigious sporting events such as the Dubai World Cup horse race, the Dubai Tennis Championship and the Dubai Desert Classic golf tournament, itself part of the European PGA tour. Overall the developments resemble what Sassen (2008: 480) has termed 'high income gentrification', with the added advantage of beaches and sea, still one of the staple attractions for holidaymakers, especially during the winter months in Europe, while Mansfield and Winckler (2007: 345) point out that Dubai is also an attractive destination for mixing business and pleasure travel.

It would seem then that Dubai has plenty to offer; however, figures for hotel occupancy show a dominance of the short stay and hence stopover market, with an average length of hotel stay of just over 2.5 days, and apartment stay of 3.7 days. It needs to be kept in mind, however, that at the time these figures were compiled there were fewer tourist apartments than hotel bedspaces. The emphasis that the tourist authority places on the quality of experience together with the kinds of development and the profile of the hotel stock clearly indicate the intent of the emirate to become a world class upmarket resort (Anwar and Sohail 2004). Altogether there are 12,000 five-star rooms, 6,000 four-star rooms and just over 4,000 three-star rooms, (Department of Tourism and Commerce Marketing 2008), although this number will have increased significantly with the opening of the Atlantis, which adds another 1,539 rooms to the five-star category. Hotel occupancy figures also show that that the largest proportion of visitors come from Europe (32 per cent), closely followed by the Arab countries (30 per cent) and then Asia (22 per cent); in terms of particular country of origin, the largest national group are UK tourists with a total of 508,000 visitors in 2006, almost half the European total of 1.17 million, followed by tourists from the United States with 218,952 and Saudi Arabia with 206,000 (Department of Tourism and Commerce Marketing 2008). Tourist flows into the emirate are dominated by inter-regional movement from Europe and Asia, which reflects Dubai's strategic location; however there are also significant flows from other countries within the region, which is probably caused by the variety of pursuits and attractions on offer, which outstrip those of its closest neighbours in scale and variety.

A key element that we need to take account of is the way in which culture, as a resource, can be incorporated into the political economy. As noted above, tourism exhibits a number of aspects that are not found in other sectors of the economy, in particular the ways in which value is extracted from both the aesthetics of place and material culture. In addition, the less tangible qualities of people and place can act both as an economic resource as well as a means to create and maintain a sense of identity. This is not a new phenomenon (see, for example, Phillips 1998) nor one that we can attribute solely to the condition of contemporary globalization (see Rydell and Kroes 2005). The crucial issue here is one of power: who owns and who controls. Drache and Froese (2006: 375), for example, point out that states 'equate protection of identity with their continued political viability' and there are many examples of states using tourism as a means of promoting specific claims to both people and place (see, for example, Kolas 2004). Although Dubai is pitching for a cosmopolitan market, national identity is an important element, but there is also evidence of some tensions that exist across many parts of the Arabic world between economic growth and Westernization, often equated with Americanization, and the desire to maintain a distinctly Arabic and Islamic identity (Moussalli 2007). In cultural terms Dubai is a relatively liberal and open state; there is no prohibition on the sale of alcohol within hotels, and the practice of other religions, although not the preaching of them, is also tolerated. However, it is not a place in which to take a holiday of unbridled hedonism; strict laws govern sexual behaviour, and tourists, particularly women, are advised to dress modestly when outside the confines of the European residential area and hotel precincts. It is unclear if such relative tolerance is the result of the long-standing contact between Dubai and Europe, or a pragmatic response to the rather unusual situation in which the indigenous population is heavily outnumbered by temporary migrant workers, even if they hold all the cards.

Conclusions

Dubai has a particular if not unique political system; it is a micro-state within a larger federation with an autocratic government that is prepared to invest large amounts of revenue into the built environment. Although this has been achieved though a mixture of public and private funding, and although elements of a free market neoliberal approach are evident, the role of the state, or more precisely the ruling elite, has not been compromised but actually strengthened. What this example shows is that under certain circumstances globalization enhances the power of the state seeking to control the flows and networks of finance and people, which are as important as control over territory.

In this case, what kind of flows and networks are we dealing with? First, the flows of tourists are both inter- and intra-regional. With a small population the UAE as a whole will not develop a sizable domestic tourism sector, even if the Emirati citizens benefit from the provision of new services and infrastructure. The pattern of tourism in Dubai is a reflection of both its role and location and its specific political economy. As a regional travel hub located midway between Asia and Europe, Dubai attracts significant numbers of tourists from both those regions, as well as significant intra-regional tourism. Small tourist numbers from the Americas (excluding the United States) and South-East Asia/Oceania indicate that Dubai is not a significant long-haul destination in itself. What is on offer is a mix of upmarket retail with periodic sporting events that is designed to appeal to an affluent and cosmopolitan market segment, and, like other urban developments, is more suited to the short break or stopover market, although the new palm developments offer an upmarket version of the traditional sun, sand and sea holiday. Although local culture is preserved and utilized as a tourist resource it does not have the same prominence you can find in other Middle Eastern states.

This has been possible for a number of reasons. With a relatively small historic urban core there is plenty of land available for large-scale developments, Also there was no established pattern or tradition of tourism to build on; in effect, by diversifying its economy, Dubai developed its tourism infrastructure in a very short time from nothing, but in a controlled manner by the provision of a business-friendly environment. This has been achieved by both a mixture of public–private funding and encouraging speculative off-plan property development, especially since the granting of freehold rights to migrants. The single most important factor has been the structure of government. With few external checks and balances, and with no organized political opposition, the ruling elite can implement policies and strategy in a very short space of time, while the granting of work and residency permits that do not confer permanent right of settlement also means that the work-force can be rapidly adjusted to suit market conditions.

The property boom required a workforce that was drawn predominantly from the state of Kerala in South-West India, where we can also see a reverse financial flow of remittances having a substantial effect on the local economy. However, the Kerala workers in effect act as a reserve army of labour and, like other expatriates, have no right of permanent residence; in this sense there is a clear centre–periphery relationship with regard to unskilled and semi-skilled labour, whereas other expatriate workers in higher-skilled occupations are more likely to be recruited from a more geographically dispersed population. Another factor we need to consider is the rentier redistributive function of the state and the dependency of many Dubai citizens on high public sector salaries and their reluctance to enter the private sector, which will no doubt be reflected in the hotel sector workforce.

In terms of financial flows the picture is a complex one. Tourist revenues flow into Dubai and play an important role in the economy, and, as noted, there is a definable reverse flow from Dubai to Kerala, and indeed to other states where the workforce has been recruited from. What is more difficult to judge is the amount of leakage from Dubai to overseas through profits accrued on the speculative property market and extracted as rents from apartments and hotel profits. As much of the development has been off plan, it is likely that many properties would have been purchased for resale once they had accrued sufficient returns, perhaps without even being completed. Since freehold property rights were granted to non-UAE nationals it is not unreasonable to expect that ownership of Dubai real estate is now distributed around the globe, even though in the current climate its value has fallen significantly.

Whether or not the downturn will have a significant effect on Dubai's tourism is hard to say, but the latest United Nations World Tourism Organization forecast predicts a global decline in long-haul travel. In the first quarter of 2009 international tourist arrivals declined by 8 per cent compared with the previous year, and tourist arrivals in the Middle East declined by 18 per cent (United Nations World Tourism Organization 2009). Such changes may in fact strengthen regional or national markets, and could also signal a shift towards more competitively priced destinations.[4]

Tourism has weathered other financial and security crises before, and long term is likely to recover, but whether or not Dubai's long-term strategy will be compromised remains to be seen. The current slowdown has not resulted in the collapse of the current global economic system, although we are certainly entering a period of increasing financial regulation in which, in some cases, the role of the state will be significantly strengthened. In the case of Dubai, however, the state was central to the whole process, not only as a distributor of its rentier-generated income, but also as an enabler and facilitator, encouraging direct foreign investment and speculative development that gave rise to Dubai's sudden rise to prominence as a global tourist destination.

Notes

1 Some service sector industries and retail may be highly influenced by locational aesthetics.
2 The other main approaches are typically described as the 'sceptics' who doubt that globalization is new, and the 'hyperglobalizers' who view the role of the state as being severely curtailed. See Glenn (2007).
3 Human Rights Watch gives the figure at US$175.
4 As I am writing this, an advert in my local paper is offering discount short stays in the Atlantis Hotel.

References

Al Abed, I. (2001) 'The historical background and constitutional basis to the federation', in I. Al Abed and P. Hillyer (eds) *United Arab Emirates: A new perspective*, London: Trident Press.

Al Ali, J. (2008) 'Emiratisation: Drawing UAE nationals into their surging economy', *International Journal of Sociology and Social Policy*, 28: 365–379.

Al Sageh, F. (2004) 'Post 9/11 changes in the Gulf: The case of the UAE', *Middle East Policy*, 11: 107–124.

Anwar, S. A. and Sohail, M. S. (2004) 'Festival tourism in the United Arab Emirates: First time versus repeat visitor perceptions', *Journal of Vacation Marketing*, 10: 161–170.

Bagaeen, S. (2007) 'Brand Dubai: The instant city or the instantly recognizable city', *International Planning Studies*, 12: 173–197.

Beblawi, H. (1990) 'The rentier state in the Arab world', in G. Luciani (ed.) *The Arab State*, London: Routledge.

Biersteker, T. (2000) 'Globalization as a mode of thinking in major institutional actors', in N. Woods (ed.) *The Political Economy of Globalization*, Basingstoke: Macmillan.

Davidson, C. (2006) 'After Shaikh Zayed: The politics of succession in Abu Dhabi and the UAE', *Middle East Policy*, 13: 42–59.

Davidson, C. (2007) 'The emirates of Abu Dhabi and Dubai: Contrasting roles in the international system', *Asian Affairs*, 38: 33–48.

Department of Tourism and Commerce Marketing (2008) 'Analysis of 2006 Dubai hotel statistics'. Online. Available at http://www.dubaitourism.ae/EServices/Statistics/HotelStatistics/tabid/167/language/en-US/Default.aspx (accessed 5 March 2010).

Department of Tourism and Commerce Marketing (2009) 'UAE population estimates 2008'. Online. Available at http://www.dubaitourism.ae/EServices/Statistics/PopulationStatistics/tabid/169/language/en-US/Default.aspx (accessed 5 March 2010).

Dicken, P. (2003) *Global Shift: Reshaping the global economic map in the 21st century*, London: Sage.

Drache, D. and Froese, M. D. (2006) 'Globalisation, world trade and the cultural commons: Identity, citizenship and pluralism', *New Political Economy*, 11: 361–382.

Gallant, M. and Pounder, J. S. (2008) 'The employment of female nationals in the United Arab Emirates', *Education, Business and Society: Contemporary Middle Eastern Issues*, 1: 26–33.

Ghimire, K. B. (2001) *The Native Tourist: Mass tourism within developing countries*, London: Earthscan.

Glenn, J. (2007) *Globalization: North–South perspectives*, London: Routledge.

Gopinathan Nair, P. R. (1999) 'Return of overseas contract workers and their rehabilitation and development in Kerala, India', *International Migration*, 37: 209–242.

Gray, M. (1997) 'The political economy of tourism in Syria: State, society and economic liberalisation', *Arab Studies Quarterly*, 19: 57–73.

Hannigan, J. (1998) *Fantasy City: Pleasure and profit in the postmodern metropolis*, Routledge: London.

Harrison, D. (2001) *Tourism and the Less Developed Word: Issues and case studies*. CABI: Wallingford.

Hazbun, W. (2004) 'Globalisation, reterritorialisation and the political economy of tourism development in the Middle East', *Geopolitics*, 9: 310–341.

Hazbun, W. (2006) 'Explaining the Arab Middle East tourism paradox', *The Arab World Geographer*, 9: 206–218.

Henderson, J. C. (2006a) 'Destination development: Singapore and Dubai compared', *Journal of Travel and Tourism Marketing*, 20: 33–45.

Henderson, J. C. (2006b) 'Tourism in Dubai: Overcoming barriers to destination development', *International Journal of Tourism Research*, 8: 87–99.

Herb, M. (2008) 'Parliaments, rentier labor markets and economic diversification in Kuwait and the UAE', paper presented at the Annual Meeting of the American Political Science Association, Boston, August.

Human Rights Watch (2006) *Building Towers, Cheating Workers: Exploitation of migrant construction workers in the United Arab Emirates*, New York: Human Rights Watch.

Hvidt, M. (2007) 'Public–private ties and their contribution to development: The case of Dubai', *Middle Eastern Studies*, 43: 557–577.

Kolas, A. (2004) 'Tourism and the making of place in Shangri-la', *Tourism Geographies*, 6: 262–278.

Mansfield, Y. and Winckler, O. (2007) 'The tourism industry as an alternative for GCC oil-based rentier economics', *Tourism Economics*, 13: 333–360.

Matly, M. and Dillon, L. (2007) 'Dubai Strategy: Past, present, future', Harvard Business School. Online. Available at http://belfercenter.ksg.harvard.edu/publication/3159/dubai_strategy.html (accessed 5 March 2010).

Moussalli, A. S. (2007) 'Regional realities in the Arab World', in H. Anheier and Y. R. Isar (eds) *Conflicts and Tensions*, London: Sage.

Nelson, C. (2004) *UAE National Women at Work in the Private Sector: Conditions and constraints*, Dubai: Centre for Labour Market Research and Information.

Okruhlik, G. (1999) 'Rentier wealth, unruly law, and the rise of opposition: The political economy of oil states', *Comparative Politics*, 31: 295–315.

Pacione. M (2005) 'City profile Dubai', *Cities*, 22: 255–265.

Phillips, R. (1998) *Trading Identities: The souvenir in native North American art from the Northeast 1700–1900*, Seattle: University of Washington Press.

Porter, R. (1998) 'Clusters and the new economics of competition', *Harvard Business Review*, November/December, pp. 77–90.

Prakash, B. (1998) 'Gulf migration and its economic impact: The Kerala experience', *Economic and Political Weekly*, 33: 3209–3213.

Rydell, R. W, and Kroes, R. (2005) *Buffalo Bill in Bologna: The Americanization of the world 1869–1922*, Chicago: University of Chicago Press.

Sassen, S. (2008) 'Two steps in today's new global geographies: Shaping novel labor supplies and employment regimes', *American Behavioral Scientist*, 52: 457–496.

Shambayati, H. (1994) 'The rentier state, interest groups and the paradox of autonomy: State and business in Turkey and Iran', *Comparative Politics*, 26: 307–331.

Sharpley, R. (2008) 'Planning for tourism: The case of Dubai', *Tourism and Hospitality Planning & Development*, 5: 13–30.

Shihab, M. (2001) 'Economic development in the UAE', in I. Al-Abed and P. Hillyer (eds) *United Arab Emirates: A new perspective*, London: Trident.

Singh, S. (ed.) (2009) *Domestic Tourism in Asia: Diversity and divergence*, London: Earthscan.

The Times (21 November 2008) 'Crisis? What crisis? Dubai's Atlantis hotel opens with £13m party'. Online. Available at http://www.timesonline.co.uk/tol/news/world/middle_east/article5201601.ece (accessed 16 September 2010).

UAEinteract (2007) 'Dubai population makes big surge'. Online. Available at http://www.uaeinteract.com/docs/Dubai_population_makes_big_surge/24196.htm (accessed 17 May 2010).

UAEinteract (2008) 'Expat growth widens UAE demographic gap'. Online. Available at http://uaeinteract.com/docs/Expat_growth_widens_UAE_demographic_gap__/32128. htm (accessed 17 May 2010).

United Nations World Tourism Organization (2009) *UNWTO Tourism Barometer*, 7 (2), June. Online. Available at http://www.unwto.org/facts/eng/barometer.htm (accessed 5 March 2010).

Urry, J. (2000) *The Tourist Gaze*, 2nd edn, London: Sage.

Vesperman, J., Wald, A. and Gleich, R. (2008) 'Aviation growth in the Middle East: Impacts on incumbent players and potential strategic reactions', *Journal of Transport Geography*, 16: 388–394.

Willoughby, J. (2005) 'Ambivalent anxieties of the South Asian–Gulf Arab Labor Exchange', American University, Washington DC, Working Paper 2005–2. Online. Available at http://www.american.edu/cas/economics/research/papers.cfm (accessed 5 March 2010).

Woods, N. (2000) *The Political Economy of Globalization*, Basingstoke: Macmillan.

Zachariah, K. C and Irudaya Rajan, S. (2007) *Economic and Social Dynamics of Migration in Kerala 1999–2004*, Working Paper 384, Thiruvananthapuram, Kerala: Centre for Development Studies.

Zachariah, K. C., Prakash, B. A. and Irudaya Rajan, S. (2002) *Gulf Migration Study: Employment, wages and working conditions of Kerala emigrants in the United Arab Emirates*, Working Paper 326, Thiruvananthapuram, Kerala: Centre for Development Studies.

Zachariah, K. C., Prakash, B. A. and Irudaya Rajan, S. (2003) 'The impact of immigration policy on Indian contract migrants: The case of the United Arab Emirates', *International Migration*, 41: 161–172.

Part III

Tourism and spatial contexts of political economy

12 Negotiating business interests and a community's 'greater good'

Community-based tourism planning and stakeholder involvement in the Catlins, New Zealand

Julia N. Albrecht

Political economy and tourism planning

Political economy in the context of tourism has been tentatively explored since the early 1990s when Britton's (1991) seminal paper likened tourism to a production system incorporating economic activities aiming to market a destination, social, cultural and physical elements and governing regulating agencies. There are numerous inter-relationships between the aforementioned activities and tourism planning and, indeed, tourism planning has a significant part in the tourism production system. At the same time, however, the planning process itself is affected by that system.

As a theoretical tradition, political economy is fundamentally concerned with decision-making, the choice between different alternatives and the outcomes of these processes. A political economy perspective lends itself to the exploration of tourism planning as the related processes are rife with interaction and decision-making of stakeholders, their prioritizing and choice between different alternatives, questions of who represents whose and which interests, and the need to assess the outcomes of these processes. Acknowledging how significant aspects of both plan formulation and plan implementation have been removed from the realm of governments and have found their way into civil society, Friedmann (1998) has posited a new political economy of planning. Similar developments can be recognized in tourism strategy and planning and it is hoped that a political economy perspective will help in illuminating some salient aspects.

This chapter seeks to provide a political economy perspective on rural community tourism planning and implementation. Investigating an example of a community-based tourism planning strategy in the rural region of the Catlins, New Zealand, stakeholders, in particular small and medium tourism enterprises (SMTEs), and their roles are examined. The focus is on how actors partake in the process, how they articulate and represent their interests, and what the outcomes are in terms of the negotiation of personal and business objectives and what can be described as general community goals, for example the preservation of the natural and social environments. The chapter starts with a short review of the literature on community-based tourism planning and SMTE characteristics and performance. After introducing the case study and research project, the findings are presented and discussed in the context of a prominent paradigm in political economy, namely rational choice. The choice of this paradigm is inspired by the following statement from Krippendorf (1987: 20): 'Everybody wants more business, a larger share of the market. They will all move heaven and earth and use well-contrived methods to reach their goal . . . Their primary interest is the short-term growth of their own business and not the long-term development of a well balanced tourist trade.'

Rational choice assumes that actors aim to benefit from their behaviour. Although it is acknowledged that this benefit does not necessarily need to be economic (Smelser 1992), Krippendorf's (1987) declaration that tourism companies are and act as businesses and not charitable institutions holds true and economic gain is undoubtedly the major inducement for the tourism business operator. Krippendorf implicitly suggests that SMTE representatives in tourism planning may tend to favour their business interests over community interests or the 'greater good'. Regional government representatives, such as economic development agencies (EDAs) whose main task lies in fostering local business success, may agree that economically based rational choice between various business options is the most logical course of action for tourism business owners and will also benefit the whole community. Other stakeholders may favour different interests such as protection of the natural and social environment. The community's 'greater good' is a highly disputed conception and, as Hall (2005: 2) states for the context of peripheral areas, '[w]hat may be economically rational is not necessarily politically rational, particularly when one adopts a philosophy that the "public good" is not necessarily to be equated with "economic good"'.

SMTE stakeholders in community-based tourism planning

SMTEs have an important role in the tourism industry and small-scale and family-owned tourism businesses can form a significant part of the tourism product in small and/or rural destinations. Such companies potentially struggle with a variety of difficulties. Some of the problems, such as seasonality, difficulties in attracting skilled staff or issues related to infrastructure, result from the characteristics of the destination region itself; others, for example lack of professionalism, difficulties in marketing or financial problems, lie in the company itself (Buhalis 1999). SMTE owners are known to invest a significant amount of their personal wealth in the company (Page *et al.* 1999) and are therefore under pressure to succeed. Short-term business planning that does not incorporate or allow for a long-term community perspective is common for SMTEs (Ioannides 2001). Even though it would be desirable from the destination and community viewpoint (Carey and Gountas 1997), such small and potentially struggling enterprises cannot be expected to comply with societal marketing approaches.

Since Murphy's (1985, 1988) call for a community focus in tourism, intensive community involvement and a focus on the local context in tourism planning have been emphasized throughout the tourism literature (e.g. Prentice 1993; Jamal and Getz 1995; Timothy and White 1999; Tosun 2000; Mitchell and Reid 2001). It is generally accepted that the local level needs to be involved in tourism planning to some degree but whether this refers to the community as such or whether it is restricted to local government, administration or tourism agencies is debatable. Whereas Elliott (1997: 101) calls for general local, grassroots or 'impact level' involvement, Dredge (2006: 563) is more specific and outlines consequences of local government activity without public support: 'The planning or policy product, while well articulated, justified and defensible, can remain a desktop exercise with little or no implementation and can remain contested within the community despite "adoption" by local agencies'.

Community-based tourism planning is employed in practice in different ways and for different reasons: first, to empower a community to take an active role in regional planning and development; second, to thus enable residents to identify with the aforementioned developments and to achieve community acceptance of resulting outcomes; and third, as a means to increase the sustainability of said planning outcomes. It goes beyond mere community participation in that the residents are expected not only to state their opinions on certain projects or strategies but also to take ownership of the entire planning process from the initiation or plan-making stage to the planning results and their enactment and evaluation. Joppe (1996) states that financial resources and influence (or lack thereof) are factors that affect potential participation of stakeholders at the community level. Cases in which stakeholders may choose to participate as a result of their specific financial situation (and with a view to improve it) are thus conceivable and likely.

In her study of community planning, McAreavey (2006: 86) describes how individuals decide to become involved 'because they believe they have a valid contribution to make to a particular situation as well as a benefit to be gained'. This implies that these individuals see themselves as being capable of making a valuable contribution; it also means that the interests that they pursue do not necessarily relate to the 'greater good' of the community, but can in fact be their own private or business interests.

The project and case study

This research is part of a project that investigates tourism strategy implementation and uses the rural region of the Catlins, New Zealand, as a case study. The Catlins is an emerging destination on New Zealand's South Island. Since roughly 2002, tourist numbers have been rising, not least as a result of the main road through the area being sealed and allowing more travellers to access the area. Some residents of the Catlins, in collaboration with local government agencies, have successfully lobbied for the formulation of a tourism strategy and the carrying out of tourism planning projects. The Catlins Tourism Strategy has been prepared by the University of Otago Department of Tourism (2004), acting as a consultant. The strategy document responds to some residents' concerns that tourism may impact negatively on both the natural and the social environments. Aiming to establish tourism in the Catlins in a sustainable manner, the strategy addresses issues related to the protection of natural and cultural resources, increasing the economic value of tourism through product and infrastructure development and service quality, hospitality and communication with the visitor, visitor research and marketing and promotion (University of Otago, Department of Tourism 2004). As the initial impetus for the strategy was in maintaining community values while at the same time getting involved in tourism, the document is described by one Tourism Catlins member as being a 'conservation and community document' (Interview 2) as opposed to being growth-oriented. Nevertheless, the document does take into consideration the significance of tourism businesses in achieving such goals and contains numerous recommendations on how to increase business success (e.g. increased EDA advice and involvement, the establishment of a mentoring programme).

As the initiation of the strategy came from community members and attempts have been made to intensively involve the Catlins community in every step during strategy formulation, most community members subscribe to the goals outlined in the final strategy document. Strategy and project implementation are located at the community level and the document mentions the establishment of a 'Tourism Catlins' group as the first objective to be implemented. This group consists of six community members who frequently receive assistance from members of the local government and representatives from EDAs. Tourism Catlins board membership is for two years and, on average, half of the board members own and/or operate businesses that directly or indirectly benefit from tourists.

During the formulation of the Catlins Tourism Strategy, a survey of a small sample of tourism businesses was conducted. It was found that these display characteristics that are typical for a destination in the early stages of its life cycle. Most tourism products are either guided tours, often focusing on the natural environment and recreation opportunities, or small-scale accommodation businesses. Key characteristics of tourism businesses in the Catlins are (University of Otago, Department of Tourism 2004: 20):

- The majority of tourism businesses operate between October and April.
- Financial turnover varies significantly among businesses, from as little as NZ$2,000 to as much as NZ$800,000 per annum for some businesses.
- Most tourism businesses are small scale, employing few people on a full-time basis.
- Tourism businesses expenditure ranged from as little as NZ$200 to as high as NZ$40,500 per annum.
- Spending on advertising ranged from as little as NZ$100 up to NZ$6,000 per annum.

Shared community goals?

Common goals that are shared by all community members are not only considered an asset in the achievement of sustainable tourism (World Tourism Organization 2004), they also render the process of strategy implementation simple and straightforward. But as planning goals are shared only by parts of a community and/or only to a degree, the representation of interests, both personal and business, becomes relevant. One EDA representative (Interview 10) suggests that in some cases there may be more agreement among community members than anticipated and that communication difficulties between various stakeholders may account for non-agreement:

> It is important that everybody has common goals. That's just a matter of communicating those goals, common language and a method that fits everybody . . . Because the farmer in the middle of the Catlins, he might not understand all the big words that the academic may use, or the concepts, or the methodologies but you are probably both working towards the same outcome.

In most cases of disagreement, differing opinions and visions for the area seem to be present. Different stakeholders, from Tourism Catlins members to local government representatives (Interviews 7, 8 and 12), highlight the wide range of possible views in the process. Their comments highlight the degree to which conflict can occur as well as the need for balance:

> You have a lot of different fractions and they are all buying for their own agendas first. [. . .] Some parts of the community do not want to see growth. They are quite happy with the way it is. And those agendas will never go away.
>
> (Interview 8)
>
> And in the Catlins, you've got the Old Group, [mentions family names], who are trying to kind of, slow the Catlins down and not really overexpose the Catlins. [. . .] It's a pretty tight clique group. There's a lot of interesting things and dynamics going on in the Catlins right now. You've got investors coming into the Catlins. [. . .] There's the [. . .] really tight environmental group and the other group who are trying to actually build some resources out there.
>
> (Interview 12)
>
> You need a good group of people which is balanced and you can't have it balanced in the favour of tourism and you can't have it balanced in the favour of farming and business or environmentalists. It needs to have this balance and then you need to have people who can compromise on what they feel.
>
> (Interview 7)

Although a fair representation of all possible relevant stakeholder groups would be ideal and desirable in order to achieve balanced views across all actors, this is hardly feasible. Stakeholders differ not only in their own viewpoints on certain projects and matters but also in their opinions on who else should be involved. In this case the decision over which stakeholders to involve rested to a certain degree with local government and EDA representatives, as these financed the preparation of the strategy document and provided assistance throughout the community participation processes. These actors also had a function in publicizing participation events and workshops and were therefore perceived as significant stakeholders by many. The University of Otago moderated these meetings as a consultant because the EDAs and local government did not want to get involved in potential conflict situations: 'This was where University did well, in facilitating that engagement, the community felt comfortable. [Name of EDA] didn't want to get involved in conflicts. They can only assist in finding a resolution' (Interview 5). One EDA representative put these occurrences into perspective, stating 'When there's politics, local government politics involved, there's always tensions and there's always parochialism' (Interview 5). Indeed, the strength of business interest representation that thus arises in the local policy arena has been linked to increased political clout of businesses (Dodds 2005). Perhaps this is even convenient for some government institutions because, as Hall (1994: 48) states, 'the increased range of demands placed on governments makes it increasingly difficult for government to satisfy those demands'. This perception is confirmed by some stakeholders who highlight their view of what the role of tourism businesses in the planning process should be like.

Perceptions of the role of businesses

Although it is established that there are differing opinions relating to the interests of tourism business owners and their motivations for becoming involved with the community-based tourism strategy, what the entrepreneurs' roles in tourism planning and implementation *should be* was perceived in various ways too. Although, in general, EDA and local government representatives seemed to be for business involvement and see themselves in a collaborative role (Interview 10), one EDA representative (Interview 17) goes so far as to suggest a lead role for tourism businesses in tourism planning:

> I think in general, where the community wants projects to happen, I don't think budgetary or other issues stand in the way. If the group is interested and motivated, either by vested interest, which is probably the best kind of interest [. . .] They're the kind of people that want to see the other projects develop and the industry develops. So, a lot of it is kind of out of our hands, to a certain degree, we can make them look at opportunities and make gestures but the private sector then needs to [take action].

Another EDA representative goes so far as to equal business benefit and community benefit: 'Whatever happens, it's the operators who should benefit, you know, the local community' (Interview 5). Indeed, one interviewee (Interview 8) openly admits that he merely became involved with Tourism Catlins because he owned a tourism business at the time. This opinion is unlikely to be supported or shared by a large part of the community and needs to be viewed in a more differentiated way. Although it is understandable that some local tourism business owners ['Business will always trump anything that local bodies do' (Interview 12)] argue in favour of tourism development and call upon local bodies and EDAs to provide further business support (Interview 12), business owners who are involved with Tourism Catlins' work hold a more balanced view. One interviewee (Interview 11) who would herself benefit economically from increasing tourist numbers and expenditure puts these extreme approaches into perspective and states rather pragmatically: 'If you have one body that comes together and tries to implement without any connection between these businesses, it's not going to work'. This is in line with Wilson *et al.*'s (2001) view that tourism operators are instrumental to successful tourism development. Indeed, there seems to be a fine line between what is widely perceived in the community as 'beneficial vested interest' from the community perspective and mere egoism and focus on one's own economic success.

The next two sections examine other situations in which 'vested interests' were perceived negatively in the community-based tourism planning process. The cases show that 'vested interests' are not necessarily related to personal financial gain and business success.

Personal status and power as a motivation

Another emerging case of an implementation process participant illustrates how vested interest does not inevitably imply financial gain. One Tourism Catlins group member who became involved immediately after the release of the tourism strategy in 2004 was seen by the community not only to push his business agenda but also to try and raise his status as a community member:

> One problem is, and I think this is a general problem, is that you get individuals who join up for the wrong reasons. It's not on the group now, that's for sure, but in the past, people joined it because they thought this was a way they could raise their status in the community. And they thought they could get some power by what they thought was a burgeoning tourism area. So it was a power thing. They didn't see it for what it really was.
>
> (Interview 2)

However, according to four interviewees (Interviews 1, 2, 3 and 15) this did not work in the person's favour and he lasted only one year in the group.

McAreavey (2006: 85) investigates the 'micro-politics' of rural development and examines processes that govern community group interactions and the resulting process outcomes. She describes how micro-politics often extend the policy issue in question and go beyond what goes on during meetings; instead they include trust, local customs, perceptions and social networks but also social pressure, both local and individual values and considerations for people's status and their personalities (McAreavey 2006). Although most of these features are apparent in many planning contexts, they are particularly obvious in small groups in which people know each other very well.

Too much concern for the 'greater good'? Another perspective on 'vested interests'

This case is interesting as it involves a stakeholder who is perceived by many (Interviews 1, 3, 7 and 15) as being exceptionally community focused to the degree of being altruistic in spending most of his time working on various community committees concerned with the preservation of the natural and social environment

as well as being involved with Tourism Catlins. He is also an eco-tourism operator. This person's involvement with Tourism Catlins is controversial because of
potentially conflicting affiliations:

> He had too many vested interests. He sits on the Conservation Board so he
> has kind of a . . . And I don't mean this in a disrespectful way at all because
> I really admire him . . . But it's pretty hard for him to go to the Ministry of
> Conservation and say "Get your shit together", we've got three DoC staff
> down here and it's not a happening thing when he sits on the management
> board on a local level.
>
> (Interview 7)

Another interviewee associates his main interests with tourism instead of conservation and finds: '[Name of person] is so involved with tourism that perhaps
he doesn't always see the ordinary person's view. And the ordinary person thinks
he's so involved in it that he only sees it that way. I think that might be one of the
problems' (Interview 3). Others are less forgiving; one interviewee (Interview 12)
describes him as 'ultra-green' and 'pushing his agenda'. In this particular case, the
contentious issue not only emerged and was discussed at the community level, the
regional newspaper also published an article that discussed the person's various
involvements and potential implications for the groups he was working with (*The
Southland Times*, 1 August 2005, p. 2). The person himself denies any conflicting
roles, stating that he does what he believes in for the community.

Another interviewee (Interview 15) highlights the instrumental role of the
person stating that: 'There might have been suggestions that it was driven by
[name of Tourism Catlins member] and therefore meeting his business needs
but that didn't really come through strongly . . . In fact, if [he] hadn't driven
it, it wouldn't probably have happened at all'. Such experiences are not uncommon in rural contexts. Keen (2004: 148) describes a case in the rural region of
the Maniototo on New Zealand's South Island in which a 'social entrepreneur'
achieved both successful community projects as well as the establishment of her
own successful business. Keen goes on to illustrate a relative lack of economic
motivation in the formation of some rural businesses and highlights the social
and community benefits of operating the businesses that are perceived by social
entrepreneurs. Although this planning-oriented study also identifies social and
community benefits as incentives to partake in the planning process, many stakeholders are clearly economically motivated.

Vested interests in tourism strategy implementation by volunteers

The above examples illustrate a number of issues that relate to vested interests and
action towards strategy implementation at the local level. First, they demonstrate
how businesses and their representation of interests in a community tourism strategy process are perceived in a positive light by some whereas others are critical
about the implications of their actions. In addition to this, the display of vested

interests is by no means restricted to financial or economic considerations but can include status and power. Potentially overlapping interests, despite all being in favour of what is seen by some as the 'greater community good', can be viewed in a negative way too. This is particularly relevant when the tourism businesses' views of what constitutes the 'greater community good' differ strongly from the perspectives of others (regardless of what local policy or, as in this case, a tourism strategy may envisage).

At any rate, a number of incentives to become involved with tourism strategy at the local level that transcend community benefit can be identified. As one EDA representative puts it:

> When you have a lot of operators driving an initiative or implementation for the wider community benefit there's always that [. . .] factor of objectivity. Or are they in it for themselves? [. . .] How much is it community good versus personal good that they are pushing?'
>
> (Interview 5)

At the same time this person is aware that stakeholder involvement that could actually hinder the achievement of community good, as well as benefit at the personal level only, will be identified and brought to an end by the other actors: '[People who push their personal agenda] get found out pretty quickly anyway and it's normally their peers who will deal with it before anything else has to happen' (Interview 5).

One strategy maker (Interview 15, who does not live in the region himself) contemplates varying degrees of social constraints among participants as being a reason for varying displays of vested interests. One Tourism Catlins member, who participated in the process at an early stage, had no hesitation in putting his business interests first and using the strategy to inform his business decisions and to try to steer Tourism Catlins' work in a direction that would suit his plans (Interview 12). This person was a new resident of the Catlins who had bought businesses (tourism and other) in the area only two years before the tourism strategy process was initiated. As social constraints to openly displaying vested interests have an important role in local politics (McAreavey 2006), one interviewee (Interview 15) suggests that such a course of action and behaviour would not have been expected from anybody else in the community, certainly not from a community member:

> I don't think you can group all tourism operators into one homogenous group. And there are people like [names or operators] who . . . their interests are for the community and the environment. Whereas other tourism operators who I alluded to earlier . . . Their sole interest is the bottom-line and generating income for themselves. [. . .] But that was a rarity in that process. [. . .] Many of those people [referring to business owners] were long-standing community members and I think it would be way out of line for them to [have taken] an economic approach representing their own interest. They would have never done that because they know very clearly what the ramifications would have been for them in the community if they had done that.

Indeed, as McAreavey (2006: 90) states, '[community group] membership should not automatically be taken at face value. Just as some are involved for very specific reasons, others may not be involved or end their involvement for reasons that go beyond the lack of time to devote effort to an initiative'. In this statement, which, again, rightly calls for scepticism as to community members' involvement with the achievement of what can broadly be perceived as 'community goals', McAreavey (2006) also alludes to time constraints of community-level involvement and, indeed, many relevant stakeholders during strategy implementation at the community level were volunteers.

As one EDA representative (Interview 5) fittingly states: 'We are dealing with a voluntary community-based type of group [. . .], operating for the greater good of the community'. As, however, the previous occurrences during strategy implementation showed, the 'greater good of the community' is a contested notion. The fact that most actors who are involved are volunteers also raises questions as to their motives. Is it not fair that if people spend their spare time on community projects that they should get something out of it? Something beyond the satisfaction of having contributed to the 'greater community good'? Even though there is literature that supports the notion of selflessness as a motivation for volunteering at the community level (Lotz and MacIntyre 2003), assuming that volunteers participate for the greater good of the community displays degrees of naivety. There is a fine line between contributing for the good of the community because one is a member of that community and working towards one's own objectives and having the community benefit from such personal gain.

Collaboratively achieving the greater community good?

This contribution has already established the difficulty of achieving representative community participation, but the question as to what factors influence stakeholder participation remains unanswered. Contemplating how current actors became involved, one Tourism Catlins advisor (Interview 10) states that:

> I think you are always going to get people that have more time to be involved and that's just the nature of things and volunteers as well. [. . .] I think you've always got people that are passionately for something whether it's wildlife or to run a business or promoting the area. And everybody has their own interests as well.

Community participation can thus be assumed to be almost random and subject to a variety of external conditions as well. For example, local politics are known to rely to a high degree on personal relations (McAreavey 2006). As one interviewee (Interview 8) states, 'It comes down to getting the right people to talk to the right people to get what you want'. Blackstock (2005: 42) confirms that, 'However, most communities are heterogeneous, stratified and sites of power relations. This conceptualisation of community ignores how "community" groups can act out of self-interest rather than for collective good'. One interviewee is aware of this arbitrariness and optimistically states that, 'At the end of the day, there's always potential for democracy to work' (Interview 5).

Overall, there was low local government involvement during the making and implementation of the Catlins Tourism Strategy. To a certain degree, this is a result of a lack of capacity (Interview 9), and, indeed, difficulties in plan implementation and the establishment of control mechanisms are not uncommon (Wisansing *et al.* 2004). One incident in the Catlins, however, shows that local government representatives are subject to 'local politics' to a considerable degree and with relevant implications. They can act as individuals rather than representing the interests of the local government body and thus have a large influence on strategy implementation and related projects, as one interviewee complains:

> And so I just think that [name of local government representative] sought his bureaucratic revenge because what he did was nothing. Effectively he just did nothing. It's not that he did anything wrong. [. . .] I'm so angry about it, I'm so livid because I personally put a lot into it. And I was emphatic that you could trust these bureaucrats. They had a brief to do this. They were contracted to do the right thing. You know, I never believed for a moment that they wouldn't until I left and then they did nothing.

Negotiations related to the 'greater community good' therefore take place at a variety of levels: at the individual level where an actor may have to negotiate potentially contradicting affiliations, at the community group level where strategy aims may be interpreted and enacted in various ways, and at the level of outside advisors and local government where strategy goals may be seen in a broader picture and are by no means mandatory policy.

As tourist numbers are expected to rise in the Catlins, the divergence between what is perceived as the 'greater community good', business interests and the preservation of the natural and cultural environment may increase. There may come a point when more involvement from local government will be needed to moderate and mediate various interests and to regulate tourism development in the region. Hall (2000: 143–144) calls for strengthened government positions to regulate the impact and influence of private sector decisions and states that:

> If government is meant to occupy the role of general interest protector, and more particularly, if public tourism planning is meant to protect the interests of the wider community rather that just short-term sectoral tourism interests, then increasing attention also needs to be given to the manner in which the institutional arrangements of government involvement in tourism are organized and the instruments by which government intervenes to achieve tourism planning and community goals.

Although increased government involvement potentially results in more transparency in planning and implementation processes and heightened effectiveness and efficiency because of a streamlining of processes, community acceptance may be at stake, and bottom-up processes as envisaged, for example, during strategy-making in the Catlins may be skewed. On the other hand, if there is no common perception of what the 'greater community good' is, then in a situation in which civil society is indeed in charge (even though within their limited means) the 'greater community good' is whatever the community implements, regardless of its being representative of community wants and needs.

A wider political economy perspective

Decision-making and negotiations of priorities with respect to tourism strategy implementation occur for a variety of issues. These are not restricted to strategy implementation but include related issues such as the desired overall degree of tourism development for the region as well as environmental issues. Both political economy perspectives in general and rational choice in particular allow for an individual (person, business or agency) to be the unit of observation (Coleman 1990). As rational choice assumes that actors aim to benefit (economically or otherwise; Smelser 1992) from their behaviour this is a logical level of observation as individuals' decisions do not necessarily equal those of, for example, an agency that they may represent (as the sometimes differing opinions of the EDA representatives in this study illustrate).

At the same time, rational choice perspectives face ontological and epistemological problems. Even individuals who engage with, as in this case, an implementation process related to a document that is known to all participants hold differing views on what constitutes a rational proceeding; indeed, from one rational being's viewpoint another rational being's viewpoint and actions may seem rather illogical and irrational. Rational proceedings may imply different actions and outcomes for varying actors in different positions. Who represents the 'greater community good'? At both methodical and epistemological levels this also poses the following questions: Whose rationality is taken into consideration in a study (such as this)? How is it operationalized (and, well, rationalized) in order to achieve an understanding of the rational being's actions? At the methodical level, the concept of the *homo economicus* as the epitome of a rational actor is simplified to a degree that allows for theoretical modelling but not for an understanding of the real world.

Rational choice perspectives are associated with various perspectives on market situations and, in general, situations that involve decision-making and negotiations. The most well known, and also the most contradicting, is Smith's (1991 [1776]) metaphor of the *invisible hand* and Hardin's 'Tragedy of the Commons' (1968). The *invisible hand* is an allegory coined by Adam Smith (1991 [1776]) in his influential *The Wealth of Nations*. According to Smith, any individual that pursues his self-interest in a free market environment implicitly acts towards the good of his community; Smith refers to the phenomenon of the self-regulating nature of a market as the *invisible hand*. Although circumstances under which to equate the above-described strategy implementation situation to an economic market environment are thinkable, this would only be appropriate if a merely economic viewpoint was the research focus (which despite the focus on SMTEs would be one-dimensional and not provide a comprehensive picture). The metaphor of the *invisible hand* has also rightly been criticized for not taking into account environmental variables; Stiglitz (1985, 2002) explains how actions of an individual that do not imply immediate economic (monetary) value flaw a market situation or negotiation. He is also critical of the assumption that humans can behave rationally (by whichever perception of rationality) at all.

The 'Tragedy of the Commons' dilemma is well known; it is used here to represent the other end of the spectrum. In a nutshell, it assumes that, as a result of rational decision-making by individuals, common goods are used and exploited to a degree that is in the long term disadvantageous for all. Although countless studies have proven tourism's threats to host communities, it is still often community members in key governmental or business positions who have lead roles in pursuing economic growth at all costs.

For the context of tourism strategy at a community level, this study suggests that community 'greater good' is negotiated through social mechanisms that strongly depend on social control as well as coincidence (e.g. when stakeholder participation is dependent on interests as well as dispensable time). Whereas many actors display what might be described as rational action towards goals that they may benefit from (at economic, financial, social or professional levels), many of these actions seem to mitigate each other so that a balance is achieved (however, this occurs at the cost of change and, perhaps, what a majority might perceive as successful project implementation). Whether such a phenomenon should be described as an *invisible hand* is open to debate but, indeed, the political economy of tourism planning at a rural community level is subject to the influence of individuals as well as to serendipity. In this study, negotiations of goals and priorities neither occurred often nor openly; instead, it was often the realities of external influences that finally determined which stakeholder could achieve their goal at a particular moment. Some social effects, such as the fact that collaboration and cooperation at the Tourism Catlins group level would result in more support (financial support as well as advice), were recognized and acted upon.

This chapter focuses on actors in a rural community tourism strategy implementation process. Using a political economy and rational choice perspective, it openly and implicitly examines negotiations of the actors' interests and power relationships. There is no doubt that SMTEs are a vital part of the tourism production system and that some of their representatives assume a wide-reaching governance role for the destination community. The significant role of SMTE representatives at a practical level of tourism strategy implementation is apparent:

> And I suppose the view that we came to largely around implementation was that if the key movers and shakers were convinced they would make things happen to the extent they were comfortable with. And by and large, they were the people that had the capital, the infrastructure, the personal motivation to succeed and they were key leaders in the community.
>
> (Interview SI 1 in Albrecht 2009).

At the same time, the interactions *within* this group of stakeholders have wide-reaching impacts on the processes of strategy implementation. Stevenson *et al.* (2008: 733) allude to relevant implications at a conceptual level, stating that 'A policy conceptualization includes those interactions and processes associated with making policies, and the continual negotiations required to enact them'. Using political economy perspectives to analyse and explain stakeholders' behaviour patterns, this chapter argues that ultimately negotiations at the grassroots level of policy implementation reveal and bring into being (tourism) policy.

References

Albrecht, J. N. (2009) 'The implementation of tourism strategies – a critical analysis of two New Zealand case studies', unpublished thesis, University of Otago.

Blackstock, K. (2005) 'A critical look at community based tourism', *Community Development Journal*, 40: 39–49.

Britton, S. (1991) 'Tourism, capital, and place: Towards a critical geography of tourism', *Environment and Planning D: Society and Space*, 9: 451–478.

Buhalis, D. (1999) 'Limits of tourism development in peripheral destinations: Problems and challenges', *Tourism Management*, 20: 183–185.

Carey, S., and Gountas, Y. (1997) 'Tour operators and destination sustainability', *Tourism Management*, 18: 425–431.

Coleman, J. (1990) *Foundations of Social Theory*, Cambridge: Belknap Press of Harvard University Press.

Dodds, R. (2005) 'Barriers to the implementation of sustainable tourism policy in destinations', unpublished thesis, University of Surrey.

Dredge, D. (2006) 'Networks, conflict and collaborative communities', *Journal of Sustainable Tourism*, 14: 562–581.

Elliott, J. (1997) *Tourism: Politics and public sector management*, London: Routledge.

Friedmann, J. (1998) 'The new political economy of planning: The rise of civil society', in M. Douglass and J. Friedmann (eds) *Cities for Citizens: Planning and the rise of civil society in a global age*, Chichester: John Wiley and Sons.

Hall, C. M. (1994) *Tourism and Politics: Policy, power and place*, Chichester: John Wiley and Sons.

Hall, C. M. (2000) *Tourism Planning – Policies, Processes and Relationships*, Harlow: Prentice Hall.

Hall, C. M. (2005) 'Competing from the periphery: Mobility, toursim and regional development', University of Otago Working Papers in Competitiveness, UOWP2005.3. Dunedin: School of Business, University of Otago.

Hardin, G. (1968) 'The tragedy of the commons', *Science*, 162: 1243–1248.

Ioannides, D. (2001) 'Sustainable development and the shifting of tourism stakeholders: Towards a dynamic framework', in S. F. McCool and R. N. Moisey (eds) *Tourism, Recreation and Sustainability*, Wallingford: CABI International.

Jamal, T. B. and Getz, D. (1995) 'Collaboration theory and community tourism planning', *Annals of Tourism Research*, 22: 186–204.

Joppe, M. (1996) 'Sustainable community tourism development revisited', *Tourism Management*, 17: 475–479.

Keen, D. (2004) 'The interaction of community and small tourism businesses in rural New Zealand', in R. Thomas (ed.) *Small Firms in Tourism: International perspectives*, Amsterdam: Elsevier.

Krippendorf, J. (1987) *The Holidaymakers*, London: Butterworth-Heinemann.

Lotz, J. and MacIntyre, G. A. (2003) *Sustainable People: A new approach to community development*, Sydney, Nova Scotia: Cape Breton University Press.

McAreavey, R. (2006) 'Getting close to the action', *Sociologia Ruralis*, 46: 85–103.

Mitchell, R. E. and Reid, D. G. (2001) 'Community integration: Island tourism in Peru', *Annals of Tourism Research*, 28: 113–139.

Murphy, P. (1988) 'Community driven tourism planning', *Tourism Management*, 9: 96–104.

Murphy, P. E. (1985) *Tourism: A community approach*. London: Methuen.

Page, S. J., Forer, P. and Lawton, G. R. (1999) 'Small business development and tourism: Terra incognita?', *Tourism Management*, 20: 435–459.

Prentice, R. (1993) 'Community-driven tourism planning and residents' preferences', *Tourism Management*, 14: 218–227.

Smelser, N. J. (1992) 'The rational choice perspective: A theoretical assessment', *Rationality and Society*, 4: 381–410.

Smith, A. (1991 (1776) *The Wealth of Nations*, New York: Alfred A. Knopf.

Stevenson, N., Airey, D. and Miller, G. (2008) 'Tourism policy making: The policymakers' perspectives', *Annals of Tourism Research*, 35: 732–750.

Stiglitz, J. E. (1985) 'Information and economic analysis: A perspective', *The Economic Journal*, 95 (Supplement: Conference Papers): 21–41.

Stiglitz, J. E. (2002) 'There is no *invisible hand*', *The Guardian*, 20 December.

Timothy, D. J. and White, K. (1999) 'Community-based ecotourism development on the periphery of Belize', *Current Issues in Tourism*, 2: 226–242.

Tosun, C. (2000) 'Limits to community participation in the tourism development process in developing countries', *Tourism Management*, 21: 613–633.

University of Otago, Department of Tourism (2004) 'Catlins Tourism Strategy', unpublished, University of Otago.

Wilson, S., Fesenmaier, D. R., Fesenmaier, J. and van Es, J. C. (2001) 'Factors for success in rural tourism development', *Journal of Travel Research*, 40: 132–138.

Wisansing, J., Simmons, D. G. and McIntosh, A. (2004) 'Community driven tourism marketing: Tensions towards implementation and lessons learned from Thailand', paper presented at the 2nd Asia Pacific CHRIE Conference and the 6th Biennial Conference on Tourism in Asia, Phuket, Thailand, May.

World Tourism Organization (2004) *Indicators of Sustainable Development for Tourism Destinations A Guidebook*, Madrid: World Tourism Organization.

13 Tourism, neoliberal policy and competitiveness in the developing world

The case of the Master Plan of Marrakech

Nicolai Scherle

> If we want to make tourism a veritable motor of development then every single Moroccan must see himself as a tourism promoter mobilised to win the wager.
>
> (H. M. King Mohammed VI)

'*Mon rhythme est celui du Maroc*', Morocco's young king, Mohammed VI, the secular and religious leader (*amir al-mu'minin*) of his country, explained to a French reporter a good year after his enthronement (Le Figaro 2001): his political rhythm was that of his country. And this was not the rhythm that certain foreign observers wished to impose upon his country and him, who, like Abdullah II in Jordan and Hamad bin Isa in Bahrain, is considered one of a new reform-oriented group of Arab rulers.

The Arab world is changing. It is without a doubt in a phase of radical historical change, but it is not necessarily changing as fast, as profoundly and as comprehensively as large parts of the young generation wish, as foreign experts or business people consider necessary and as some long-established elites fear (Stewart 2009; Perthes 2002). The message of the Moroccan king is clear, and it stands not only for the westernmost outpost of the Arab hemisphere, but also for almost all Arab states in which a change in power has occurred in the past years.

The change in generation at the top of the political scale that has taken place in Morocco, Jordan and Syria and will occur in further Arab states in the coming years is only one element in the upheaval that the region is currently experiencing. This phase of upheaval is characterized by massive socio-economic changes that are often lumped together under the slogan globalization, particularly by the press (e.g. Ehteshami 2008; Sayan 2009). Like states in other regions (in particular Eastern Europe and Southern Asia) and in competition with them, the states of the Arab world are endeavouring to establish themselves as attractive locations for investment. For this they are opening their markets and negotiating with each other and with international actors, especially the European Union, about free trade and tariff reductions (Perthes 2002; Sekkat and Véganzonès-Varoudakis 2004). As a result the boundaries of the states in question have become more permeable, though for the time being more for goods and capital than for people.

The main development lines of Morocco's economic opening, or rather its economic policy, are more apparent in tourism than in almost any other sector.

The most obvious symbol of the process is the Master Plan of Marrakech, which was adopted in 2001. It elevated tourism to the leading sector in the economic development of the country and in many respects it heralded a paradigm shift with regard to the strategic orientation of tourism policies. The Master Plan is, however, not only a complex conceptual framework that was designed to improve the competitiveness of the destination in light of current transformation processes, for example the accelerated internationalization of the structures of tourism supply and increasingly fragmented and hybrid consumption patterns (Knowles *et al.* 2001; Wahab and Cooper 2001; Buhalis 2001). It can also be interpreted as a document that bears impressive testimony to a largely uninhibited neoliberalism, which has increasingly come under attack since the outbreak of the worldwide financial crisis in 2008, if not earlier.

The following contribution will examine the current Moroccan tourism policies in light of the adoption of the Master Plan of Marrakech from a problem-based perspective. First I will try to give a concise insight into selected economic conditions in Morocco that are still linked to an economic system, so-called rent capitalism, that differs quite considerably from the classical Western economic systems, particularly from an intercultural perspective. Nevertheless, Morocco has opened its economy to the West more than almost any other North African state has, especially to the EU, and has experienced a neoliberal penetration that will be outlined in an appropriate section and that is reflected truly paradigmatically in the kingdom's tourism policies. The genesis and strategic goals of the Master Plan will then be examined in more detail, as will selected assessments by tourism actors and experts. The subsequent section will introduce selected current developments in Moroccan tourism in relation to three closely linked examples that are connected with the underlying concept of the Master Plan of Marrakech. The first example includes selected assessments of the subject from the perspective of incoming agencies that cooperate with German tour organizers in consideration of the intensified internationalization of Moroccan tourism actors postulated in the Master Plan. The second example has to do with the liberalization of air traffic that was called for in the Master Plan and has been realized meanwhile, and the third example examines the process of gentrification of Moroccan medinas, which was initiated primarily by Europeans and North Americans and facilitated by the liberalization of air traffic. This not only involves a functional reallocation of former town houses into second homes and boutique hotels, but also has massive socio-cultural implications. Finally, in the discussion and conclusion, the Master Plan of Marrakech will be critically appraised with explicit reference to the transformation processes associated with it.

Morocco's economic structures between rent capitalism and neoliberalism

The Islamic world, and thus Morocco, the subject of this contribution, is traditionally associated with an economic system referred to as rent capitalism, which was analysed especially extensively by German-speaking researchers working in the field of Islamic studies (e.g. Bobek 1959; Wirth 1956, 1988). It is beyond the scope of this contribution to try to elucidate the entire complexity of this exceedingly diverse economic system. Consequently the following remarks will be restricted to some basic information selected on the basis of the following considerations. For one thing, the following explanations will help us to contextualize the current economic structures and processes in Morocco from a historical-genetic perspective. For another thing, it is becoming apparent that economic systems are decidedly process-related constructs and that in a globalized world they are subject to continuous transformation processes.

From a Western perspective classical rent capitalism has decidedly feudalistic tendencies. All profits that exceed the margin of subsistence of the *fellahin*, craftsmen or other dependents, who as a rule are highly indebted, are siphoned off by the usually urban 'capitalists'. Investments to maintain or even increase the productivity of an operation are largely alien to rent capitalism (Bhagwati 1982; Chatelus 1987). Thus in many cases this economic system has a definitely parasitic character, and as a rule the siphoning off of the profits leads to over-exploitation, which thwarts progress (Mensching and Wirth 1989). In this situation the involved persons show relatively little interest in increasing production or in innovations or intensifications, because they would not benefit from the increased production themselves. Only the 'capitalist' would. Table 13.1 shows the most important characteristics of rent capitalism in condensed form.

From the standpoint of development theory rent capitalism implies not only a deformation of the economic structures and the orientation of society as a whole, but also the formation of a rent-seeking mentality, particularly among the elite, but also among the native businesspeople (Buchanan 1980; Krueger 1974; Kuran 2004). In this view the efficiency principle loses its validity and is replaced by lobbying, while market awareness is less important than having the correct connections. A lack of internal communication or cooperation between the actors of

Table 13.1 Chief characteristics of so-called rent capitalism

- An economic system that is mainly associated with the Islamic world and with nation-state structures
- Profits (rents) siphoned off by the owners of the means of production on a continuous basis without investments to maintain or increase productivity
- Marked statist structures and a highly developed clientele system
- Paternalistic business structures and considerable state influence on key companies and sectors
- Highly culturally determined activity patterns (e.g. the influence of religious structures)
- Lack of innovative spirit
- Stagnation in the development of the material forces of production and stationary nature of these societies

Source: Developed by the author after Bobek (1959), Buchanan (1980), Krueger (1974) and Kuran (2004).

economic life and a lack of mutual trust are the result. Consequently a rent-seeking mentality is held to be a grave obstacle to sustainable economic development, particularly because, following the traditions of rent capitalism, a large number of actors prefer long-term financial investment in real estate or short-term investment in loans or speculation in land or building (Laband and Sophodeus 1988; Lindner 1998).

Since the last years of the reign of Hassan II, and at the latest since his son, Mohammed VI, came to power in 1999, Morocco is increasingly rarely associated with rent capitalist structures. More than almost any other North African state, and irrespective of the persistence of economic conditions, the kingdom has gone through a socio-economic transformation process that is as remarkable as it is ambivalent and whose main characteristics are more reminiscent of a 'neoliberal model student' than a 'rent capitalist patient' (Davis 2006; Ravallion and Lokshin 2004). In many regards the economic opening of the kingdom adhered virtually paradigmatically to the ideals or concepts that are associated with the ideological, economic and social project of neoliberalism (e.g. Jessop 2002; Peck and Tickell 2002; Schmidt and Hersh 2006; Ward and England 2007). For instance, already at the beginning of the 1980s the kingdom accepted the structural adjustment programmes of the International Monetary Fund (IMF) in order to make its debt burden manageable by means of debt-rescheduling agreements and conversion of debts into capital shares. The government privatized parts of the predominantly state-run industrial and service sector, liberalized foreign trade, reduced the deficits of the public budget and became creditworthy again (Cohen and Jaidi 2006; Brenton *et al.* 2006). Furthermore, Morocco was, along with Tunisia, the first state to negotiate an association agreement with the EU within the framework of the Barcelona Process. This agreement provided for further economic opening, in particular the reduction of trade barriers, generally better access to the European market and increased European support in the attempts to prepare local businesses for integration into a larger Euro-Mediterranean economic area (Venditto 1998; Zaafrane and Mahjoub 2000).

The success of most of the economic reforms initiated in the past years in Morocco is assessed quite ambivalently, not only because many reforms were forced on the country from outside and were too hasty or not well thought out, but above all because both political and social reforms usually did not go beyond tentative first attempts (Ravallion and Lokshin 2004; Storm 2007). In these circumstances the image that Morocco projects has for several years been rather bewildering, as Ghiles accurately outlined in *Afrique* (2001: 6, author's translation) under the heading 'Hard Landing in the Global World Economy':

> The country is a crude mixture of tradition and modernity, of antiquated customs that are reminiscent of the court of Versailles and avant-garde features. The king quite definitely takes advantage of the possibilities for intervention available to him. He appoints independent committees to deal with particularly urgent questions, such as industrial and tourist development. In the process he disregards the government, which does not even protest, but sits back and watches itself losing credibility from day to day.

In the next section I will look at the development pursued by Morroco in the past years in the key industry of tourism in light of the adoption of the Master Plan of Marrakech.

Morocco's tourism policies in the context of the Master Plan of Marrakech

The 10 January 2001 proved to be a big day for Marrakech and an even bigger day for Morocco, or rather for Moroccan tourism in particular. On that day King Mohammed VI gave a speech in front of the most important representatives of the Moroccan tourism industry that attracted a great deal of attention. More than most other heads of states he is convinced that he represents the political rhythm of his country and from the beginning of his reign in 1999 he committed himself to cautious political reforms. At this point he had already signalized an – albeit cautious – departure from the authoritarian despotism of his deceased father, King Hassan II (Perthes 2002). Thus, at the time of his speech in Marrakech, Mohammed VI had already opened the so-called *jardins secrets*, a euphemism denoting nothing less than the notorious prison camps in which his father had had opposition members interned. He had also initiated a relatively progressive reform of family law that provided for an end to polygamy, among other things. In his economic policies as well, Mohammed VI, who was educated in France, emphasizes reforms that should enable his developing country to face the challenges of an increasingly globalized world. In this process tourism is considered to be a key industry.

The king's speech, which was published in *La Vie Touristique Africaine* (2001), represents one side of the medal of that first national tourism conference in Marrakech. The other side of the medal, which is less representative of the interests of the state but all the more programmatic, represents the adoption of a Master Plan that sets strategic guidelines for Moroccan tourism policy for the period from 2001 to 2010. In the following I will describe the most important reforms and goals connected with the Master Plan. These are not just supposed to prepare the destination for the increasingly complex challenges of progressively tougher competition. They should also initiate definite improvements in the Moroccan tourism structures, which so far have been assessed primarily critically (Lessmeister 2008; Scherle 2004).

The basis for the adoption of the Master Plan was an internal document of the Moroccan trade association, the Confédération Générale des Entreprises Marocaines (CGEM 2000), which was available to the author. The main subjects of this document include a kind of stocktaking of the development of Moroccan tourism during the past decades and the tourism structures involved, as well as the so-called Vision 2010, which is an ambitious scenario for how Moroccan tourism could develop until the year 2010 in view of the trends in tourism and the projected reforms. In the résumé the representatives of the trade association come to a quite explicit conclusion, as the following quotation shows (CGEM 2000: 90; author's translation): 'From both a short-term and a medium range perspective – after 15 years of structural reforms – a further development of the tourism industry promoted by us is probably the only possibility to generate dynamic economic and social growth'. In this context the authors promise not only closer ties between the kingdom and the European Union, but also a certain protection from the consequences of increasing globalization.

Only those who know how unusually immense the power of the Moroccan king and his royal household, the so-called *makhzen* (Faath 1987; Storm 2007), has always been are able to estimate how exceedingly important it was to win the support of Mohammed VI and the political and administrative elite for Vision 2010. It would not be divulging a secret to say that the Master Plan is not without controversy, in view of its ambitious (critics would say utopian) guidelines. This will become more apparent in the following remarks. See Table 13.2 for the most important strategic guidelines of the Master Plan.

The strategic guidelines associated with the Master Plan must be viewed not only against the background of increasing global challenges that must be faced by the destinations and their actors at the threshold of the twenty-first century (e.g. Fayos-Solà and Bueno 2001; Meethan 2001; Mosedale 2008), but also in light of the enormous deficits of Morocco's tourism structures. Particularly the latter aspect is addressed by the Confédération Générale des Entreprises Marocaines with truly remarkable candour and with explicit reference to the most important destinations competing with Morocco (CGEM 2000: 17; author's translation):

> Since 1992 the national tourism crisis has changed successively from a crisis of demand to a crisis of supply, which since 1995 is characterised by an investment crisis and, in association with this, a stagnation of the hotel capacities. All of this against the background of inadequate governance and intensified competition on the part of Turkey, Egypt and Tunisia.

Table 13.2 Strategic guidelines and main aims of Moroccan tourism development up to 2010

- To raise the tourism-specific proportion of the gross domestic product from approx. 7.0% (2001) to 20.0%
- To increase the number of foreign tourists to 10 million
- To increase the number of beds from approx. 75,000 to 230,000
- To generate 600,000 new jobs in tourism
- To promote the internationalization of local tourism companies and improve the investment conditions for foreign investors
- To create and develop new resorts on the Atlantic and Mediterranean coasts
- To pay for up to 50% of land acquisition costs for hotel investments
- To liberalize air traffic regulations
- To decentralize the administration and management of Moroccan tourism structures
- To promote and restructure marketing activities while simultaneously raising the budget

Source: Abridged from CGEM (2000).

In the context of the transformation from a demand to a supply crisis the authors point to a number of factors that can be considered responsible for the deficits of Moroccan tourism structures: the great age of most of the hotel facilities (a circumstance that can be attributed to a lack of willingness to invest), the high prices compared with those in many competing destinations, the inadequate marketing of Morocco in the most important source markets and last, but not least, the poor image of the tourist product. These structural deficits are reflected in the development of the volume of investment in tourism. In 1995 it still reached a value of almost 1.5 billion dirhams and had eventually in 1998, that is, two years before the report was published, sunk to around 250 million dirhams (Loverseed 2002; ONMT 2000), a value that corresponded approximately to the volumes of investment that were usual in the early and mid-1980s. In view of such deficits it is hardly surprising that over the course of the years Morocco gained a reputation among tourism actors, especially among the operators, as being a country of 'tourism standstill' or a 'monodestination' (Ungefug 2001; Pfingsten 2001). It is against this background that the following statement by the product manager of a German travel operator, who withdrew from Moroccan tourism at the beginning of 2000, should be seen. His assessment in a conversation with the author was quite bitter:

> In tourism there is nothing worse than when a country is not able to look to the future, because we cannot allow ourselves to stagnate. There are other countries that are forging ahead really fast and are much more efficient. That was never one of Morocco's strengths! You can see for yourself: X has pulled out, Y has pulled out and Z has pulled out.

The stagnating tourism at the end of the 1990s, which ultimately led to the adoption of the Master Plan, is evident, especially in the fact that even today Morocco has only a single seaside resort, Agadir, that meets international standards. Therefore, whereas Morocco has only one designated centre of international seaside tourism in its portfolio, the competing destinations such as Tunisia or Turkey have dozens of such tourist hot spots in which international investors have gathered in the past decades.

Doubtless the affected actors recognized the deficits of Moroccan tourism structures outlined above when they adopted the Master Plan. The implementation of the corresponding goals and reforms also seems, at least from the outside, to exceed a mere stocktaking. For instance, in *La Gazette du Maroc* (2003: 3), an article under the heading 'The New Deal in Motion' reads:

> Morocco's tourism policy has become a kind of strategy. In fact, nowadays Morocco wants to offer tailor-made tourism. In a word, to go from dabbling in tourism to a real industry that would make Morocco into one of the most appreciated destinations and which could also act as a shield against possible turmoil in the world.

In a similar direction, although in a slightly more nuanced light, Loverseed (2002: 31), who analysed the Moroccan tourism structures on behalf of an English management consultancy, argues:

> There is no doubt that the Moroccan government has the vision, and the will, to achieve these tourism projects. However, in the coming decade, there are likely to be strong demands on the public purse, fuelled by the country's social problems, the high unemployment rate and ongoing labour disputes which, in the past, has diverted funds from tourism development. Further privatization could, however, alleviate that problem, as would the sale (at least in part) of state-owned Royal Air Maroc, a long-standing goal of the government.

How far the expectations raised by this Master Plan, which was drawn up by the government and the trade association, can actually be fulfilled will depend to a great extent on whether it can be implemented as comprehensively and promptly as envisaged. In this context one of the main deficits of the Master Plan needs to be pointed out, namely that it concentrates much too highly on quantitative indicators at the expense of qualitative, in particular long-term, upgrading of the present structures of supply. Both of the following assessments made by two of the author's respondents, who have been advising German companies for several years in the context of their market penetration in Morocco, must be seen in this light:

> The goals are naturally very attractive; those are great specifications, and I wouldn't want to question the will of the involved persons, but I do not see the whole thing as very realistic. [. . .] I cannot imagine how they want to reach ten million guests. I do not see that coming on the basis of the statistics, nor are any concrete investment projects becoming apparent.

> The millions of tourists who are supposed to come will have to be imported from the Milky Way or perhaps be cloned. In this dimension I find it totally unrealistic. That is too bad! Why? When you design such a project for such numbers and such ambitious goals it has already failed before it has started.

This scepticism is expressed in the following quotation from the director of a Moroccan incoming agency who has been cooperating with European travel operators for several years:

> If we want to improve our product then things must work, we have to invest in infrastructure. It's not enough to say we want to have 10 million tourists by 2010. Ultimately that means that the current capacity must be multiplied by a factor of 5. What we built up over 50 years has to happen now in 9 years.

The complex dilemma of Moroccan tourism structures is reflected in this citation like in a magnifying glass: on the one side the insight that stronger efforts are required to remain competitive internationally; on the other side scarcely concealed doubts whether the projected goals can be achieved in the envisaged period and on the envisaged scale.

The development of tourism in Morocco in the light of the Master Plan of Marrakech

Going international: Moroccan incoming agencies in the context of bilateral cooperation

One of the most important goals of the Master Plan of Marrakech was not only to improve the conditions for foreign investors, but also to promote the internationalization of the local tourism companies. The expectation was that there would be substantial potential business, especially for small and medium-sized companies, particularly in the niche segments of trekking, desert tourism, golf and thalasso, which would meet the increasingly hybrid demands of the source markets (CGEM 2000; Lessmeister 2008; Pfingsten 2001). Even if the demand actually has risen in many cases, disillusionment is spreading, particularly among small and medium-sized businesses, as shown by a study by Scherle (2004) on the internationalization of Moroccan incoming agencies in the context of bilateral business cooperations with German tour operators. When expressing their concerns regarding their business future, a number of actors resorted to the slogan globalization, which doubtless is one of the key symbols of a neoliberal concept of politics and economics (Harvey 2005; Peck 2004; Smith 2005). Thus, two business managers from Agadir stated:

> Globalisation is a problem for many incoming agencies. In three or four years the huge tour operators will take over all the small agencies. That's not good at all for small destinations like Agadir. Our firm is not so much affected, because we co-operate with solid and independent enterprises. But of course that cannot rule out the possibility that one day we also might be taken over by a huge tour operator. That's really bad for a destination like Agadir.

> It is becoming more and more difficult to find business partners, as globalisation is made for those who are already strong and who become even stronger with globalisation. When you talk about globalisation you have to automatically think of the three large groups in the Moroccan market: TUI, Neckermann [now Thomas Cook] and LTU. These are the biggest, who will benefit, and for us everything will get harder.

At this point I should not fail to mention that in the past years a large number of Moroccan incoming agencies have lost their former cooperation partners to mergers and acquisitions. It was further criticized that the purchasing power of the large European and North American tour operators is becoming stronger all the time and the associated rigid price policies inevitably lead to a drop in the quality of the tourism product, as documented by the following quotation from a Moroccan respondent:

> We currently notice that there is a tremendous pressure on German tour operators to lower their prices. [. . .] At the same time that prices are to drop, they are putting pressure on us to improve the quality of our service. That cannot work. You cannot expect a Moroccan tourism actor who has invested in a hotel to keep lowering his prices. There is for example one tour operator [. . .] who decided to drop his prices by 20% this year, knowing well that his bookings account for 30% to 40% of the respective hotelier's turnover. The hotelier will be forced to agree and will have to reduce quality. [. . .] Naturally quality will drop, there will be complaints and this will certainly have an effect on demand.

In view of these developments, particularly in centres of package tourism, where the various aspects of tourism-generated income are dominated particularly highly by large-scale enterprises, there is a danger that local tourism actors will become increasingly marginalized, which if the worst comes to the worst can lead to the exclusion of certain locations and companies.

The liberalization of air traffic under the influence of an open sky policy

One of the main intentions of the tourism policies pursued by Morocco since the end of the 1990s was to promote the liberalization of air traffic. This was closely related not only to the goals of the Master Plan of Marrakech, but also to those of the structural adjustment programme of the IMF and the Euro-Mediterranean Free Trade Zone (Berriane and Popp 1998; Zaafrane and Mahjoub 2000). Thus Morocco was one of the first states to conclude an open sky agreement with the EU. Its social, economic and ecological implications are still a controversial issue, particularly in connection with low-cost airlines (e.g. Duval 2008; Gerike 2007; Goetz and Vowles 2009; Graham 1998; Manuela 2007).

Irrespective of massive reservations on the part of the state-run Royal Air Maroc, which feared losing its market-dominating position, the expectation associated with the liberalization of air traffic was not only greater integration of the Moroccan economy into world trade, but also increased mobility of expatriates residing particularly in the two former colonial powers, France and Spain (Meyer 2001). Furthermore, the liberalization of air traffic was supposed to help promote the decentralization and diversification of Moroccan tourism, whose structures of supply concentrate predominantly on one destination, namely the seaside resort of Agadir (CGEM 2000). Particularly people in Marrakech and in Ouarzazate, which could serve as starting bases for high-quality cultural, trekking and desert tourism, hoped for increased demand from foreign tourists.

The first airline to sign a cooperation agreement was Ryanair, Europe's leading low-cost carrier, which has a 20.2 per cent share of low-cost flights in the

European commercial aviation market (DLR 2008). The agreement was initially limited to five years. Especially since the middle of the 1990s Ryanair has experienced a remarkable diffusion process in Europe, and it was only a matter of time before this process spread to adjoining regions. In this case it spread to the deregulating Morocco, merely 14 kilometres from the European continent. Ryanair's Deputy Chief Executive, Michael Cawley, announced in an official press statement:

> We are delighted to make this joint announcement with the Government of Morocco. This represents a singularly important initiative in the development of tourism and the business for the country. The Government has recognised that low cost air access is a growth vehicle throughout Europe and by joining the Open skies regime and embracing Europe's leading low fares airline, the Government in Morocco has made a clear statement about its intentions to develop its tourism industry in the next five years. Ryanair's commitment to establish up to 20 routes and carry close to 1 million passengers per annum on flights to Morocco is a vote of confidence by the airline in the excellence and attractiveness of Morocco as a destination both for weekend breaks, mid-week trips and longer holidays. Our low fares will also help ex-patriate Moroccans to see their families more often and facilitate local businesses in accessing markets with low fare routes including those already announced to both Frankfurt and Marseille.
>
> (Ryanair 2006)

The announcement marked the culmination of six months of discussions between Ryanair and the Moroccan government. It reflects the government's policy of encouraging significant growth in its tourism industry as well as providing low-cost access to its citizens for business and leisure purposes. Shortly thereafter other airlines followed suit, including Easyjet, Ryanair's most important rival, and Jet4you. This generated increased demand from Europe. Thus the number of foreign tourists in 2007 rose by 13 per cent compared with the previous year, and city tourism in the royal cities benefited especially from this development (Auswärtiges Amt 2009). They can now be reached in many cases without the inconvenience of having to change planes in Agadir or Casablanca.

The gentrification of Moroccan medinas by foreign purchasers of real estate

Certainly one of the most significant and interesting phenomena that Moroccan tourism has experienced since the mid-1990s is the increasing development of Moroccan old towns (medinas) for purposes of tourism by foreign purchasers of real estate. This development was additionally intensified by the above outlined liberalization of air traffic and meanwhile has massive socio-cultural implications for the medinas, many of which are world heritage sites (Escher *et al.* 2001; Escher and Petermann 2009). In most of the other Arab states the urban planning policies of the colonial period led to dramatic changes to the building structure of the old towns under the influence of European architects. In contrast to this, the first French governor of Morocco, General Lyautey (1912–1924), pursued a strict spatial and social isolation of the medinas from the French-influenced *villes nouvelles*, which were built at some distance from the old towns. What looks today like a particularly blatant form of apartheid proved in retrospect, at least from the point of view of protecting historical heritage, to be far-sighted and lasting preservation of what was in many regards a unique cultural heritage.

After the country gained independence in 1956 the buildings in the old towns began to successively deteriorate in association with a process of socio-economic erosion. Once the French had left, the Moroccan upper class particularly, but also large parts of the middle class, left the old towns and moved into the *villes nouvelles*, which were considered modern and chic (Mandleur 1972; Naciri 1987). Marrakech had always had the reputation in Morocco of being a comparatively liberal city. It opened itself quite early to discerning and exclusive cultural and incentive tourism, stimulated by its image as an urban incarnation of 1001 nights (Widmer-Münch 1990). Here the decay of the medina has long since given way to gentrification. This is reflected primarily in a massive selling off and subsequent luxury redevelopment of traditional town houses, the so-called *riads*, which are often used as second homes, but also as chic boutique hotels.

This development was initially driven primarily by wealthy jet setters, unconventional artists and eccentric dropouts, but has long since developed into a middle-class phenomenon. The factors behind this development are exceedingly complex and are closely related to the ambitious goals of the Master Plan of Marrakech: domestic stability, administrative deregulation, legal certainty for foreign-owned real estate and comparatively low costs of investment and low living expenses plus a positive image that fits virtually paradigmatically into the discourses on imaginative geographies (e.g. Gregory 1995; Huggan 2001; Said 1978). One asset that has been instrumentalized by the tourism industry for a fairly long time is illustrated by the following quotation by Cityred (2009), one of the largest vendors of *riads*:

> Marrakech has become one of the most talked about cities of the world. Marrakech is charming, extraordinary, magical, exotic, indulging, mesmerising, and the list can go on . . . Riads in Marrakech present to you a unique selection of the finest Riads and Boutique Hotels in Marrakech. Choose a traditional Riad in the Medina, or for a more reclusive experience, stay in a Riad in the outskirts of Marrakech. Search our hand-picked boutique hotels for a holiday of sheer self-indulgence.

Marrakech is easily reached within two to three hours from a large number of European cities – thanks not least to the Moroccan open sky policy. In their extensive study on the increasing gentrification of Marrakech the research team of the German cultural geographer Escher shows impressively what new Marrakechis associate with the pertinent processes. As at least the second quotation reveals, they often show little awareness of the actual local situation (Escher *et al.* 2001: 26):

> A riad in Marrakech is the most exotic thing you can have, financially afford-able and geographically so close [author's translation].

> It's very good for the medina because these foreigners are bringing in a lot of money and are fixing up all these old houses that are falling into ruins [. . .] or are tearing them down and are building something marvellous in the place [. . .], so that's very good. [. . .] It cleans up the city. It brings a lot of money to Morocco. It employs hundreds of Moroccan workmen, and so that part is very, very good.

In any appraisal of the outlined transformation process the perspective doubt-less plays a key role (compare with other spatial contexts, for example Gough 2002; Smith 2002). Unfortunately – precisely from the perspective of tourists and investors – the negative aspects of the increasing gentrification of Moroccan cities are all too often overlooked. These include such things as rising real estate prices, intercultural tension because of divergent lifestyles and a successive displacement of the former residents. Moreover, the restoration measures are often not guided by the requirements of heritage preservation and tend to adhere more to Western notions of an idealized Orient, in the sense of Said (1978), rather than to the original architectural character. In this context it is not surprising that critics view such developments in close connection with a kind of intensified neocolonialism (Escher *et al.* 2001; Escher and Petermann 2009), in which the medina and its residents function merely as exotic and obliging backdrops.

Discussion and conclusion

History has shown that many a reform consisted not in doing something new, but in doing away with something old. The situation is not much different in the case of the Master Plan of Marrakech. Both the Moroccan government and the trade association hope its successful implementation will help the kingdom to become one of the leading destinations worldwide. All the same, the strategic guidelines or goals postulated in this document are not particularly original, let alone visionary, nor does it contain any spectacular innovations. The many impas-sioned comments accompanying this reform since it was adopted in January 2001 cannot hide this fact. Many of them embody nothing more than propaganda for a regime that has, it is true, launched some tentative political and socio-economic reforms. Nevertheless, in the opinion of many critics (Perthes 2002; Storm 2007) it still has definitely autocratic features, as shown by the strong focus of its politi-cal and administrative structures on the authority of the king, and it only conforms to democratic concepts to a limited degree. Certainly, the youthful king, who received a doctorate in France and likes to surround himself with Western think tanks, has given this regime a fresher, perhaps even more humane, face, but to date it has not experienced any lasting structural change.

As this contribution has made clear, in many respects what the Master Plan of Marrakech shows is that the Moroccan tourism policies are being consistently geared to the interests of a rampant neoliberalism that, at least until the current economic and financial crisis, was the mantra of a successful economic policy (Coates 2005; Hall and Soskice 2001). In this context, under the patronage of Mohammed VI Morocco followed with a certain delay many other emerging and developing countries, such as Thailand or the Dominican Republic, that had already committed themselves to this trend much earlier. The pertinent characteristics or instruments differ only marginally and are labelled with more or less interchangeable slogans, such as privatization, liberalization, deregulation or decentralization, which, as the case of the Moroccan liberalization of air traffic has shown, are supposed to lead to increased commitment of foreign businesses.

In the context of the adoption of the Master Plan of Marrakech it was expected that the optimized conditions for the tourism industry would lead not only to increased commitment of foreign tour operators to the destination, but also – and this is related – to intensified internationalization of the kingdom's tourist actors. As the assessments on the part of some managers of Moroccan incoming agencies have documented, it is apparent that, whether rational or not, massive fears of the increasingly internationalized market mechanisms exist, and these fears are voiced through the slogan globalization. This case reveals once again the widespread, though diffuse, fear in the Arab world of being forced into a marginalized role or even being cut off (Mernissi 2002).

Probably the most serious consequences that Morocco is currently experiencing in the context of the Master Plan of Marrakech can be seen in the appropriation and gentrification of Moroccan medinas, primarily by Europeans and North Americans. The old towns are often under the patronage of UNESCO, and until well into the 1990s owning real estate in them was a rare privilege. As a result of administrative deregulation, guaranteed legal certainty for foreign-owned real estate and comparatively low investment costs and living expenses it has developed into a phenomenon that is financially viable even for large parts of the middle class. This development was accelerated not least by the open sky policy postulated in the Master Plan. The increased commitment of low-cost carriers has led not only to an increase in flight frequencies, but also to lower flight prices. It is thus hardly surprising that critical observers, such as Escher and Petermann (2009), no longer speak in this connection of neoliberalism but rather of neocolonialism, a neocolonialism that is gaining ground half a century after the end of the French–Spanish colonial era in an – ostensibly – exotic setting.

Those who are familiar with the complex structural deficits of Moroccan tourism know that substantial improvements are required, not only in the area of infrastructure, which is particularly critical for the investment climate (Lessmeister 2008; Troin 2002), but also in comparatively 'soft' site-related factors that play an increasingly important role in international competition. This refers above all to the professionalization of tourist training courses and a stronger orientation towards service and quality in human resource management (e.g. Jones and Haven-Tang 2005; Williams and Buswell 2003). Unfortunately, precisely these aspects play only a marginal role in the Master Plan of Marrakech, and this is particularly critical in a service industry such as tourism that depends on well-trained employees more than most industries. Once again the suspicion arises that, as befitting a neoliberal economic view, employees are perceived primarily as an expense factor.

As already mentioned, I can and do not wish to question the legitimacy of the reform package of the Master Plan of Marrakech per se. In view of the lack of profile and coordination of its tourism policies, around the turn of the century Morocco was indeed in danger of missing out on promising development trends and of falling behind in the increasingly internationalized competition between the various destinations. The fact that the Master Plan of Marrakech definitely views the future tourist positioning of Morocco as a coordinated effort and that it attempts for the first time in the postcolonial history of the country to address and integrate all relevant stakeholders gives ground for optimism. Whether, however, the strong focus on quantitative indicators is a successful strategy can be questioned, at least from a long-term perspective. Or perhaps the guiding principle will be a kind of constructive pragmatism that is reflected truly paradigmatically in the final quotation from a high-ranking official in the administration of Mohammed VI, who gave the following response to critical questions regarding the realistic implementation of the envisaged operating figures:

> For me it is not the number that is important – whether it is five, six, or eight million tourists. In my opinion the most important thing is that we should aim not for mass tourism but for quality tourism, tourism that perhaps brings fewer tourists, but more money, i.e. high-calibre tourism.

Quality instead of quantity, class instead of mass – the creed of sustainable quality tourism is possibly a realistic perspective that can protect from exaggerated expectations.

References

Auswärtiges Amt (2009) ‚Marokko Wirtschaft'. Online. Available at http://www.auswaertiges-amt.de/diplo/de/Laenderinformationen/Marokko/Wirtschaft.html (accessed 24 May 2009).

Berriane, M. and Popp, H. (eds) (1998) *Migrations Internationals entre le Maghreb et l'Europe*, Passau: Maghreb-Studien.

Bhagwati, J. N. (1982) 'Directly unproductive, profit-seeking (DUP) activities', *Journal of Political Economy*, 90: 988–1002.

Bobek, H. (1959) 'Die Hauptstufen der Gesellschafts- und Wirtschaftsentfaltung aus geographischer Sicht', *Die Erde*, 90: 259–298.

Brenton, P., Baroncelli, E. and Malouche, M. (2006) *Trade and Investment Integration of the Maghreb*, Washington DC: World Bank.

Buchanan, J. M. (1980) 'Rent seeking and profit seeking', in J. M. Buchanan, G. Tullock and R. Tollison (eds) *Toward a Theory of the Rent-Seeking Society*, College Station: Texas A & M University Press.

Buhalis, D. (2001) 'The tourism phenomenon: The new tourist and consumer', in S. Wahab and C. Cooper (eds) *Tourism in the Age of Globalisation*, London: Routledge.

CGEM (Confédération Générale des Entreprises Marocaines) (2000) 'Contrat Programme 2000–2010. La relance de la croissance du Royaume à travers un développement accéléré de son tourisme', Internal ministerial study, unpublished.

Chatelus, M. (1987) 'Rentier or producer economy in the Middle East? The Jordanian response', in B. Khader and A. Badran (eds) *The Economic Development of Jordan*, London: Croom Helm.

Cityred (2009) 'Marrakech riads and hotels'. Online. Available at http://www.riadsinmarrakech.com (accessed 18 May 2009).

Coates, D. (ed.) (2005) *Varieties of Capitalism, Varieties of Approaches*, London: Palgrave Macmillan.

Cohen, S. and Jaidi, L. (2006) *Morocco: Globalization and its consequences*, London: Routledge.

Davis, D. K. (2006) 'Neoliberalism, environmentalism, and agricultural restructuring in Morocco', *Geographical Journal*, 172: 88–105.

DLR (2008) 'Low cost monitor'. Online. Available at http://www.dlr.de/fw/desktopdefault.aspx/tabid-2937/4472_read-17278 (accessed 20 May 2009).

Duval, D. T. (2008) 'Aeropolitics, global aviation networks and the regulation of international visitor flows', in T. Coles and C. M. Hall (eds) *International Business and Tourism: Global issues, contemporary interactions*, London: Routledge.

Ehteshami, A. (2008) *Globalization and Geopolitics in the Middle East. Old games, new rules*, London: Routledge.

Escher, A., Petermann, S. and Clos, B. (2001) 'Gentrification in der Medina von Marrakech', *Geographische Rundschau*, 53: 24–31.

Escher, A. and Petermann, S. (2009) *Tausendundein Fremder im Paradies? Ausländer in der Medina von Marrakech*, Würzburg: Ergon.

Faath, S. (1987) *Marokko. Die innen- und außenpolitische Entwicklung seit der Unabhängigkeit*, Hamburg: Deutsches Orient-Institut.

Fayos-Solà, E. and Bueno, A. P. (2001) 'Globalization, national tourism policy and international organizations', in S. Wahab and C. Cooper (eds) *Tourism in the Age of Globalisation*, London: Routledge.

Gerike, R. (2007) 'Ecological and economical impacts of low cost airlines', in S. Groß and A. Schröder (eds) *Handbook of Low Cost Airlines: Strategies, business processes and market environment*, Berlin: Schmidt.

Ghiles, F. (2001) 'Harte Landung in der Weltwirtschaft', *Afrique*, March 20/26: 6–7.

Goetz, A. R. and Vowles, T. M. (2009) 'The good, the bad, and the ugly: 30 years of US airline deregulation', *Journal of Transport Geography*, 17: 251–263.

Gough, J. (2002) 'Neoliberalism and socialisation in the contemporary city: Opposites, complements and instabilities', in N. Brenner and N. Theodore (eds) *Spaces of Neoliberalism. Urban restructuring in North America and Western Europe*, Malden: Blackwell.

Graham, B. (1998) 'Liberalization, regional economic development and the geography of demand for air transport in the European Union', *Journal of Transport Geography*, 6: 87–104.

Gregory, D. (1995) 'Imaginative geographies', *Progress in Human Geography*, 19: 447–485.

Hall, P. and Soskice, D. (eds) (2001): *Varieties of Capitalism: The institutional foundations of comparative advantage*, Oxford: Oxford University Press.

Harvey, D. (2005) *A Brief History of Neoliberalism*, Oxford: Oxford University Press.

Huggan, G. (2001) *The Post-Colonial Exotic: Marketing the margins*, London: Routledge.

Jessop, B. (2002) 'Liberalism, neoliberalism, and urban governance: A state-theoretical perspective', *Antipode*, 34: 452–472.

Jones, E. and Haven-Tang, C. (eds) (2005) *Tourism SMEs, Service Quality and Destination Competitveness*, Wallingford: CABI.

Knowles, T., Dimiantis, D. and Bey El-Mourhabi, J. (2001) *The Globalization of Tourism and Hospitality: A strategic perspective*, London: Continuum.

Krueger, A. (1974) 'The political economy of the rent-seeking society', *American Economic Review*, 64: 291–303.

Kuran, T. (2004) *Islam and Mammon: The economic predicaments of Islamism*, Princeton, NJ: Princeton University Press.

Laband, D. N. and Sophodeus, J. P. (1988) 'The social cost of rent-seeking: First estimates', *Public Choice*, 58: 269–275.

La Gazette du Maroc (2003) 'The new deal in motion', 8 March, p. 3.

La Vie Touristique Africaine (2001) 'Orientations royales pour relancer le tourisme', 15 January: 4–5.

Le Figaro (2001) 'Royalement vôtre'. Online. Available at http://www.maroc-hebdo.press. ma/MHinternet/Archives_476/html_476/royalem.html (accessed 24 May 2009).

Lessmeister (2008) 'Governance and organisation structure in special interest tourism – buyer-driven or producer-driven value chains? The case of trekking tourism in the Moroccan mountains', *Erdkunde*, 62: 143–158.

Lindner, P. (1998) 'Innovator oder Rentier? Anmerkungen zu einem entwicklungstheoretischen Paradigma aus empirischer Perspektive: das Beispiel Palästina', *Erdkunde*, 52: 201–218.

Loverseed, H. (2002) *Travel and Tourism in Morocco*, London: Mintel.

Mandleur, A. (1972) 'Croissance et urbanisation de Marrakech', *Revue de Géographie du Maroc*, 22: 31–59.

Manuela, E. S. (2007) 'Airline liberalization effects on fares: The case of the Philippines', *Journal of Business Research*, 60: 161–167.

Meethan, K. (2001) *Tourism in Global Society: Place, culture, consumption*, Basingstoke: Palgrave.

Mensching, H. and Wirth, E. (1989) *Nordafrika und Vorderasien*, Frankfurt: Fischer.

Mernissi, F. (2002) *Islam and Democracy: Fear of the modern world*, Cambridge: Perseus.

Meyer, F. (2001) 'Euro-mediterrane Partnerschaft oder Konfrontation?', *Geographische Rundschau*, 53: 32–37.

Mosedale, J. (2008) 'The internationalisation of tourism commodity chains', in T. Coles and C. M. Hall (eds) *International Business and Tourism. Global issues, contemporary interactions*, London: Routledge.

Naciri, M. (1987) 'L'aménagement des villes et ses enjeux', *Le Maroc des Années 80 – Maghreb-Machrek*, 118: 56–70.

ONMT (Office National Marocain du Tourisme) (2000) *La République Féderale d'Allemagne: Données et statistiques*, Düsseldorf: ONMT.

Peck, J. (2004) 'Geography and public policy: Constructions of neoliberalism', *Progress in Human Geography*, 28: 392–405.

Peck, J. and Tickell, A. (2002) 'Neoliberalizing space', *Antipode*, 34: 380–404.

Perthes, V. (2002) *Geheime Gärten. Die neue arabische Welt*, Berlin: Siedler.

Pfingsten, S. (2001) 'Monodestination Marokko', *touristik aktuell*, September: 119.

Ravallion, M. and Lokshin, M. (2004) *Gainers and Losers from Trade Reform in Morocco*, Washington DC: World Bank.

Ryanair (2006) 'Ryanair announces long term agreement with the government of Morocco'. Online. Available at http://www.ryanair.com/site/EN/news.php?yr=06&month=may&story=gen-en-250506 (accessed 15 June 2009).

Said, E. (1978) *Orientalism*, London: Routledge.

Sayan, S. (2009) *Economic Performance in the Middle East and North Africa: Institutions, corruption and reform*, London: Routledge.

Scherle, N. (2004) 'International bilateral business in the tourism industry: Perspectives from German–Moroccan co-operations', *Tourism Geographies*, 6: 229–256.

Schmidt, J. D. and Hersh, J. (2006) 'Neoliberal globalization: Workfare without welfare', *Globalizations*, 3: 69–89.

Sekkat, K. and Véganzonès-Varoudakis, M.-A. (2004) *Trade and Foreign Exchange Liberalization, Investment Climate and FDI in the MENA Countries*, Washington DC: World Bank.

Smith, N. (2002) 'New globalism, new urbanism: Gentrification as global urban strategy', in N. Brenner and N. Theodore (eds) *Spaces of Neoliberalism. Urban restructuring in North America and Western Europe*, Malden: Blackwell.

Smith, N. (2005) *The Endgame of Globalization*, New York: Routledge.

Stewart, D. (2009) *The Middle East Today: Political, geographical and cultural perspectives*, London: Routledge.

Storm, L. (2007) *Democratization in Morocco. The political elite and struggles for power in the post-independence state*, London: Routledge.

Troin, J.-F. (2002) *Maroc: Régions, pays, territoires*. Paris: Maisonneuve & Larose.

Ungefug, H.-G. (2001) 'Aufbruch in Agadir: Tourismus bekommt in Marokko höheren Stellenwert', *fvw*, 13 July, 19: 50

Venditto, B. (1998) 'Is the Euromediterranean free trade area still a convincing instrument for regional co-operation?', *The Maghreb Review*, 23: 87–101.

Wahab, S. and Cooper, C. (2001) 'Tourism, globalisation and the competitive advantage of nations', in Wahab, S. and Cooper, C. (eds) *Tourism in the Age of Globalisation*, London: Routledge.

Ward, K. and England, K. (2007) 'Introduction: Reading neoliberalisation', in K. England and K. Ward (eds) *Neoliberalisation: States, networks, peoples*, Oxford: Blackwell.

Widmer-Münch, R. (1990) *Der Tourismus in Fès und Marrakech. Strukturen und Prozesse in bipolaren Urbanräumen des islamischen Orients*, Basel: Wepf.

Williams, C. and Buswell, J. (2003) *Service Quality in Leisure and Tourism*, Wallingford: CABI.

Wirth, E. (1956) 'Der heutige Irak als Beispiel orientalischen Wirtschaftsgeistes', *Die Erde*, 8: 30–50.

Wirth, E. (1988) 'German geographical research in the Middle East and North Africa', in E. Wirth (ed.) *German Geographical Research Overseas*, Tübingen: VCH.

Zaafrane, H. and Mahjoub, A. (2000) 'The Euro-Mediterranean free trade zone: Economic challenges and social impacts on the countries of the South and East Mediterranean', *Mediterranean Politics*, 5: 9–32.

14 The political economy of trade in international air transport services

David Timothy Duval and John Macilree[1]

International commercial air transport operates within a dense framework of political, economic and regulatory institutions. The institutional framework (the 'rules of the game') can roughly be characterized as the aeropolitical operating environment. A critical reality that is perhaps not immediately apparent in the study of international tourism – although this is changing (e.g. Forsyth 2006) – is that much of the global flow of tourists remains constrained by complex international arrangements that regulate access by airlines. Aeropolitics is thus broadly concerned with the regulatory environment within which international air transport (particularly scheduled services) operates. It helps explain economic and safety oversight, as well as the often contested nature of access rights, services and limits on foreign ownership and control of airlines. Not unlike other aspects of international trade, there are issues of protection of local or domestic interests that may need to be considered for reasons of national economic stability, policy and political risk. Understanding the arcane mechanisms by which aeropolitics is manifested thus helps explain and predict patterns of visitor flows worldwide.

At the time of writing, serious challenges exist across the global air transport sector. Many carriers around the world have struggled for survival in the two-year period beginning in March 2008 as a result of negative externalities such as volatile oil prices, the H1N1 flu pandemic, volcanic ash from Iceland and the global economic recession. Nonetheless, the size and value of the commercial air transport sector remains huge. A study conducted by Oxford Economics in 2008 for the International Air Transport Association found that global air transport supports 32 million and creates 5.5 million jobs, moves 2.2 billion passengers annually, and generates US$3.5 trillion in economic impacts (equating to 7.5 per cent of global gross domestic product). Commercial air transport is a fundamental component of the tourism system as it connects many destinations to origins.

The purpose of this chapter is to review the complex and multifaceted system of international aeropolitics. It provides a multidisciplinary assessment of the legal and political parameters for national government policies on foreign relations, trade, commerce and tourism that culminate in air access negotiations, treaties and understandings (using a continuum of restrictive and open access policies). The chapter sketches the relationship between these broad parameters that, together, form the regulatory and aeropolitical landscape and political economy of global commercial aviation. Although broad in its intent, specific examples are offered to demonstrate how governance of access is managed and negotiated and the consequences for tourism flows.

The recognition of the value of air services to tourism is certainly not new (e.g. Graham *et al*. 2008; Forsyth 2006; Turton and Mutambirwa 1996). What has yet to be fully explored, however, is an overview of the precise nature of the negotiation and settlement of arrangements for air service provision between two or more states and their resulting impact on travel flows. To be sure, the political and legal aspects of these arrangements consider tourism flows carefully and precisely, and utilize principles such as 'true origin–destination' (TOD) and 'full uplift–discharge' (FUD) to map flows in anticipation of securing exchanges of traffic rights that are mutually beneficial to two or more states.

Legal and political parameters: the basis of aeropolitics

We have combined the two parameters of law and politics because together they shape the flows of passenger traffic through air transport networks. In brief, but to be expanded upon below, politics governs airline access between states, while treaties and understandings (the legal instruments that together we call 'arrangements'), established through negotiation, dictate the particular details of that access. International tourism flows, or at least those by air, are thus governed by underlying political and diplomatic trade in air services rights. The basis of this trade is not unlike the basis of trade in other goods and services in that a balance of equity and fairness is sought. When rights to provide international air transport services are exchanged, however, there is often an even stricter focus on reciprocity.

The network of international commercial air linkages is governed by an institutional framework that dates back to the early twentieth century. The principle of sovereignty over airspace was firmly established in the 1919 Paris Convention and a special conference held in Chicago in 1944 while World War II – which did much to accelerate the development of aircraft technology and skills – was heading towards its conclusion (Cheng 1962). At the Chicago conference (where what is commonly referred to as the Chicago Convention was negotiated) the United States – which, with a well-developed airline industry, advocated a free market approach – along with the more cautious United Kingdom and fifty-three other countries (Germany, Japan and Russia did not attend) sought to establish the institutions for the postwar development of aviation. Thus, the 1944 Chicago Convention established a safety standard-setting system for international aviation and the International Civil Aviation Organization (ICAO).

At Chicago, the International Air Services Transit Agreement (IASTA) was also relatively widely accepted. This treaty granted to signatories the right of airlines to overfly states and to make technical stops (e.g. refuelling). An agreement for a wider multilateral exchange of access rights for international airlines, however, received minimal acceptance, and thus there would be no equivalent of the maritime freedom of the seas for aviation. For the next few decades, the future of international aviation would be more protectionist in nature, harking back to the English Navigation Acts of the seventeenth century that restricted third-country (notably Dutch) access to England's sea transport markets (Levi and Ali 1998).

It was left to individual states to establish bilateral air services agreements (ASAs) to exchange air rights based on a structure that is still very much in place today. Although not the first (that was a reciprocal arrangement reached between Germany and France in 1913) the bilateral arrangements negotiated by the United States and the United Kingdom in Bermuda in 1946 established a model that became widely followed.

Today, the political and legal negotiations that shape the existing structure of air service access help determine, for example, whether an airline of state A has the right to uplift and discharge passengers at an airport in state B and vice versa (Mendelsohn 2004). A key feature here is the principle of 'fair and equal opportunity', which translates into the reciprocal exchange of rights for the airlines of both countries concerned (Abeyratne 2005/2006; Dempsey 2006; Cheng 1962). Collectively the various rights that are agreed between two or more states and which are central to this follow a pattern that is known as the 'freedoms of the air', of which nine are now generally identified but not always provided for in arrangements between states (see Table 14.1). Transit rights are encapsulated within the first two freedoms, while the remaining seven are generally referred to as traffic rights.

The first five freedoms were specified at Chicago. Four additional freedoms have since been defined, but these are not in any global regulatory agreement (hence they are often described as 'so-called' freedoms). They are instead a feature of some bilateral agreements.

Although the first, second, third and fourth freedom rights are normally included as a matter of course in most ASAs, it is the exchanging of fifth freedom rights that is perhaps the most interesting from an aeropolitical perspective. A refusal to exchange such rights is essentially a protectionist action that reserves carriage between two countries for the carriers of those two countries.

The nature of individual exchanges of the 'freedoms of the air' can certainly have an influence on the degree of competition and, by extension, flows of tourist traffic across networks. With notable exceptions (e.g. the EU's Third Package liberalization gives 'community' carriers unfettered access throughout the EU), countries will attempt to optimize ASAs to their own advantage (Clarke 1998) and generally fall short of complete liberalization of access. But restrictive exchanges of 'freedoms of the air' are generally not carried out in isolation. There are other components to the set of rights that countries exchange that we must also consider.

The elements of air services agreements

Air services agreements – usually having treaty status in international law – and their related, sometimes confidential, memoranda of understanding (MoUs) constitute an arrangement between two (or more) states that outlines various conditions attached to access to both states by designated carriers of those (or other)

Table 14.1 The nine freedoms

First freedom	The right or privilege granted by one state for the airline(s) of another state or states to fly across its territory without landing
Second freedom	The right granted by one state for the airline(s) of another state or states to land in its territory for non-traffic purposes (e.g. fuel or other technical/maintenance reasons)
Third freedom	The right or privilege granted by one state for the airline(s) of another state to put down, in the territory of the first state, traffic coming from the home state of the carrier; that is, the right for an airline of country A to carry passengers from country A to country B
Fourth freedom	The right or privilege granted by one state for the airline(s) of another state to take on, in the territory of the first state, traffic destined for the home state of the carrier; that is, the right for an airline of country A to bring back passengers from country B to country A
Fifth freedom	The right or privilege granted by one state for the airline(s) of another state to put down and to take on, in the territory of the first state, traffic coming from or destined to a third state on a service that originates or terminates in the home country of the foreign carrier (e.g. Air New Zealand carrying passengers between Los Angeles and London on its services that originate in Auckland). Note that this will require separate arrangements between state A and state C and between state A and state B. Note also that an arrangement between state B and state C is not required (e.g. the arrangements between the European Union and the United States are not relevant to the Air New Zealand services between Los Angeles and London)
Sixth freedom	The combination of third and fourth freedoms, 'resulting in the ability of an airline to uplift traffic from a foreign state and transport it to another foreign state via an intermediate stop – probably involving a change of plane and/or flight number – in its home country' (Holloway 2003: 218) (e.g. Emirates carrying passengers between Sydney and London via its Dubai hub)
Seventh freedom	The right or privilege granted by one state to another state of transporting traffic between the territory of the granting state and any third state with no requirement to include on such operation any point in the territory of the airline's home state. Seventh freedom rights are more commonly exchanged for cargo-only services and are much less common for passenger services. Again note that for an airline of country A to operate services solely between countries B and C this will require an agreement between country A and country B, as well as an agreement between country A and country C, but not an agreement between country B and country C
Eighth freedom ('consecutive' cabotage)	The right or privilege of transporting cabotage traffic between two points in the territory of the granting state on a service that originates or terminates in the home country of the foreign carrier or (in connection with the so-called seventh freedom of the air) outside the territory of the granting state

Ninth freedom ('stand-alone' cabotage)	The right or privilege of transporting cabotage traffic of the granting state on a service performed entirely within the territory of the granting state. Thus, an airline outside stated ownership and control restrictions (which would otherwise allow it to be treated as a national carrier) can operate domestic services without initiating or terminating a service in its home country. Although rare, it may be granted as a matter of foreign investment policy rather than exchanged in air services arrangements. Recent examples include the Singaporean-owned Tiger Australia operation within Australia and the New Zealand–United Kingdom air services agreement of 2005, which exchanges all nine freedoms

Source: Based on International Civil Aviation Organization (2004), Cheng (1962), Doganis (2001) and Duval (2007).

states. These bilateral arrangements are numerous, with in excess of 2,200 ASAs registered with ICAO and currently in force today [although the World Trade Organization (2006) estimates that around two-thirds of global international air traffic is carried under just 100 of these ASAs]. In addition to formalizing the rights of access alongside the framework of the 'freedoms of the air' discussed above, a number of other regulatory elements within bilateral arrangements make up the sets of rights that are exchanged in most air services agreements. These are:

- *Grant of traffic rights*: These are generally the rights of access as described above. First, second and third/fourth freedoms are common, fifth freedom is less so, and seventh and eighth freedoms are rare. Sixth freedom rights may be granted, but are generally not essential. Restrictions on fifth freedom rights might take the form of limiting traffic to less than 50 per cent of capacity or a specified number of seats per year.
- *Routes*: Specific routes may be included in a route schedule to the ASA, detailing the points (airports) available to be served by the partner's airline in the granting country's territory (e.g. this could be limited to only one airport or a specified number of airports or access could be granted to all airports), and at intermediate and beyond points in third countries, but this may not give the full picture. For example, the granting of traffic rights might be route specific and thus some points are specifically named in the associated MoU.
- *Capacity*: A capacity clause stipulates the principles for determining the amount of capacity for the agreed services. Limits are based primarily on the third/fourth freedom traffic. More restrictive ASAs may provide for limited capacity whereas more liberal ASAs will not include such limits. Predetermination of capacity is normally specified in an attached MoU and is based on flight frequency or seat numbers on a particular route. Aircraft types that may be used are sometimes specified.
- *Tariff regulation*: In many arrangements, dual approval of tariffs (all fare levels charged by the airlines and the related conditions) is still required

(i.e. both states must agree) before tariffs are set on specific services. Recent tariff regulation models include 'country of origin', in which the regulator of each country approves tariffs only for travel from that country to the other country, and 'double disapproval', in which both regulators must decline a tariff within a set period of time for it not to automatically be deemed to be approved. Liberal ASAs allow airlines the freedom to set prices according to their perception of demand in the market. Explicit residual power for government intervention may be limited to, for example, predatory behaviour (generally difficult to prove in a timely way) and subsidization. There may also be an explicit provision within an ASA which states that an airline carrying fifth freedom traffic should not undercut the fares charged for any third or fourth freedom traffic over the same route. Past attempts to restrict sixth freedom tariffs have proved to be particularly controversial (e.g. by Australia in the late 1970s, which led to a major dispute with ASEAN countries). The implications for tourism are clear in this regard: the restriction of tariffs can distort natural demand for services within a market. It is, however, difficult to enforce the sale of only approved tariffs and, if market restrictions are to be imposed, capacity restrictions can provide a simpler solution for countries wishing to restrict competition.

• *Withholding criteria*: This set of clauses generally outlines the effective constraints on foreign ownership and control of an international airline. Restrictive conditions may in practice require substantial ownership and effective control (SO&EC) of an international airline by nationals of the state designating that airline under an ASA. Otherwise the bilateral partner has the right to refuse operation authorization to an airline that does not meet the criteria. 'Effective control' can refer to the nationality of an airline's board members and even senior management. 'Substantial ownership' refers to the proportion of share ownership in the hands of foreign nationals. More liberal withholding criteria substitute 'principal place of business' (PPoB) and 'effective regulatory control' (ERC) (Chang *et al.* 2004). Such criteria prevent the circumvention of restrictions contained in ASAs. For example, if country A grants the airlines of country B unlimited access but has a more restrictive reciprocal ASA with country C, the nationals/airlines of country C should not necessarily be able to gain access to country A by owning/controlling airlines of country B. With airline privatization and shares freely traded on stock exchanges and a general expectation in almost all other industries in the developed world at least that foreign takeovers are possible, this has become a difficult area for aviation policy and a focus for the International Air Transport Association's 'Agenda for Freedom' (IATA 2010). Some creative solutions have had to be developed, including legislated restrictions on foreign ownership, licence provisions and 'golden' shares. The EU's 'horizontal' agreements in which bilateral partners in effect agree not to challenge the ownership and control of EU airlines if foreign ownership is held within any EU member states is one example. The existence of multiple ASAs governing an international airline's network means that practical progress in liberalizing in this area will likely be slow in creating opportunities for international airlines to freely access global equity markets and allow for cross-border consolidation.

- *Designation*: The number of carriers that a state may designate for operation on a route can be constrained. Designation is related to the concept of national flag carrier, although designated 'flag carriers' may be entirely state owned, fully privatized or a combination of the two. If a country has more than one international airline and rights under an ASA are restricted, regulatory mechanisms will provide for a government to allocate to its international airlines the rights that it has secured in its ASAs.
- *Data and statistics*: The sharing of information between states, often for the purposes of monitoring and setting capacity limits, can be a requirement (Piermartini and Rousova 2008).

Code sharing

A significant aspect of ASAs that has an impact on tourist flows is the provision for code sharing (Hassin and Shy 2004). Code sharing between airlines refers to one airline operating the service(s), with one or more other airlines placing their code and marketing/selling seats on the service (Doganis 2001). The importance of this is closely related to the development of global airline alliances (e.g. Star Alliance, oneworld and SkyTeam). Alliance-centred code sharing allows airlines to coordinate scheduling and operations, and consolidate costs (and benefits) across a wider network of operations (Brueckner 2001), which may often raise issues of anti-trust (Schlangen 2000). Code sharing is also a means by which an airline can gain access to a route that it may not be able to operate directly, perhaps for reasons of limitations on the existing ASA or MOU. As code sharing involves the exercise of traffic rights just as much as an airline operating its own aircraft on a route, it can generally be carried out only if provided for in an ASA.

In some arrangements, airlines may be restricted to bilateral code sharing. Thus, under an ASA between countries A and B, the airlines of country A may code share with the airlines of country B but not with the airlines of any other country. This can protect the route from additional competition from third-country airlines. Less restrictive arrangements will permit third-country code sharing in which the marketing (non-operating) airline is permitted to code share between points in a bilateral partner and in a third country. The usual stipulation is that all carriers involved must hold the necessary traffic rights. Exchanging this right can be of particular significance when an airline from country A has an alliance partner in country C but not country B, and it would be uneconomic for the airline of country A to operate between countries B and C, and/or because it does not have the necessary fifth freedom rights.

A further option may be that a marketing carrier is permitted to carry 'own stopover' traffic. For example, in an ASA between countries A and B, the airlines of A are not granted fifth freedom rights between B and country C but may, as marketing carriers, code share between B and C by carrying their own passengers that have stopped over in B en route between A and C. Exchanging this right can also be of particular significance when an airline from country A has an alliance partner in country C but not in country B.

Code sharing can also be used to grant access to additional domestic points without having to exchange cabotage rights. For example, under an ASA between country A and country B, an airline of country A may be given the right to code share as marketing carrier on the domestic services of an airline of country B between an international gateway airport and interior points within country B provided that the passengers have also travelled on the country A airline's international services, and vice versa.

Charter services

One key point relating to the above discussion on ASAs that can have profound implications for tourist flows is the role of charter (non-scheduled) international air services. Airlines establish charter services as a means of competing directly with networked and scheduled carriers. Such services often operate outside of ASAs because most ASAs only cover scheduled services, although this is changing. Charter airlines were traditionally successful because of substantially lower unit costs, although the development in the last two decades of low-cost, non-network carriers has supplanted this competitive advantage to some extent (Williams 2001). Charter services are usually vertically integrated with existing tour company offerings (Buck and Lei 2004), as has been the case, for example, with many Spanish tour operators (Forsyth 2006).

'Open skies' versus quantitative economic regulation: where to strike the balance?

As is to be expected, there is considerable variation in the content of bilateral air services agreeements. To this end, some agreements are overtly less restrictive than others, reflecting differing government aviation policies in these situations. For example, an agreement between two states may allow for almost unfettered access to international airports in both states with unlimited frequency and capacity. Such liberalized agreements have actually become more common worldwide in the past few decades (largely modelled after US-led initiatives) and are now referred to in many instances as 'open skies' agreements. These have very few restrictive elements within the agreement that would prevent access to designated carriers. However, even these differ in character. The following are generally considered features of open skies arrangements:

- fifth freedom intermediate and beyond rights;
- seventh freedom passenger* and/or cargo rights;
- cabotage* rights – eighth freedom;
- all points exchanged (an open route schedule);

- capacity unrestricted;
- tariffs filing not required;
- liberal airline ownership provisions* – principal place of business;
- multiple designation – no restriction on number of airlines;
- the right to code share, including on third-country airlines;

(*not part of the US bilateral 'open skies' model and are rare)

Governments establish how 'open' their policies of access will be with respect to foreign carriers in the context of their own need to secure access to foreign states for their own airline(s). Several questions thus emerge. For example, does a state intentionally pursue policies of openness with respect to access for foreign carriers for the benefit of trade in goods and services (particularly tourism)? Is a state prepared to agree to 'open skies' with all other states and if not what criteria does it use to establish when to opt for a more restrictive relationship or none at all? If agreeing to 'open skies', what impact might this have on the state's own airline industry that, as a result, may face open competition from foreign carriers with lower costs bases and more efficient operations? (How this is possible is discussed below.)

Some states may elect to adopt a protectionist stance regarding access by foreign carriers, such that they are prepared to exchange only limited capacity and/or route rights. In these cases, the question remains as to what impacts such policies have on the trade in goods and services involving that state and in particular their tourism industries. Several states (for instance, the United States, New Zealand, Singapore and the United Arab Emirates) have explicitly liberal policies towards international air services.

Other states' policies may broadly be liberal, but may retain some restrictions to access in situations in which such access is not considered to provide 'fair and equal opportunity' for their carrier(s) (Kasper 1988). Canada and Hong Kong are examples of this latter approach as is Japan, although its approach is changing for airports outside of the Tokyo region. Australia is another example in which a generally liberal access policy (including providing for foreign ownership of domestic carriers – so-called ninth freedom) nonetheless has retained some limits with all states except New Zealand and the United States. Australia has, for example, precluded Singaporean and Canadian carriers from accessing routes between Australia and the United States by refusing to grant the necessary fifth freedom rights (Duval 2008).

In addition to government policy, which as noted above determines the degree of liberal access by foreign carriers, there is the other consideration of geographical positioning of a particular state, which will have some bearing on the extent of liberalization contained within its policies on air access. In some situations, geography can restrict the natural development of open markets and competition given the presence of 'thin routes' (i.e. routes for which demand is limited and that therefore attract few competitors) (Fageda and Fernandez-Villadangos 2009; Hazledine 2008; Nolan *et al.* 2005). These represent limited opportunities and therefore seem less attractive in an exchange. Examples of such countries are those on the Antarctic Rim, such as Australia, New Zealand, Chile, Argentina and South Africa, that often need fifth freedom rights at intermediate points to enable their airlines to access major tourism markets yet have more limited fifth freedom opportunities to trade in exchange with countries that enjoy sixth freedom opportunities in those same markets. Australia and New Zealand, for example, depend heavily on tourist traffic from the United Kingdom as one of their largest source markets.

Exchanges of rights: two states

To consider how the sets of rights that may be exchanged are put together, let us now examine a simple sector (A–B) and the related exchange of third/fourth freedom traffic rights between states A and B. There are a range of different options that could make up the set of rights. Third/fourth freedom rights would almost always be part of any exchange. Routes might be restricted to specified airports or all international airports in both countries could be made available. Limits on the supply of capacity able to be operated might be predetermined, based on an estimate of the market demand on the route, and shared 50:50 between the airlines of the two countries by specifying the maximum number of flights per week or seats per year on particular routes between the two countries, or there might be no such limits.

In addition, the two states might require their airlines to gain the approval of both states for any tariffs, only wish to approve the tariffs for passengers originating in their territory or not have any requirement for the specific approval of tariffs. If the two states concerned favour airline cooperation over competition, there might even be agreement between the states for the airlines of the two countries to pool the revenue they earn, something that was more common in the past (e.g. Qantas and Air New Zealand more than once operated trans-Tasman services on this basis). In essence, and recalling the key concept of 'fair and equal opportunity', the result is a reciprocal, 'equal' exchange of rights between the two states.

Of course, we do not live in a world of only two countries. For example, state A might favour a capacity restriction if it considered that the A–B market was of limited value, the airlines of state B would enjoy sixth freedom opportunities between state A and larger third countries that were not fully available to state A's airlines and/or the lack of a capacity restriction could limit market access for its airlines to third countries. In such a case state A could seek a capacity limit based on the number of passengers whose true origin and destination was in states A and B. State B, however, might seek to reach an agreement that bases any capacity limit on the full uplift and discharge of traffic carried between A and B so that the sixth freedom traffic its airlines carry from third countries via B to A is not excluded from consideration in setting capacity limits (we expand on this point below). Depending on whether a state advocates a TOD or FUD approach to traffic rights there could be differing views as to what is 'fair'. In this sense it is not necessary for the airlines of both countries to be operating on the routes between A and B. Rather than a balance of benefits (although such considerations may influence the negotiators), the exchange is a balance of opportunities (Goldstein 2001; ICAO 2004).

Exchange of rights: three states

Clearly the exchange of rights can become quite complex when factors such as geography (is a country centrally located between major markets?) and aircraft technology (aircraft range and size) are taken into account. Third-country considerations amplify this complexity through the exchange of fifth and sixth freedom rights. Consider the negotiation of access between three states, A, B and C, and an air route (A–B–C) involving these three states. This would involve bilateral air services agreements between A and B, A and C, and B and C.

Suppose that state A wishes to have the rights for its designated airline(s) to access state C because there is a strong potential for tourist and business flows between the two countries. If non-stop flights between state A and state C are not possible from a technological (increasingly less likely as aircraft ranges have increased) and/or market viability perspective, not only will arrangements be required that allow third/fourth freedom traffic to be carried between states A and C but also state A will most likely need to secure fifth freedom rights separately from both state B and state C. Historically, key stopover airports, such as Gander in Newfoundland (independent until 1949) for trans-Atlantic air services and Honolulu in the United States for trans-Pacific services, gave their respective states considerable negotiating leverage. A recent example involving shorter routes is across the Tasman Sea between Australia and New Zealand. This route encompasses one of the most competitive markets in the world, following the willingness of New Zealand and, separately, Australia to grant fifth freedom access to airlines from third countries such as Argentina, Brunei, Chile and the United Arab Emirates (airlines from Indonesia, Malaysia and Thailand have also exercised these rights across the Tasman Sea).

Suppose current aircraft technology still does not allow economic non-stop access between states A and C (e.g. the United Kingdom and Australia or New Zealand); in other words, existing aircraft are not able to traverse the distance required without stopping for refuelling (a first freedom technical stop). As such, state A will seek arrangements with state B (e.g. Hong Kong, Singapore, Thailand or the United States) for access beyond state B to state C. State A could secure the fifth freedom right to pick up and drop off passengers in state B en route to state C (e.g. Air New Zealand now competes freely in the Los Angeles–London market). Here, if capacity is to be restricted, the TOD and FUD concepts introduced earlier become directly relevant, with state B – the intermediate point on the route – likely to favour the FUD concept when determining capacity if it is to be restricted and states A and C likely to favour the TOD concept.

In this example a separate arrangement is needed between state A and state C that provides for fifth freedom traffic rights to allow for an airport in state B to be an intermediate point where a carrier from state A can pick up and drop off passengers for carriage between state B and state C. For airlines of state A to operate with traffic rights on the route A–B–C, recall that any bilateral arrangements between state B and state C are not required. The two separate arrangements that state A forms, one with state C and the other with state B, give the carrier of state A the rights to move traffic between states A, B and C.

Now, as we have noted above, there are three sets of negotiations between the states to consider: A with C, A with B and B with C. Let us assume that state B is agreeable to entering into a reciprocal exchange with state A. In return, state B may be given by state A access to airports in state A, including access to points beyond state A. Whether this is acceptable to state B will in part depend on how valuable the traffic flows between state A and state B are to a carrier from state B, and by extension how valuable traffic beyond state A is to a state B carrier. As well as exchanging fifth freedom rights, by exchanging third and fourth freedom rights states A and B in effect are exchanging sixth freedom rights. States A and B may also reach an understanding to restrict capacity. One common form of restriction is to impose in a MoU a quota on the carriage of any fifth freedom traffic, as noted earlier. The question arises as to how to measure (TOD or FUD) and enforce any such restriction. For example, do passengers briefly stopping over in state B get counted against any fifth freedom quota? This is not the case if passengers are counted on a TOD basis.

For illustrative purposes, suppose that the value to state B of services to and from state A and beyond is not the same as the value to state A of services to state C via state B. For our purposes, assume that state B is amenable to a state A carrier to have state B as an intermediate point in traffic between state A and state C, but logically may be looking for rights of roughly equal value for its own carrier(s). In the exchange of rights as outlined, state B might not move forward with the agreement as its carriers, in its view, would not be securing rights that would allow the exchange to be 'fair and equal'.

Suppose, however, that state B is willing to exchange reciprocal third/fourth freedom rights with state A and also access to points beyond in third states. (State B's preparedness to do so may depend on its ability to separately secure the rights of access to those beyond points, which is irrespective of its agreement with state A – we expand on this example involving four states below.) State A will not wish to grant unlimited access to state B if this is going to impact on its ability to secure separate access to state C. Faced with state B being unwilling to grant fifth freedom access except on very restricted terms, a likely response of state A is to consider its 'best alternative to no agreement' (BATNA) (Malhotra and Bazerman 2007) and deal with neighbouring states to state B that are willing to enter into a more open exchange of rights. A common result is that smaller state B states, who may benefit from their geographical location and have airlines that are more reliant on sixth freedom carriage, have proved to be more willing to enter into 'open skies' arrangements. An illustration of this was the strategy adopted by the United States in entering into 'open skies' agreements with the Netherlands and South Korea, in part with the aim of encouraging Germany and Japan, respectively, to enter into 'open skies' agreements.

Overall, adopting a tough line in favour of the FUD approach may protect state B's airline(s) but this is likely to be at the expense of its tourism and airport industries as passenger flows will be directed elsewhere. A key consideration here is to what extent the respective governments and their air rights negotiators are taking into account the interests of the various other stakeholders apart from their airline(s). A test of this is who is involved in the negotiations. Quite often this may be limited to air transport officials, diplomats and airlines, but the questions remain as to what extent the interests of airports, unions, the tourism industry and consumers are taken into account during the negotiations.

Exchange of rights: four states

To illustrate how complex air rights exchanges can become, we offer a real-world example involving four states along an air route A–B–C–D, in which a failure to reach agreement between the two central states, B and C, over exchanging fifth freedom rights for a time indirectly frustrated the aspirations of a carrier from state A to serve state C via state B (see Figure 14.1). Diplomatic sensitivities prevent us from naming the actual states involved. In each case, one of the two parties required to agree to a fifth freedom rights exchange was not prepared to do so.

State A had already exchanged rights with state B to give state A's airlines fifth

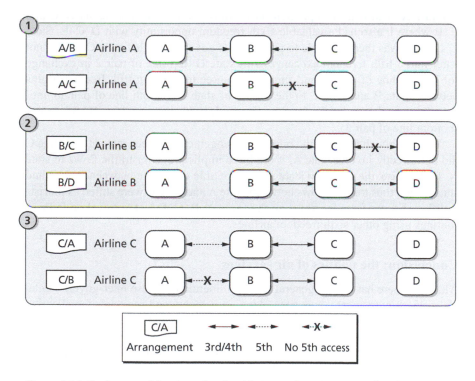

Figure 14.1 Exchanges of freedoms involved between four states, grouping the necessary fifth freedom exchanges in three pairs, numbered 1, 2 and 3.

freedom (beyond) rights between state B and states C (top line of pair 1) and D. For an airline of state A to have fifth freedom rights between state B and state C, recall that state A must also gain these rights from state C (bottom line of pair 1). To gain these fifth freedom rights in exchange state A was prepared to grant state C's airlines fifth freedom (intermediate) rights between state A and state B (top line of pair 3).

State B was seeking from state C fifth freedom access beyond state C to state D (top line of pair 2) having already exchanged the necessary rights with state D (bottom line of pair 2). In exchange, state B was prepared to either grant state C fifth freedom (beyond) rights between state B and state A or withhold them as a bargaining chip (bottom line of pair 3). Note that these exchanges do not directly involve state A.

When negotiating such exchanges, it is useful to examine the likely alternatives from the different perspectives of the different stakeholders who will influence the positions taken by the air services negotiators. In this case, for state C's airline the sector C–D was particularly valuable as state D is a major tourism source market and it did not want to face additional competition from a state B airline exercising fifth freedom rights on this sector. In addition, it was also happy to see the sector C–B restricted to the airlines of states C and B. It took the attitude that being able to serve the route C–B–A with full traffic rights was not worth the value that it would lose with extra competition on its third/fourth freedom sectors D–C and C–B where it also had a valuable sixth freedom opportunity with D–C–B. State C's airline was therefore able to persuade its government that state C should not enter into a fifth freedom exchange with state B (top line of pair 2 in exchange for bottom line of pair 3) and should not agree to granting fifth freedom rights between state B and state C to the carrier of state A (bottom line of pair 1) until state B granted state C fifth freedom (beyond) rights between state B and state A (bottom line of pair 3).

Thus, although this specific bilateral arrangement between state B and state C did not directly involve state A, it did have implications for traffic flows to state A. In this case, the airline of state A was not able to operate between state B and state C, and thus tourism flows between state A and state C were stifled as tourists wanting cheaper fares for travel on the route A–B–C–D had to travel on indirect routings using other sixth freedom airlines.

Conclusion: the politics of air services

Although there has been a general trend to liberalizing these inter-governmental air services agreements, and open skies agreements and regional liberalization are now more common, the structure of the international airline industry is still tightly constrained by a set of rules that are now well over six decades old and cannot easily be disentangled. This complex framework of traffic rights has arguably had a major influence on the development of airline industry networks, such that intensive competition seems to be correlated with regions (e.g. EU) where open skies agreements feature. As a natural outcome of the general reluctance, as illustrated earlier, of some states to grant fifth freedom access, some of the most successful carriers (e.g. Emirates, Singapore Airlines) are those that are in a position to take advantage of both home state geography and pairs of third and fourth freedom rights to gain sixth freedom opportunities through their hubs, thus shuttling traffic from major origin and destination regions.

Although almost every book covering international airlines will make reference to the 'freedoms of the air' and the role of governments in negotiating air rights, the relationships between the various components of ASAs have received only limited treatment in the academic literature, in part because the MoUs that detail specific limits on routings and access are often not made public. That said, insights as to what the full rights exchanges do and do not include are sometimes revealed when the ASAs are signed, when airlines – often thwarted by restrictions – seek public attention in another country in an attempt to gain wider stakeholder support from interests such as the tourism and airport industries, and when consumers (often subsequently) apply political pressure (e.g. Singapore Airlines has attempted this in Australia with the objective of gaining fifth freedom access to the Australia–US market, whilst Emirates is lobbying in Canada for greater capacity).

In this chapter we have examined how various regulatory, legal and economic conditions associated with commercial air transport shape global tourist flows. We have shown that economic regulation, through government policy regarding air access as implemented through the negotiation of ASAs, can still play a significant role. The complex patchwork of global economic regulation of air services has major implications for tourism, and sometimes can have more of an impact on tourist flows than marketing budgets, development policies and strategic planning combined. International airlines cannot simply begin services between any two airports without having been allocated the necessary rights that must first be negotiated by their governments, and ensuring that the proper economic (and safety) regulatory provisions have been satisfied is the proverbial 'elephant in the room' when global tourist traffic flows are analysed.

Note

1   John Macilree is responsible for negotiating air services agreements on behalf of the New Zealand government. The views expressed in this chapter do not necessarily reflect the views of the New Zealand government or the New Zealand Ministry of Transport, but are the personal opinion of the authors.

References

Abeyratne, R. (2005/2006) 'Competition in air transport – the need for shift in focus', *Transportation Law Journal*, 33: 29–110.

Brueckner, J. K. (2001) 'The economics of international codesharing: An analysis of airline alliances', *International Journal of Industrial Organization*, 19: 1475–1498.

Buck, S. and Lei, Z. (2004) 'Charter airlines: Have they a future?', *Tourism and Hospitality Research*, 5 :72–78.

Chang, Y.-C., Williams, G. and Hsu, C.-J. (2004) 'The evolution of airline ownership and control provisions', *Journal of Air Transport Management*, 10: 161–172.

Cheng, B. (1962) *The Law of International Air Transport*, London: Stevens.

Clarke, H. (1998) 'Optimal air service agreements', *Economic Analysis and Policy*, 28: 169–186.

Dempsey, P. S. (2006) 'The evolution of air transport agreements', *Annals of Air and Space Law*, 33: 127–193.

Doganis, R. (2001) *The Airline Business in the 21st Century*, London: Routledge.

Duval, D. T. (2007) *Tourism and Transport: Modes, Networks and Flows*, Clevedon: Channel View.

Duval, D. T. (2008) 'Regulation, competition and the politics of air access across the Pacific', *Journal of Air Transport Management*, 14: 237–242.

Fageda, X. and Fernandez-Villadangos, L. (2009) 'Triggering competition in the Spanish airline market: The role of airport capacity and low-cost carriers', *Journal of Air Transport Management*, 15: 36–40.

Forsyth, P. (2006) 'Tourism benefits and aviation policy', *Journal of Air Transport Management*, 12: 3–13.

Goldstein, A. (2001) 'Infrastructure development and regulatory reform in sub-Saharan Africa: The case of air transport', *The World Economy*, 24: 221–248.

Graham, A., Papatheodorou, A. and Forsyth, P. (2008) *Aviation and Tourism: Implications for leisure travel*, Aldershot: Ashgate.

Hassin, O. and Shy, O. (2004) 'Code-sharing agreements and interconnections in markets for international flights', *Review of International Economics*, 12: 337–352.

Hazledine, T. (2008) 'Competition and competition policy in the trans-Tasman air travel market', *Australian Economic Review*, 41: 337–348.

Holloway, S. (2003) *Straight and Level: Practical airline economics*, Aldershot: Ashgate.

International Air Transport Association (IATA) (2010) 'Agenda For freedom'. Online. Available at http://www.agenda-for-freedom.aero (accessed 16 May 2010).

International Civil Aviation Organization (ICAO) (2004) 'Manual on the Regulation of International Air Transport', Doc 9626, Montreal: International Civil Aviation Organization.

Kasper, D. M. (1988) 'Liberalizing airline services: How to get from here to there', *The World Economy*, 11: 91–108.

Levi, J. S. and Ali, S. (1998) 'From commercial competition to strategic rivalry to war: The evolution of the Anglo-Dutch rivalry, 1609–1652', in P. F. Diehl (ed.) *The Dynamics of Enduring Rivalries,* Urbana: University of Illinois Press.

Malhotra D. and Bazerman, M. H. (2007) *Negotiation Genius: How to overcome obstacles and achieve brilliant results at the bargaining table and beyond*, New York: Bantam.

Mendelsohn, A. I. (2004) 'The USA and the EU – aviation relations: An impasse or an opportunity?', *Air and Space Law*, 29: 263–279.

Nolan, J., Ritchie, P. and Rowcroft, J. (2005) 'Small market air service and regional policy', *Journal of Transport Economics and Policy*, 38: 363–378.

Piermartini, R. and Rousova, L. (2008) 'Liberalization of air transport services and passenger traffic', World Trade Organization Staff Working Paper ERSD-2008–06. Unpublished

Schlangen, C. (2000) 'Differing views of competition: Antitrust review of international airline alliances', *University of Chicago Legal Forum* 2000: 413–446.

Turton, B. J. and Mutambirwa, C. C. (1996) 'Air transport services and the expansion of international tourism in Zimbabwe', *Tourism Management* 17: 453–462.

Williams, G. (2001) 'Will Europe's charter carriers be replaced by "no-frills" scheduled airlines?', *Journal of Air Transport Management*, 7: 277–286.

World Trade Organization (WTO) (2006) 'Second review of the Air Transport Annex: Developments in the air transport sector (Part Two), Quantitative air services agreements review (QUASAR)', Volume I, document S/C/W/270/Add.1. Unpublished

15 Tourism regulation and relational geography

The global, local and everything in between

Jan Mosedale and Julia N. Albrecht

All too often within the tourism context, globalization is viewed as consisting of dichotomous geographical scales: 'the global', that is, the rise of transnational tourism corporations (see the 1990 special issue on tourism and transnationalism in *Tourism Management*), as well as 'the local', that is, unique local factors influencing tourism development (see Chang *et al.* 1996; Teo and Li 2003). However, one of the characteristics of globalization is the increasing connectivity of social relations across time and space: 'the stretching and deepening of social relations and institutions' (Held 1995: 20). This spatiality permeates beyond essentialist views of geographical scale and the influence of globalization on place and space indicates the need for 'a new ontology of place/space relations' (Amin 2002: 385). Such relational thinking is particularly important for tourism regulation as hierarchically organized institutions (at international, national and local scales) aim to regulate relational, non-scalar processes. This chapter therefore aims to offer a brief overview of tourism regulation before examining in more detail the recently advocated concept of relational geography in relation to tourism.

Governance and tourism regulation

As outlined by Cornelissen (see Chapter 3, this volume), regulation focuses on the transformations of social relations in capitalist production and the regulatory responses to these transformations. Accordingly, regulation is used

> to denote a specific local and historical collection of structural forms or institutional arrangements within which individual and collective behaviour unfolds and a particular configuration of market adjustments through which privately made decisions are coordinated and which give rise to elements of regularity in economic life.
>
> (Dunford 1990: 306)

Regulation is primarily concerned with stabilizing an unstable regime of accumulation that cannot guarantee its own reproduction (Jessop 2000). As a social process (depending on interpretations of value) regulation is dynamic, occasionally contradictory and suffers from occasional crises (Goodwin and Painter 1996), particularly when the mode of regulation is no longer adequate for the current regime of accumulation. The increasing globalization of the economy has been perceived by some to represent a crisis. As transnational firms are able to take advantage of differences in regulation between countries (such as in the level of tariffs, assistance with public financing, environmental and labour regulations, taxes, profit remittance), national governments are no longer in the position to regulate their national economies. This leads Hedley (1999: 226) to conclude that 'In today's world, in contrast to the historical effects of differences among nations, variability among states diminishes sovereignty'. Given the international nature of capitalism and the exploitation of variations in national regulations, Hedley (1999) supports trans- or supranational legislation in order to effectively regulate firm practices across national borders.

However, such re-regulation includes a process whereby powers formerly assigned to the nation-state are transferred to other scales of regulation towards the international or transnational scale as well as the subnational. Jessop (2000: 352) has termed this 'hollowing out of the state'. This process is not as simple as national governments merely transferring their capabilities of governance upwards or downwards. Shaw and Williams (2004), for instance, contend that the argument of the curtailment of the state as a location of regulatory power is overstated. Instead they posit that there has indeed been transformation in the importance and role of the nation-state, because of increasing institutional connections between scales, yet 'the state exists in new and more complex relations – including partnership and multi-level governance – with other tiers of state regulation and with other bodies' (Shaw and Williams 2004: 47). This transformation also involves a shift from government to governance; an extension from governing by way of elected bodies to the involvement of public, public–private and voluntary agencies not just at the national scale, but involving subnational and supranational scales as well (Goodwin and Painter 1996). Such 'diffuse' governance has 'further complicated the relationship between the spatial scale of "the local" and the processes and institutions which affect localities' (Goodwin and Painter 1996: 636). Similarly, Church *et al.* (2000: 330) recognize the multiplicity of actors and spatial scales involved in tourism policy: 'Tourism is a diverse and at times chaotic policy arena . . . [with] numerous policy strands at a variety of geographical scales but without an overall strategic underpinning'. In addition to this messy scalar delineation of responsibilities, neoliberal policies resulted in a reduced state involvement as unregulated markets are seen to be the optimal strategy for economic development and growth. For instance, the institutional restructuring of tourism institutions in Peru following a change of government in 1990 provides a good example of the effects of neoliberal strategies on tourism development (Desforges 2000). Although the state was actively engaged in tourism development up to 1990, it has largely withdrawn from tourism planning and privatized key state functions in order to reduce public spending, leaving questions about its ability to adequately control the sharp increase in tourist numbers. The implications of a shift from state-centred or interventionist tourism development (through state-owned businesses or subsidies to private enterprise) towards a withdrawal of the nation-state in support of a more market-led approach are also highlighted by Clancy (1999) in the case of Mexico. These examples suggest a continuously evolving role of the nation-state in terms of its function to regulate economic processes. As actors take on different roles and the scales of tourism governance shift towards both the supranational and local scale, the nation-state may simply be reduced to 'play a central role in mediating the mechanics, ethos and outcomes of this [collaborative governance] process' (Church *et al.* 2000: 332).

Since the nation-state is just one of many institutions that frame public policy related to tourism, the complex system of regulatory relations requires an analysis that extends beyond the nation-state to include relationships between different institutions and scales of regulation.

Examining the role and increasing significance of supranational organizations in tourism governance, development and regulation, Hall (2005a) argues that non-tourism-specific supranational bodies are increasingly acting to regulate tourism and are active in creating institutional arrangements governing human mobility. International organizations dealing with trade issues that can be of relevance to tourism, among other sectors and industries, include the International Monetary Fund (IMF), the Organisation for Economic Co-operation and Development (OECD) and the World Trade Organization (WTO). The United Nations World Tourism Organization (UNWTO), in contrast, has a specific interest in tourism and defines its role as promoting tourism as a tool for economic development, job creation and education (UNWTO 2002).

At the same time, local destinations have the capacity to contest and harness globalization. Gotham (2002: 1752), for instance, demonstrates how New Orleans has positioned itself as 'a themed landscape of entertainment' for the consumption of tourists by 'using' global brands to promote Mardi Gras (and by association New Orleans) in the brands' imagery and advertising. Using the case of New Orleans, Gotham (2005: 322) argues against the homogenizing force of globalization and underlines the contesting power of place: 'Tourism is an uneven and contested process that involves a set of global forces imposed from above in conjunction with localized actions and organizations attempting to preserve place difference, local traditions and indigenous cultures'.

The diverse spatial scales that influence places lead Hall (2005b) to present a case for a multiscalar approach to tourism policy and regulation, which highlights the relationships between regulatory structures and institutions at different scales. Similarly, Pearce (1997) adopts an interorganizational framework that recognizes the importance of both spatial scales and time to examining the organizational structure of Spanish tourism. Following an open-system approach, he sets the network of tourism organization in the context of the wider social, political and economic environment. The regulatory network therefore does not only span the institutional scalar settings of tourism organizations but also transcends into what Pearce (1997) calls 'the wider environment' through exchanges and social relations. By including time as an additional dimension of the framework, Pearce

(1997) acknowledges the dynamic nature and interdependency of these relationships. In context of the Middle East, Hazbun (2004: 336) contends that

> the physical and cultural space tourists now inhabit in the Middle East is not the product of an unchanging natural or historical landscape, but instead an ever changing political construction, the product of struggles between state, societal and transnational actors over the control of transnational flows, the use of space and the nature of cultural representations.

Milne and Ateljevic (2001) discuss the spatial organization of production and regulation in relation to a nexus of global and local processes of economic development. They view tourism as a transaction process that transcends the scalar notions of space as it is influenced by 'global priorities of multi-national corporations, geo-political forces and broader forces of economic change and the complexities of the local – where residents, visitors, workers, governments and entrepreneurs interact at the industry "coal face"' (Milne and Ateljevic 2001: 372). However, their focus is not solely set on the global–local dichotomy but includes the interaction between multiple 'nested scales': '[tourism] is essentially a global process, which manifests itself *locally* and *regionally* and explicitly involves the construction of place' (Milne and Ateljevic 2001: 386, emphasis added).

Current consensus in tourism research seems to be that a number of scales interact in the current restructuring of the tourism system: on the one hand, institutions stretch and deepen their social relations over space and time, and on the other hand they are embedded in local networks that link as well as transcend spatial scales, thus raising the connectivity within the system through flows of tourists, ideas and information. Tourism destinations are thereby interpreted as 'sites within networks of varying geographical composition [and as] spaces of movement and circulation (of goods, technologies, knowledge, people, finance, information)' (Amin *et al.* 2003: 25). Yet previous tourism research has been surprisingly silent on the theoretical discussions of space and their implications for tourism regulation. The next section addresses theoretical discussions on the spatialities of political economy.

Spatialities of political economy

For Cox (1998, 2002: 106), the problem with a regulationist approach to economic globalization and the state's changing scalar fixes in response is its obsession with order rather than struggle, which 'cannot be forced into a simple national–international or local–global understanding of geographic scale'. Held *et al.* (1999: 16) describe globalization as a 'process which embodies a transformation in the spatial organization of social relations and transactions – assessed in terms of their extensity, intensity, velocity and impact – generating transcontinental or inter-regional flows and networks of activity, interaction and the exercise of power'. Although this statement elucidates how space and geography are at the forefront of the globalization process, there is disagreement over the ontology of space and the relations between spatial scales associated with these transformations and their implications for government and governance. As spatial scales are viewed as socially constructed (i.e. not as fixed entities), they are being continually transformed by the dominant discourse and resulting conflict with non-dominant discourses [Marston (2000) provides a comprehensive review of the literature on spatial scales]: 'spatial scales are never fixed, but are perpetually redefined, contested and restructured' (Swyngedouw 2004: 33).

The relationship between scales is indeed being questioned and some researchers such as Jessop (2000) and Swyngedouw (1997) argue that globalization processes result in a tension between socially constructed scales. Jessop (2000: 343), for instance, stresses the notion of the 'relativization of scale', as old scales are being transformed and re-ordered; new spaces and new scales of organization emerge, so that there is 'no pregiven set of places, spaces or scales'. Swyngedouw (1997) identifies a simultaneous shift in the place of regulatory power away from the national state and towards both the supranational and the local scale. He calls this concept 'glocalization', on one level signifying the breakdown of the national scale and the reconstitution of the local as well as the global. This is exemplified by the growing importance of supranational organizations such as the EU, the WTO or the North American Free Trade Agreement (NAFTA), as well as the emergence of local/regional governance as illustrated by, for example, devolution in the United Kingdom. At the same time, neoliberal policies have positioned the state in the background and put the onus on private enterprise, thus redefining the boundaries between public and private, as shown in transformations of the Keynesian welfare state. This mirrors Jessop's (2000: 352) notion of the 'hollowing out of the state':

> de- and reterritorialization are occurring. Given the primacy of the national scale in the advanced capitalist economies in the era of Atlantic Fordism, this can be described as the 'hollowing out' of the national state or, in more formal terms, as the denationalization of statehood.

Amin (2002) bases his concept of spatial organization on Jessop's (2000: 341) notion of globalization as a socio-spatial process signifying the 'creation and/or restructuring of scale as a social relation and as a site of social relations'. But in contrast to Jessop's (2000) scalar view of the globalization process as multiscalar, multitemporal and multicentric, Amin (2002, 2004) advocates a non-scalar perception of global economic changes and proposes a relational understanding of the interaction between scales and social and economic relations between them. Amin (2002: 389) distances himself from the scalar notion of globalization and argues that globalization has created a non-scalar landscape of social relations:

> I take it to suggest a topological sense of space and place, a sense of geographies constituted through the folds, undulations and overlaps that natural and social practices normally assume, without any a priori assumption of geographies or relations nested in territorial or geometric space.

In contrast to a hierarchical view (Swyngedouw 1997) or the relativization of scales (Jessop 2000), Amin's (2002) interpretation of the spatialities of globalization is based on the concept of networks that transcend spatial scales. Indeed, the territorial aspect of local, national and global scales is replaced with a relational understanding of scales as a nexus of social relations within fields of influence (Amin 1997). As networks transcend space and hence different scales, places attached to these networks become linked to each other across space: 'Therefore, places are more than what they contain and what happens in them is more than the sum of localized practices and powers and actions at other "spatial scales"' (Amin 2002: 395). However, adopting such a conceptual position towards spatial scales does not imply a universal rejection of scales as such but provides an alternative organization within networks while still recognizing the existence of scalar organization in certain practices and in institutional frameworks.

In a similar vein to Amin (2002), Sheppard (2002) proposes a positional perspective of economic and social organization across space and time. In his argumentation he draws on the feminist theory of a researcher's positionality and situatedness in terms of gender, race, class, sexuality, etc., by highlighting the geographical situatedness of entities within the global economy; in other words, how different economic institutions are positioned in relation to each other. This perspective is based on three aspects of connectivity: first, positionality is relational in that the actions of an agent are dependent on his/her position in relation to others in the network; second, this automatically involves power relations in terms of exerting influence over others and, in keeping with situated knowledge, challenging the power of 'objectivity'; and, third, this positionality is (re)produced as it is path-dependent yet, at the same time, subject to change through imperfect repetition (Sheppard 2002).

Healey (2004) goes beyond the notion of scale in delineating the relational from the essentialist concept; she incorporates five other criteria that she perceives to be the key differences between the two concepts and which are similar to the key concepts of cultural political economy (as discussed in Chapter 6): position, regionalization, materiality and identity, development and representational form (see Table 15.1).

Healey (2004) views *positionality* not as a traditional geographical characteristic in terms of geographical location, but rather in relational terms according to the relative distance (spatial and temporal) from significant nodes in the multiple networks of social relations. The relational range crosses scales and in the process connects multiple sites to networks of social relations. However, these processes not only transcend scales, but they intersect and interact in and with space and different scales. Healey (2004: 49) extends this analysis of spatial scale and positionality within the relational system to include the organization of locales or sites (*regionalization*), in which 'nodes are actively constructed by mobilization effort and boundaries established by mental maps of place qualities'. This interpretation of the organization of place stands in contrast to the essentialist socio-spatial organization differentiated by the physical fabric of place and recognizes the 'fragmentation and splintering of social relations' (Healey 2004: 49).

Table 15.1 Comparison of essentialist and relational views of spatial scales

Criterion	Essentialist conception	Relational conception
Treatment of scale	Nested hierarchy	Relational reach in different networks
Treatment of position	Hierarchy and borders	Different positions in different networks
Regionalization	An integrated, differentiated physical fabric	Fragmented, folded conceptions of space; multiple networks co-exist
Materiality and identity	A material physical future can be built; meshed with social relations in an integrated way	Materialities are co-existent with conceptions of identity and iconographies of space/place
Concept of development	An integrated linear trajectory	Multiple, non-linear, continually emergent trajectories
Representational form	Material metaphors of functional integration, expressed in maps	Metaphors of movement and ambience, expressed in multiple ways

Source: Adapted from Healey (2004: 48).

She sets these social relations in the context of the physical fabric, which result in a dynamic system of multiple and interconnected layers of social relations.

The third criterion distinguishing relational geography from its essentialist predecessor is concerned with the *materiality of spatial relations* and its role in constructing identities. Healey (2004) contends that a relational perspective is also associated with a social-constructivist view, in that objects and materialities are infused with meaning, which influences the multiple identities and naming of spatialities: 'the formation of the spatial patterning of the materialities of social relations and place qualities is co-emergent with the "naming" of these spatialities and qualities' (Healey 2004: 49).

Networks traversing spatial scales

Networks are inherently dynamic as they are set within ongoing social processes and 'constituted, transformed and reproduced through asymmetrical and evolving power relations by intentional social actors and their intermediaries' (Dicken *et al.* 2001: 105). A specific network is therefore situated within a time- and space-specific broader network of 'society' and can span across multiple spatial scales. As social relations are not bound to localities, they 'can have many geographies, from being localized and rooted in local social tradition to being spread across space' (Ettlinger 2003: 160).

According to Dicken *et al.* (2001: 91), 'Networks are essentially *relational processes*, which when realized empirically within distinct time- and space-specific contexts, produce observable patterns in the global economy'. This view of the economy as relational networks changes the unit of analysis from individuals, firms, institutions, nation-states, etc. to the networks of which they are a part of. An analysis of relational networks therefore requires a deep understanding of the socio-spatial foundation of actors and organizations in order to portray the multiple forms of relationships that constitute the network. Such a relational view with an emphasis on interconnectedness offers opportunities for discovering pluralities of scalar interactions and meanings.

Although social relations in and between networks are not bound by geographical scale, they do not operate in a spatial vacuum. Coe *et al.* (2008: 279) underline the importance of the institutional and geographical environments [as appear in Pearce's (1997) framework] in which networks function, are shaped and originate: 'every element in a . . . network – every firm, every function – is, quite literally, *grounded* in specific locations. Such grounding is both material (the fixed assets of production) and also less tangible (localized social relationships and distinctive institutions and cultural practices)'.

Network analysis has also being employed in tourism to analyse practices of and social relations inherent in networks of governance (see, for instance, Scott *et al.* 2008). Yet many of the analyses are still framed within specific hierarchical scalar organization (see, for example, Pforr 2006; Tyler and Dinan 2001). Although Saxena (2005: 279) considers sustainable tourism to be 'territorially embedded' through its cultural context of social networks and relationships, her emphasis is the analytic shift from 'products and firms to people, organisations and social processes'. This notion of networks requires an ontological change from conceptualizing organizational units (e.g. firms or public institutions) as separate identities (i.e. black boxes) to understanding them as 'a constellation of network relations governed by social actors through both material and discursive practices' (Yeung 2000: 12). Social relationships between actors and organizations and discursive representation are additional elements in the consideration of relational planning. Drawing from Healey's (2004) work on relational planning, the next section outlines implications for governance and planning.

Spatial discourse and imaginaries

Finally, Healey (2004) turns to the *representation of spatiality* used to illustrate spatial relationships or processes. This is closely associated with the 'naming' of spatialities mentioned in context of materiality and identity above. Healey (2004) is particularly interested in these implications of a relational perspective as she compares the academic debates on spatial scalarity in the social science with the use of spatial concepts, vocabulary and representations in practice within European strategic spatial plans. Her analysis of the spatial vocabulary and representations used in these plans reveals the shifting discourse by some planning authorities in Europe from an essentialist to a relational view of spatial scales. However, this shifting discourse is only possible if support is present in the institutional framework:

shifting a planning discourse will be hard without other supporting shifts in
the institutional context which makes a new discourse more welcome . . . If
it is so difficult to change the spatial content of a planning discourse, is there
any merit in seeking to shift the geographical imagination from traditional,
essentialist conceptions to the new relational geography?

(Healey 2004: 64).

On the one hand her study demonstrates the shifting discursive politics of
spatial organization in European planning; on the other hand, it also shows the
discursive power carried by the traditional hierarchical categories (Barnes 1996;
Gibson-Graham 1996; Kelly 1997, 1999). Cox (2002: 105), for instance, argues
that regulationist interpretations of globalization are skewed as they view globalization as a process that is merely imposed on nation-states without recognizing
that governments (as well as many other actors) are actively engaged in creating
spatial discourse and thus contribute to the shaping of space:

the way in which the state has been involved in the construction of globalization, not just materially but also discursively and how it has exaggerated its
effects for its own purposes, is missed. Instead of examining as the starting
point capital's restructuring strategies in the context of the long downturn and
as they are mediated by the state, globalization is introduced as, in effect, a
deus ex machina.

Spatial organization is socially constructed (Marston 2000) and is therefore
apparent through discourses about spaces. These discourses are specific to socio-
spatio-temporal interpretations of 'representations of space, which are tied to
the relations of production and to the "order" which those relations impose, and
hence to knowledge, to signs, to codes, and to "frontal" relations' (Lefebvre 1991:
33). In the realm of policy-making, spatial metaphors, imaginaries and narratives
are created and reproduced to legitimate and justify a certain spatial approach
and politics (González 2006). Especially discourses about globalization include
a variety of spatial imaginaries either to support or to oppose the dominance of
the global: 'Spatial metaphors serve as important hermeneutical devices for the
social–spatial constructions of globalization tendencies without which globalization would face a crisis of legitimation' (Cox 2005: 185).

Larner (1998) and González (2006) analyse the discursive spatial dimension
of policy-making in New Zealand and Bilbao, respectively, and demonstrate
that spatial imaginaries are employed in a political strategy to promote a new
understanding of governance (both the practices *and* the sites of governing).
Using discursive imaginaries of spatial organization, New Zealand, for instance,
re-oriented its economic networks to the Asia-Pacific region in the late 1980s
(Larner 1998), whereas Bilbao has followed academic discourse on global-city
regions, glocalization and the spaces of flows to frame, promote and justify urban
regeneration based on tourism and conspicuous architecture (González 2006).

These two cases demonstrate that sites of governance are not merely reacting to an imposed spatial organization, but instead are actively engaged in framing political decisions within spatial discourses amenable to their particular positions. González (2006: 838) refers to politics of scales as 'strategies used by actors to explain, justify, defend and even try to impose the link between a particular scale or scalar configuration and a political project'.

This implies that it is necessary to analyse spatial discourses, imaginaries and narratives in order to understand how spatial organization is framed and inserted into the formatting of new forms of governance in different times and contexts.

Conclusion: researching relational geographies in tourism

Amin (2002) puts forward the topological view that social relations stretch across space and therefore transcend the scalar organization of space. Places are therefore not reduced to being separate sites connected to each other through geographical links, but are rather constituted by social practices that create place regardless of predetermined territorial organization. The conceptual implications of this understanding of spatial organization are manifold for tourism governance and planning; taking a relational approach towards geographical organization has important implications for ontologies, epistemologies and resulting research methodologies (Amin 2002). With a relational understanding of space, territorially bounded research finds itself on shaky ground. See Macleod and Jones (2007) for an interesting discussion on the implications of a relational geography for the subdiscipline of regional geography, with distinguishable regions within nation-states being its object of enquiry.

Networks and social relations become key features in understanding how practices may transcend – but are possibly also bound within – geographical scales. Processes of governance and regulation take on meaning within the context of cultural, social and political relations (Lee and Wills 1997). Data needs therefore encompass qualitative relational data as research focuses on the characteristics of relationships in order to unravel the relational geographies between actors (Yeung 2003).

With the increasing acceptance of the importance of networks and positionality within these networks over traditional concepts of scalar boundaries and the changing nature of economic ordering or struggle it has also become necessary to re-theorize the implications for regulation and governance. As Milne and Ateljevic (2001: 387) state for the context of tourism:

> A new configuration of articulated economic spaces and scales of governance is emerging in the tourism industry. Our challenge as tourism researchers is to embrace this complexity and not to shy away from dealing with a world of constant evolution and change.

What, then, are the consequences of a relational approach and socio-economic view for the study of tourism regulation? Regulation is set in networks of social relations as well as within the scalarity of the institutional framework that is predominantly structured according to hierarchically organized space (i.e. into supranational, national and subnational scales) (Hall 2005b). Indeed, Gotham (2005: 311) highlights that interactions and processes within the tourism sector occur across and within multiple scales:

> The generalized processes of commodification and homogenization that characterize the international tourism industry are not monolithic but are mediated at various spatial and institutional levels, from the macro-level of globalized institutions to the micro-level of people's day-to-day lives.

In light of the relational perspective on spatiality and Healey's (2004) research on the vocabularies of European planning documents, the principal questions to be considered in tourism regulation are whether the practices and organization of regulatory institutions have also shifted to better reflect network relations across places and space. As Massey (2004: 9) observes: 'In this world so often described as a space of flows, so much of our formal democratic politics is organized territorially'. This raises the question whether territorially bound tourism regulation can still be successful or whether an increasing significance of social relations demands a changing orientation and organization of tourism regulation beyond spatial scales. This chapter has aimed to demonstrate the need to take spatial organization seriously in context of tourism regulation and that a cultural political economy has to be conscious of discourses about spatiality. Spatial imaginaries have repercussions on the notions of governance that are presented within the discourse (see, for instance, discourses on globalization and the linked strategy of neoliberal governance). It is therefore imperative for a cultural political economy of tourism regulation to analyse the various discourses on space and to examine how they are represented and employed strategically within a politics of scale in order to implement a particular policy.

References

Amin, A. (1997) 'Placing globalization', *Theory, Culture, Society: Explorations in Critical Social Science*, 14: 123–137.

Amin, A. (2002) 'Spatialities of globalisation', *Environment and Planning A*, 34: 385–399.

Amin, A., Massey, D. and Thrift, N. (2003) *Decentering the Nation: A radical approach to regional inequality*, London: Catalyst.

Barnes, T. J. (1996) *Logics of Dislocation: Models, metaphors and meanings of economic space*, New York: Guilford Press.

Chang, T. C., Milne, S., Fallon, D. and Pohlmann, C. (1996) 'Urban heritage tourism: The global–local nexus', *Annals of Tourism Research*, 23: 1–19.

Church, A., Ball, R. and Bull, C. (2000) 'Public policy engagement with British tourism: The national, local and the European Union', *Tourism Geographies*, 2: 312–336.

Clancy, M. (1999) 'Tourism and development: Evidence from Mexico', *Annals of Tourism Research*, 26: 1–20.

Coe, N. M., Dicken, P. and Hess, M. (2008) 'Global production networks: Realizing the potential', *Journal of Economic Geography*, 8: 271–295.

Cox, K. R. (1998) 'Spaces of dependence, spaces of engagement and the politics of scale or: Looking for local politics', *Political Geography*, 17: 1–24.

Cox, K. R. (2002) '"Globalization", the "regulation approach" and the politics of scale', in A. Herod and M. W. Wright (eds) *Geographies of Power: Placing scale*, Oxford: Blackwell.

Cox, K. R. (2005) 'Local: Global', in P. J. Cloke and R. Johnston (eds) *Spaces of Geographical Thought: Deconstructing human geography's binaries*, London: Sage.

Desforges, L. (2000) 'State tourism institutions and neo-liberal development: A case study of Peru', *Tourism Geographies*, 2: 177–192.

Dicken, P., Kelly, P. F., Olds, K. and Yeung, H. W.-C. (2001) 'Chains and networks, territories and scales: Towards a relational framework for analysing the global economy', *Global Networks*, 1: 89–112.

Dunford, M. (1990) 'Theories of regulation', *Environment and Planning D: Society and Space*, 8: 297–321.

Ettlinger, N. (2003) 'Cultural economic geography and a relational and microspace approach to trusts, rationalities, networks and change in collaborative workplaces', *Journal of Economic Geography*, 3: 145–171.

Gibson-Graham, J. K. (1996) *The End of Capitalism (as We Knew It): A feminist critique of political economy*, Oxford: Blackwell.

González, S. (2006) 'Scalar narratives in Bilbao: A cultural politics of scales approach to the study of urban policy', *International Journal of Urban and Regional Research*, 30: 836–857.

Goodwin, M. and Painter, J. (1996) 'Local governance, the crises of Fordism and the changing geographies of regulation', *Transactions of the Institute of British Geographers*, 21: 635–648.

Gotham, K. F. (2002) 'Marketing Mardi Gras: Commodification, spectacle and the political economy of tourism in New Orleans', *Urban Studies*, 39: 1735–1756.

Gotham, K. F. (2005) 'Tourism from above and below: Globalization, localization and New Oreans's Mardi Gras', *International Journal of Urban and Regional Research*, 29: 309–326.

Hall, C. M. (2005a) 'Supranational tourism governance: Analysing new domains of regulatory power in tourism', paper presented at at the RGS-Ibg Annual Conference, London, August/September.

Hall, C. M. (2005b) *Tourism: Rethinking the social science of mobility*, Harlow: Pearson.

Hazbun, W. (2004) 'Globalisation, reterritorialisation and the political economy of tourism development in the Middle East', *Geopolitics*, 9: 310–341.

Healey, P. (2004) 'The treatment of space and place in the new strategic spatial planning in Europe', *International Journal of Urban and Regional Research*, 28: 45–67.

Hedley, R. A. (1999) 'Transnational corporations and their regulation: Issues and strategies', *International Journal of Comparative Sociology*, 40: 215–230.

Held, D. (1995) *Democracy and the Global Order*, Cambridge: Polity Press.

Held, D., McGrew, A., Goldblatt, D. and Perraton, J. (1999) *Global Transformations: Politics, economics and culture*, Cambridge: Polity Press.

Jessop, B. (2000) 'The crisis of the national spatio-temporal fix and the tendential ecological dominance of globalizing capitalism', *International Journal of Urban and Regional Research*, 24: 323–360.

Kelly, P. F. (1997) 'Globalization, power and the politics of scale in the Philippines', *Geoforum*, 28: 151–171.

Kelly, P. F. (1999) 'The geographies and politics of globalization', *Progress in Human Geography*, 23: 379–400.

Larner, W. (1998) 'Hitching a ride on the tiger's back: Globalisation and spatial imaginaries in New Zealand', *Environment and Planning D: Society and Space*, 16: 599–614.

Lee, R. and Wills, J. (1997) *Geographies of Economies*, London: Edward Arnold.

Lefebvre, H. (1991) *The Production of Space*, Oxford: Blackwell.

Macleod, G. and Jones, M. (2007) 'Territorial, scalar, networked, connected: In what sense a "regional world"?', *Regional Studies*, 41: 1177–1191.

Marston, S. A. (2000) 'The social construction of scale', *Progress in Human Geography*, 24: 219–241.

Massey, D. (2004) 'Geographies of responsibility', *Geografiska Annaler B*, 86: 5–18.

Milne, S. and Ateljevic, I. (2001) 'Tourism, economic development and the global–local nexus: Theory embracing complexity', *Tourism Geographies*, 3: 369–393.

Pearce, D. (1997) 'Tourism and the autonomous communities in Spain', *Annals of Tourism Research*, 24: 156–177.

Pforr, C. (2006) 'Tourism policy in the making: An Australian network study', *Annals of Tourism Research*, 33: 87–108.

Saxena, G. (2005) 'Relationships, networks and the learning regions: Case evidence from the Peak District National Park', *Tourism Management*, 26: 277–289.

Scott, N., Baggio, R. and Cooper, C. (2008) *Network Analysis and Tourism: From theory to practice*. Clevedon: Channel View.

Shaw, G. and Williams, A. M. (2004) *Tourism and Tourism Spaces*, London: Sage.

Sheppard, E. (2002) 'The spaces and times of globalization: Place, scale, networks and positionality', *Economic Geography*, 78: 307–330.

Swyngedouw, E. (1997) 'Neither global nor local: "Glocalization" and the politics of scale', in K. Cox (ed.) *Spaces of Globalization: Reasserting the power of the local*, New York: Guilford Press.

Swyngedouw, E. (2004) 'Globalisation or "glocalisation"? Networks, territories and re-scaling', *Cambridge Review of International Affairs*, 17: 25–48.

Teo, P. and Li, L. H. (2003) 'Global and local interactions in tourism', *Annals of Tourism Research*, 30: 287–306.

Tourism Management (1990) Special issue on tourism and transnationalism, 11: 287–372.

Tyler, D. and Dinan, C. (2001) 'The role of interested groups in England's emerging tourism policy network', *Current Issues in Tourism*, 4: 210–252.

UNWTO (2002) *Tourism in the Age of Alliances, Mergers and Acquisitions*, Madrid: United Nations World Tourism Organization.

Yeung, H. W-C. (2000) 'Reconceptualising the "firm" in new economic geographies: An organisational perspective', paper presented at the workshop on '"The Firm" in Economic Geography', University of Portsmouth, 9–11 March.

Yeung, H. W.-C. (2003) 'Practicing new economic geographies: A methodological examination', *Annals of the Association of American Geographers*, 93: 442–462.

Index

Lightning Source UK Ltd.
Milton Keynes UK
UKOW06f0311150916

283002UK00014B/325/P